Beginning Android 4

Grant Allen

Apress®

Beginning Android 4

ISBN-13 (pbk): 978-1-4302-3984-0

ISBN-13 (electronic): 978-1-4302-3985-7

President and Publisher: Paul Manning
Lead Editor: Steve Anglin
Development Editor: Jonathan Gennick
Technical Reviewers: Nikhil Gopal and Michael Thomas
Editorial Board: Steve Anglin, Mark Beckner, Ewan Buckingham, Gary Cornell, Morgan Ertel, Jonathan Gennick, Jonathan Hassell, Robert Hutchinson, Michelle Lowman, James Markham, Matthew Moodie, Jeff Olson, Jeffrey Pepper, Douglas Pundick, Ben Renow-Clarke, Dominic Shakeshaft, Gwenan Spearing, Matt Wade, Tom Welsh
Coordinating Editor: Jessica Belanger
Copy Editor: William McManus
Compositor: MacPS, LLC
Indexer: John Collin
Artist: April Milne
Cover Designer: Anna Ishchenko

Distributed to the book trade worldwide by Springer Science+Business Media, LLC., 233 Spring Street, 6th Floor, New York, NY 10013. Phone 1-800-SPRINGER, fax 201-348-4505, e-mail orders-ny@springer-sbm.com, or visit www.springeronline.com.

For information on translations, please e-mail rights@apress.com, or visit www.apress.com.

Apress and friends of ED books may be purchased in bulk for academic, corporate, or promotional use. eBook versions and licenses are also available for most titles. For more information, reference our Special Bulk Sales–eBook Licensing web page at www.apress.com/bulk-sales.

Any source code or other supplementary materials referenced by the author in this text is available to readers at www.apress.com. For detailed information about how to locate your book's source code, go to http://www.apress.com/source-code/.

Contents at a Glance

Contents

About the Author

Grant Allen has worked in the IT field for over 20 years as a CTO, enterprise architect, and database architect. Grant's roles have covered private enterprise, academia, and the government sector around the world, specializing in global-scale systems design, development, and performance. He is a frequent speaker at industry and academic conferences, on topics ranging from data mining to compliance, and technologies such as databases (DB2, Oracle, SQL Server, and MySQL), content management, collaboration, disruptive innovation, and mobile ecosystems like Android.

His first Android application was a task list to remind him to finish all his other unfinished Android projects.

Grant works for Google, and in his spare time is completing a PhD on building innovative high-technology environments.

Grant is the author of *Beginning DB2: From Novice to Professional* (Apress, 2008), and lead author of *Oracle SQL Recipes: A Problem-Solution Approach* (Apress, 2010) and *The Definitive Guide to SQLite*, 2nd Edition (Apress, 2010).

About the Technical Reviewers

Michael Thomas has worked in software development for over 20 years as an individual contributor, team lead, program manager, and Vice President of Engineering. Michael has over 10 years experience working with mobile devices. His current focus is in the medical sector using mobile devices to accelerate information transfer between patients and health care providers.

Nikhil Gopal is a director of software development at Intelligene, LLC. He works on machine learning and genomics/bioinformatics applications. In the past, he has worked in the biotechnology and software industries, primarily in the role of a programmer scientist. He has contributed to a number of open source projects pertaining to bioinformatics, genomics, and unix-based operating systems. He graduated from UC Davis with a B.S. in Biotechnology/Bioinformatics. He enjoys playing the guitar, riding motorcycles, and a number of outdoor activities. He currently lives in the San Francisco bay area.

Core Concept

1

The Big Picture

Android is everywhere. Phones. Tablets. TVs and set-top boxes powered by Google TV. Soon, Android will be in cars, in in-flight entertainment systems on planes, and even in robots!

However, the general theme of Android devices will be smaller screens and/or no hardware keyboard. And, by the numbers, Android will probably be associated mostly with smartphones for the foreseeable future. For developers, this has both benefits and drawbacks, as described next. This chapter also describes the main components in an Android application and the Android features that you can exploit when developing your applications.

Benefits and Drawbacks of Smartphone Programming

On the plus side, Android-style smartphones are sexy. Offering Internet services over mobile devices dates back to the mid-1990s and the Handheld Device Markup Language (HDML). However, only in recent years have phones capable of Internet access taken off. Now, thanks to trends like text messaging and products like Apple's iPhone, phones that can serve as Internet-access devices are rapidly gaining popularity. So, working on Android applications gives you experience with an interesting technology (Android) in a fast-moving market segment (Internet-enabled phones), which is always a good thing.

The problem comes when you actually have to program the darn things.

Anyone with experience in programming for PDAs or phones has felt the pain of phones simply being *small* in all sorts of dimensions:

■ Screens are small (you will not get comments like, "Is that a 24-inch LCD in your pocket, or . . . ?").

■ Keyboards, if they exist, are small.

- Pointing devices, if they exist, are annoying (as anyone who has lost their stylus will tell you) or inexact (large fingers and "multitouch" LCDs can sometimes be . . . problematic).

- CPU speed and memory are always behind what's available on desktops and servers.

Moreover, applications running on a phone have to deal with the fact that they're *on a phone*.

People with mobile phones tend to get very irritated when those phones do not work. Similarly, those same people will get irritated if your program "breaks" their phones by

- Tying up the CPU such that calls can't be received.

- Not quietly fading into the background when a call comes in or needs to be placed, because the program doesn't work properly with the rest of the phone's operating system.

- Crashing the phone's operating system, such as by leaking memory like a sieve.

Hence, developing programs for a phone is a different experience than developing desktop applications, web sites, or back-end server processes. The tools look different, the frameworks behave differently, and you have more limitations on what you can do with your programs.

What Android tries to do is meet you halfway:

- You get a commonly used programming language (Java) with some commonly used libraries (e.g., some Apache Commons APIs), with support for tools you may be used to using (Eclipse).

- You get a fairly rigid and uncommon framework in which your programs need to run so they can be "good citizens" on the phone and not interfere with other programs or the operation of the phone itself.

As you might expect, much of this book deals with that framework and how you write programs that work within its confines and take advantage of its capabilities.

What Androids Are Made Of

When you write a desktop application, you are "master of your own domain." You launch your main window and any child windows—like dialog boxes—that are needed. From your standpoint, you are your own world, leveraging features supported by the operating system, but largely ignorant of any other program that may be running on the computer at the same time. If you do interact with other programs, it is typically through an application programming interface (API), such as Java Database Connectivity (JDBC), or frameworks atop it, to communicate with MySQL or another database.

Android has similar concepts, but they are packaged differently and structured to make phones more crash-resistant:

- *Activities*: The building block of the user interface is the activity. You can think of an activity as being the Android analogue for the window or dialog box in a desktop application or the page in a classic web application. Android is designed to support lots of cheap activities, so you can allow users to keep tapping to open new activities and tapping the Back button to back up, just like they do in a web browser.

- *Services*: Activities are short-lived and can be shut down at any time. Services, on the other hand, are designed to keep running, if needed, independent of any activity, akin to the notion of services or daemons on other operating systems. You might use a service to check for updates to an RSS feed or to play back music even if the controlling activity is no longer operating. You will also use services for scheduled tasks ("cron jobs") and for exposing custom APIs to other applications on the device, though those are relatively advanced capabilities.

- *Content providers*: Content providers provide a level of abstraction for any data stored on the device that is accessible by multiple applications. The Android development model encourages you to make your own data available to other applications, as well as your own applications. Building a content provider lets you do that, while maintaining complete control over how your data gets accessed. Content providers can be anything from web feeds, to local SQLite databases, and beyond.

- *Intents*: Intents are system messages that run around the inside of the device and notify applications of various events, from hardware state changes (e.g., an SD card was inserted), to incoming data (e.g., a Short Message Service [SMS] message arrived), to application events (e.g., your activity was launched from the device's main menu). Intents are much like messages or events on other operating systems. Not only can you respond to an Intent, but you can create your own to launch other activities or to let you know when specific situations arise (e.g., raise such-and-so Intent when the user gets within 100 meters of this-and-such location).

Stuff at Your Disposal

- *Storage*: You can package data files with your application for things that do not change, such as icons or help files. You also can carve out a small bit of space on the device itself, for databases or files containing user-entered or retrieved data needed by your application. And, if the user supplies bulk storage, like an SD card, you can read and write files on there as needed.

■ *Network*: Android devices generally are Internet-ready, through one communications medium or another. You can take advantage of the Internet access at any level you wish, from raw Java sockets all the way up to a built-in WebKit-based web browser widget you can embed in your application.

■ *Multimedia*: Android devices have the ability to play back and record audio and video. While the specifics may vary from device to device, you can query the device to learn its capabilities and then take advantage of the multimedia capabilities as you see fit, whether that is to play back music, take pictures with the camera, or use the microphone for audio note-taking.

■ *Location services*: Android devices frequently have access to location providers, such as GPS and cell triangulation, which can tell your applications where the device is on the face of the Earth. In turn, you can display maps or otherwise take advantage of the location data, such as to track a device's movements if the device has been stolen.

■ *Phone services*: Because Android devices are typically phones, your software can initiate calls, send and receive SMS messages, and do everything else you expect from a modern bit of telephony technology.

The Big Picture...of This Book

Now that you have the Android big picture, here is what's coming in the rest of this book:

■ The next two chapters are designed to get you going quickly with the Android environment, through a series of step-by-step, tutorial-style instructions for setting up the tools you need, creating your first project, and getting that first project running on the Android emulator.

■ The three chapters that follow explain a bit more about what just happened in Chapters 2 and 3. We examine the Android project that we created, talk a bit more about Eclipse, and discuss some things we could add to the project to help it run on more devices and enhance its capabilities.

■ The bulk of the book explores the various capabilities of the Android APIs—how to create components like activities, how to access the Internet and local databases, how to get your location and show it on a map, and so forth.

Chapter 2

How to Get Started

Without further ado, let's get you set up with the pieces and parts necessary to build an Android app.

> **NOTE:** The instructions presented here are accurate as of the time of this writing. However, the tools change rapidly, so these instructions may be out of date by the time you read this. Please refer to the Android Developers web site for current instructions, using this as a base guideline of what to expect.

Step 1: Set Up Java

When you write Android applications, you typically write them in Java source code. That Java source code is then turned into the stuff that Android actually runs (Dalvik bytecode in an Android package [APK] file).

Hence, the first thing you need to do is get set up with a Java development environment so that you are prepared to start writing Java classes.

Install the JDK

You need to obtain and install the official Oracle Java SE Development Kit (JDK). You can obtain this from the Oracle Java web site for Windows and Linux, and from Apple for Mac OS X. The plain JDK (sans any "bundles") should suffice. Follow the instructions supplied by Oracle or Apple for installing it on your machine. At the time of this writing, Android supports Java 5 and Java 6, with Java 7 likely to be supported by the time you are reading this.

ALTERNATIVE JAVA COMPILERS

In principle, you are supposed to use the official Oracle JDK. In practice, it appears that OpenJDK also works, at least on Ubuntu. However, the further removed you get from the official Oracle implementation, the less likely it is that it will work. For example, the GNU Compiler for Java (GCJ) may not work with Android.

Learn Java

This book, like most books and documentation on Android, assumes that you have basic Java programming experience. If you lack this, you really should consider spending a bit of time on Java fundamentals before you dive into Android. Otherwise, you may find the experience to be frustrating.

If you are in need of a crash course in Java to get involved in Android development, here are the concepts you need to learn, presented in no particular order:

- Language fundamentals (flow control, etc.)
- Classes and objects
- Methods and data members
- Public, private, and protected
- Static and instance scope
- Exceptions
- Threads and concurrency control
- Collections
- Generics
- File I/O
- Reflection
- Interfaces

One of the easiest ways of acquiring this knowledge is to read *Learn Java for Android Development* by Jeff Friesen (Apress, 2010).

Step 2: Install the Android SDK

The Android SDK gives you all the tools you need to create and test Android applications. It comes in two parts: the base tools, and version-specific SDKs and related add-ons.

Install the Base Tools

You can find the Android developer tools on the Android Developers web site at http://developer.android.com. Download the ZIP file that is appropriate for your platform and unzip it in a logical location on your machine—no specific path is required. Windows users also have the option of running a self-installing EXE file.

Install the SDKs and Add-ons

Inside the tools/ directory of your Android SDK installation from the previous step, you will see an android batch file or shell script. If you run that, you will be presented with the Android SDK and AVD Manager, shown in Figure 2–1.

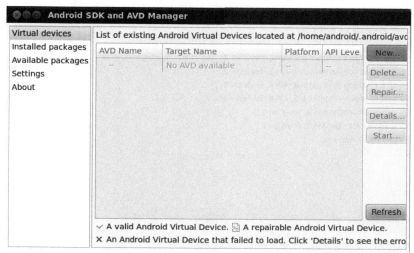

Figure 2–1. *Android SDK and AVD Manager*

At this point, you have some of the build tools, but you lack the Java files necessary to compile an Android application. You also lack a few additional build tools, and the files necessary to run an Android emulator. To address this, click the Available packages option on the left to open the screen shown in Figure 2–2.

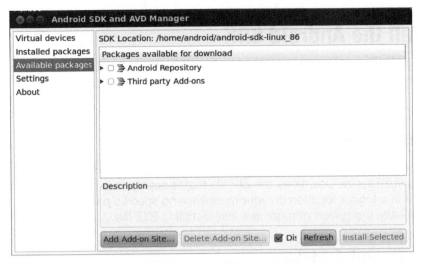

Figure 2–2. *Android SDK and AVD Manager available packages*

Open the Android Repository branch of the tree. After a short pause, you will see a screen similar to Figure 2–3.

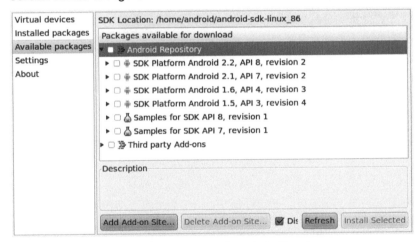

Figure 2–3. *Android SDK and AVD Manager available Android packages*

Check the boxes for the following items:

- "SDK Platform" for all Android SDK releases you want to test against

- "Documentation for Android SDK" for the latest Android SDK release

- "Samples for SDK" for the latest Android SDK release, and perhaps for older releases if you wish

Then, open the Third party Add-ons branch of the tree. After a short pause, you will see a screen similar to Figure 2–4.

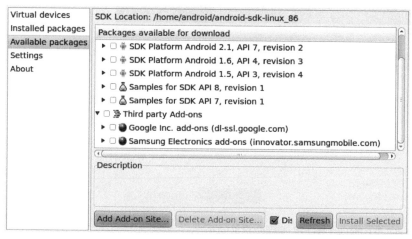

Figure 2–4. *Android SDK and AVD Manager available third-party add-ons*

Click the "Google Inc. add-ons" branch to open it, as shown in Figure 2–5.

Figure 2–5. *Android SDK and AVD Manager available Google add-ons*

Most likely, you will want to check the boxes for the "Google APIs by Google Inc." items that match up with the SDK versions you selected in the Android Repository branch. The Google APIs include support for well-known Google products, such as Google Maps, both from your code and in the Android emulator.

After you have checked all the items you want to download, click the Install Selected button, which brings up a license confirmation dialog box, shown in Figure 2–6.

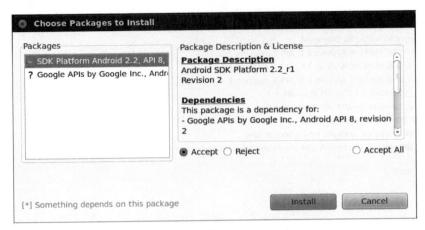

Figure 2–6. *Android SDK and AVD Manger license agreement screen*

Review and accept the licenses if you agree with the terms, and then click the Install button. At this point, this is a fine time to go get lunch or dinner. Unless you have a substantial Internet connection, downloading all of this data and unpacking it will take a fair bit of time.

When the download is complete, you can close the SDK and AVD Manager if you wish, though you will use it to set up the emulator in Step 5 of this chapter.

Step 3: Install the ADT for Eclipse

If you will not be using Eclipse for your Android development, you can skip to the next section. If you will be using Eclipse but have not yet installed it, you will need to do that first. Eclipse can be downloaded from the Eclipse web site, `www.eclipse.org/`. The Eclipse IDE for Java Developers package will work fine.

Next, you need to install the Android Developer Tools (ADT) plug-in. To do this, open Eclipse and choose Help ►► Install New Software. Then, in the Install dialog box, click the Add button to add a new source of plug-ins. Give it a name (e.g., Android) and supply the following URL: `https://dl-ssl.google.com/android/eclipse/`. That should trigger Eclipse to download the roster of plug-ins available from that site (see Figure 2–7).

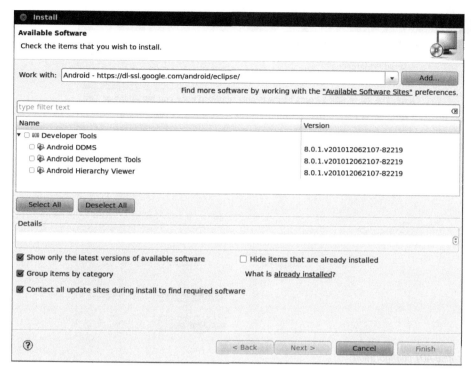

Figure 2–7. *Eclipse ADT plug-in installation*

Check the Developer Tools check box and click the Next button. Follow the rest of the wizard steps to review the tools to be downloaded and review and accept their respective license agreements. When the Finish button is enabled, click it, and Eclipse will download and install the plug-ins. When it's done, Eclipse will ask to restart; let it do so.

Then, you need to show ADT where to locate your Android SDK installation from the preceding section. To do this, choose Window ➤➤ Preferences from the Eclipse main menu (or the equivalent Preferences option for Mac OS X). Click the Android entry in the list pane of the Preferences dialog box, as shown in Figure 2–8.

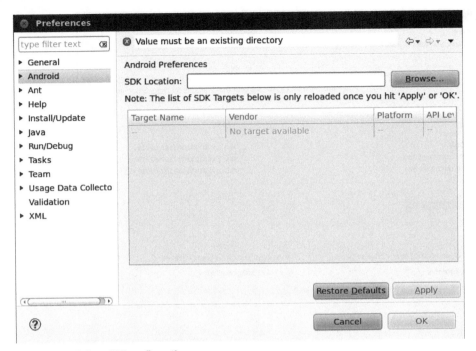

Figure 2–8. *Eclipse ADT configuration*

Then, click the Browse button to find the directory where you installed the SDK. After choosing it, click Apply in the Preferences dialog box, and you should see the Android SDK versions you installed previously. Then, click OK, and the ADT will be ready for use.

Step 4: Install Apache Ant

If you will be doing all of your development from Eclipse, you can skip to the next section. If you wish to develop using command-line build tools, you need to install Apache Ant. You may have this installed already from previous Java development work, as it is fairly common in Java projects. However, you need Ant version 1.8.1 or later, so check your current copy (e.g., `ant -version`).

If you do not have Ant or do not have the correct version, you can obtain it from the Apache Ant web site, at `http://ant.apache.org/`. Full installation instructions are available in the Ant manual, but the basic steps are as follows:

1. Unpack the ZIP archive in a logical place on your machine.
2. Add a `JAVA_HOME` environment variable, pointing to where your JDK is installed, if you do not have one already.
3. Add an `ANT_HOME` environment variable, pointing to the directory where you unpacked Ant in step 1.
4. Add `$JAVA_HOME/bin` and `$ANT_HOME/bin` to your `PATH`.
5. Run `ant -version` to confirm that Ant is installed properly.

Step 5: Set Up the Emulator

The Android tools include an *emulator*, a piece of software that pretends to be an Android device. This is very useful for development because it not only enables you to get started on your Android development without a device, but also enables you to test device configurations for devices that you do not own.

The Android emulator can emulate one or several Android devices. Each configuration you want is stored in an Android Virtual Device (AVD). The Android SDK and AVD Manager, which you used to download the SDK components earlier in this chapter, is where you create these AVDs.

If you do not have the SDK and AVD Manager running, you can run it via the `android` command from your SDK's `tools/` directory, or via Window ➤ SDK and AVD Manager from Eclipse. It opens with a screen listing the AVDs you have available; initially, the list will be empty, as shown in Figure 2–9.

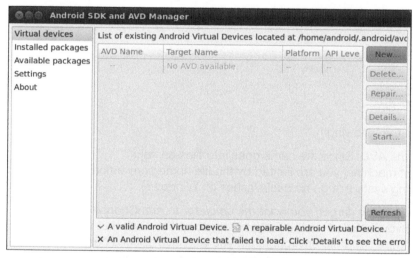

Figure 2–9. *Android SDK and AVD Manager Android Virtual Devices list*

Click the New button to create a new AVD file. This opens the dialog box shown in Figure 2–10, where you can configure how this AVD should look and work.

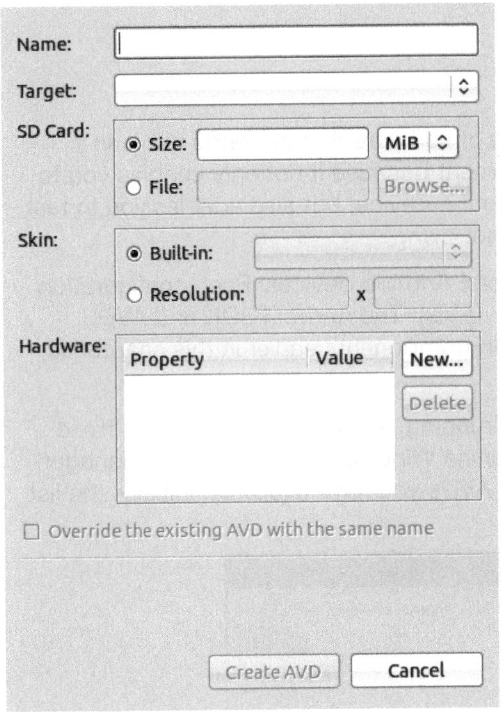

Figure 2–10. *Adding a new AVD*

You need to provide the following:

- *A name for the AVD*: Since the name goes into files on your development machine, you are limited by the file name conventions for your operating system (e.g., no backslashes on Windows).

- *The Android version (target) you want the emulator to run*: Choose one of the SDKs you installed via the Target drop-down list. Note that in addition to "pure" Android environments, you will have options based on the third-party add-ons you selected. For example, you probably have some options for setting up AVDs containing the Google APIs, and you will need such an AVD for testing an application that uses Google Maps.

- *Details about the SD card the emulator should emulate*: Since Android devices invariably have some form of external storage, you probably want to set up an SD card, by supplying a size in the associated field. However, since a file will be created on your development machine of whatever size you specify for the card, you probably do not want to create a 2GB emulated SD card. 32MB is a nice starting point, though you can go larger if needed.

■ *The "skin" or resolution the emulator should run in*: The skin options you have available depend upon what target you chose. The skins let you choose a typical Android screen resolution (e.g., WVGA800 for 800×480). You can also manually specify a resolution when you want to test a nonstandard configuration.

You can skip the Hardware section of the dialog box for now, as changing those settings is usually only required for advanced configurations.

The resulting dialog box might look something like Figure 2–11.

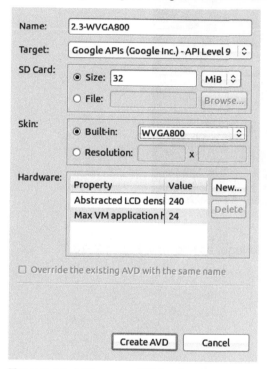

Figure 2–11. *Adding a new AVD (continued)*

Click the Create AVD button, and your AVD stub will be created.

To start the emulator, select it in the Android Virtual Devices list and click Start. You can skip the launch options for now and just click Launch. The first time you launch a new AVD, it will take a long time to start up. The second and subsequent times you start the AVD, it will come up a bit faster, and usually you need to start it only once per day (e.g., when you start development). You do not need to stop and restart the emulator every time you want to test your application, in most cases.

The emulator will go through a few startup phases, the first of which displays a plain-text ANDROID label, as shown in Figure 2–12.

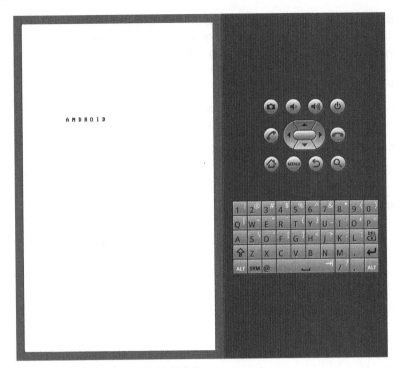

Figure 2-12. *Android emulator, initial startup segment*

The second phase displays a graphical Android logo, as shown in Figure 2–13.

Figure 2–13. *Android emulator, secondary startup segment*

Finally, the emulator reaches the home screen (the first time you run the AVD; see Figure 2–14) or the keyguard (see Figure 2–15).

Figure 2–14. *Android home screen*

If you get the keyguard, press the Menu button or slide the green lock on the screen to the right, to get to the emulator's home screen.

Figure 2–15. *Android keyguard*

Step 6: Set Up the Device

With an emulator set up, you do not need an Android device to get started in Android application development. Having one is a good idea before you try to ship an application (e.g., upload it to the Android Market). But perhaps you already have a device—maybe that is what is spurring your interest in developing for Android.

The first step to make your device ready for use with development is to go into the Settings application on the device. From there, choose Applications, then Development. That should give you a set of check boxes for choosing development-related options, similar to what's shown in Figure 2–16.

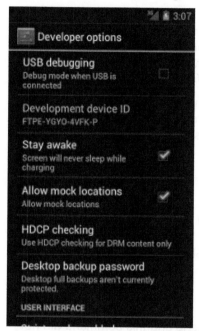

Figure 2–16. *Android device development settings*

Generally, you will want to enable USB debugging so that you can use your device with the Android build tools. You can leave the other settings alone for now if you wish, though you may find the Stay awake option to be handy, as it saves you from having to unlock your phone repeatedly while it is plugged into USB.

Next, you need to set up your development machine to talk to your device. That process varies by the operating system of your development machine, as covered in the following sections.

Windows

When you first plug in your Android device, Windows attempts to find a driver for it. It is possible that, by virtue of other software you have installed, the driver is ready for use. If Windows finds a driver, you are probably ready to go.

If Windows doesn't find the driver, here are some options for getting one:

- *Windows Update*: Some versions of Windows (e.g., Vista) prompt you to search Windows Update for drivers. This is certainly worth a shot, though not every device manufacturer will have supplied its device's driver to Microsoft.

- *Standard Android driver*: In your Android SDK installation, you will find a google-usb_driver directory, containing a generic Windows driver for Android devices. You can try pointing the driver wizard at this directory to see if it thinks this driver is suitable for your device.

- *Manufacturer-supplied driver*: If you still do not have a driver, search the CD that came with the device (if any) or search the web site of the device manufacturer. Motorola, for example, has drivers available for all of its devices in one spot for download.

Mac OS X and Linux

Odds are decent that simply plugging in your device will "just work." You can see if Android recognizes your device by running adb devices in a shell (e.g., OS X Terminal), where adb is in your platform-tools/ directory of your SDK. If you get output similar to the following, Android detected your device:

```
List of devices attached
HT9CPP809576  device
```

If you are running Ubuntu (or perhaps another Linux variant) and this command did not work, you may need to add some udev rules. For example, here is a 51-android.rules file that will handle the devices from a handful of manufacturers:

```
SUBSYSTEM=="usb", SYSFS{idVendor}=="0bb4", MODE="0666"
SUBSYSTEM=="usb", SYSFS{idVendor}=="22b8", MODE="0666"
SUBSYSTEM=="usb", SYSFS{idVendor}=="18d1", MODE="0666"
SUBSYSTEMS=="usb", ATTRS{idVendor}=="18d1", ATTRS{idProduct}=="0c01", MODE="0666", ↵
  OWNER="[me]"
SUBSYSTEM=="usb", SYSFS{idVendor}=="19d2", SYSFS{idProduct}=="1354", MODE="0666"
SUBSYSTEM=="usb", SYSFS{idVendor}=="04e8", SYSFS{idProduct}=="681c", MODE="0666"
```

Drop that in your /etc/udev/rules.d directory on Ubuntu, and then either reboot the computer or otherwise reload the udev rules (e.g., sudo service udev reload). Then, unplug the device, plug it in again, and see if it is detected.

Chapter 3

Your First Android Project

Now that you have the Android SDK, it is time to make your first Android project. The good news is that this requires zero lines of code—Android's tools create a "Hello, world!" application for you as part of creating a new project. All you need to do is build it, install it, and watch it open on your emulator or device.

Step 1: Create the New Project

Android's tools can create a complete skeleton project for you, with everything you need for a complete (albeit very trivial) Android application. The process differs depending on whether you are using an IDE like Eclipse or the command line.

Eclipse

From the Eclipse main menu, choose File ➤ New ➤➤ Project to open the New Project dialog box, which gives you a list of project type wizards to choose from. Expand the Android option and click Android Project, as shown in Figure 3–1.

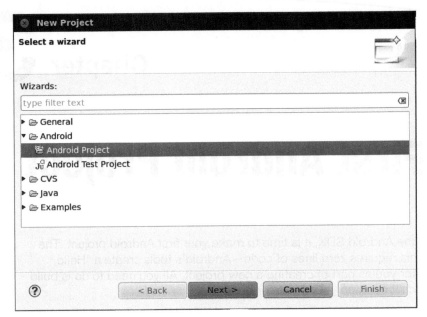

Figure 3–1. *Selecting a wizard in the Eclipse New Project dialog box*

Click Next to advance to the first page of the New Android Project wizard, shown in Figure 3–2.

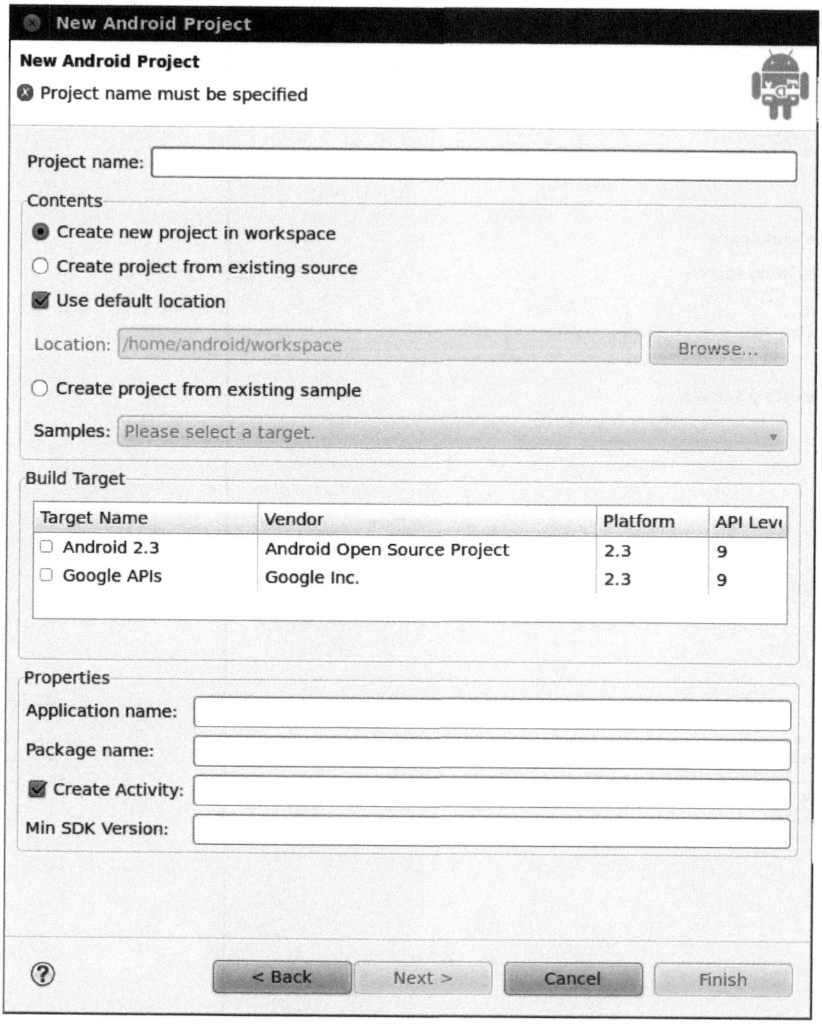

New Android Project

New Android Project

❌ Project name must be specified

Project name: [   ]

Contents
- ⦿ Create new project in workspace
- ○ Create project from existing source
- ☑ Use default location

Location: [/home/android/workspace]   Browse...

- ○ Create project from existing sample

Samples: [Please select a target.   ▾]

Build Target

Target Name	Vendor	Platform	API Lev(
☐ Android 2.3	Android Open Source Project	2.3	9
☐ Google APIs	Google Inc.	2.3	9

Properties

Application name: [   ]

Package name: [   ]

☑ Create Activity: [   ]

Min SDK Version: [   ]

⑦   [< Back]   [Next >]   [Cancel]   [Finish]

Figure 3–2. *Eclipse New Android Project wizard, ready to fill in*

Fill in the following and leave the default settings otherwise (the completed example for this project is shown in Figure 3–3):

- *Project name*: The name of the project (e.g., Now)

- *Build Target*: The Android SDK you wish to compile against (e.g., Google APIs for Android 2.3.3)

- *Application name*: The display name of your application, which will be used for the caption under your icon in the launcher (e.g., Now)

- *Package name*: The name of the Java package in which this project belongs (e.g., com.commonsware.android.skeleton)

- *Create Activity*: The name of the initial activity to create (e.g., Now)

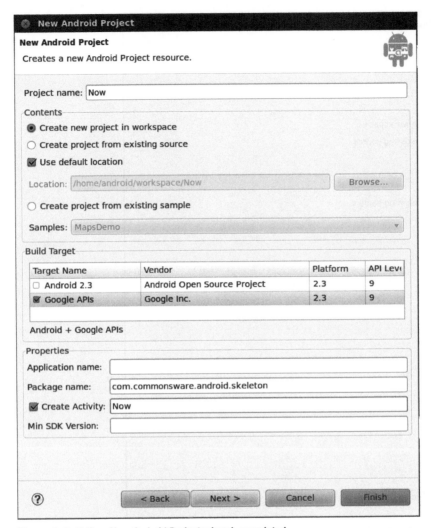

Figure 3–3. *Eclipse New Android Project wizard, completed*

At this point, click Finish to create your Eclipse project.

Command Line

Here is a sample command that creates an Android project from the command line:

```
android create project --target "Google Inc.:Google APIs:7" --path Skeleton/Now
  --activity Now --package com.commonsware.android.skeleton
```

This creates an application skeleton for you, complete with everything you need to build your first Android application: Java source code, build instructions, and so forth. However, you'll probably need to customize this somewhat. Here are what those command-line switches mean:

- `--target`: Indicates which version of Android you are targeting in terms of your build process. You need to supply the ID of a target that is installed on your development machine, one you downloaded via the Android SDK and AVD Manager. You can find out which targets are available via the `android list targets` command. Typically, your build process will target the newest version of Android that you have available.

- `--path`: Indicates where you want the project files to be generated. Android will create a directory if the one you name does not exist. For example, in the preceding command, a `Skeleton/Now/` directory will be created (or used if it exists) under the current working directory, and the project files will be stored there.

- `--activity`: Indicates the Java class name of your first activity for this project. Do not include a package name, and make sure the name meets Java class-naming conventions.

- `--package`: Indicates the Java package in which your first activity will be located. This package name also uniquely identifies your project on any device on which you install it, and it must be unique on the Android Market if you plan on distributing your application there. Hence, typically, you should construct your package based on a domain name you own (e.g., `com.commonsware.android.skeleton`), to reduce the odds of an accidental package name collision with somebody else.

For your development machine, you need to pick a suitable target, and you may wish to change the path. You can ignore the activity and package for now.

Step 2: Build, Install, and Run the Application in Your Emulator or Device

Having a project is nice and all, but it would be even better if you could build and run it, whether on the Android emulator or on your Android device. Once again, the process differs somewhat depending on whether you are using Eclipse or the command line.

Eclipse

With your project selected on the Package Explorer panel of Eclipse, click the green play button in the Eclipse toolbar to run your project. The first time you do this, you have to go through a few steps to set up a run configuration, so Eclipse knows what you want to do.

First, in the Run As dialog box, choose Android Application, as shown in Figure 3–4.

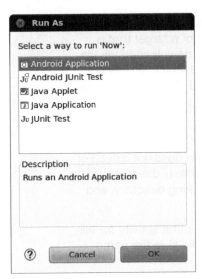

Figure 3–4. *Choosing to run as an Android application in the Eclipse Run As dialog box*

Click OK. If you have more than one emulator AVD or device available, you will then get an option to choose which you wish to run the application on. Otherwise, if you do not have a device plugged in, the emulator will start up with the AVD you created earlier. Then, Eclipse will install the application on your device or emulator and start it.

Command Line

For developers who are not using Eclipse, in your terminal, change into the Skeleton/Now directory, then run the following command:

```
ant clean install
```

The Ant-based build should emit a list of steps involved in the installation process, which looks like this:

```
Buildfile: /home/some-balding-guy/projects/Skeleton/Now/build.xml
    [setup] Android SDK Tools Revision 10
    [setup] Project Target: Android 1.6
    [setup] API level: 4
    [setup]
    [setup] ------------------
    [setup] Resolving library dependencies:
    [setup] No library dependencies.
    [setup]
    [setup] ------------------
    [setup]
    [setup] WARNING: No minSdkVersion value set. Application will install on all Android
versions.
    [setup]
    [setup] Importing rules file: tools/ant/main_rules.xml

clean:
```

```
    [delete] Deleting directory /home/some-balding-guy/projects/Skeleton/Now/bin
    [delete] Deleting directory /home/some-balding-guy/projects/Skeleton/Now/gen

-debug-obfuscation-check:

-set-debug-mode:

-compile-tested-if-test:

-pre-build:

-dirs:
     [echo] Creating output directories if needed...
    [mkdir] Created dir: /home/some-balding-guy/projects/Skeleton/Now/bin
    [mkdir] Created dir: /home/some-balding-guy/projects/Skeleton/Now/gen
    [mkdir] Created dir: /home/some-balding-guy/projects/Skeleton/Now/bin/classes

-aidl:
     [echo] Compiling aidl files into Java classes...

-renderscript:
     [echo] Compiling RenderScript files into Java classes and RenderScript bytecode...

-resource-src:
     [echo] Generating R.java / Manifest.java from the resources...

-pre-compile:

compile:
    [javac] /opt/android-sdk-linux/tools/ant/main_rules.xml:384: warning:
'includeantruntime' was not set, defaulting to build.sysclasspath=last; set to false for
repeatable builds
    [javac] Compiling 2 source files to /home/some-balding-
guy/projects/Skeleton/Now/bin/classes

-post-compile:

-obfuscate:

-dex:
     [echo] Converting compiled files and external libraries into /home/some-balding-
guy/projects/Skeleton/Now/bin/classes.dex...

-package-resources:
     [echo] Packaging resources
     [aapt] Creating full resource package...

-package-debug-sign:
[apkbuilder] Creating Now-debug-unaligned.apk and signing it with a debug key...

debug:
     [echo] Running zip align on final apk...
     [echo] Debug Package: /home/some-balding-guy/projects/Skeleton/Now/bin/Now-
debug.apk

install:
```

```
    [echo] Installing /home/some-balding-guy/projects/Skeleton/Now/bin/Now-debug.apk
onto default emulator or device...
    [exec] 98 KB/s (4626 bytes in 0.045s)
    [exec] pkg: /data/local/tmp/Now-debug.apk
    [exec] Success

BUILD SUCCESSFUL
Total time: 10 seconds
```

Note the BUILD SUCCESSFUL message at the bottom—that is how you know the application compiled successfully.

When you have a clean build, in your emulator or device, open the application launcher, shown in Figure 3–5, which typically is found at the bottom of the home screen.

Figure 3–5. *Android emulator application launcher*

Notice there is an icon for your Now application. Click it to open it and see your first activity in action. To leave the application and return to the launcher, press the Back button, which is located to the right of the Menu button and looks like an arrow pointing to the left.

Chapter 4

Examining Your First Project

The previous chapter stepped you through creating a stub project. This chapter describes what is inside of this project, so you understand what Android gives you at the outset and what the roles are for the various directories and files.

Project Structure

The Android build system is organized around a specific directory tree structure for your Android project, much like any other Java project. The specifics, though, are fairly unique to Android—the Android build tools do a few extra things to prepare the actual application that will run on the device or emulator. Here's a quick primer on the project structure, to help you make sense of it all, particularly for the sample code referenced in this book.

Root Contents

When you create a new Android project (e.g., via `android create project`), you get several items in the project's root directory, including the following:

- `AndroidManifest.xml`: An XML file that describes the application being built and what components (activities, services, etc.) are being supplied by that application

- `bin/`: The directory that holds the application once it is compiled

- `libs/`: The directory that holds any third-party JARs your application requires

- `res/`: The directory that holds resources, such as icons, GUI layouts, and the like, that are packaged with the compiled Java in the application

- `src/`: The directory that holds the Java source code for the application

In addition to the preceding file and directories, you may find any of the following in Android projects:

- `assets/`: The directory that holds other static files that you want packaged with the application for deployment onto the device

- `gen/`: The directory in which Android's build tools place source code that they generate

- `build.xml` and `*.properties`: Files that are used as part of the Ant-based command-line build process, if you are not using Eclipse

- `proguard.cfg`: A file that is used for integration with ProGuard to obfuscate your Android code

The Sweat Off Your Brow

When you create an Android project (e.g., via android create project), you supply the fully qualified class name of the main activity for the application (e.g., com.commonsware.android.SomeDemo). You will then find that your project's src/ tree already has the namespace directory tree in place, plus a stub Activity subclass representing your main activity (e.g., src/com/commonsware/android/SomeDemo.java). You are welcome to modify this file and add others to the src/ tree as needed to implement your application.

The first time you compile the project (e.g., via ant), out in the main activity's namespace directory, the Android build chain will create R.java. This contains a number of constants tied to the various resources you placed in the res/ directory tree. You should not modify R.java yourself, but instead let the Android tools handle it for you. You will see throughout this book that many of the examples reference things in R.java (e.g., referring to a layout's identifier via R.layout.main).

And Now, the Rest of the Story

The res/ directory tree in your project holds *resources*—static files that are packaged along with your application, either in their original form or, occasionally, in a preprocessed form. Following are some of the subdirectories you will find or create under res/:

- `res/drawable/`: For images (PNG, JPEG, etc.)
- `res/layout/`: For XML-based UI layout specifications
- `res/menu/`: For XML-based menu specifications
- `res/raw/`: For general-purpose files (e.g., an audio clip or a CSV file of account information)
- `res/values/`: For strings, dimensions, and the like
- `res/xml/`: For other general-purpose XML files you wish to ship

Some of the directory names may have suffixes, like `res/drawable-hdpi/`. This indicates that the directory of resources should be used only in certain circumstances—in this case, the drawable resources should be used only on devices with high-density screens.

We will cover all of these resources, and more, in later chapters of this book.

In your initial project, you will find the following:

- `res/drawable-hdpi/icon.png`, `res/drawable-ldpi/icon.png`, and `res/drawable-mdpi/icon.png`: Three renditions of a placeholder icon for your application for high-, low-, and medium-density screens, respectively

- `res/layout/main.xml`: An XML file that describes the very simple layout of your user interface

- `res/values/strings.xml`: An XML file that contains externalized strings, notably the placeholder name of your application

What You Get Out of It

When you compile your project (via `ant` or the IDE), the results go into the `bin/` directory under your project root, as follows:

- `bin/classes/`: Holds the compiled Java classes

- `bin/classes.dex`: Holds the executable created from those compiled Java classes

- `bin/`*`yourapp`*`.ap_`: Holds your application's resources, packaged as a ZIP file (where *yourapp* is the name of your application)

- `bin/`*`yourapp`*`-*.apk`: The actual Android application (where * varies)

The `.apk` file is a ZIP archive containing the `.dex` file, the compiled edition of your resources (`resources.arsc`), any uncompiled resources (such as what you put in `res/raw/`), and the `AndroidManifest.xml` file. If you build a debug version of the application (which is the default), you will have `yourapp-debug.apk` and `yourapp-debug-aligned.apk` as two versions of your APK. The latter has been optimized with the `zipalign` utility to make it run faster.

Inside Your Manifest

The foundation for any Android application is the manifest file, `AndroidManifest.xml`, in the root of your project. This is where you declare what is inside your application—the activities, the services, and so on. You also indicate how these pieces attach themselves to the overall Android system; for example, you indicate which activity (or activities) should appear on the device's main menu (a.k.a., the launcher).

When you create your application, a starter manifest is generated for you automatically. For a simple application, offering a single activity and nothing else, the autogenerated manifest will probably work out fine, or perhaps require a few minor modifications. On the other end of the spectrum, the manifest file for the Android API demo suite is over 1,000 lines long. Your production Android applications will probably fall somewhere in the middle.

In the Beginning, There Was the Root, and It Was Good

The root of all manifest files is, not surprisingly, a manifest element:

```
<manifest xmlns:android="http://schemas.android.com/apk/res/android"
  package="com.commonsware.android.search">
...
</manifest>
```

Note the namespace declaration. Curiously, the generated manifests apply it only on the attributes, not the elements (e.g., manifest, not android:manifest). This pattern works, so, unless Android changes, you should stick with it.

The biggest piece of information you need to supply on the manifest element is the package attribute (also curiously not namespaced). Here, you can provide the name of the Java package that will be considered the "base" of your application. Then, everywhere else in the manifest file that needs a class name, you can just substitute a leading dot as shorthand for the package. For example, if you needed to refer to com.commonsware.android.search.Snicklefritz in the preceding manifest, you could just use .Snicklefritz, since com.commonsware.android.search is defined as the application's package.

As noted in the previous chapter, your package also is a unique identifier for your application. A device can have only one application installed with a given package, and the Android Market will list only one project with a given package.

Your manifest also specifies android:versionName and android:versionCode attributes. These represent the versions of your application. The android:versionName value is what the user will see in the Applications list in their Settings application. Also, the version name is used by the Android Market listing, if you are distributing your application that way. The version name can be any string value you want. The android:versionCode value, on the other hand, must be an integer, and newer versions must have higher version codes than do older versions. Android and the Android Market will compare the version code of a new APK to the version code of an installed application to determine if the new APK is indeed an update. The typical approach is to start the version code at 1 and increment it with each production release of your application, though you can choose another convention if you wish.

> **TIP:** The Android Market will present only one version (typically, the latest) of any APK. Should you ever want to deploy a different version and not have to go through the effort of recompiling from your code, you can take a backup of your APK for any given version and simply side-load it onto your device or emulator.

An Application for Your Application

In your initial project's manifest, the only child of the `<manifest>` element is an `<application>` element. The children of the `<application>` element represent the core of the manifest file.

One attribute of the `<application>` element that you may need in select circumstances is the android:debuggable attribute. This needs to be set to `true` if you are installing the application on an actual device, you are using Eclipse (or another debugger), and your device precludes debugging without this flag. For example, the Google/HTC Nexus One requires android:debuggable = "true", according to some reports.

By default, when you create a new Android project, you get a single `<activity>` element inside the `<application>` element:

```xml
<?xml version="1.0"?>
<manifest xmlns:android="http://schemas.android.com/apk/res/android"
package="com.commonsware.android.skeleton">
    <application>
        <activity android:name=".Now" android:label="Now">
            <intent-filter>
                <action android:name="android.intent.action.MAIN"/>
                <category android:name="android.intent.category.LAUNCHER"/>
            </intent-filter>
        </activity>
    </application>
</manifest>
```

This element supplies android:name for the class implementing the activity, android:label for the display name of the activity, and (frequently) an `<intent-filter>` child element describing under what conditions this activity will be displayed. The stock `<activity>` element sets up your activity to appear in the launcher, so users can choose to run it. As you'll see later in this book, you can have several activities in one project, if you so choose.

Chapter 5

A Bit About Eclipse

Eclipse is an extremely popular integrated development environment (IDE), particularly for Java development. It is also designed to be extensible via an add-in system. To top it off, Eclipse is open source, thanks to the beneficence of IBM many years back in its decision to release Eclipse to the wide world. That combination made it an ideal choice of IDE for the core Android developer team.

Specifically, to go alongside the Android SDK, Google has published some add-ins for the Eclipse environment. Primary among these is the Android Developer Tools (ADT) add-in, which gives Eclipse it core awareness of Android.

What the ADT Gives You

The ADT add-in, in essence, takes regular Eclipse operations and extends them to work with Android projects. For example, with Eclipse, you get the following features (among others):

- New project wizards to create regular Android projects, Android test projects, and so forth

- The ability to run an Android project just like you might run a regular Java application—via the green Run button in the toolbar—despite the fact that this really involves pushing the Android application over to an emulator or device, possibly even starting up the emulator if it is not running

- Tooltip support for Android classes and methods

In addition, the latest version of the ADT provides you with preliminary support for drag-and-drop GUI editing. While this book will focus on the XML files that Eclipse generates, Eclipse now lets you assemble those XML files by dragging GUI components around on the screen, adjusting properties as you go. Drag-and-drop GUI editing is fairly new, so there may be a few rough edges for a while as the community and Google identify the problems and limitations with the current implementation.

Coping with Eclipse

Eclipse is a powerful tool. Like many powerful tools, Eclipse is sometimes confounding. Determining how to solve some specific development problem can be a challenge, exacerbated by the newness of Android itself.

This section offers some tips for handling some common issues in using Eclipse with Android.

How to Import a Non-Eclipse Project

Not all Android projects ship with Eclipse project files, such as the sample projects associated with this book. However, you can easily add them to your Eclipse workspace, if you wish. Here's how to do it!

First, choose File ➤➤ New ➤➤ Project from the Eclipse main menu, as shown in Figure 5–1.

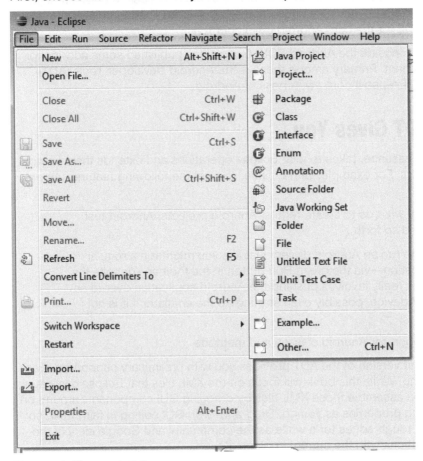

Figure 5–1. *File menu in Eclipse*

Then, choose **Android ➤➤ Android Project** from the tree of available project types, as shown in Figure 5–2, and click Next.

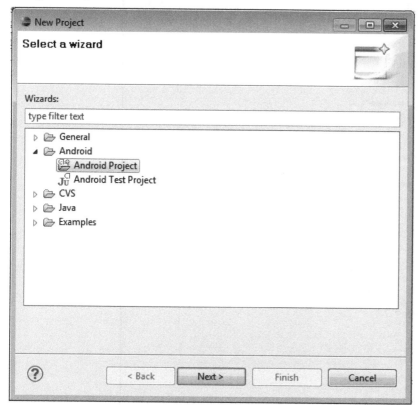

Figure 5–2. *New Project wizard in Eclipse*

NOTE: If you do not see this option, you have not installed Android Developer Tools.

Then, on the first page of the New Android Project wizard, choose the "Create project from existing source" radio button, click the Browse button, and open the directory containing your project's AndroidManifest.xml file. This will populate most of the rest of the wizard page, though you may need to also specify a build target from the table, as shown in Figure 5–3.

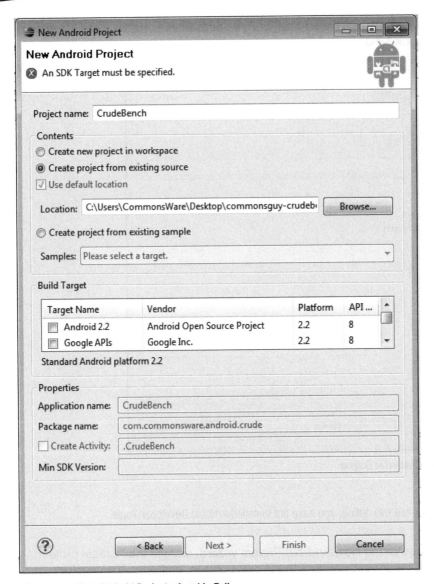

Figure 5–3. *New Android Project wizard in Eclipse*

Then, click Finish. This will return you to Eclipse, with the imported project in your workspace, as shown in Figure 5–4.

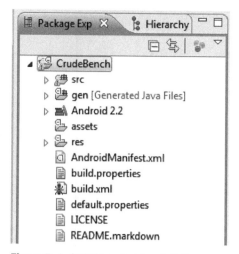

Figure 5–4. *Android project tree in Eclipse*

Next, right-click the project name and choose **Build Path** ➤➤ **Configure Build Path** from the context menu, as shown in Figure 5–5.

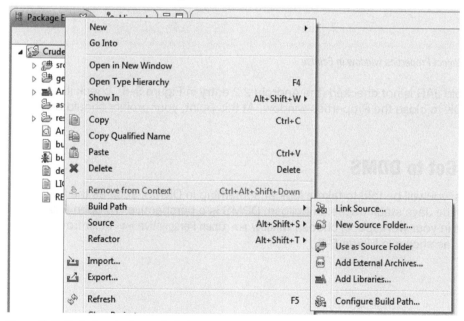

Figure 5–5. *Project context menu in Eclipse*

This brings up the Java Build Path portion of the project Properties window, as shown in Figure 5–6.

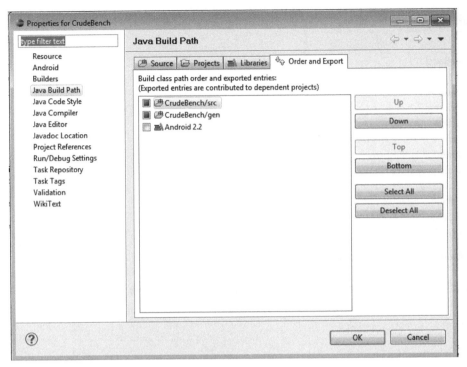

Figure 5–6. *Project Properties window in Eclipse*

If the Android JAR is not checked (the Android 2.2 entry in Figure 5–6), check it, and then click OK to close the Properties window. At this point, your project should be ready for use.

How to Get to DDMS

Many times, you will be told to take a look at something in DDMS, such as the LogCat tab to examine Java stack traces. In Eclipse, DDMS is a perspective. To open this perspective in your workspace, choose **Window ➤➤ Open Perspective ➤➤ Other** from the main menu, as shown in Figure 5–7.

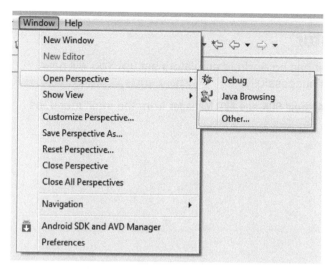

Figure 5–7. *Perspective menu in Eclipse*

Then, in the list of perspectives, shown in Figure 5–8, choose DDMS.

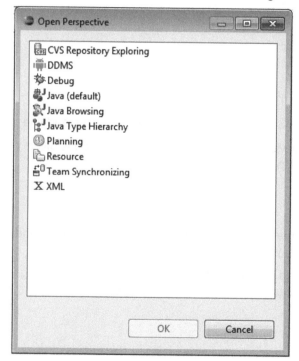

Figure 5–8. *Perspective roster in Eclipse*

This will add the DDMS perspective to your workspace and open it in your Eclipse IDE.

DDMS is covered in greater detail in a later chapter of this book.

How to Create an Emulator

By default, your Eclipse environment has no Android emulators set up. You will need one before you can run your project successfully.

To do this, first choose **Window** ➤ **Android SDK and AVD Manager** from the main menu, as shown in Figure 5–9.

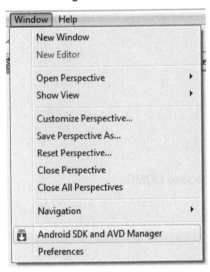

Figure 5–9. *Android SDK and AVD Manager menu option in Eclipse*

That brings up the same window as you get by running android from the command line.

You can now define an Android Virtual Device (AVD) by following the instructions given in Chapter 2, in the section "Step 5: Set Up the Emulator."

How to Run a Project

Given that you have an AVD defined, or that you have a device set up for debugging and connected to your development machine, you can run your project in the emulator.

First, click the Run toolbar button, or choose **Project** ➤ **Run** from the main menu. This brings up the Run As dialog box the first time you run the project, as shown in Figure 5–10.

Figure 5–10. *The Run As dialog box in Eclipse*

Choose Android Application and click OK. If you have more than one AVD or device available, you will be presented with a window in which you choose the desired target environment. Then, the emulator will start up to run your application. Note that you will need to unlock the lock screen on the emulator (or device) if it is locked.

How Not to Run Your Project

When you go to run your project, be sure that an XML file is not the active tab in the editor. Attempting to "run" this will result in a .out file being created in whatever directory the XML file lives in (e.g., res/layout/main.xml.out). To recover, simply delete the offending .out file and try running again, this time with a Java file as the active tab.

Alternative IDEs

If you really like Eclipse and the ADT, you may want to consider MOTODEV Studio for Android. This is another set of add-ins for Eclipse, augmenting the ADT and offering a number of other Android-related development features, including the following (among many others):

- More wizards for helping you create Android classes

- Integrated SQLite browsing, so you can manipulate a SQLite database in your emulator right from your IDE

- More validators to check for common bugs, and a library of code snippets to have fewer bugs at the outset

■   Assistance with translating your application to multiple languages

While MOTODEV Studio for Android is published by Motorola, you can use it to build applications for all Android devices, not only those manufactured by Motorola themselves. With Google's pending acquisition of Motorola, the future of MOTODEV will certainly be interesting.

Other IDEs are slowly getting their equivalents of the ADT, albeit with minimal assistance from Google. For example, IntelliJ's IDEA has a module for Android. It was originally commercial, but now it is part of the open source community edition of IDEA as of version 10.

And, of course, you do not need to use an IDE at all. While this may sound sacrilegious to some, IDEs are not the only way to build applications. Much of what is accomplished via the ADT can be accomplished through command-line equivalents, meaning a shell and an editor are all you truly need. For example, the authors of this book do not presently use an IDE and have no intentions of adopting Eclipse any time soon.

IDEs and This Book

You are welcome to use Eclipse as you work through this book. You are welcome to use another IDE if you wish. You are even welcome to skip the IDE outright and just use an editor.

This book is focused on demonstrating Android capabilities and the APIs for exploiting those capabilities. It is not aimed at teaching the use of any one IDE. As such, the sample code shown should work in any IDE, particularly if you follow the instructions in this chapter for importing non-Eclipse projects into Eclipse.

Chapter 6

Enhancing Your First Project

The `AndroidManifest.xml` file that Android generated for your first project gets the job done. However, for a production application, you may wish to consider adding a few attributes and elements, such as those described in this chapter.

Supporting Multiple Screen Sizes

Android devices come with a wide range of screen sizes, from 2.8-inch tiny smartphones to 46-inch Google TVs. Android divides these into four categories, based on physical screen size and the distance at which they are usually viewed:

- *Small*: Under 3 inches (7.5 cm), at least 426×320dp resolution

- *Normal*: 3 inches (7.5 cm) to around 4.5 inches (11.5 cm), at least 470×320dp resolution

- *Large*: 4.5 inches (11.5 cm) to around 10 inches (25 cm), at least 640×480dp resolution

- *Extra-large*: Over 10 inches (25 cm), at least 960×720dp resolution

By default, your application will not support small screens, will support normal screens, and may support large and extra-large screens via some code built into Android that automates conversion, scaling, and resizing of an application onto larger screens.

To truly support all the screen sizes you want to target, you should consider adding a `<supports-screens>` element in your manifest file. This enumerates the screen sizes for which you have explicit support. For example, if you want to support small screens, you need to include the `<supports-screens>` element. Similarly, if you are providing custom UI support for large or extra-large screens, you will want to have the `<supports-screens>` element with appropriate subelements. So, while the default settings in the starting manifest file work, you should consider adding support for handling multiple screen sizes.

Much more information about providing solid support for all screen sizes can be found in Chapter 25.

Specifying Versions

As noted in the previous chapter, your manifest already contains some version information about your application's version. However, you probably want to add to your `AndroidManifest.xml` file a `<uses-sdk>` element as a child of the `<manifest>` element, to specify which versions of Android your application supports. By default, your application is assumed to support every Android version from 1.0 to the current 3.0 and onward to any version in the future. Most likely, that is not what you want.

The most important attribute for your `<uses-sdk>` element is `android:minSdkVersion`. This indicates what is the oldest version of Android for which you offer support. If you like, it communicates the oldest version with which you are testing your application. The value of the attribute is an integer representing the Android SDK version:

- 1: Android 1.0
- 2: Android 1.1
- 3: Android 1.5
- 4: Android 1.6
- 5: Android 2.0
- 6: Android 2.0.1
- 7: Android 2.1
- 8: Android 2.2
- 9: Android 2.3
- 10: Android 2.3.3
- 11: Android 3.0
- 12: Android 3.1
- 13: Android 3.2
- 14: Android 4.0

So, if you are testing your application only on Android 2.1 and newer versions of Android, you would set the `android:minSdkVersion` attribute to 7.

From Android 3.2 onward, an alternative method is provided to more accurately specify the space requirements of your screen layouts. These attributes specify the smallest width, sw<N>dp, available width, w<N>dp, and available height, h<N>dp (where N is the pixel count). At first, using these prescriptive options may seem more complicated, but for many designers it is more natural to design a layout and set of features, and then determine the minimum and optimum sizes to the nearest pixel for presentation requirements.

You may also wish to specify an android:targetSdkVersion attribute. This indicates which version of Android you are targeting as you are writing your code. If your application is run on a newer version of Android, Android may do some things to try to improve compatibility of your code with respect to changes made in the newer Android. So, for example, you might specify android:targetSdkVersion="10", indicating you are writing your application with Android 2.3.3 in mind; if your app someday is run on an Android 3.0 device, Android may take some extra steps to make sure your 2.3.3-centric code runs correctly on the 3.0 device. In particular, to get a tablet look and feel when running on an Android 3.0 (or higher) tablet, you need to specify a target SDK version of 11 or higher. This topic will be covered in more detail in Chapters 26 and 27.

Activities

Chapter 7

Rewriting Your First Project

The project you created in Chapter 3 is composed of just the default files generated by the Android build tools—you did not write any Java code yourself. In this chapter, you will modify that project to make it somewhat more interactive. Along the way, you will examine the basic Java code that comprises an Android activity.

> **NOTE:** The instructions in this chapter assume you followed the original instructions in Chapter 3 in terms of the names of packages and files. If you used different names, you will need to adjust the names in the following steps to match yours.

The Activity

Your project's `src` directory contains the standard Java-style tree of directories based on the Java package you used when you created the project (e.g., `com.commonsware.android` results in `src/com/commonsware/android/`). Inside the innermost directory you should find a pregenerated source file named Now.java, which is where your first activity will go.

Open Now.java in your editor and paste in the following code (or, if you downloaded the source files from the Apress web site, you can just use the `Skeleton/Now` project directly):

```
package com.commonsware.android.skeleton;

import android.app.Activity;
import android.os.Bundle;
import android.view.View;
import android.widget.Button;
import java.util.Date;
```

```
public class Now extends Activity implements View.OnClickListener {
  Button btn;

  @Override
  public void onCreate(Bundle icicle) {
    super.onCreate(icicle);
    btn=new Button(this);
    btn.setOnClickListener(this);
    updateTime();
    setContentView(btn);
  }

  public void onClick(View view) {
    updateTime();
  }

  private void updateTime() {
    btn.setText(new Date().toString());
  }
}
```

Dissecting the Activity

Let's examine this Java code piece by piece, starting with the package declaration and imported classes:

```
package com.commonsware.android.skeleton;
```

```
import android.app.Activity;
import android.os.Bundle;
import android.view.View;
import android.widget.Button;
import java.util.Date;
```

The package declaration needs to be the same as the one you used when creating the project. Then, as with any other Java project, you need to import any classes you reference. Most of the Android-specific classes are in the android package.

NOTE: Not every Java SE class is available to Android programs. Visit the Android class reference to see what is and is not available.

Activities are public classes, inheriting from the android.app.Activity base class. In this case, the activity holds a button (btn):

```
public class Now extends Activity implements View.OnClickListener {
  Button btn;
```

Since, for simplicity, we want to trap all button clicks just within the activity itself, we also have the activity class implement OnClickListener.

The onCreate() method is invoked when the activity is started. The first thing you should do is chain upward to the superclass, so the stock Android activity initialization can be done:

```
@Override
public void onCreate(Bundle icicle) {
  super.onCreate(icicle);

  btn=new Button(this);
  btn.setOnClickListener(this);
  updateTime();
  setContentView(btn);
}
```

In our implementation, we then create the button instance btn (via new Button(this)), tell it to send all button clicks to the activity instance itself (via setOnClickListener()), call a private updateTime() method, and then set the activity's content view to be the button itself (via setContentView()). We will take a look at that magical Bundle icicle in a later chapter. For the moment, consider it an opaque handle that all activities receive upon creation.

```
public void onClick(View view) {
  updateTime();
}
```

In Java's traditional Swing UI world, a JButton click raises an ActionEvent, which is passed to the ActionListener configured for the button. In Android, a button click causes onClick() to be invoked in the OnClickListener instance configured for the button. The listener has passed to it the view that triggered the click (in this case, the button). All we do here is call that private updateTime() method:

```
private void updateTime() {
  btn.setText(new Date().toString());
}
```

When we open the activity (onCreate()) or when the button is clicked (onClick()), we update the button's label to be the current time via setText(), which functions much the same as the JButton equivalent.

Building and Running the Activity

To build the activity, use your IDE's built-in Android packaging tool, or run ant clean install in the base directory of your project (as described in Chapter 3). Then, run the activity. It should be launched for you automatically if you are using Eclipse; otherwise, find the activity in the home screen launcher. You should see an activity akin to what's shown in Figure 7–1.

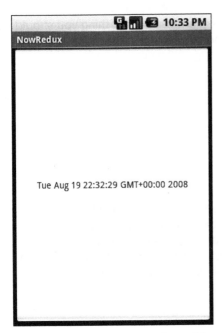

Figure 7–1. *The Now demonstration activity*

Clicking the button—in other words, clicking pretty much anywhere on the device's screen—will update the time shown in the button's label.

Note that the label is centered horizontally and vertically, as those are the default styles applied to button captions. We can control that formatting, which will be covered in a later chapter.

After you are finished gazing at the awesomeness of Advanced Push-Button Technology, you can click the Back button on the emulator to return to the launcher.

Chapter **8**

Using XML-Based Layouts

While it is technically possible to create and attach widgets to your activity purely through Java code, as we did in the preceding chapter, the more common approach is to use an XML-based layout file. Dynamic instantiation of widgets is reserved for more complicated scenarios, where the widgets are not known at compile time (e.g., populating a column of radio buttons based on data retrieved from the Internet).

With that in mind, it's time to break out the XML and learn how to lay out Android activity views that way.

What Is an XML-Based Layout?

As the name suggests, an XML-based layout is a specification of widgets' relationships to each other—and to containers—encoded in XML format. Specifically, Android considers XML-based layouts to be resources, and as such, layout files are stored in the `reslayout` directory inside your Android project.

Each XML file contains a tree of elements specifying a layout of widgets and containers that make up one `View`. The attributes of the XML elements are properties, describing how a widget should look or how a container should behave. For example, if a `Button` element has an attribute value of `android:textStyle = "bold"`, that means that the text appearing on the face of the button should be rendered in a boldface font style.

Android's SDK ships with a tool (aapt) that uses the layouts. This tool should be automatically invoked by your Android tool chain (e.g., Eclipse or Ant's `build.xml`). Of particular importance to you as a developer is that aapt generates the `R.java` source file within your project's gen directory, allowing you to access layouts and widgets within those layouts directly from your Java code, as will be demonstrated later in this chapter.

Why Use XML-Based Layouts?

Most everything you do using XML layout files can be achieved through Java code. For example, you could use `setTypeface()` to have a button render its text in bold, instead of using a property in an XML layout. Since XML layouts are yet another file for you to keep track of, we need good reasons for using such files.

Perhaps the biggest reason is to assist in the creation of tools for view definition, such as a GUI builder in an IDE like Eclipse or a dedicated Android GUI designer like DroidDraw. Such GUI builders could, in principle, generate Java code instead of XML. The challenge is rereading the definition in the design tool to support edits, which is far simpler when the data is in a structured format like XML rather than in a programming language. Moreover, keeping the generated bits separated from handwritten code makes it less likely that somebody's custom-crafted source will get clobbered by accident when the generated bits get regenerated. XML forms a nice middle ground between something that is easy for tool writers to use and something that is easy for programmers to work with by hand as needed.

Also, XML as a GUI definition format is becoming more commonplace. Microsoft's Extensible Application Markup Language (XAML), Adobe's Flex, Google's Google Web Toolkit (GWT), and Mozilla's XML User Interface Language (XUL) all take a similar approach to that of Android: put layout details in an XML file and put programming smarts in source files (e.g., JavaScript for XUL). Many less-well-known GUI frameworks, such as ZK, also use XML for view definition. While "following the herd" is not necessarily the best policy, it does have the advantage of helping to ease the transition to Android from any other XML-centered view description language.

OK, So What Does It Look Like?

Here is the `Button` from the previous chapter's sample application, converted into an XML layout file, found in the `Layouts/NowRedux` sample project:

```
<?xml version="1.0" encoding="utf-8"?>
<Button xmlns:android="http://schemas.android.com/apk/res/android"
    android:id="@+id/button"
    android:text=""
    android:layout_width="fill_parent"
    android:layout_height="fill_parent"/>
```

The class name of the widget, `Button`, forms the name of the XML element. Since `Button` is an Android-supplied widget, we can just use the bare class name. If you create your own widgets as subclasses of `android.view.View`, you will need to provide a full package declaration as well (e.g., `com.commonsware.android.MyWidget`).

The root element needs to declare the Android XML namespace:

```
xmlns:android="http://schemas.android.com/apk/res/android"
```

All other elements will be children of the root and will inherit that namespace declaration.

Because we want to reference this button from our Java code, we need to give it an identifier via the `android:id` attribute. We will cover this concept in greater detail in the next section.

The remaining attributes are properties of this `Button` instance:

- `android:text`: Indicates the initial text to be displayed on the button face (in this case, an empty string)
- `android:layout_width` and `android:layout_height`: Tell Android to have the button's width and height fill the parent, which in this case is the entire screen

These attributes will be covered in greater detail in Chapter 10.

Since this single widget is the only content in our activity's view, we need only this single element. Complex views will require a whole tree of elements, representing the widgets and containers that control their positioning. All the remaining chapters of this book will use the XML layout form whenever practical, so there are dozens of other examples of more complex layouts for you to peruse.

What's with the @ Signs?

Many widgets and containers need to appear only in the XML layout file and do not need to be referenced in your Java code. For example, a static label (`TextView`) frequently needs to be in the layout file only to indicate where it should appear. These sorts of elements in the XML file do not need to have the `android:id` attribute to give them a name.

Anything you *do* want to use in your Java source, though, needs an `android:id`.

The convention is to use `@+id/...` as the id value, where the ... represents your locally unique name for the widget in question, for the first occurrence of a given id value in your layout file. In the XML layout example in the preceding section, `@+id/button` is the identifier for the `Button` widget. The second and subsequent occurrences in the same layout file should drop the + sign—a feature we will use in Chapter 10.

Android provides a few special `android:id` values, of the form `@android:id/....` You will see some of these values in various examples throughout this book.

And How Do We Attach These to the Java?

Given that you have painstakingly set up the widgets and containers for your view in an XML layout file named `main.xml` stored in `res/layout`, all you need is one statement in your activity's `onCreate()` callback to use that layout:

```
setContentView(R.layout.main);
```

This is the same `setContentView()` we used earlier, passing it an instance of a `View` subclass (in that case, a `Button`). The Android-built `View`, constructed from our layout, is accessed from that code-generated `R` class. All of the layouts are accessible under `R.layout`, keyed by the base name of the layout file; for example, `res/layout/main.xml` results in `R.layout.main`.

To access your identified widgets, use `findViewById()`, passing it the numeric identifier of the widget in question. That numeric identifier was generated by Android in the R class as `R.id.something` (where `something` is the specific widget you are seeking). Those widgets are simply subclasses of View, just like the Button instance we created in the previous chapter.

The Rest of the Story

In the original Now demo, the button's face would show the current time, which would reflect when the button was last pushed (or when the activity was first shown, if the button had not yet been pushed). Most of that logic still works, even in this revised demo (NowRedux). However, rather than instantiating the Button in our activity's `onCreate()` callback, we can reference the one from the XML layout:

```
package com.commonsware.android.layouts;

import android.app.Activity;
import android.os.Bundle;
import android.view.View;
import android.widget.Button;
import java.util.Date;

public class NowRedux extends Activity
  implements View.OnClickListener {
  Button btn;

  @Override
  public void onCreate(Bundle icicle) {
    super.onCreate(icicle);

    setContentView(R.layout.main);

    btn=(Button)findViewById(R.id.button);
    btn.setOnClickListener(this);
    updateTime();
  }

  public void onClick(View view) {
    updateTime();
  }

  private void updateTime() {
    btn.setText(new Date().toString());
  }
}
```

The first difference is that, rather than setting the content view to be a view we created in Java code, we set it to reference the XML layout (`setContentView(R.layout.main)`). The R.java source file will be updated when we rebuild this project to include a reference to our layout file (stored as `main.xml` in our project's `res/layout` directory).

The other difference is that we need to get our hands on our Button instance, for which we use the `findViewById()` call. Since we identified our button as `@+id/button`, we can reference the button's identifier as R.id.button. Now, with the Button instance in hand, we can set the callback and set the label as needed.

The results look the same as with the original Now demo, as shown in Figure 8–1.

Figure 8–1. *The NowRedux sample activity*

Chapter 9

Employing Basic Widgets

Every GUI toolkit has some basic widgets: fields, labels, buttons, and so forth. Android's toolkit is no different in scope, and the basic widgets provide a good introduction to how widgets work in Android activities.

Assigning Labels

The simplest widgets the label, referred to in Android as a `TextView`. As in most GUI toolkits, labels are bits of text that can't be edited directly by users. Typically, labels are used to identify adjacent widgets (e.g., a "Name:" label next to a field where the user fills in a name

In Java, you can create a label by creating a `TextView` instance. More commonly, though, you will create labels in XML layout files by adding a `TextView` element to the layout, with an `android:text` property to set the value of the label itself. If you need to swap labels based on certain criteria, such as internationalization, you may wish to use a string resource reference in the XML instead, as will be described later in this book.

`TextView` has numerous other properties of relevance for labels, such as the following

- `android:typeface`: Sets the typeface to use for the label (e.g., monospace)

- `android:textStyle`: Indicates that the typeface should be made bold (bold), italic (italic), or bold and italic (bold_italic)

- `android:textSize`: Specifies the size of the font, in one of several measures: sp (scaled pixels), dip (density-independent pixels), px (raw pixels), in (inches), mm (millimeters). The recommend approach is to use sp, and this is appended to the size, such as 12sp.

- `android:textColor`: Sets the color of the label's text, in RGB hex format (e.g., #FF0000 for red)

For example, in the Basic/Label project, you will find the following layout file:

```xml
<?xml version="1.0" encoding="utf-8"?>
<TextView xmlns:android="http://schemas.android.com/apk/res/android"
  android:layout_width="fill_parent"
  android:layout_height="wrap_content"
  android:text="You were expecting something profound?"
  />
```

Just that layout alone, with the stub Java source provided by Android's project builder (e.g., android create project), gives you the result shown in Figure 9–1.

Figure 9–1. *The LabelDemo sample application*

In our XML responsible for the LabelDemo, you'll note we used two width and height directives. The first, fill_parent, indicates we want our UI element to completely fill its parent space, minus any padding or border. The second, wrap_content, ensures that only enough space within the parent to show our content is used, and no more. These will become clearer as we step through more examples in the coming chapters.

Button, Button, Who's Got the Button?

You've already seen the use of the Button widget the previous two chapters. As it turns out, Button is a subclass of TextView, so everything discussed in the preceding section also applies to formatting the face of the button.

Android offers you two approaches when you are dealing with the on-click listener for a Button. The first option is the "classic" way of defining some object (such as the activity) as implementing the View.OnClickListener interface. Even better than the classic method is the contemporary Android way of simplifying things. This simple option has two steps:

1. Define some method on your `Activity` that holds the button that takes a single `View` parameter, has a `void` return value, and is `public`.

2. In your layout XML, on the `Button` element, include the `android:onClick` attribute with the name of the method you defined in the previous step.

For example, we might have a method on our `Activity` that looks like this:

```
public void someMethod(View theButton) {
  // do something useful here
}
```

Then, we could use this XML declaration for the `Button` itself, including `android:onClick`:

```
<Button
  android:onClick="someMethod"
  ...
/>
```

This is enough for Android to wire together the `Button` with the click handler. At first you may not feel this is any simpler than the traditional approach. But consider the ease with which this method opens up options to change the `Activity` for a given `Button` through simple dint of differing options in your XML specification—for instance, under different language locales, screen sizes, and so forth. We will talk more about these options in coming chapters.

Fleeting Images

Android has two widgets to help you embed images in your activities: `ImageView` and `ImageButton`. As the names suggest, they are image-based analogues to `TextView` and `Button`, respectively.

Each widget takes an `android:src` attribute (in an XML layout) to specify which picture to use. These attributes usually reference a drawable resource, described in greater detail in Chapter 23, which discusses resources.

`ImageButton`, a subclass of `ImageView`, mixes in the standard `Button` behaviors, for responding to clicks and whatnot. For example, take a peek at the `main.xml` layout from the `Basic/ImageView` sample project:

```
<?xml version="1.0" encoding="utf-8"?>
<ImageView xmlns:android="http://schemas.android.com/apk/res/android"
    android:id="@+id/icon"
    android:layout_width="fill_parent"
    android:layout_height="fill_parent"
    android:adjustViewBounds="true"
    android:src="@drawable/molecule"
    />
```

The result, just using the code-generated activity, is simply the image, as shown in Figure 9–2.

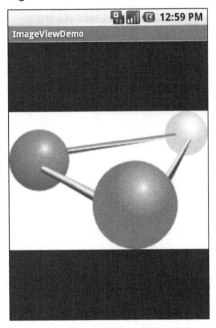

Figure 9–2. *The ImageViewDemo sample application*

Fields of Green...or Other Colors

Along with buttons and labels, fields are the third anchor of most GUI toolkits. In Android, they are implemented via the EditText widget, which is a subclass of the TextView used for labels.

Along with the standard TextView properties (e.g., android:textStyle), EditText has many other properties that will be useful to you in constructing fields, including the following:

- android:autoText: Controls if the field should provide automatic spelling assistance

- android:capitalize: Controls if the field should automatically capitalize the first letter of entered text (e.g., in name and city fields)

- android:digits: Configures the field to accept only certain digits

- android:password: Configures the field to display password dots as characters are typed into the field, hiding the typed characters

- android:singleLine: Controls if the field is for single-line input or multiple-line input (e.g., does pressing Enter move you to the next widget or add a newline?)

Most of the preceding properties are also available from the new android:inputType attribute, added in Android 1.5 as part of adding "soft keyboards" to Android (discussed in Chapter 11).

For example, from the Basic/Field project, here is an XML layout file showing an EditText widget:

```xml
<?xml version="1.0" encoding="utf-8"?>
<EditText xmlns:android="http://schemas.android.com/apk/res/android"
  android:id="@+id/field"
  android:layout_width="fill_parent"
  android:layout_height="fill_parent"
  android:singleLine="false"
  />
```

Note that android:singleLine is set to "false", so users will be able to enter several lines of text.

For this project, the FieldDemo.java file populates the input field with some prose:

```java
package com.commonsware.android.field;

import android.app.Activity;
import android.os.Bundle;
import android.widget.EditText;

public class FieldDemo extends Activity {
  @Override
  public void onCreate(Bundle icicle) {
    super.onCreate(icicle);
    setContentView(R.layout.main);

    EditText fld=(EditText)findViewById(R.id.field);
    fld.setText("Licensed under the Apache License, Version 2.0 " +
            "(the \"License\"); you may not use this file " +
            "except in compliance with the License. You may " +
            "obtain a copy of the License at " +
            "http://www.apache.org/licenses/LICENSE-2.0");
  }
}
```

The result, once built and installed into the emulator, is shown in Figure 9–3.

Another flavor of field is one that offers autocompletion, to help users supply a value without typing in the whole text. That is provided in Android as the AutoCompleteTextView widget, discussed in greater detail in Chapter 12.

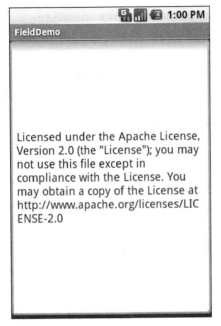

Figure 9–3. *The FieldDemo sample application*

Just Another Box to Check

The classic check box has two states: checked and unchecked. Clicking the check box toggles between those states to indicate a choice (e.g., "Add rush delivery to my order").

In Android, there is a CheckBox widget to meet this need. It has TextView as an ancestor, so you can use TextView properties like android:textColor to format the widget.

Within Java, you can invoke the following:

- isChecked(): Determines if the check box has been checked
- setChecked(): Forces the check box into a checked or unchecked state
- toggle(): Toggles the check box as if the user checked it

Also, you can register a listener object (in this case, an instance of OnCheckedChangeListener) to be notified when the state of the check box changes.

For example, from the Basic/CheckBox project, here is a simple check box layout:

```
<?xml version="1.0" encoding="utf-8"?>
<CheckBox xmlns:android="http://schemas.android.com/apk/res/android"
    android:id="@+id/check"
    android:layout_width="wrap_content"
    android:layout_height="wrap_content"
    android:text="This checkbox is: unchecked" />
```

The corresponding CheckBoxDemo.java retrieves and configures the behavior of the check box:

```
public class CheckBoxDemo extends Activity
  implements CompoundButton.OnCheckedChangeListener {
  CheckBox cb;

  @Override
  public void onCreate(Bundle icicle) {
    super.onCreate(icicle);
    setContentView(R.layout.main);

    cb=(CheckBox)findViewById(R.id.check);
    cb.setOnCheckedChangeListener(this);
  }

  public void onCheckedChanged(CompoundButton buttonView,
                               boolean isChecked) {
    if (isChecked) {
      cb.setText("This checkbox is: checked");
    }
    else {
      cb.setText("This checkbox is: unchecked");
    }
  }
}
```

Note that the activity serves as its own listener for check box state changes, since it implements the OnCheckedChangeListener interface (via cb.setOnCheckedChangeListener(this)). The callback for the listener is onCheckedChanged(), which receives the check box whose state has changed and the new state. In this case, we update the text of the check box to reflect what the actual box contains.

The result? Clicking the check box immediately updates its text, as shown in Figures 9–4 and 9–5.

Figure 9–4. *The CheckBoxDemo sample application, with the check box unchecked*

Figure 9–5. *The same application, now with the check box checked*

Throw the Switch, Igor

New to Android 4.0 (Ice Cream Sandwich) is a variant of the CheckBox. This is a two-state toggle Switch that enables the user to swipe or drag with their finger as if they were toggling a light switch. They can also tap the Switch widget as if it were a CheckBox to change its state.

The Switch provides an android:text property to display associated text with the Switch state, which is controlled via the setTextOn() and setTextOff() methods of the Switch.

Other useful methods available for a Switch include:

- getTextOn(): Returns the text used when the Switch is on

- getTextOff(): Returns the text used when the Switch is off

- setChecked(): Changes the current Switch state to on (just like CheckBox)

For example, from the Basic/Switch project, here is a simple Switch layout:

```xml
<?xml version="1.0" encoding="utf-8"?>
<Switch xmlns:android="http://schemas.android.com/apk/res/android"
    android:id="@+id/switchdemo"
    android:layout_width="wrap_content"
    android:layout_height="wrap_content"
    android:text="This switch is: off" />
```

Note that we couldn't call the widget "switch" because of reserved-word conventions in Java. The corresponding SwitchActivity.java retrieves and configures the behavior of the switch We once again configure our class to implement the OnCheckChangedListener interface, and it takes care of calling our onCheckedChanged method:

```java
public class SwitchDemo extends Activity
  implements CompoundButton.OnCheckedChangeListener {
  Switch sw;

  @Override
  public void onCreate(Bundle icicle) {
    super.onCreate(icicle);
    setContentView(R.layout.main);

    sw=(Switch)findViewById(R.id.switchdemo);
    sw.setOnCheckedChangeListener(this);
  }

  public void onCheckedChanged(CompoundButton buttonView,
                               boolean isChecked) {
    if (isChecked) {
      sw.setTextOn("This switch is: on");
    }
    else {
      sw.setTextOff("This switch is: off");
    }
  }
}
```

}

You can see from the general structure, use of parent methods, and behavior that the Switch operates in very similar ways to the CheckBox. Our results are shown in Figures 9–6 and 9–7 with the switch in each possible state.

Figure 9–6. *The SwitchDemo sample application, with the switch off*

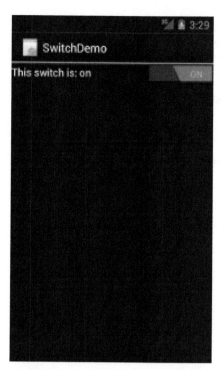

Figure 9–7. *The same application, now with the switch on*

Turn Up the Radio

As with other implementations of radio buttons in other toolkits, Android's radio buttons are two-state, like check boxes and switches, but can be grouped such that only one radio button in the group can be checked at any time.

Like CheckBox, RadioButton inherits from CompoundButton, which in turn inherits from TextView. Hence, all the standard TextView properties for font face, style, color, and so forth are available for controlling the look of radio buttons. Similarly, you can call isChecked() on a RadioButton to see if it is selected, toggle() to select it, and so on, as you can with a CheckBox.

Most times, you will want to put your RadioButton widgets inside a RadioGroup. The RadioGroup indicates a set of radio buttons whose state is tied, meaning only one button in the group can be selected at any time. If you assign an android:id to your RadioGroup in your XML layout, you can access the group from your Java code and invoke the following:

- check(): Checks a specific radio button via its ID (e.g., group.check(R.id.radio1))

- clearCheck(): Clears all radio buttons, so none in the group is checked

- getCheckedRadioButtonId(): Gets the ID of the currently checked radio button (or -1 if none is checked)

Note that the mutual-exclusion feature of RadioGroup applies only to RadioButton widgets that are immediate children of the RadioGroup. You cannot have other containers—discussed in the next chapter—between the RadioGroup and its RadioButton widgets.

For example, from the Basic/RadioButton sample application, here is an XML layout showing a RadioGroup wrapping a set of RadioButton widgets:

```xml
<?xml version="1.0" encoding="utf-8"?>
<RadioGroup
  xmlns:android="http://schemas.android.com/apk/res/android"
  android:orientation="vertical"
  android:layout_width="fill_parent"
  android:layout_height="fill_parent"
  >
    <RadioButton android:id="@+id/radio1"
      android:layout_width="wrap_content"
      android:layout_height="wrap_content"
      android:text="Rock" />

    <RadioButton android:id="@+id/radio2"
      android:layout_width="wrap_content"
      android:layout_height="wrap_content"
      android:text="Scissors" />

    <RadioButton android:id="@+id/radio3"
      android:layout_width="wrap_content"
      android:layout_height="wrap_content"
      android:text="Paper" />
</RadioGroup>
```

Using the stock Android-generated Java for the project and this layout, you get the result shown in Figure 9–8.

Note that the radio button group is initially set to be completely unchecked at the outset. To preset one of the radio buttons to be checked, use either setChecked() on the RadioButton or check() on the RadioGroup from within your onCreate() callback in your activity.

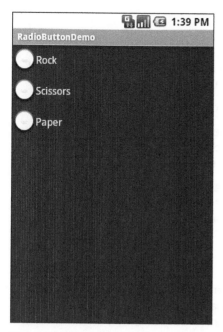

Figure 9–8. *The RadioButtonDemo sample application*

It's Quite a View

All widgets, including the ones shown in the previous sections, extend View, which gives all widgets an array of useful properties and methods beyond those already described.

Padding

Widgets have a minimum size, which may be influenced by what is inside of them. So, for example, a Button will expand to accommodate the size of its caption. You can control this size by using padding. Adding padding will increase the space between the contents (e.g., the caption of a Button) and the edges of the widget.

Padding can be set once in XML for all four sides (android:padding) or on a per-side basis (android:paddingLeft, etc.). Padding can also be set in Java via the setPadding() method.

The value of any of these is a dimension, a combination of a unit of measure and a count. So, 5px is 5 pixels, 10dip is 10 density-independent pixels, and 2mm is 2 millimeters. We will examine dimension in greater detail in Chapter 25.

Other Useful Properties

In addition to the properties presented in this chapter and in the next chapter, some of the other properties of View that are most likely to be used include the following:

- android:visibility: Controls whether the widget is initially visible

- android:nextFocusDown, android:nextFocusLeft, android:nextFocusRight, and android:nextFocusUp: Control the focus order if the user uses the D-pad, trackball, or similar pointing device

- android:contentDescription: Roughly equivalent to the alt attribute on an HTML <img> tag, used by accessibility tools to help people who cannot see the screen navigate the application

Useful Methods

You can toggle whether or not a widget is enabled via setEnabled() and see whether or not it is enabled via isEnabled(). One common use pattern for this is to disable some widgets based on a CheckBox or RadioButton selection.

You can give a widget focus via requestFocus() and see if it is focused via isFocused(). You might use this in concert with disabling widgets to ensure the proper widget has the focus once your disabling operation is complete.

To help navigate the tree of widgets and containers that make up an activity's overall view, you can use:

- getParent(): Finds the parent widget or container

- findViewById(): Finds a child widget with a certain ID

- getRootView(): Gets the root of the tree (e.g., what you provided to the activity via setContentView())

Colors

There are two types of color attributes in Android widgets. Some, like android:background, take a single color (or a graphic image to serve as the background). Others, like android:textColor on TextView (and subclasses), can take a ColorStateList, including via the Java setter (in this case, setTextColor()).

A ColorStateList allows you to specify different colors for different conditions. For example, a TextView can have one text color when it is the selected item in a list and another color when it is not selected (Chapter 12 covers selection widgets). This is handled via the default ColorStateList associated with TextView.

If you wish to change the color of a TextView widget in Java code, you have two main choices:

- Use `ColorStateList.valueOf()`, which returns a `ColorStateList` in which all states are considered to have the same color, which you supply as the parameter to the `valueOf()` method. This is the Java equivalent of the `android:textColor` approach, to make the `TextView` always a specific color regardless of circumstances.

- Create a `ColorStateList` with different values for different states, either via the constructor or via an XML drawable resource, a concept discussed in Chapter 23.

Chapter 10

Working with Containers

A container pours a collection of widgets (and possibly child containers) into a specific structure of your choosing. If you want a form with labels on the left and fields on the right, you need a container. If you want OK and Cancel buttons to be beneath the rest of the form, next to one another, and flush to the right side of the screen, you need a container. Just from a pure XML perspective, if you have multiple widgets (beyond RadioButton widgets in a RadioGroup), you need a container just to have a root element in which to place the widgets.

Most GUI toolkits have some notion of layout management, frequently organized into containers. In Java/Swing, for example, you have layout managers like BoxLayout and containers that use them (e.g., Box). Some toolkits, such as XUL and Flex, stick strictly to the box model, figuring that any desired layout can be achieved through the right combination of nested boxes. Android, through LinearLayout, also offers a box model, but in addition supports a range of containers that provide different layout rules.

In this chapter, we will look at four commonly used containers, LinearLayout (the box model), RelativeLayout (a rule-based model), and TableLayout (the grid model), along with the all-new GridLayout (the infinite fine-line model) released with Ice Cream Sandwich (ICS). We'll also look at ScrollView, a container designed to assist with implementing scrolling containers.

Thinking Linearly

As just noted, LinearLayout is a box model—widgets or child containers are lined up in a column or row, one after the next. This works similarly to FlowLayout in Java/Swing, vbox and hbox in Flex and XUL, and so forth.

Flex and XUL use the box as their primary unit of layout. If you want, you can use LinearLayout in much the same way, eschewing some of the other containers. Getting the visual representation you want is mostly a matter of identifying where boxes should nest and which properties those boxes should have, such as their alignment relative to other boxes.

LinearLayout Concepts and Properties

To configure a LinearLayout, you have five main areas of control besides the container's contents: the orientation, the fill model, the weight, the gravity, and the padding.

Orientation

Orientation indicates whether the LinearLayout represents a row or a column. Just add the android:orientation property to your LinearLayout element in your XML layout, and set the value to be horizontal for a row or vertical for a column.

The orientation can be modified at runtime by invoking setOrientation() on the LinearLayout, supplying it either HORIZONTAL or VERTICAL.

Fill Model

Imagine a row of widgets, such as a pair of radio buttons. These widgets have a "natural" size based on their text. Their combined size probably does not exactly match the width of the Android device's screen—particularly since screens come in various sizes. We then have the issue of what to do with the remaining space.

All widgets inside a LinearLayout must supply android:layout_width and android:layout_height properties to help address this issue. These properties' values have three flavors:

- You can provide a specific dimension, such as 125dip, to indicate the widget should take up exactly a certain size.

- You can provide wrap_content, which means the widget should fill up its natural space, unless that is too big, in which case Android can use word-wrap as needed to make it fit.

- You can provide fill_parent, which means the widget should fill up all available space in its enclosing container, after all other widgets are taken care of.

The latter two flavors are the most common, as they are independent of screen size, allowing Android to adjust your view to fit the available space.

> **NOTE:** In API level 8 (Android 2.2), fill_parent was renamed to match_parent, for unknown reasons. You can still use fill_parent, as it will be supported for the foreseeable future. However, at such point in time as you are supporting only API level 8 or higher (e.g., android:minSdkVersion="8" in your manifest), you should probably switch over to match_parent.

Weight

But what happens if we have two widgets that should split the available free space? For example, suppose we have two multiline fields in a column, and we want them to take up the remaining space in the column after all other widgets have been allocated their space.

To make this work, in addition to setting android:layout_width (for rows) or android:layout_height (for columns) to fill_parent, you must also set android:layout_weight. This property indicates the proportion of the free space that should go to that widget. For example, if you set android:layout_weight to be the same nonzero value for a pair of widgets (e.g., 1), the free space will be split evenly between them. If you set it to be 1 for one widget and 2 for the other widget, the second widget will use up twice the free space that the first widget does. And so on. The weight for a widget is 0 by default.

Another pattern for using weights is to allocate sizes on a percentage basis. To use this technique for, say, a horizontal layout, do the following:

- Set all the android:layout_width values to be 0 for the widgets in the layout.
- Set the android:layout_weight values to be the desired percentage size for each widget in the layout.
- Make sure all those weights add up to 100.

Gravity

By default, everything in a LinearLayout is left- and top-aligned. So, if you create a row of widgets via a horizontal LinearLayout, the row will start flush on the left side of the screen. If that is not what you want, you need to specify a gravity value. Using android:layout_gravity on a widget (or calling setGravity() at runtime on the widget's Java object), you can tell the widget and its container how to align vis-à-vis the screen.

For a column of widgets, common gravity values are left, center_horizontal, and right for left-aligned, centered, and right-aligned widgets, respectively.

For a row of widgets, the default is for them to be aligned so their text is aligned on the baseline (the invisible line that letters seem to "sit on"). You can specify a gravity of center_vertical to center the widgets along the row's vertical midpoint.

Margins

By default, widgets are tightly packed next to each other. You can change this via the use of margins, a concept that is similar to that of padding, described in Chapter 9.

The difference between padding and margins is apparent only for widgets with a nontransparent background. For widgets with a transparent background—like the default look of a TextView—padding and margins have similar visual effect, increasing the space between the widget and adjacent widgets. For widgets with a nontransparent background—like a Button—padding is considered to be inside the background, while margins are considered to be outside the background. In other words, adding padding will increase the space between the contents (e.g., the caption of a Button) and the edges, while adding margins increases the empty space between the edges and adjacent widgets.

Margins can be set in XML, either on a per-side basis (e.g., android:layout_marginTop) or on all sides via android:layout_margin. As with padding, the value of any of these is a dimension—a combination of a unit of measure and a count, such as 5px for 5 pixels.

LinearLayout Example

Let's look at an example (Containers/Linear) that shows LinearLayout properties set both in the XML layout file and at runtime. Here is the layout:

```xml
<?xml version="1.0" encoding="utf-8"?>
<LinearLayout
  xmlns:android="http://schemas.android.com/apk/res/android"
  android:orientation="vertical"
  android:layout_width="fill_parent"
  android:layout_height="fill_parent"
  >
  <RadioGroup android:id="@+id/orientation"
    android:orientation="horizontal"
    android:layout_width="wrap_content"
    android:layout_height="wrap_content"
    android:padding="5dip">
    <RadioButton
      android:id="@+id/horizontal"
      android:text="horizontal" />
    <RadioButton
      android:id="@+id/vertical"
      android:text="vertical" />
  </RadioGroup>
  <RadioGroup android:id="@+id/gravity"
    android:orientation="vertical"
    android:layout_width="fill_parent"
    android:layout_height="wrap_content"
    android:padding="5dip">
    <RadioButton
      android:id="@+id/left"
      android:text="left" />
    <RadioButton
      android:id="@+id/center"
      android:text="center" />
    <RadioButton
      android:id="@+id/right"
      android:text="right" />
  </RadioGroup>
</LinearLayout>
```

Note that we have a LinearLayout wrapping two RadioGroup sets. RadioGroup is a subclass of LinearLayout, so our example demonstrates nested boxes as if they were all LinearLayout containers.

The top RadioGroup sets up a row (android:orientation = "horizontal") of RadioButton widgets. The RadioGroup has 5dip of padding on all sides, separating it from the other RadioGroup, where dip stands for density-independent pixels (think of them as ordinary pixels for now—we will get into the distinction later in the book). The width and height are both set to wrap_content, so the radio buttons will take up only the space that they need.

The bottom RadioGroup is a column (android:orientation = "vertical") of three RadioButton widgets. Again, we have 5dip of padding on all sides and a natural height (android:layout_height = "wrap_content"). However, we have set android:layout_width to be fill_parent, meaning the column of radio buttons claims the entire width of the screen.

To adjust these settings at runtime based on user input, we need some Java code:

```java
package com.commonsware.android.linear;

import android.app.Activity;
import android.os.Bundle;
import android.view.Gravity;
import android.text.TextWatcher;
import android.widget.LinearLayout;
import android.widget.RadioGroup;
import android.widget.EditText;

public class LinearLayoutDemo extends Activity
  implements RadioGroup.OnCheckedChangeListener {
  RadioGroup orientation;
  RadioGroup gravity;

  @Override
  public void onCreate(Bundle icicle) {
    super.onCreate(icicle);
    setContentView(R.layout.main);

    orientation=(RadioGroup)findViewById(R.id.orientation);
    orientation.setOnCheckedChangeListener(this);
    gravity=(RadioGroup)findViewById(R.id.gravity);
    gravity.setOnCheckedChangeListener(this);
  }

  public void onCheckedChanged(RadioGroup group, int checkedId) {
    switch (checkedId) {
      case R.id.horizontal:
        orientation.setOrientation(LinearLayout.HORIZONTAL);
        break;

      case R.id.vertical:
        orientation.setOrientation(LinearLayout.VERTICAL);
        break;
```

```
    case R.id.left:
      gravity.setGravity(Gravity.LEFT);
      break;

    case R.id.center:
      gravity.setGravity(Gravity.CENTER_HORIZONTAL);
      break;

    case R.id.right:
      gravity.setGravity(Gravity.RIGHT);
      break;
  }
 }
}
```

In onCreate(), we look up our two RadioGroup containers and register a listener on each, so we are notified when the radio buttons change state (setOnCheckedChangeListener(this)). Since the activity implements OnCheckedChangeListener, the activity itself is the listener.

In onCheckedChanged() (the callback for the listener), we see which RadioButton had a state change. Based on the clicked-upon item, we adjust either the orientation of the first LinearLayout or the gravity of the second LinearLayout.

Figure 10–1 shows the result when the demo is first launched inside the emulator.

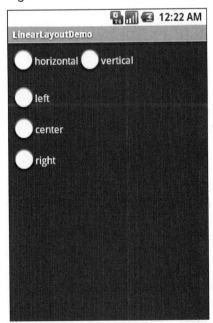

Figure 10–1. *The LinearLayoutDemo sample application, as initially launched*

If we toggle on the "vertical" radio button, the top RadioGroup adjusts to match, as shown in Figure 10–2.

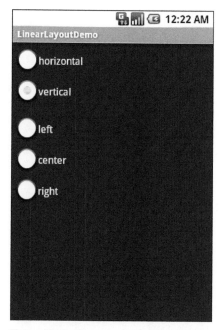

Figure 10–2. *The same application, with the vertical radio button selected*

If we toggle the "center" or "right" radio button, the bottom `RadioGroup` adjusts to match, as shown in Figures 10–3 and 10–4.

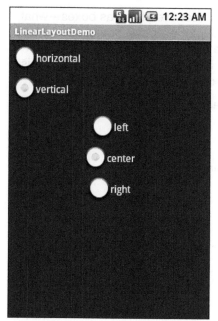

Figure 10–3. *The same application, with the vertical and center radio buttons selected*

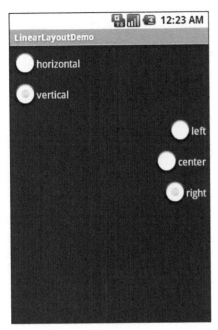

Figure 10–4. *The same application, with the vertical and right radio buttons selected*

The Box Model

As noted earlier in this chapter, some GUI frameworks treat everything as boxes—what Android calls LinearLayout containers. In Flex and XUL, for example, you create boxes and indicate how big they should be, as a percentage of the available space, and then you put widgets in the boxes. A similar pattern exists in Android for LinearLayout, as is demonstrated in the Containers\LinearPercent project.

Here we have a layout XML file that contains a vertical LinearLayout wrapping three Button widgets:

```
<?xml version="1.0" encoding="utf-8"?>
<LinearLayout
  xmlns:android="http://schemas.android.com/apk/res/android"
  android:orientation="vertical"
  android:layout_width="fill_parent"
  android:layout_height="fill_parent"
  >
  <Button
    android:text="Fifty Percent"
    android:layout_width="fill_parent"
    android:layout_height="0dip"
    android:layout_weight="50"
  />
  <Button
    android:text="Thirty Percent"
    android:layout_width="fill_parent"
    android:layout_height="0dip"
```

```
      android:layout_weight="30"
  />
  <Button
    android:text="Twenty Percent"
    android:layout_width="fill_parent"
    android:layout_height="0dip"
    android:layout_weight="20"
  />
</LinearLayout>
```

Each of the three widgets will take up a certain percentage of the vertical space for the LinearLayout. Since the LinearLayout is set to fill the screen, this means that the three widgets will divide up the screen based on their requested percentages.

To request a percentage, each Button does the following:

- Sets its android:layout_height to be 0dip (note that we use height here because it is a vertical LinearLayout we are subdividing)

- Sets its android:layout_weight to be the desired percentage (e.g., android:layout_weight="50")

So long as the weights sum to 100, as they do in this case, you will get your desired breakdown by percentage, as shown in Figure 10–5.

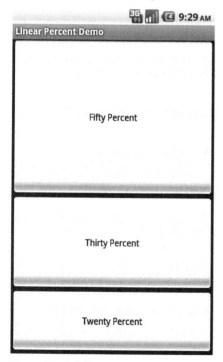

Figure 10–5. *A LinearLayout split among three Buttons by percentage*

All Things Are Relative

RelativeLayout, as the name suggests, lays out widgets based on their relationship to other widgets in the container and the parent container. You can place widget X below and to the left of widget Y, have widget Z's bottom edge align with the bottom edge of the container, and so on. This is reminiscent of James Elliot's RelativeLayout for use with Java/Swing.

RelativeLayout Concepts and Properties

To make all this work, we need ways to reference other widgets within an XML layout file, plus ways to indicate the relative positions of those widgets.

Positions Relative to Container

The easiest relationships to set up are those that tie a widget's position to that of its container, using the following properties:

- android:layout_alignParentTop: Aligns the widget's top with the top of the container

- android:layout_alignParentBottom: Aligns the widget's bottom with the bottom of the container

- android:layout_alignParentLeft: Aligns the widget's left side with the left side of the container

- android:layout_alignParentRight: Aligns the widget's right side with the right side of the container

- android:layout_centerHorizontal: Positions the widget horizontally at the center of the container

- android:layout_centerVertical: Positions the widget vertically at the center of the container

- android:layout_centerInParent: Positions the widget both horizontally and vertically at the center of the container

All of these properties take a simple Boolean value (true or false).

Note that the padding of the widget is taken into account when performing these various alignments. The alignments are based on the widget's overall cell (combination of its natural space plus the padding).

Relative Notation in Properties

The remaining properties of relevance to RelativeLayout take as a value the identity of a widget in the container. To do this:

1. Assign identifiers (android:id attributes) to all elements that you will need to address.

2. Reference other widgets using the same identifier value.

The first occurrence of an id value should include the plus sign (@+id/widget_a); the second and subsequent times that id value is used in the layout file, the plus sign should be omitted (@id/widget_a). This allows the build tools to better help you catch typos in your widget id values—if you do not have a plus sign for a widget id value that has not been seen before, that will be caught at compile time.

For example, if widget A is identified as @+id/widget_a, widget B can refer to widget A in one of its own properties via the identifier @id/widget_a.

Positions Relative to Other Widgets

The following four properties control the position of a widget relative to other widgets:

- android:layout_above: Indicates that the widget should be placed above the widget referenced in the property

- android:layout_below: Indicates that the widget should be placed below the widget referenced in the property

- android:layout_toLeftOf: Indicates that the widget should be placed to the left of the widget referenced in the property

- android:layout_toRightOf: Indicates that the widget should be placed to the right of the widget referenced in the property

Beyond those four properties, five additional properties can be used to control one widget's alignment relative to another:

- android:layout_alignTop: Indicates that the widget's top edge should be aligned with the top edge of the widget referenced in the property

- android:layout_alignBottom: Indicates that the widget's bottom edge should be aligned with the bottom edge of the widget referenced in the property

- android:layout_alignLeft: Indicates that the widget's left edge should be aligned with the left edge of the widget referenced in the property

- android:layout_alignRight: Indicates that the widget's right edge should be aligned with the right edge of the widget referenced in the property

- android:layout_alignBaseline: Indicates that the baseline of the two widgets should be aligned (where the baseline is the invisible line that text appears to sit on)

The android:layout_alignBaseline property is useful for aligning labels and fields so that the text appears natural. Since fields have a box around them and labels do not, android:layout_alignTop would align the top edge of the field's box with the top edge of the label, causing the text of the label to be higher on the screen than the text entered into the field.

So, if we want widget B to be positioned to the right of widget A, in the XML element for widget B, we need to include android:layout_toRightOf = "@id/widget_a" (assuming @id/widget_a is the identity of widget A).

Order of Evaluation

Android formerly used a single pass to process RelativeLayout-defined rules. That meant you could not reference a widget (e.g., via android:layout_above) until it had been declared in the XML. This made defining some layouts a bit complicated. Starting in Android 1.6, Android uses two passes to process the rules, so you can now safely have forward references to as-yet-undefined widgets.

RelativeLayout Example

With all that in mind, let's examine a typical form with a field, a label, and a pair of buttons labeled OK and Cancel. Here is the XML layout, pulled from the Containers/Relative sample project:

```xml
<?xml version="1.0" encoding="utf-8"?>
<RelativeLayout
  xmlns:android="http://schemas.android.com/apk/res/android"
  android:layout_width="fill_parent"
  android:layout_height="wrap_content">
<TextView android:id="@+id/label"
  android:layout_width="wrap_content"
  android:layout_height="wrap_content"
  android:text="URL:"
  android:layout_alignBaseline="@+id/entry"
  android:layout_alignParentLeft="true"/>
<EditText
  android:id="@id/entry"
  android:layout_width="fill_parent"
  android:layout_height="wrap_content"
  android:layout_toRightOf="@id/label"
  android:layout_alignParentTop="true"/>
<Button
  android:id="@+id/ok"
```

```
    android:layout_width="wrap_content"
    android:layout_height="wrap_content"
    android:layout_below="@id/entry"
    android:layout_alignRight="@id/entry"
    android:text="OK" />
  <Button
    android:id="@+id/cancel"
    android:layout_width="wrap_content"
    android:layout_height="wrap_content"
    android:layout_toLeftOf="@id/ok"
    android:layout_alignTop="@id/ok"
    android:text="Cancel" />
</RelativeLayout>
```

First, we open the RelativeLayout. In this case, we want to use the full width of the screen (android:layout_width = "fill_parent") and only as much height as we need (android:layout_height = "wrap_content").

Next, we define the label as a TextView. We indicate that we want its left edge aligned with the left edge of the RelativeLayout (android:layout_alignParentLeft="true") and its baseline aligned with the baseline of the yet-to-be-defined EditText. Since the EditText has not been declared yet, we use the + sign in the ID (android:layout_alignBaseline="@+id/entry").

After that, we add in the field as an EditText. We want the field to be to the right of the label, have the field be aligned with the top of the RelativeLayout, and have the field take up the rest of this "row" in the layout. These requirements are handled by the following three properties, respectively:

- android:layout_toRightOf = "@id/label"

- android:layout_alignParentTop = "true"

- android:layout_width = "fill_parent"

Then, the OK button is set to be below the field (android:layout_below = "@id/entry") and have its right side align with the right side of the field (android:layout_alignRight = "@id/entry"). The Cancel button is set to be to the left of the OK button (android:layout_toLeft = "@id/ok") and have its top aligned with the OK button (android:layout_alignTop = "@id/ok").

With no changes to the autogenerated Java code, the emulator gives us the result shown in Figure 10–6.

Figure 10–6. *The RelativeLayoutDemo sample application*

Overlap

RelativeLayout also has a feature that LinearLayout lacks—the ability to have widgets overlap one another. Later children of a RelativeLayout are "higher in the Z axis" than are earlier children, meaning that later children will overlap earlier children if they are set up to occupy the same space in the layout.

This will be clearer with an example. Here is a layout, from Containers/RelativeOverlap, with a RelativeLayout holding two Button widgets:

```
<?xml version="1.0" encoding="utf-8"?>
<RelativeLayout
  xmlns:android="http://schemas.android.com/apk/res/android"
  android:layout_width="fill_parent"
  android:layout_height="fill_parent"
  >
  <Button
    android:text="I AM BIG"
    android:textSize="120dip"
    android:textStyle="bold"
    android:layout_width="fill_parent"
    android:layout_height="fill_parent"
  />
  <Button
    android:text="I am small"
    android:layout_width="wrap_content"
    android:layout_height="wrap_content"
    android:layout_centerInParent="true"
  />
```

```
</RelativeLayout>
```

The first Button is set to fill the screen. The second Button is set to be centered inside the parent and to take up only as much space as is needed for its caption. Hence, the second Button will appear to float over the first Button, as shown in Figure 10–7.

Figure 10–7. *The RelativeOverlap sample application*

Both Button widgets can still be clicked, though clicking the smaller Button does not also click the bigger Button. Your clicks will be handled by the widget on top in the case of an overlap like this.

Tabula Rasa

If you like HTML tables, spreadsheet grids, and similar layout options, you will like Android's TableLayout, which allows you to position your widgets in a grid to your specifications. You control the number of rows and columns, which columns might shrink or stretch to accommodate their contents, and so on.

TableLayout works in conjunction with TableRow. TableLayout controls the overall behavior of the container, with the widgets themselves poured into one or more TableRow containers, one per row in the grid.

TableLayout Concepts and Properties

For your table layout to work as you intend, you need to understand how widgets work with rows and columns, and how to handle widgets that live outside of rows.

Putting Cells in Rows

Rows are declared by you, the developer, by putting widgets as children of a TableRow inside the overall TableLayout. You, therefore, control directly how many rows appear in the table.

The number of columns is determined by Android; you control the number of columns in an indirect fashion. First, there will be at least one column per widget in your longest row. So if you have three rows—one with two widgets, one with three widgets, and one with four widgets—there will be at least four columns. However, you can have a widget take up more than one column by including the android:layout_span property, indicating the number of columns the widget spans. This is akin to the colspan attribute one finds in table cells in HTML. In this XML layout fragment, the field spans three columns:

```
<TableRow>
  <TextView android:text="URL:" />
  <EditText
    android:id="@+id/entry"
    android:layout_span="3"/>
</TableRow>
```

Ordinarily, widgets are put into the first available column. In the preceding fragment, the label would go in the first column (column 0, as columns are counted starting from 0), and the field would go into a spanned set of three columns (columns 1 through 3). However, you can put a widget into a different column via the android:layout_column property, specifying the 0-based column the widget belongs to:

```
<TableRow>
  <Button
    android:id="@+id/cancel"
    android:layout_column="2"
    android:text="Cancel" />
  <Button android:id="@+id/ok" android:text="OK" />
</TableRow>
```

In the preceding XML layout fragment, the Cancel button goes in the third column (column 2). The OK button then goes into the next available column, which is the fourth column.

Non-Row Children of TableLayout

Normally, TableLayout contains only TableRow elements as immediate children. However, it is possible to put other widgets in between rows. For those widgets, TableLayout behaves a bit like LinearLayout with vertical orientation. The widgets automatically have their width set to fill_parent, so they will fill the same space that the longest row does.

One pattern for this is to use a plain View as a divider. For example, you could use <View android:layout_height = "2dip" android:background = "#0000FF" /> as a two-pixel-high blue bar across the width of the table.

Stretch, Shrink, and Collapse

By default, each column will be sized according to the natural size of the widest widget in that column (taking spanned columns into account). Sometimes, though, that does not work out very well, and you need more control over column behavior.

You can place an android:stretchColumns property on the TableLayout. The value should be a single column number (again, 0-based) or a comma-delimited list of column numbers. Those columns will be stretched to take up any available space on the row. This helps if your content is narrower than the available space.

Conversely, you can place an android:shrinkColumns property on the TableLayout. Again, this should be a single column number or a comma-delimited list of column numbers. The columns listed in this property will try to word-wrap their contents to reduce the effective width of the column—by default, widgets are not word-wrapped. This helps if you have columns with potentially wordy content that might cause some columns to be pushed off the right side of the screen.

You can also leverage an android:collapseColumns property on the TableLayout, again with a column number or comma-delimited list of column numbers. These columns will start out collapsed, meaning they will be part of the table information but will be invisible. Programmatically, you can collapse and uncollapse columns by calling setColumnCollapsed() on the TableLayout. You might use this to allow users to control which columns are of importance to them and should be shown versus which ones are less important and can be hidden.

You can also control stretching and shrinking at runtime via setColumnStretchable() and setColumnShrinkable().

TableLayout Example

The XML layout fragments previously shown, when combined, give us a TableLayout rendition of the form we created for RelativeLayout, with the addition of a divider line between the label/field and the two buttons (found in the Containers/Table demo):

```
<?xml version="1.0" encoding="utf-8"?>
<TableLayout
  xmlns:android="http://schemas.android.com/apk/res/android"
  android:layout_width="fill_parent"
  android:layout_height="fill_parent"
  android:stretchColumns="1">
  <TableRow>
    <TextView
```

```
                android:text="URL:" />
        <EditText android:id="@+id/entry"
            android:layout_span="3"/>
    </TableRow>
    <View
        android:layout_height="2dip"
        android:background="#0000FF" />
    <TableRow>
        <Button android:id="@+id/cancel"
            android:layout_column="2"
            android:text="Cancel" />
        <Button android:id="@+id/ok"
            android:text="OK" />
    </TableRow>
</TableLayout>
```

When compiled against the generated Java code and run on the emulator, we get the result shown in Figure 10–8.

Figure 10–8. *The TableLayoutDemo sample application*

Scrollwork

Phone screens tend to be small, which requires developers to use some tricks to present a lot of information in the limited available space. One trick for doing this is to use scrolling, so that only part of the information is visible at one time, and the rest is available via scrolling up or down.

ScrollView is a container that provides scrolling for its contents. You can take a layout that might be too big for some screens, wrap it in a ScrollView, and still use your existing layout logic. The user can see only part of your layout at one time, and see the rest via scrolling.

For example, here is a `ScrollView` used in an XML layout file (from the Containers/Scroll demo):

```xml
<?xml version="1.0" encoding="utf-8"?>
<ScrollView
  xmlns:android="http://schemas.android.com/apk/res/android"
  android:layout_width="fill_parent"
  android:layout_height="wrap_content">
  <TableLayout
    android:layout_width="fill_parent"
    android:layout_height="fill_parent"
    android:stretchColumns="0">
    <TableRow>
      <View
        android:layout_height="80dip"
        android:background="#000000"/>
      <TextView android:text="#000000"
        android:paddingLeft="4dip"
        android:layout_gravity="center_vertical" />
    </TableRow>
    <TableRow>
      <View
        android:layout_height="80dip"
        android:background="#440000" />
      <TextView android:text="#440000"
        android:paddingLeft="4dip"
        android:layout_gravity="center_vertical" />
    </TableRow>
    <TableRow>
      <View
        android:layout_height="80dip"
        android:background="#884400" />
      <TextView android:text="#884400"
        android:paddingLeft="4dip"
        android:layout_gravity="center_vertical" />
    </TableRow>
    <TableRow>
      <View
        android:layout_height="80dip"
        android:background="#aa8844" />
      <TextView android:text="#aa8844"
        android:paddingLeft="4dip"
        android:layout_gravity="center_vertical" />
    </TableRow>
    <TableRow>
      <View
        android:layout_height="80dip"
        android:background="#ffaa88" />
      <TextView android:text="#ffaa88"
        android:paddingLeft="4dip"
        android:layout_gravity="center_vertical" />
    </TableRow>
    <TableRow>
      <View
```

```
        android:layout_height="80dip"
        android:background="#ffffaa" />
      <TextView android:text="#ffffaa"
        android:paddingLeft="4dip"
        android:layout_gravity="center_vertical" />
    </TableRow>
    <TableRow>
      <View
        android:layout_height="80dip"
        android:background="#ffffff" />
      <TextView android:text="#ffffff"
        android:paddingLeft="4dip"
        android:layout_gravity="center_vertical" />
    </TableRow>
  </TableLayout>
</ScrollView>
```

Without the ScrollView, the table would take up at least 560 pixels (seven rows at 80 pixels each, based on the View declarations). Some devices have screens capable of showing that much information, such as tablets, but the screens of many devices will be smaller. The ScrollView lets us keep the table as is, but present only part of it at a time.

On the stock Android emulator, when the activity is first viewed, it appears as shown in Figure 10–9.

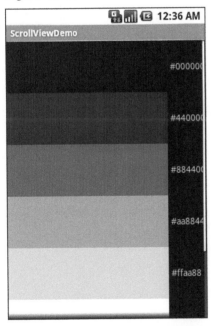

Figure 10–9. *The ScrollViewDemo sample application*

Notice how only five rows and part of the sixth are visible. By pressing the up/down buttons on the D-pad, you can scroll up and down to see the remaining rows. Also note how the right side of the content is clipped by the scrollbar—be sure to put some padding on that side or otherwise ensure your own content does not get clipped in that fashion.

Android 1.5 introduced HorizontalScrollView, which works like ScrollView, but horizontally. This is useful for forms that might be too wide rather than too tall. Note that neither ScrollView nor HorizontalScrollView will give you bidirectional scrolling, so you have to choose vertical or horizontal.

Also, note that you cannot put scrollable items into a ScrollView. For example, a ListView widget—which we will see in upcoming chapters—already knows how to scroll. If you put a ListView in a ScrollView, it will not work very well.

Take Them to the Grid

A TableLayout appeals to those who yearn for HTML- or CSS-style pixel precision (or lack thereof). Often you'll find that you know how you'd like the elements of your layout to appear relative to one another, or need more finesse when it comes to specifying the placement of widgets in your layout. Enter the all-new GridLayout, released with Android 4 Ice Cream Sandwich (ICS).

GridLayout is a layout that places its children onto a grid of infinitely detailed lines that separate the area into cells. The key to GridLayout's fine control is that the number of cells or, more accurately, grid lines used to describe the cells has no limit or threshold—you specify how many or how few grid lines your GridLayout should have, using rowSpec and columnSpec properties. This means you could create a layout that mimics a simple table with a few cells (that is, rows and columns) or, for those demanding situations where you need fantastically fine precision, you could go crazy specifying thousands or even millions of cells.

> **NOTE:** To complement GridLayout's different view of the UI world, it uses android:layout_gravity in place of android:layout_weight.

As an example, here is a GridLayout used in an XML layout file (from the Containers/Grid demo):

```
<?xml version="1.0" encoding="utf-8"?>
<GridLayout
 xmlns:android="http://schemas.android.com/apk/res/android"
 android:orientation="vertical"
 android:layout_width="fill_parent"
 android:layout_height="fill_parent"
>
  <Button
    android:text="Defying gravity!"
    android:layout_gravity="top"
  />
  <Button
    android:text="Falling like an apple"
    android:layout_gravity="bottom"
  />
</GridLayout>
```

In an ICS Android emulator, we see the activity using our GridLayout, as shown in Figure 10–10.

Figure 10–10. *The GridDemo sample application*

Our buttons have followed their various gravity directions to place themselves on the GridLayout, using the defaults for rowSpec and columnSpec counts. We can observe the utility of the GridLayout not needing the somewhat tedious static layout directives of the TableLayout by adding another button to our declarations in main.xml

```
...
  <Button
    android:text="Defying gravity!"
    android:layout_gravity="top"
  />
  <Button
    android:text="Floating middle right"
    android:layout_gravity="right|center_vertical"
  />
  <Button
    android:text="Falling like an apple"
    android:layout_gravity="bottom"
  />
...
```

Figure 10–11 shows how our GridLayout adapts to display its children.

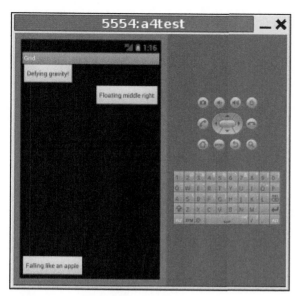

Figure 10–11. *The GridDemo revised*

Chapter 11

The Input Method Framework

Android 1.5 introduced the input method framework (IMF), which is commonly referred to as *soft keyboards*. However, this term is not necessarily accurate, as IMF could be used for handwriting recognition or other means of accepting text input via the screen.

Keyboards, Hard and Soft

Some Android devices have a hardware keyboard that is visible some of the time (when it is slid out). A few Android devices have a hardware keyboard that is always visible (so-called "bar" or "slab" phones). Most Android devices, though, have no hardware keyboard at all. The IMF handles all of these scenarios.

In short, if there is no hardware keyboard, an input method editor (IME) will be available to the user when they tap an enabled EditText widget. If the default functionality of the IME is what you want to offer, you don't need to make any code changes to your application. Fortunately, Android is fairly smart about guessing what you want, so you may simply need to test with the IME and make no specific code changes.

But the IME may not quite behave how you would like it to for your application. For example, in the Basic/Field sample project, the FieldDemo activity has the IME overlaying the multiple-line EditText, as shown in Figure 11–1. It would be nice to have more control over how this appears, and to be able to control other behavior of the IME. Fortunately, the IMF as a whole gives you many options for this, as described in this chapter.

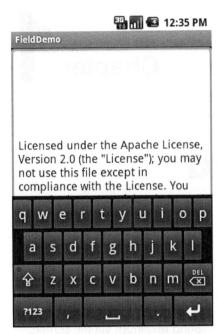

Figure 11–1. *The input method editor, as seen in the FieldDemo sample application*

Tailored to Your Needs

Android 1.1 and earlier offered many attributes on EditText widgets to control their style of input, such as android:password to indicate a field should be for password entry (shrouding the password keystrokes from prying eyes). Starting in Android 1.5, with the IMF, many of these attributes have been combined into a single android:inputType attribute.

The android:inputType attribute takes a class plus modifiers, in a pipe-delimited list (where | is the pipe character). The class generally describes what the user is allowed to input, and this determines the basic set of keys available on the soft keyboard. The available classes are as follows:

- text (the default)
- number
- phone
- datetime
- date
- time

Many of these classes offer one or more modifiers to further refine what the user will be allowed to enter. To get a better understanding of how these modifiers work, take a look at the res/layout/main.xml file from the InputMethod/IMEDemo1 project:

```xml
<?xml version="1.0" encoding="utf-8"?>
<TableLayout xmlns:android="http://schemas.android.com/apk/res/android"
  android:layout_width="fill_parent"
  android:layout_height="fill_parent"
  android:stretchColumns="1"
  >
  <TableRow>
    <TextView
      android:text="No special rules:"
    />
    <EditText
    />
  </TableRow>
  <TableRow>
    <TextView
      android:text="Email address:"
    />
    <EditText
      android:inputType="text|textEmailAddress"
    />
  </TableRow>
  <TableRow>
    <TextView
      android:text="Signed decimal number:"
    />
    <EditText
      android:inputType="number|numberSigned|numberDecimal"
    />
  </TableRow>
  <TableRow>
    <TextView
      android:text="Date:"
    />
    <EditText
      android:inputType="date"
    />
  </TableRow>
  <TableRow>
    <TextView
      android:text="Multi-line text:"
    />
    <EditText
      android:inputType="text|textMultiLine|textAutoCorrect"
      android:minLines="3"
      android:gravity="top"
    />
  </TableRow>
</TableLayout>
```

This shows a TableLayout containing five rows, each demonstrating a slightly different flavor of EditText:

- The first row has no attributes at all on the EditText, meaning you get a plain text-entry field.

- The second row has android:inputType = "text|textEmailAddress", meaning it is a text-entry field that specifically seeks an e-mail address.

- The third row allows for signed decimal numeric input, via android:inputType = "number|numberSigned|numberDecimal".

- The fourth row is set up to allow for data entry of a date (android:inputType = "date").

- The last row allows for multiline input with autocorrection of probable spelling errors (android:inputType = "text|textMultiLine|textAutoCorrect").

The class and modifiers tailor the keyboard. For example, a plain text-entry field results in a plain soft keyboard, as shown in Figure 11–2.

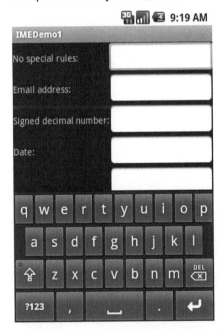

Figure 11–2. *A standard input method editor (a.k.a. soft keyboard)*

An e-mail address field might put the @ symbol on the soft keyboard, at the cost of a smaller spacebar, as shown in Figure 11–3.

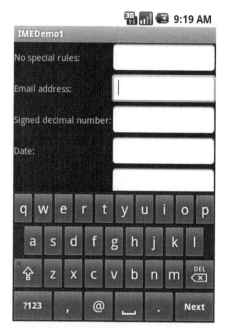

Figure 11–3. *The input method editor for e-mail addresses*

Note that this behavior is specific to the IME. Some editors might put the @ symbol on the primary keyboard for an e-mail field. Some might put a .com button on the primary keyboard. Some might not react at all. It is up to the implementation of the IME—all you can do is supply the hint.

Number and date fields restrict the keys to numeric keys, plus a set of symbols that may or may not be valid on a given field, as shown in Figure 11–4.

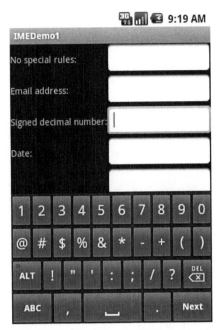

Figure 11-4. *The input method editor for signed decimal numbers*

These are just a few examples of the possible IMEs. By choosing the appropriate android:inputType, you can give users a soft keyboard that best suits the type of data they should be entering.

Tell Android Where It Can Go

You may have noticed a subtle difference between the IME shown in Figure 11-2 and the IME shown in Figure 11-3, beyond the addition of the @ key. The lower-right corner of the soft keyboard in Figure 11-3 has a Next button, whereas the one in Figure 11-2 has a newline button. This points out two things:

- EditText widgets are multiline by default if you do not specify android:inputType.

- You can control what goes on with that lower-right button, called the *accessory* button.

By default, on an EditText widget where you have specified android:inputType, the accessory button will be Next, moving you to the next EditText widget in sequence, or Done, if you are on the last EditText widget on the screen. You can manually stipulate what the accessory button will be labeled via the android:imeOptions attribute. For example, in the res/layout/main.xml file from InputMethod/IMEDemo2, you will see an augmented version of the previous example, where two input fields specify what their accessory button should look like:

```xml
<?xml version="1.0" encoding="utf-8"?>
<ScrollView xmlns:android="http://schemas.android.com/apk/res/android"
  android:layout_width="fill_parent"
  android:layout_height="fill_parent"
>
  <TableLayout
    android:layout_width="fill_parent"
    android:layout_height="fill_parent"
    android:stretchColumns="1"
    >
    <TableRow>
      <TextView
        android:text="No special rules:"
      />
      <EditText
      />
    </TableRow>
    <TableRow>
      <TextView
        android:text="Email address:"
      />
      <EditText
        android:inputType="text|textEmailAddress"
        android:imeOptions="actionSend"
      />
    </TableRow>
    <TableRow>
      <TextView
        android:text="Signed decimal number:"
      />
      <EditText
        android:inputType="number|numberSigned|numberDecimal"
        android:imeOptions="actionDone"
      />
    </TableRow>
    <TableRow>
      <TextView
        android:text="Date:"
      />
      <EditText
        android:inputType="date"
      />
    </TableRow>
    <TableRow>
      <TextView
        android:text="Multi-line text:"
      />
      <EditText
        android:inputType="text|textMultiLine|textAutoCorrect"
        android:minLines="3"
        android:gravity="top"
      />
    </TableRow>
  </TableLayout>
</ScrollView>
```

Here, we attach a Send action to the accessory button for the e-mail address (android:imeOptions = "actionSend"), and the Done action on the middle field (android:imeOptions = "actionDone").

By default, Next moves the focus to the next EditText and Done closes the IME. However, for those actions, or for any others like Send, you can use setOnEditorActionListener() on EditText (technically, on the TextView superclass) to get control when the accessory button is clicked or the user presses the Enter key. You are provided with a flag indicating the desired action (e.g., IME_ACTION_SEND), and you can then do something to handle that request (e.g., send an e-mail to the supplied e-mail address).

Fitting In

Notice that the IMEDemo2 layout shown in the preceding section has another difference from its IMEDemo1 predecessor: the use of a ScrollView container wrapping the TableLayout. This ties into another level of control you have over the IMEs: what happens to your activity's own layout when the IME appears. There are three possibilities, depending on circumstances:

- Android can "pan" your activity, effectively sliding the whole layout up to accommodate the IME, or overlaying your layout, depending on whether the EditText being edited is at the top or bottom. This has the effect of hiding some portion of your UI.

- Android can resize your activity, effectively causing it to shrink to a smaller screen dimension, allowing the IME to sit below the activity itself. This is great when the layout can readily be shrunk (e.g., it is dominated by a list or multiline input field that does not need the whole screen to be functional).

- Android may display the IME full-screen, obscuring your entire activity. This allows for a bigger keyboard and generally easier data entry.

Android controls the full-screen option using its historic defaults. And, by default, Android will choose between pan and resize modes depending on what your layout looks like. If you want to specifically choose between pan and resize, you can do so via an android:windowSoftInputMode attribute on the <activity> element in your AndroidManifest.xml file. For example, here is the manifest from IMEDemo2:

```
<?xml version="1.0" encoding="utf-8"?>
<manifest xmlns:android="http://schemas.android.com/apk/res/android"
package="com.commonsware.android.imf.two" android:versionCode="1"
android:versionName="1.0">
    <application android:label="@string/app_name" android:icon="@drawable/cw">
        <activity android:name=".IMEDemo2" android:label="@string/app_name"
android:windowSoftInputMode="adjustResize">
            <intent-filter>
                <action android:name="android.intent.action.MAIN"/>
                <category android:name="android.intent.category.LAUNCHER"/>
            </intent-filter>
```

```
            </activity>
          </application>
        <supports-screens android:largeScreens="true" android:normalScreens="true"
      android:smallScreens="true" android:anyDensity="true"/>
      </manifest>
```

Because we specified resize, Android will shrink our layout to accommodate the IME. With the ScrollView in place, this means the scroll bar will appear as needed, as shown in Figure 11–5.

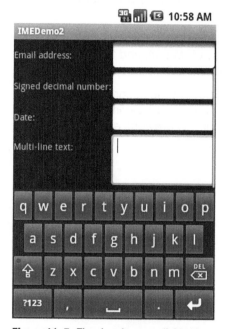

Figure 11–5. *The shrunken, scrollable layout*

You can control Android's behavior to maximize screen real-estate by using the additional methods introduced in Honeycomb, and refined in Ice Cream Sandwich. Use the Java method setSystemUiVisibility() with the STATUS_BAR_HIDDEN option to hide the System Bar and allow even larger full-screen modes, or use the method setDimAmount() to tweak the brightness of the home buttons to remove distractions from your regularly resized full-screen layout.

Jane, Stop This Crazy Thing!

Sometimes, you need the IME to just go away. For example, if you make the accessory button a Search button, the IME won't be hidden automatically when the user taps that button, whereas you may want it to be hidden. To hide the IME, you need to make a call to the InputMethodManager, a system service that controls these IMEs:

```
InputMethodManager mgr=(InputMethodManager)getSystemService(INPUT_METHOD_SERVICE);
```

```
mgr.hideSoftInputFromWindow(fld.getWindowToken(), 0);
```

(In the preceding line, `fld` is the `EditText` whose IME you want to hide.)

This will always close the designated IME. However, bear in mind that there are two ways a user can open the IME in the first place:

- If the user's device does not have a hardware keyboard exposed, and the user taps the `EditText`, the IME should appear.

- If the user previously dismissed the IME or is using the IME for a widget that does not normally pop one up (e.g., `ListView`), and the user presses the Menu button, the IME should appear.

If you want to close the IME only for the first scenario, but not the second, use `InputMethodManager.HIDE_IMPLICIT_ONLY` as a flag for the second parameter to your call to `hideSoftInputFromWindow()`, instead of the 0 shown in the previous example.

Chapter 12

Using Selection Widgets

In Chapter 11, you saw how fields could have constraints placed on them to limit possible input, such as numeric-only or phone-number-only. These sorts of constraints help users "get it right" when entering information, particularly on mobile devices with cramped keyboards.

Of course, the ultimate in constrained input is to allow selection only from a set of items, such as a group of radio buttons. Classic UI toolkits have list boxes, combo boxes, drop-down lists, and the like for that very purpose. Android provides many of the same sorts of widgets, plus others of particular interest for mobile devices (e.g., the Gallery for examining saved photos).

Moreover, Android offers a flexible framework for determining which choices are available in these widgets. Specifically, Android offers a framework of data adapters that provides a common interface for selection lists, ranging from static arrays to database contents. Selection views—widgets for presenting lists of choices—are handed an adapter to supply the actual choices.

Adapting to the Circumstances

In the abstract, adapters provide a common interface to multiple disparate APIs. More specifically, in Android's case, adapters provide a common interface to the data model behind a selection-style widget, such as a list box. This use of Java interfaces is fairly common (e.g., Java/Swing's model adapters for JTable), and Java is far from the only environment offering this sort of abstraction (e.g., Flex's XML data-binding framework accepts XML inlined as static data or retrieved from the Internet).

Android's adapters are responsible not only for providing the roster of data for a selection widget, but also for converting individual elements of data into specific views to be displayed inside the selection widget. The latter facet of the adapter system may sound a little odd, but in reality, it is not that different from other GUI toolkits' ways of overriding default display behavior. For example, in Java/Swing, if you want a JList-backed list box to actually be a checklist (where individual rows are a check box plus label, and clicks adjust the state of the check box), you inevitably wind up calling setCellRenderer() to supply your own ListCellRenderer, which in turn converts strings for the list into JCheckBox-plus-JLabel composite widgets.

The easiest adapter to use is ArrayAdapter. You simply wrap one of these around a Java array or java.util.List instance, and you have a fully functioning adapter:

```
String[] items={"this", "is", "a",
                "really", "silly", "list"};
new ArrayAdapter<String>(this,
  android.R.layout.simple_list_item_1, items);
```

One flavor of the ArrayAdapter constructor takes three parameters:

- The Context to use (typically this will be your activity instance)

- The resource ID of a view to use (such as a built-in system resource ID, as shown in the preceding example)

- The actual array or list of items to show

By default, the ArrayAdapter will invoke toString() on the objects in the list and wrap each of those strings in the view designated by the supplied resource. android.R.layout.simple_list_item_1 simply turns those strings into TextView objects. Those TextView widgets, in turn, will be shown in the list, spinner, or whatever widget uses this ArrayAdapter. If you want to see what android.R.layout.simple_list_item_1 looks like, you can find a copy of it in your SDK installation—just search for simple_list_item_1.xml.

In Chapter 13, you'll see how to subclass an adapter and override row creation, to give you greater control over how rows appear.

Lists of Naughty and Nice

The classic list box widget in Android is known as ListView. Include one of these in your layout, invoke setAdapter() to supply your data and child views, and attach a listener via setOnItemSelectedListener() to find out when the selection has changed. With that, you have a fully functioning list box.

However, if your activity is dominated by a single list, you might consider creating your activity as a subclass of ListActivity, rather than the regular Activity base class. If your main view is just the list, you do not even need to supply a layout—ListActivity will construct a full-screen list for you. If you do want to customize the layout, you can, as long as you identify your ListView as @android:id/list, so ListActivity knows which widget is the main list for the activity.

For example, here is a layout pulled from the Selection/List sample project, a simple list with a label on top to show the current selection:

```xml
<?xml version="1.0" encoding="utf-8"?>
<LinearLayout
  xmlns:android="http://schemas.android.com/apk/res/android"
  android:orientation="vertical"
  android:layout_width="fill_parent"
  android:layout_height="fill_parent" >
  <TextView
    android:id="@+id/selection"
    android:layout_width="fill_parent"
    android:layout_height="wrap_content"/>
  <ListView
    android:id="@android:id/list"
    android:layout_width="fill_parent"
    android:layout_height="fill_parent"
    android:drawSelectorOnTop="false"
    />
</LinearLayout>
```

The Java code to configure the list and connect the list with the label is as follows:

```java
public class ListViewDemo extends ListActivity {
  private TextView selection;
  private static final String[] items={"lorem", "ipsum", "dolor",
          "sit", "amet",
          "consectetuer", "adipiscing", "elit", "morbi", "vel",
          "ligula", "vitae", "arcu", "aliquet", "mollis",
          "etiam", "vel", "erat", "placerat", "ante",
          "porttitor", "sodales", "pellentesque", "augue", "purus"};

  @Override
  public void onCreate(Bundle icicle) {
    super.onCreate(icicle);
    setContentView(R.layout.main);
    setListAdapter(new ArrayAdapter<String>(this,
                        android.R.layout.simple_list_item_1,
                        items));
    selection=(TextView)findViewById(R.id.selection);
  }

  public void onListItemClick(ListView parent, View v, int position,
                              long id) {
    selection.setText(items[position]);
  }
}
```

With ListActivity, you can set the list adapter via setListAdapter()—in this case, providing an ArrayAdapter wrapping an array of nonsense strings. To find out when the list selection changes, override onListItemClick() and take appropriate steps based on the supplied child view and position—in this case, updating the label with the text for that position. The results are shown in Figure 12–1.

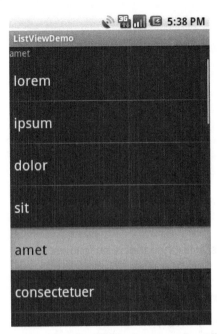

Figure 12–1. *The ListViewDemo sample application*

The second parameter to our ArrayAdapter, android.R.layout.simple_list_item_1, controls the appearance of the rows. The value used in the preceding example provides the standard Android list row: big font, a lot of padding, and white text.

Selection Modes

By default, ListView is set up to simply collect clicks on list entries. If you want a list that tracks a user's selection, or possibly multiple selections, ListView can handle that as well, but it requires a few changes.

First, you need to call setChoiceMode() on the ListView in Java code to set the choice mode, supplying either CHOICE_MODE_SINGLE or CHOICE_MODE_MULTIPLE as the value. You can get your ListView from a ListActivity via getListView(). You can also declare this via the android:choiceMode attribute in your layout XML.

Then, instead of using android.R.layout.simple_list_item_1 as the layout for the list rows in your ArrayAdapter constructor, you need to use either android.R.layout.simple_list_item_single_choice or android.R.layout.simple_list_item_multiple_choice for single-choice or multiple-choice lists, respectively.

For example, here is an activity layout from the Selection/Checklist sample project:

```xml
<?xml version="1.0" encoding="utf-8"?>
<ListView
xmlns:android="http://schemas.android.com/apk/res/android"
  android:id="@android:id/list"
  android:layout_width="fill_parent"
  android:layout_height="fill_parent"
  android:drawSelectorOnTop="false"
  android:choiceMode="multipleChoice"
/>
```

It is a full-screen ListView, with the android:choiceMode="multipleChoice" attribute to indicate that we want multiple-choice support.

Our activity simply uses a standard ArrayAdapter on our list of nonsense words, but uses android.R.layout.simple_list_item_multiple_choice as the row layout:

```java
package com.commonsware.android.checklist;

import android.os.Bundle;
import android.app.ListActivity;
import android.widget.ArrayAdapter;
import android.widget.ListView;

public class ChecklistDemo extends ListActivity {
  private static final String[] items={"lorem", "ipsum", "dolor",
          "sit", "amet",
          "consectetuer", "adipiscing", "elit", "morbi", "vel",
          "ligula", "vitae", "arcu", "aliquet", "mollis",
          "etiam", "vel", "erat", "placerat", "ante",
          "porttitor", "sodales", "pellentesque", "augue", "purus"};

  @Override
  public void onCreate(Bundle icicle) {
    super.onCreate(icicle);
    setContentView(R.layout.main);
    setListAdapter(new ArrayAdapter<String>(this,
                      android.R.layout.simple_list_item_multiple_choice,
                      items));
  }
}
```

The user sees the list of words on the left with check boxes down the right edge, as shown in Figure 12–2.

Figure 12–2. *Multiple-select mode*

If we wanted to, we could call getCheckedItemPositions() on our ListView to find out which items the user checked, or setItemChecked() to check (or uncheck) a specific entry ourselves.

Spin Control

In Android, the Spinner is the equivalent of the drop-down selector you might find in other toolkits (e.g., JComboBox in Java/Swing). Pressing the center button on the D-pad pops up a selection dialog box from which the user can choose an item. The Spinner basically provides list selection capabilities without taking up all the screen space of a ListView, at the cost of an extra click or screen tap to make a change.

As with ListView, you provide the adapter for data and child views via setAdapter(), and hook in a listener object for selections via setOnItemSelectedListener().

If you want to tailor the view used when displaying the drop-down perspective, you need to configure the adapter, not the Spinner widget. Use the setDropDownViewResource() method to supply the resource ID of the view to use.

For example, culled from the Selection/Spinner sample project, here is an XML layout for a simple view with a Spinner:

```
<?xml version="1.0" encoding="utf-8"?>
<LinearLayout
    xmlns:android="http://schemas.android.com/apk/res/android"
```

```
  android:orientation="vertical"
  android:layout_width="fill_parent"
  android:layout_height="fill_parent"
  >
  <TextView
    android:id="@+id/selection"
    android:layout_width="fill_parent"
    android:layout_height="wrap_content"
    />
  <Spinner android:id="@+id/spinner"
    android:layout_width="fill_parent"
    android:layout_height="wrap_content"
    android:drawSelectorOnTop="true"
  />
</LinearLayout>
```

This is the same view as shown in the previous section, but with a Spinner instead of a ListView. The Spinner property android:drawSelectorOnTop controls whether the arrow is drawn on the selector button on the right side of the Spinner UI.

To populate and use the Spinner, we need some Java code:

```
public class SpinnerDemo extends Activity
  implements AdapterView.OnItemSelectedListener {
  private TextView selection;
  private static final String[] items={"lorem", "ipsum", "dolor",
          "sit", "amet",
          "consectetuer", "adipiscing", "elit", "morbi", "vel",
          "ligula", "vitae", "arcu", "aliquet", "mollis",
          "etiam", "vel", "erat", "placerat", "ante",
          "porttitor", "sodales", "pellentesque", "augue", "purus"};

  @Override
  public void onCreate(Bundle icicle) {
    super.onCreate(icicle);
    setContentView(R.layout.main);
    selection=(TextView)findViewById(R.id.selection);

    Spinner spin=(Spinner)findViewById(R.id.spinner);
    spin.setOnItemSelectedListener(this);

    ArrayAdapter<String> aa=new ArrayAdapter<String>(this,
                        android.R.layout.simple_spinner_item,
                        items);

    aa.setDropDownViewResource(
      android.R.layout.simple_spinner_dropdown_item);
    spin.setAdapter(aa);
  }

  public void onItemSelected(AdapterView<?> parent,
                              View v, int position, long id) {
    selection.setText(items[position]);
  }

  public void onNothingSelected(AdapterView<?> parent) {
    selection.setText("");
```

```
  }
}
```

Here, we attach the activity itself as the selection listener
(spin.setOnItemSelectedListener(this)). This works because the activity implements
the OnItemSelectedListener interface. We configure the adapter not only with the list of
fake words, but also with a specific resource to use for the drop-down view (via
aa.setDropDownViewResource()). Also note the use of
android.R.layout.simple_spinner_item as the built-in View for showing items in the
spinner itself.

Finally, we implement the callbacks required by OnItemSelectedListener to adjust the
selection label based on user input. Figures 12–3 and 12–4 show the results.

Figure 12–3. *The SpinnerDemo sample application, as initially launched*

Figure 12–4. *The same application, with the spinner drop-down list displayed*

Grid Your Lions (or Something Like That...)

As the name suggests, GridView gives you a two-dimensional grid of items to choose from. You have moderate control over the number and size of the columns; the number of rows is dynamically determined based on the number of items the supplied adapter says are available for viewing.

There are a few properties that, when combined, determine the number of columns and their sizes:

- android:numColumns: Indicates how many columns there are, or, if you supply a value of auto_fit, Android will compute the number of columns based on the available space and the following properties in this list.

- android:verticalSpacing and android:horizontalSpacing: Indicate how much whitespace should exist between items in the grid.

- android:columnWidth: Indicates how many pixels wide each column should be.

- android:stretchMode: Indicates, for grids with auto_fit for android:numColumns, what should happen for any available space not taken up by columns or spacing. This can be columnWidth, to have the columns take up available space, or spacingWidth, to have the whitespace between columns absorb extra space.

Otherwise, the GridView works much like any other selection widget—use setAdapter() to provide the data and child views, invoke setOnItemSelectedListener() to register a selection listener, and so on.

For example, here is an XML layout from the Selection/Grid sample project, showing a GridView configuration:

```
<?xml version="1.0" encoding="utf-8"?>
<LinearLayout
  xmlns:android="http://schemas.android.com/apk/res/android"
  android:orientation="vertical"
  android:layout_width="fill_parent"
  android:layout_height="fill_parent"
  >
  <TextView
    android:id="@+id/selection"
    android:layout_width="fill_parent"
    android:layout_height="wrap_content"
    />
  <GridView
    android:id="@+id/grid"
    android:layout_width="fill_parent"
    android:layout_height="fill_parent"
    android:verticalSpacing="40dip"
    android:horizontalSpacing="5dip"
    android:numColumns="auto_fit"
    android:columnWidth="100dip"
    android:stretchMode="columnWidth"
    android:gravity="center"
    />
</LinearLayout>
```

For this grid, we take up the entire screen except for what our selection label requires. The number of columns is computed by Android (android:numColumns = "auto_fit") based on our horizontal spacing (android:horizontalSpacing = "5dip") and column width (android:columnWidth = "100dip"), with the columns absorbing any "slop" width left over (android:stretchMode = "columnWidth").

The Java code to configure the GridView is as follows:

```
package com.commonsware.android.grid;

import android.app.Activity;
import android.content.Context;
import android.os.Bundle;
import android.view.View;
import android.widget.AdapterView;
import android.widget.ArrayAdapter;
import android.widget.GridView;
import android.widget.TextView;

public class GridDemo extends Activity
  implements AdapterView.OnItemSelectedListener {
  private TextView selection;
  private static final String[] items={"lorem", "ipsum", "dolor",
            "sit", "amet",
```

```
               "consectetuer", "adipiscing", "elit", "morbi", "vel",
               "ligula", "vitae", "arcu", "aliquet", "mollis",
               "etiam", "vel", "erat", "placerat", "ante",
               "porttitor", "sodales", "pellentesque", "augue", "purus"};

  @Override
  public void onCreate(Bundle icicle) {
    super.onCreate(icicle);
    setContentView(R.layout.main);
    selection=(TextView)findViewById(R.id.selection);

    GridView g=(GridView) findViewById(R.id.grid);
    g.setAdapter(new ArrayAdapter<String>(this,
                        R.layout.cell,
                        items));
    g.setOnItemSelectedListener(this);
  }

  public void onItemSelected(AdapterView<?> parent, View v,
                              int position, long id) {
    selection.setText(items[position]);
  }

  public void onNothingSelected(AdapterView<?> parent) {
    selection.setText("");
  }
}
```

The grid cells are defined by a separate res/layout/cell.xml file, referenced in our
ArrayAdapter as R.layout.cell:

```
<?xml version="1.0" encoding="utf-8"?>
<TextView
  xmlns:android="http://schemas.android.com/apk/res/android"
  android:layout_width="wrap_content"
  android:layout_height="wrap_content"
  android:textSize="14dip"
/>
```

With the vertical spacing from the XML layout (android:verticalSpacing = "40dip"), the
grid overflows the boundaries of the emulator's screen, as shown in Figures 12–5 and
12–6.

Figure 12–5. *The GridDemo sample application, as initially launched*

Figure 12–6. *The same application, scrolled to the bottom of the grid*

Fields: Now with 35% Less Typing!

The AutoCompleteTextView is sort of a hybrid between the EditText (field) and the Spinner. With autocompletion, as the user types, the text is treated as a prefix filter, comparing the entered text as a prefix against a list of candidates. Matches are shown in a selection list that drops down from the field (as with Spinner). The user can either type the full entry (e.g., something not in the list) or choose an item from the list to be the value of the field.

AutoCompleteTextView subclasses EditText, so you can configure all the standard look-and-feel aspects, such as font face and color. In addition, AutoCompleteTextView has an android:completionThreshold property, to indicate the minimum number of characters a user must enter before the list filtering begins.

You can give AutoCompleteTextView an adapter containing the list of candidate values via setAdapter(). However, since the user could type something that is not in the list, AutoCompleteTextView does not support selection listeners. Instead, you can register a TextWatcher, as you can with any EditText widget, to be notified when the text changes. These events will occur either because of manual typing or from a selection from the drop-down list.

The following is a familiar XML layout, this time containing an AutoCompleteTextView (pulled from the Selection/AutoComplete sample application):

```xml
<?xml version="1.0" encoding="utf-8"?>
<LinearLayout
  xmlns:android="http://schemas.android.com/apk/res/android"
  android:orientation="vertical"
  android:layout_width="fill_parent"
  android:layout_height="fill_parent"
  >
  <TextView
    android:id="@+id/selection"
    android:layout_width="fill_parent"
    android:layout_height="wrap_content"
    />
  <AutoCompleteTextView android:id="@+id/edit"
      android:layout_width="fill_parent"
      android:layout_height="wrap_content"
      android:completionThreshold="3"/>
</LinearLayout>
```

The corresponding Java code is as follows:

```java
package com.commonsware.android.auto;

import android.app.Activity;
import android.os.Bundle;
import android.text.Editable;
import android.text.TextWatcher;
import android.view.View;
import android.widget.AdapterView;
import android.widget.ArrayAdapter;
import android.widget.AutoCompleteTextView;
```

```
import android.widget.TextView;

public class AutoCompleteDemo extends Activity
  implements TextWatcher {
  private TextView selection;
  private AutoCompleteTextView edit;
  private static final String[] items={"lorem", "ipsum", "dolor",
        "sit", "amet",
        "consectetuer", "adipiscing", "elit", "morbi", "vel",
        "ligula", "vitae", "arcu", "aliquet", "mollis",
        "etiam", "vel", "erat", "placerat", "ante",
        "porttitor", "sodales", "pellentesque", "augue", "purus"};

  @Override
  public void onCreate(Bundle icicle) {
    super.onCreate(icicle);
    setContentView(R.layout.main);
    selection=(TextView)findViewById(R.id.selection);
    edit=(AutoCompleteTextView)findViewById(R.id.edit);
    edit.addTextChangedListener(this);

    edit.setAdapter(new ArrayAdapter<String>(this,
                        android.R.layout.simple_dropdown_item_1line,
                        items));
  }

  public void onTextChanged(CharSequence s, int start, int before,
                            int count) {
    selection.setText(edit.getText());
  }

  public void beforeTextChanged(CharSequence s, int start,
                                int count, int after) {
    // needed for interface, but not used
  }

  public void afterTextChanged(Editable s) {
    // needed for interface, but not used
  }
}
```

This time, our activity implements TextWatcher, which means our callbacks are onTextChanged(), beforeTextChanged(), and afterTextChanged(). In this case, we are interested only in onTextChanged(), and we update the selection label to match the AutoCompleteTextView's current contents. Figures 12–7, 12–8, and 12–9 show the results.

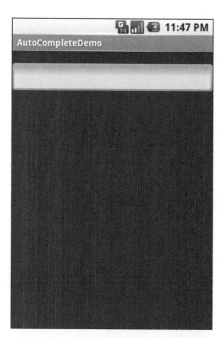

Figure 12–7. *The AutoCompleteDemo sample application, as initially launched*

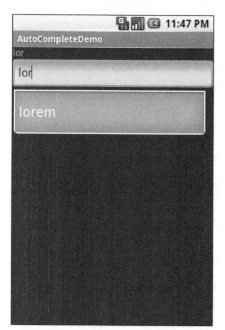

Figure 12–8. *The same application, after a few matching letters were entered, showing the autocomplete drop-down*

Figure 12–9. *The same application, after the autocomplete value was selected*

Galleries, Give or Take the Art

The Gallery widget is not one ordinarily found in GUI toolkits. It is, in effect, a list box that is laid out horizontally. One choice follows the next across the horizontal plane, with the currently selected item highlighted. On an Android device, the user rotates through the options via the left and right D-pad buttons.

Compared to the ListView, the Gallery takes up less screen space, while still showing multiple choices at one time (assuming they are short enough). Compared to the Spinner, the Gallery always shows more than one choice at a time.

The quintessential example use for the Gallery is image preview. Given a collection of photos or icons, the Gallery lets people preview the pictures in the process of choosing one.

Code-wise, the Gallery works much like a Spinner or GridView. In your XML layout, you have a few properties at your disposal:

■ android:spacing: Controls the number of pixels between entries in the list.

■ android:spinnerSelector: Controls what is used to indicate a selection. This can either be a reference to a Drawable (see the resources chapter) or an RGB value in #AARRGGBB or similar notation.

android:drawSelectorOnTop: Indicates if the selection bar (or Drawable) should be drawn before (false) or after (true) drawing the selected child. If you choose true, be sure that your selector has sufficient transparency to show the child through the selector; otherwise, users will not be able to read the selection.

Chapter 13

Getting Fancy with Lists

The humble ListView is one of the most important widgets in all of Android, simply because it is used so frequently. Whether choosing a contact to call, an e-mail message to forward, or an e-book to read, ListView widgets are employed in a wide range of activities. Of course, it would be nice if they were more than just plain text.

The good news is that Android lists can be as fancy as you want, within the limitations of a mobile device's screen, of course. However, making them fancy takes some work, requiring the features of Android that are covered in this chapter.

Getting to First Base

The classic Android ListView is a plain list of text—solid but uninspiring. Basically, we hand the ListView a bunch of words in an array and tell Android to use a simple built-in layout for pouring those words into a list.

However, we can have a list whose rows are made up of icons, icons and text, check boxes and text, or whatever we want. It is merely a matter of supplying enough data to the adapter and helping the adapter to create a richer set of View objects for each row.

For example, suppose we want a ListView whose entries are made up of an icon, followed by some text. We could construct a layout for the row that looks like this, found in res/layout/row.xml in the FancyLists/Static sample project:

```
<?xml version="1.0" encoding="utf-8"?>
<LinearLayout
          xmlns:android="http://schemas.android.com/apk/res/android"
          android:orientation="vertical"
          android:layout_width="fill_parent"
          android:layout_height="fill_parent" >
          <TextView
                    android:id="@+id/selection"
                    android:layout_width="fill_parent"
                    android:layout_height="wrap_content"/>
          <ListView
                    android:id="@android:id/list"
                    android:layout_width="fill_parent"
```

```
                                   android:layout_height="fill_parent"
                                   android:drawSelectorOnTop="false"
                                   />
</LinearLayout>
```

This layout uses a LinearLayout to set up a row, with the icon on the left and the text (in a nice big font) on the right.

However, by default, Android has no idea that we want to use this layout with our ListView. To make the connection, we need to supply our Adapter with the resource ID of the custom layout shown previously:

```
public class StaticDemo extends ListActivity {
  private TextView selection;
  private static final String[] items={"lorem", "ipsum", "dolor",
          "sit", "amet",
          "consectetuer", "adipiscing", "elit", "morbi", "vel",
          "ligula", "vitae", "arcu", "aliquet", "mollis",
          "etiam", "vel", "erat", "placerat", "ante",
          "porttitor", "sodales", "pellentesque", "augue", "purus"};

  @Override
  public void onCreate(Bundle icicle) {
    super.onCreate(icicle);
    setContentView(R.layout.main);
    setListAdapter(new ArrayAdapter<String>(this,
                       R.layout.row, R.id.label,
                       items));
    selection=(TextView)findViewById(R.id.selection);
  }

  public void onListItemClick(ListView parent, View v,
                             int position,  long id) {
    selection.setText(items[position]);
  }
}
```

This follows the general structure for the previous ListView sample. The key difference here is that we have told ArrayAdapter that we want to use our custom layout (R.layout.row) and that the TextView where the word should go is known as R.id.label within that custom layout.

> **NOTE:** Remember that to reference a layout (row.xml), use R.layout as a prefix on the base name of the layout XML file (R.layout.row).

The result is a ListView with icons down the left side; in this example, all the icons are the same, as shown in Figure 13–1.

Figure 13–1. *The StaticDemo application*

A Dynamic Presentation

As shown in the previous section, the technique of supplying an alternative layout to use for rows handles simple cases very nicely. However, what if we want the icon to change based on the row data? For example, suppose we want to use one icon for small words and a different icon for large words. In the case of ArrayAdapter, we will need to extend it, creating our own custom subclass (e.g., IconicAdapter) that incorporates our business logic. In particular, it will need to override getView().

The getView() method of an Adapter is what an AdapterView (like ListView or Spinner) calls when it needs the View associated with a given piece of data the Adapter is managing. In the case of an ArrayAdapter, getView() is called as needed for each position in the array—"get me the View for the first row," "get me the View for the second row," and so forth.

As an example, let's rework the code in the preceding section to use getView(), so we can show different icons for different rows—in this case, one icon for short words and one for long words (from the FancyLists/Dynamic sample project):

```
public class DynamicDemo extends ListActivity {
  TextView selection;
  private static final String[] items={"lorem", "ipsum", "dolor",
        "sit", "amet",
        "consectetuer", "adipiscing", "elit", "morbi", "vel",
```

```
                    "ligula", "vitae", "arcu", "aliquet", "mollis",
                    "etiam", "vel", "erat", "placerat", "ante",
                    "porttitor", "sodales", "pellentesque", "augue", "purus"};

    @Override
    public void onCreate(Bundle icicle) {
      super.onCreate(icicle);
      setContentView(R.layout.main);
      setListAdapter(new IconicAdapter());
      selection=(TextView)findViewById(R.id.selection);
    }

    public void onListItemClick(ListView parent, View v,
                                int position, long id) {
      selection.setText(items[position]);
    }

    class IconicAdapter extends ArrayAdapter<String> {
      IconicAdapter() {
        super(DynamicDemo.this, R.layout.row, R.id.label, items);
      }

      public View getView(int position, View convertView,
                          ViewGroup parent) {
        View row=super.getView(position, convertView, parent);
        ImageView icon=(ImageView)row.findViewById(R.id.icon);

        if (items[position].length()>4) {
          icon.setImageResource(R.drawable.delete);
        }
        else {
          icon.setImageResource(R.drawable.ok);
        }

        return(row);
      }
    }
  }
}
```

Our IconicAdapter—an inner class of the activity—has two methods. First, it has the constructor, which simply passes to ArrayAdapter the same data we used in the ArrayAdapter constructor in StaticDemo. Second, it has our getView() implementation, which does two things:

■ It chains to the superclass's implementation of getView(), which returns to us an instance of our row View, as prepared by ArrayAdapter. In particular, our word has already been put into the TextView, since ArrayAdapter does that normally.

■ It finds our ImageView and applies a business rule to set which icon should be used, referencing one of two drawable resources (R.drawable.ok and R.drawable.delete).

The result of our revised example is shown in Figure 13–2.

Figure 13–2. *The DynamicDemo application*

Inflating Rows Ourselves

The preceding version of the DynamicDemo application works fine. However, sometimes ArrayAdapter cannot be used even to set up the basics of our row. For example, it is possible to have a ListView where the rows are materially different, such as category headers interspersed among regular rows. In that case, we may need to do all the work ourselves, starting with inflating our rows. We will do that after a brief introduction to inflation.

A Sidebar About Inflation

"Inflation" means the act of converting an XML layout specification into the actual tree of View objects the XML represents. This is undoubtedly a tedious bit of code: take an element, create an instance of the specified View class, walk the attributes, convert those into property setter calls, iterate over all child elements, lather, rinse, and repeat.

The good news is that the fine folks on the Android team wrapped up all that into a class called LayoutInflater, which we can use ourselves. When it comes to fancy lists, for example, we want to inflate a View for each row shown in the list, so we can use the convenient shorthand of the XML layout to describe what the rows are supposed to look like.

For example, let's look at a slightly different implementation of the DynamicDemo class, from the FancyLists/DynamicEx project:

```java
public class DynamicDemo extends ListActivity {
  TextView selection;
  private static final String[] items={"lorem", "ipsum", "dolor",
          "sit", "amet",
          "consectetuer", "adipiscing", "elit", "morbi", "vel",
          "ligula", "vitae", "arcu", "aliquet", "mollis",
          "etiam", "vel", "erat", "placerat", "ante",
          "porttitor", "sodales", "pellentesque", "augue", "purus"};

  @Override
  public void onCreate(Bundle icicle) {
    super.onCreate(icicle);
    setContentView(R.layout.main);
    setListAdapter(new IconicAdapter());
    selection=(TextView)findViewById(R.id.selection);
  }

  public void onListItemClick(ListView parent, View v,
                              int position, long id) {
    selection.setText(items[position]);
  }

  class IconicAdapter extends ArrayAdapter<String> {
    IconicAdapter() {
      super(DynamicDemo.this, R.layout.row, items);
    }

    public View getView(int position, View convertView,
                        ViewGroup parent) {
      LayoutInflater inflater=getLayoutInflater();
      View row=inflater.inflate(R.layout.row, parent, false);
      TextView label=(TextView)row.findViewById(R.id.label);

      label.setText(items[position]);

      ImageView icon=(ImageView)row.findViewById(R.id.icon);

      if (items[position].length()>4) {
        icon.setImageResource(R.drawable.delete);
      }
      else {
        icon.setImageResource(R.drawable.ok);
      }

      return(row);
    }
  }
}
```

Here we inflate our R.layout.row layout by use of a LayoutInflater object, obtained from our Activity via getLayoutInflater(). This gives us a View object back, which, in reality, is our LinearLayout with an ImageView and a TextView, just as R.layout.row specifies. However, rather than having to create all those objects ourselves and wire them together, the XML and LayoutInflater handle the "heavy lifting" for us.

And Now, Back to Our Story

So we have used LayoutInflater to give us a View representing the row. This row is "empty," since the static layout file has no idea what actual data goes into the row. It is our job to customize and populate the row as we see fit before returning it, as follows:

- Fill in the text label for our label widget, using the word at the supplied position

- See if the word is longer than four characters and, if so, find our ImageView icon widget and replace the stock resource with a different one

The user sees nothing different—we have simply changed how those rows are being created. Obviously, this was a fairly contrived example, but you can see that this technique could be used to customize rows based on any sort of criteria.

Better. Stronger. Faster.

The getView() implementation shown in the FancyLists/DynamicEx project works, but it's inefficient. Every time the user scrolls, we have to create a bunch of new View objects to accommodate the newly shown rows. This is bad in terms of both overhead and perceived performance.

It might be bad for the immediate user experience if the list appears to be sluggish. More likely, though, it will be bad due to battery usage—every bit of CPU that is used eats up the battery. This is compounded by the extra work the garbage collector needs to do to get rid of all those extra objects we create. So the less efficient our code, the more quickly the phone's battery will be drained, and the less happy the user will be. And we want happy users, right?

So, let's take a look at a few tricks to make our fancy ListView widgets more efficient.

Using convertView

The getView() method receives, as one of its parameters, a View named, by convention, convertView. Sometimes, convertView will be null. In those cases, we need to create a new row View from scratch (e.g., via inflation), just as we did in the previous example. However, if convertView is not null, then it is actually one of our previously created View objects! This will happen primarily when the user scrolls the ListView. As new rows appear, Android will attempt to recycle the views of the rows that scrolled off the other end of the list, to save us from having to rebuild them from scratch.

Assuming that each of our rows has the same basic structure, we can use findViewById() to get at the individual widgets that make up our row and change their contents, and then return convertView from getView(), rather than create a whole new row. For example, here is the getView() implementation from the earlier example, now optimized via convertView (from the FancyLists/Recycling project):

```java
public class RecyclingDemo extends ListActivity {
  private TextView selection;
  private static final String[] items={"lorem", "ipsum", "dolor",
        "sit", "amet",
        "consectetuer", "adipiscing", "elit", "morbi", "vel",
        "ligula", "vitae", "arcu", "aliquet", "mollis",
        "etiam", "vel", "erat", "placerat", "ante",
        "porttitor", "sodales", "pellentesque", "augue", "purus"};

  @Override
  public void onCreate(Bundle icicle) {
    super.onCreate(icicle);
    setContentView(R.layout.main);
    setListAdapter(new IconicAdapter());
    selection=(TextView)findViewById(R.id.selection);
  }

  public void onListItemClick(ListView parent, View v,
                              int position, long id) {
    selection.setText(items[position]);
  }

  class IconicAdapter extends ArrayAdapter<String> {
    IconicAdapter() {
      super(RecyclingDemo.this, R.layout.row, items);
    }

    public View getView(int position, View convertView,
                        ViewGroup parent) {
      View row=convertView;

      if (row==null) {
        LayoutInflater inflater=getLayoutInflater();

        row=inflater.inflate(R.layout.row, parent, false);
      }

      TextView label=(TextView)row.findViewById(R.id.label);

      label.setText(items[position]);

      ImageView icon=(ImageView)row.findViewById(R.id.icon);

      if (items[position].length()>4) {
        icon.setImageResource(R.drawable.delete);
      }
      else {
        icon.setImageResource(R.drawable.ok);
      }

      return(row);
    }
  }
}
```

Here, we check to see if the convertView is null. If so, we inflate our row; otherwise, we just reuse it. The work to fill in the contents (icon image and text) is the same in either case. The advantage is that we avoid the potentially expensive inflation step. In fact, according to statistics cited by Google at the 2010 Google I|O conference, a ListView that uses a recycling ListAdapter will perform 150 percent faster than one that does not. For complex rows, that might even understate the benefit.

Not only is this faster, but it uses much less memory. Each widget or container—in other words, each subclass of View—holds onto up to 2kB of data, not counting things like images in ImageView widgets. Each of our rows, therefore, might be as big as 6kB. For our list of 25 nonsense words, consuming as much as 150kB for a nonrecycling list (25 rows at 6kB each) would be inefficient but not a huge problem. A list of 1000 nonsense words, though, consuming as much as 6MB of RAM, would be a much bigger issue. Bear in mind that your application may have only 16MB of Java heap memory to work with, especially if you are targeting older devices with constrained resources. Recycling allows us to handle arbitrary list lengths with only as much View memory consumed as is needed for the rows visible onscreen.

Note that row recycling is an issue only if we are creating the rows ourselves. If we let ArrayAdapter create the rows, by leveraging its implementation of getView(), as shown in the FancyLists/Dynamic project, then it deals with the recycling.

Using the Holder Pattern

Another somewhat expensive operation commonly done with fancy views is calling findViewById(). This dives into our inflated row and pulls out widgets by their assigned identifiers, so we can customize the widget contents (e.g., to change the text of a TextView or change the icon in an ImageView). Since findViewById() can find widgets anywhere in the tree of children of the row's root View, this could take a fair number of instructions to execute, particularly if we need to find the same widgets repeatedly.

In some GUI toolkits, this problem is avoided by having the composite View objects, like rows, be declared totally in program code (in this case, Java). Then, accessing individual widgets is merely a matter of calling a getter or accessing a field. And we can certainly do that with Android, but the code gets rather verbose. What would be nice is a way that enables us still to use the layout XML, yet cache our row's key child widgets so that we need to find them only once. That's where the holder pattern comes into play, in a class we'll call ViewHolder.

All View objects have getTag() and setTag() methods. These allow us to associate an arbitrary object with the widget. The holder pattern uses that "tag" to hold an object that, in turn, holds each of the child widgets of interest. By attaching that holder to the row View, every time we use the row, we already have access to the child widgets we care about, without having to call findViewById() again.

So, let's take a look at one of these holder classes (taken from the FancyLists/ViewHolder sample project):

```
package com.commonsware.android.fancylists.five;

import android.view.View;
import android.widget.ImageView;

class ViewHolder {
  ImageView icon=null;

  ViewHolder(View base) {
    this.icon=(ImageView)base.findViewById(R.id.icon);
  }
}
```

ViewHolder holds onto the child widgets, initialized via findViewById() in its constructor. The widgets are simply package-protected data members, accessible from other classes in this project, such as a ViewHolderDemo activity. In this case, we are holding onto only one widget—the icon—since we will let ArrayAdapter handle our label for us.

Using ViewHolder is a matter of creating an instance whenever we inflate a row and attaching said instance to the row View via setTag(), as shown in this rewrite of getView(), found in ViewHolderDemo:

```
public View getView(int position, View convertView,
                    ViewGroup parent) {
  View row=super.getView(position, convertView, parent);
  ViewHolder holder=(ViewHolder)row.getTag();

  if (holder==null) {
    holder=new ViewHolder(row);
    row.setTag(holder);
  }

  if (getModel(position).length()>4) {
    holder.icon.setImageResource(R.drawable.delete);
  }
  else {
    holder.icon.setImageResource(R.drawable.ok);
  }

  return(row);
}
```

Here, we go back to allowing ArrayAdapter to handle our row inflation and recycling for us. If the call to getTag() on the row returns null, we know we need to create a new ViewHolder, which we then attach to the row via setTag() for later reuse. Then, accessing the child widgets is merely a matter of accessing the data members on the holder. The first time the ListView is displayed, all new rows need to be inflated, and we wind up creating a ViewHolder for each. As the user scrolls, rows get recycled, and we can reuse their corresponding ViewHolder widget caches.

Using a holder helps performance, but the effect is not as dramatic. Whereas recycling can give you a 150 percent performance improvement, adding in a holder increases the improvement to 175 percent. Hence, while you may wish to implement recycling up front when you create your adapter, adding in a holder might be something you deal with later, when you are working specifically on performance tuning.

In this particular case, we certainly could simplify all of this by skipping ViewHolder and using getTag() and setTag() with the ImageView directly. This example is written as it is to demonstrate how to handle a more complex scenario, where you might have several widgets that would need to be cached via the holder pattern.

Interactive Rows

Lists with pretty icons next to them are all fine and well. But, can we create ListView widgets whose rows contain interactive child widgets instead of just passive widgets like TextView and ImageView? For example, there is a RatingBar widget that allows users to assign a rating by clicking on a set of star icons. Could we combine the RatingBar with text to allow people to scroll a list of, say, songs and rate them right inside the list? There is good news and bad news.

The good news is that interactive widgets in rows work just fine. The bad news is that it is a little tricky, specifically when it comes to taking action when the interactive widget's state changes (e.g., a value is typed into a field). We need to store that state somewhere, since our RatingBar widget will be recycled when the ListView is scrolled. We need to be able to set the RatingBar state based on the actual word being viewed as the RatingBar is recycled, and we need to save the state when it changes so it can be restored when this particular row is scrolled back into view.

What makes this interesting is that, by default, the RatingBar has absolutely no idea which item in the ArrayAdapter it represents. After all, the RatingBar is just a widget, used in a row of a ListView. We need to teach the rows which item in the ArrayAdapter they are currently displaying, so when their RatingBar is checked, they know which item's state to modify.

So, let's see how this is done, using the activity in the FancyLists/RateList sample project. We will use the same basic classes that we used in our previous example. We are displaying a list of nonsense words, which can then be rated. In addition, words given a top rating are put in all caps.

```
package com.commonsware.android.fancylists.six;

import android.app.Activity;
import android.os.Bundle;
import android.app.ListActivity;
import android.view.View;
import android.view.ViewGroup;
import android.view.LayoutInflater;
import android.widget.AdapterView;
import android.widget.ArrayAdapter;
import android.widget.RatingBar;
import android.widget.LinearLayout;
import android.widget.ListView;
import android.widget.TextView;
import java.util.ArrayList;
```

```java
public class RateListDemo extends ListActivity {
  private static final String[] items={"lorem", "ipsum", "dolor",
          "sit", "amet",
          "consectetuer", "adipiscing", "elit", "morbi", "vel",
          "ligula", "vitae", "arcu", "aliquet", "mollis",
          "etiam", "vel", "erat", "placerat", "ante",
          "porttitor", "sodales", "pellentesque", "augue", "purus"};

  @Override
  public void onCreate(Bundle icicle) {
    super.onCreate(icicle);

    ArrayList<RowModel> list=new ArrayList<RowModel>();

    for (String s : items) {
      list.add(new RowModel(s));
    }

    setListAdapter(new RatingAdapter(list));
  }

  private RowModel getModel(int position) {
    return(((RatingAdapter)getListAdapter()).getItem(position));
  }

  class RatingAdapter extends ArrayAdapter<RowModel> {
    RatingAdapter(ArrayList<RowModel> list) {
      super(RateListDemo.this, R.layout.row, R.id.label, list);
    }

    public View getView(int position, View convertView,
                        ViewGroup parent) {
      View row=super.getView(position, convertView, parent);
      ViewHolder holder=(ViewHolder)row.getTag();

      if (holder==null) {
        holder=new ViewHolder(row);
        row.setTag(holder);

        RatingBar.OnRatingBarChangeListener l=
                    new RatingBar.OnRatingBarChangeListener() {
          public void onRatingChanged(RatingBar ratingBar,
                                      float rating,
                                      boolean fromTouch)  {
            Integer myPosition=(Integer)ratingBar.getTag();
            RowModel model=getModel(myPosition);

            model.rating=rating;

            LinearLayout parent=(LinearLayout)ratingBar.getParent();
            TextView label=(TextView)parent.findViewById(R.id.label);

            label.setText(model.toString());
          }
        };
```

```
      holder.rate.setOnRatingBarChangeListener(l);
    }

    RowModel model=getModel(position);

    holder.rate.setTag(new Integer(position));
    holder.rate.setRating(model.rating);

    return(row);
  }
}
class RowModel {
  String label;
  float rating=2.0f;

  RowModel(String label) {
    this.label=label;
  }

  public String toString() {
    if (rating>=3.0) {
      return(label.toUpperCase());
    }

    return(label);
  }
}
}
```

The following list explains what is different in this activity and getView() implementation from before:

- We are still using String[] items as the list of nonsense words, but instead of pouring that String array straight into an ArrayAdapter, we turn it into a list of RowModel objects. RowModel is the mutable model: it holds the nonsense word plus the current checked state. In a real system, these might be objects populated from a database, and the properties would have more business meaning.

- We updated utility methods such as onListItemClick() to reflect the change from a pure-String model to use a RowModel.

- The ArrayAdapter subclass (RatingAdapter), in getView(), lets ArrayAdapter inflate and recycle the row, and then checks to see if we have a ViewHolder in the row's tag. If not, we create a new ViewHolder and associate it with the row. For the row's RatingBar, we add an anonymous onRatingChanged() listener that looks at the row's tag (getTag()) and converts that into an Integer, representing the position within the ArrayAdapter that this row is displaying. Using that, the rating bar can get the actual RowModel for the row and update the model based on the new state of the rating bar. It also updates the text adjacent to the RatingBar when checked, to match the rating bar state.

■ We always make sure that the RatingBar has the proper contents and has a tag (via setTag()) pointing to the position in the adapter the row is displaying.

The row layout is very simple, just a RatingBar and a TextView inside a LinearLayout:

```xml
<?xml version="1.0" encoding="utf-8"?>
<LinearLayout xmlns:android="http://schemas.android.com/apk/res/android"
  android:layout_width="fill_parent"
  android:layout_height="wrap_content"
  android:orientation="horizontal"
>
  <RatingBar
    android:id="@+id/rate"
    android:layout_width="wrap_content"
    android:layout_height="wrap_content"
    android:numStars="3"
    android:stepSize="1"
    android:rating="2" />
  <TextView
    android:id="@+id/label"
    android:padding="2dip"
    android:textSize="18sp"
    android:layout_gravity="left|center_vertical"
    android:layout_width="fill_parent"
    android:layout_height="wrap_content"/>
</LinearLayout>
```

The ViewHolder is similarly simple, just extracting the RatingBar out of the row View for caching purposes:

```java
package com.commonsware.android.fancylists.six;

import android.view.View;
import android.widget.RatingBar;

class ViewHolder {
  RatingBar rate=null;

  ViewHolder(View base) {
    this.rate=(RatingBar)base.findViewById(R.id.rate);
  }
}
```

And the result is what you would expect, visually, as shown in Figure 13–3.

Figure 13–3. *The RateListDemo application, as initially launched*

Figure 13–4 shows a toggled rating bar turning its word into all caps.

Figure 13–4. *The same application, showing a top-rated word*

Chapter 14

Still More Widgets and Containers

This book has covered a number of widgets and containers so far. This chapter is the last that focuses exclusively on widgets and containers, covering a number of popular options, from date and time widgets to tabs. Subsequent chapters introduce new widgets occasionally, but in the context of some other topic, such as introducing the ProgressBar in Chapter 20 (covering threads).

Pick and Choose

With limited-input devices like phones, having widgets and dialog boxes that are aware of the type of stuff a user is supposed to be entering is very helpful. They minimize keystrokes and screen taps and reduce the chance that a user will make some sort of error (e.g., entering a letter somewhere only numbers are expected).

As shown in Chapter 9, EditText has content-aware flavors for entering numbers and text. Android also supports widgets (DatePicker and TimePicker) and dialog boxes (DatePickerDialog and TimePickerDialog) for helping users enter dates and times.

DatePicker and DatePickerDialog allow you to set the starting date for the selection, in the form of a year, month, and day of month value. Note that the month runs from 0 for January through 11 for December. Most importantly, both DatePicker and DatePickerDialog let you provide a callback object (OnDateChangedListener or OnDateSetListener) to notify you when a user has selected a new date. It is up to you to store that date someplace, particularly if you are using the dialog box, since there is no other way for you to access the chosen date later.

Similarly, TimePicker and TimePickerDialog let you do the following:

- Set the initial time the user can adjust, in the form of an hour (0 through 23) and a minute (0 through 59)

- Indicate if the selection should be in 12-hour mode with an AM/PM toggle or in 24-hour mode (what is thought of in the United States as "military time" and in much of the rest of the world as "the way times are supposed to be")

- Provide a callback object (OnTimeChangedListener or OnTimeSetListener) to be notified of when the user has chosen a new time, which is supplied to you in the form of an hour and minute

As an example of using date and time pickers, from the Fancy/Chrono sample project, here's a trivial layout containing a label and two buttons, which will pop up the dialog box flavors of the date and time pickers:

```xml
<?xml version="1.0" encoding="utf-8"?>
<LinearLayout
  xmlns:android="http://schemas.android.com/apk/res/android"
  android:orientation="vertical"
  android:layout_width="fill_parent"
  android:layout_height="fill_parent"
  >
  <TextView android:id="@+id/dateAndTime"
    android:layout_width="fill_parent"
    android:layout_height="wrap_content"
    />
  <Button android:id="@+id/dateBtn"
    android:layout_width="fill_parent"
    android:layout_height="wrap_content"
    android:text="Set the Date"
    android:onClick="chooseDate"
    />
  <Button android:id="@+id/timeBtn"
    android:layout_width="fill_parent"
    android:layout_height="wrap_content"
    android:text="Set the Time"
    android:onClick="chooseTime"
    />
</LinearLayout>
```

The more interesting stuff comes in the Java source:

```java
package com.commonsware.android.chrono;

import android.app.Activity;
import android.os.Bundle;
import android.app.DatePickerDialog;
import android.app.TimePickerDialog;
import android.view.View;
import android.widget.DatePicker;
import android.widget.TimePicker;
import android.widget.TextView;
import java.text.DateFormat;
import java.util.Calendar;

public class ChronoDemo extends Activity {
  DateFormat fmtDateAndTime=DateFormat.getDateTimeInstance();
  TextView dateAndTimeLabel;
  Calendar dateAndTime=Calendar.getInstance();
```

```
@Override
public void onCreate(Bundle icicle) {
  super.onCreate(icicle);
  setContentView(R.layout.main);

  dateAndTimeLabel=(TextView)findViewById(R.id.dateAndTime);

  updateLabel();
}

public void chooseDate(View v) {
  new DatePickerDialog(ChronoDemo.this, d,
                       dateAndTime.get(Calendar.YEAR),
                       dateAndTime.get(Calendar.MONTH),
                       dateAndTime.get(Calendar.DAY_OF_MONTH))
    .show();
}

public void chooseTime(View v) {
  new TimePickerDialog(ChronoDemo.this, t,
                       dateAndTime.get(Calendar.HOUR_OF_DAY),
                       dateAndTime.get(Calendar.MINUTE),
                       true)
    .show();
}

private void updateLabel() {
  dateAndTimeLabel.setText(fmtDateAndTime
                        .format(dateAndTime.getTime()));
}

DatePickerDialog.OnDateSetListener d=new DatePickerDialog.OnDateSetListener() {
  public void onDateSet(DatePicker view, int year, int monthOfYear,
                        int dayOfMonth) {
    dateAndTime.set(Calendar.YEAR, year);
    dateAndTime.set(Calendar.MONTH, monthOfYear);
    dateAndTime.set(Calendar.DAY_OF_MONTH, dayOfMonth);
    updateLabel();
  }
};

TimePickerDialog.OnTimeSetListener t=new TimePickerDialog.OnTimeSetListener() {
  public void onTimeSet(TimePicker view, int hourOfDay,
                        int minute) {
    dateAndTime.set(Calendar.HOUR_OF_DAY, hourOfDay);
    dateAndTime.set(Calendar.MINUTE, minute);
    updateLabel();
  }
};
}
```

The model for this activity is just a Calendar instance, initially set to be the current date and time. We pour it into the view via a DateFormat formatter. In the updateLabel() method, we take the current Calendar, format it, and put it in the TextView.

Each button has a corresponding method that will get control when the user clicks it (chooseDate() and chooseTime()). When the button is clicked, either a DatePickerDialog or a TimePickerDialog is shown. In the case of the DatePickerDialog, we give it an OnDateSetListener callback that updates the Calendar with the new date (year, month, and day of month). We also give the dialog box the last-selected date, getting the values from the Calendar. In the case of the TimePickerDialog, it gets an OnTimeSetListener callback to update the time portion of the Calendar, the last-selected time, and a value of true indicating we want 24-hour mode on the time selector.

With all this wired together, the resulting activity looks like Figures 14–1, 14–2, and 14–3.

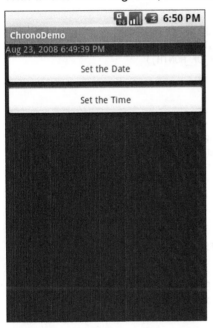

Figure 14–1. *The ChronoDemo sample application, as initially launched*

Figure 14–2. *The same application, showing the date picker dialog box*

Figure 14–3. *The same application, showing the time picker dialog box*

Time Keeps Flowing Like a River

If you want to display the time, rather than have users enter the time, you may wish to use the DigitalClock widget or the AnalogClock widget. These widgets are extremely easy to use, as they automatically update with the passage of time. All you need to do is put them in your layout and let them do their thing.

For example, from the Fancy/Clocks sample application, here is an XML layout containing both DigitalClock and AnalogClock:

```xml
<?xml version="1.0" encoding="utf-8"?>
<RelativeLayout xmlns:android="http://schemas.android.com/apk/res/android"
  android:layout_width="fill_parent"
  android:layout_height="fill_parent"
  >
  <AnalogClock android:id="@+id/analog"
    android:layout_width="fill_parent"
    android:layout_height="wrap_content"
    android:layout_centerHorizontal="true"
    android:layout_alignParentTop="true"
    />
  <DigitalClock android:id="@+id/digital"
    android:layout_width="wrap_content"
    android:layout_height="wrap_content"
    android:layout_centerHorizontal="true"
    android:layout_below="@id/analog"
    />
</RelativeLayout>
```

Without any Java code other than the generated stub, we can build this project and get the activity shown in Figure 14–4.

Figure 14–4. The ClocksDemo sample application

If you are looking for more of a timer, Chronometer may be of interest. With a Chronometer, you can track elapsed time from a starting point, as shown in the example in Figure 14–5. You simply tell it when to start() and stop(), and possibly override the format string that displays the text.

Figure 14–5. *The Views/Chronometer API Demo from the Android SDK*

Seeking Resolution

The SeekBar is an input widget that allows the user to select a value along a range of possible values. Figure 14–6 shows an example.

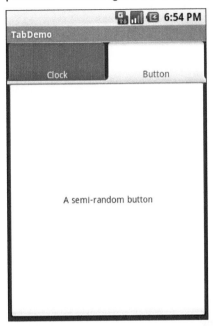

Figure 14–6. *The Views/SeekBar API Demo from the Android SDK*

The user can either drag the thumb or click on either side of the thumb to reposition it. The thumb then points to a particular value along a range. That range will be 0 to some maximum value, 100 by default, which you control via a call to setMax(). You can find out what the current position is via getProgress(), or find out when the user makes a change to the thumb's position by registering a listener via setOnSeekBarChangeListener().

We saw a variation on this theme with the RatingBar example in Chapter 13.

Putting It on My Tab

The general Android philosophy is to keep activities short and sweet. If there is more information than can reasonably fit on one screen, albeit perhaps with scrolling, then it perhaps belongs in another activity kicked off via an Intent, as will be described in Chapter 22. However, that can be complicated to set up. Moreover, sometimes there legitimately is a lot of information that needs to be collected to be processed as an atomic operation.

In a traditional UI, you might use tabs to collect and display information, such as a JTabbedPane in Java/Swing. In Android, you now have the option of using a TabHost container in much the same way. A portion of your activity's screen is taken up with tabs, which, when clicked, swap out part of the view and replace it with something else. For example, you might have an activity with a tab for entering a location and a second tab for showing a map of that location.

Some GUI toolkits refer to "tabs" as only the things that a user clicks to toggle from one view to another. Other GUI toolkits refer to "tabs" as the combination of the clickable button-like element and the content that appears when that element is chosen. Android treats the tab buttons and contents as discrete entities, so they are referred to as "tab buttons" and "tab contents" in this section.

The Pieces

You use the following widgets and containers to set up a tabbed portion of a view:

- TabHost: The overarching container for the tab buttons and tab contents.

- TabWidget: Implements the row of tab buttons, which contain text labels and, optionally, icons.

- FrameLayout: The container for the tab contents. Each tab content is a child of the FrameLayout.

This is similar to the approach that Mozilla's XUL takes. In XUL's case, the tabbox element corresponds to Android's TabHost, the tabs element corresponds to TabWidget, and tabpanels corresponds to FrameLayout.

For example, here is a layout definition for a tabbed activity, from Fancy/Tab:

```xml
<?xml version="1.0" encoding="utf-8"?>
<TabHost xmlns:android="http://schemas.android.com/apk/res/android"
  android:id="@+id/tabhost"
  android:layout_width="fill_parent"
  android:layout_height="fill_parent">
  <LinearLayout
    android:orientation="vertical"
    android:layout_width="fill_parent"
    android:layout_height="fill_parent">
  <TabWidget android:id="@android:id/tabs"
    android:layout_width="fill_parent"
    android:layout_height="wrap_content"
  />
  <FrameLayout android:id="@android:id/tabcontent"
    android:layout_width="fill_parent"
    android:layout_height="fill_parent">
    <AnalogClock android:id="@+id/tab1"
      android:layout_width="fill_parent"
      android:layout_height="fill_parent"
    />
    <Button android:id="@+id/tab2"
      android:layout_width="fill_parent"
      android:layout_height="fill_parent"
      android:text="A semi-random button"
```

```
        />
      </FrameLayout>
    </LinearLayout>
</TabHost>
```

Note that the TabWidget and FrameLayout are indirect children of the TabHost, and the FrameLayout itself has children representing the various tabs. In this case, there are two tabs: a clock and a button. In a more complicated scenario, the tabs could be some form of container (e.g., LinearLayout) with their own contents.

Wiring It Together

You can put these widgets in a regular Activity or a TabActivity. TabActivity, like ListActivity, wraps a common UI pattern (an activity made up entirely of tabs) into a pattern-aware activity subclass. If you wish to use the TabActivity, you must give the TabHost an android:id of @android:id/tabhost. Conversely, if you do not wish to use TabActivity, you need to get your TabHost via findViewById(), and then call setup() on the TabHost, before you do anything else.

The rest of the Java code needs to tell the TabHost which views represent the tab contents and what the tab buttons should look like. This is all wrapped up in TabSpec objects. You get a TabSpec instance from the host via newTabSpec(), fill it out, and then add it to the host in the proper sequence.

TabSpec has two key methods:

- setContent(): Indicates what goes in the tab content for this tab, typically the android:id of the view you want shown when this tab is selected

- setIndicator(): Sets the caption for the tab button and, in some flavors of this method, supplies a Drawable to represent the icon for the tab

Note that tab "indicators" can actually be views in their own right, if you need more control than a simple label and optional icon.

Also note that you must call setup() on the TabHost before configuring any of these TabSpec objects. The call to setup() is not needed if you are using the TabActivity base class for your activity.

For example, here is the Java code to wire together the tabs from the preceding layout example:

```java
package com.commonsware.android.fancy;

import android.app.Activity;
import android.os.Bundle;
import android.widget.TabHost;

public class TabDemo extends Activity {
  @Override
  public void onCreate(Bundle icicle) {
    super.onCreate(icicle);
    setContentView(R.layout.main);
```

```
TabHost tabs=(TabHost)findViewById(R.id.tabhost);

tabs.setup();

TabHost.TabSpec spec=tabs.newTabSpec("tag1");

spec.setContent(R.id.tab1);
spec.setIndicator("Clock");
tabs.addTab(spec);

spec=tabs.newTabSpec("tag2");
spec.setContent(R.id.tab2);
spec.setIndicator("Button");
tabs.addTab(spec);
    }
}
```

We find our TabHost via the familiar findViewById() method, and then have it set up via setup(). After that, we get a TabSpec via newTabSpec(), supplying a tag whose purpose is unknown at this time. Given the spec, we call setContent() and setIndicator(), and then call addTab() back on the TabHost to register the tab as available for use. Finally, we can choose which tab is the one to show via setCurrentTab(), providing the 0-based index of the tab.

The results are shown in Figures 14–7 and 14–8.

Figure 14–7. *The TabDemo sample application, showing the first tab*

Figure 14–8. *The same application, showing the second tab*

Note that if your application is running under an older SDK level, prior to the Honeycomb and Ice Cream Sandwich releases, then your menus will appear in the old-fashioned "button" style, as shown in Figure 14–9. You have some control over whether to use the old behavior or the new behavior by specifying android:targetSdkVersion and android:minSdkVersion in your AndroidManifest.xml. Chapter 29 has a useful list of SDK versions.

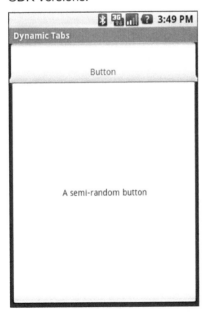

Figure 14–9. *The TabDemo sample application, showing the first tab with older-style UI*

Adding Them Up

TabWidget is set up to allow you to easily define tabs at compile time. However, sometimes you may want to add tabs to your activity during runtime. For example, imagine an e-mail client that opens each individual e-mail message in its own tab, for easy toggling between messages. In this case, you do not know how many tabs you will need or what their contents will be until runtime, when the user chooses to open a message. Fortunately, Android also supports adding tabs dynamically at runtime.

Adding tabs dynamically at runtime works much like the compile-time tabs previously described, except you use a different flavor of setContent(), one that takes a TabHost.TabContentFactory instance. This is just a callback that will be invoked. You provide an implementation of createTabContent() and use it to build and return the View that becomes the content of the tab.

Let's take a look at an example (Fancy/DynamicTab). First, here is some layout XML for an activity that sets up the tabs and defines one tab, containing a single button:

```xml
<?xml version="1.0" encoding="utf-8"?>
<TabHost xmlns:android="http://schemas.android.com/apk/res/android"
  android:id="@+id/tabhost"
  android:layout_width="fill_parent"
  android:layout_height="fill_parent">
  <LinearLayout
    android:orientation="vertical"
    android:layout_width="fill_parent"
    android:layout_height="fill_parent">
    <TabWidget android:id="@android:id/tabs"
      android:layout_width="fill_parent"
      android:layout_height="wrap_content"
    />
    <FrameLayout android:id="@android:id/tabcontent"
      android:layout_width="fill_parent"
      android:layout_height="fill_parent">
      <Button android:id="@+id/buttontab"
        android:layout_width="fill_parent"
        android:layout_height="fill_parent"
        android:text="A semi-random button"
        android:onClick="addTab"
      />
    </FrameLayout>
  </LinearLayout>
</TabHost>
```

We want to add new tabs whenever the button is clicked, which we can accomplish with the following code:

```java
package com.commonsware.android.dynamictab;

import android.app.Activity;
import android.os.Bundle;
import android.view.View;
import android.widget.AnalogClock;
import android.widget.TabHost;
```

```
public class DynamicTabDemo extends Activity {
  private TabHost tabs=null;

  @Override
  public void onCreate(Bundle icicle) {
    super.onCreate(icicle);
    setContentView(R.layout.main);

    tabs=(TabHost)findViewById(R.id.tabhost);
    tabs.setup();

    TabHost.TabSpec spec=tabs.newTabSpec("buttontab");

    spec.setContent(R.id.buttontab);
    spec.setIndicator("Button");
    tabs.addTab(spec);
  }

  public void addTab(View v) {
    TabHost.TabSpec spec=tabs.newTabSpec("tag1");

    spec.setContent(new TabHost.TabContentFactory() {
      public View createTabContent(String tag) {
        return(new AnalogClock(DynamicTabDemo.this));
      }
    });

    spec.setIndicator("Clock");
    tabs.addTab(spec);
  }
}
```

In our button's addTab() callback, we create a TabHost.TabSpec object and give it an anonymous TabHost.TabContentFactory. The factory, in turn, returns the View to be used for the tab—in this case, just an AnalogClock. The logic for constructing the tab's View could be much more elaborate, such as using LayoutInflater to construct a view from layout XML.

Initially, when the activity is launched, we just have the one tab, as shown in Figure 14–10. Figure 14–11 shows the three dynamically created tabs.

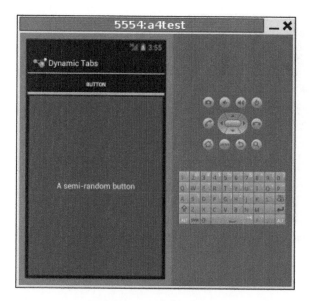

Figure 14–10. *The DynamicTab application, with the single initial tab*

Figure 14–11. *The DynamicTab application, with three dynamically created tabs*

The table handling is truly dynamic, adapting to the size of your screen. Android formats the table to fit larger-format screens such as tablets and even TVs. Figure 14–12 shows four dynamically created tabs on a larger, tablet-sized screen.

Figure 14–12. *The DynamicTab application, demonstrating adaptability on a tablet-sized screen*

Flipping Them Off

Sometimes, you want the overall effect of tabs (only some Views visible at a time) but not the actual UI implementation of tabs. Maybe the tabs take up too much screen space. Maybe you want to switch between perspectives based on a gesture or a device shake. Or maybe you just like being different. Android 4.0 Ice Cream Sandwich offers the ability to "push" your tabs up into vacant space in the action bar when space allows, such as when you rotate to landscape orientation, but that doesn't cater for those crazy "shake, rattle, and roll" ideas you might have.

The good news is that the guts of the view-flipping logic from tabs can be found in the ViewFlipper container, which can be used in other ways than the traditional tab.

ViewFlipper inherits from FrameLayout, in the same way we use it to describe the innards of a TabWidget. However, initially, ViewFlipper just shows the first child view. It is up to you to arrange for the views to flip, either manually by user interaction or automatically via a timer.

For example, here is a layout for a simple activity (Fancy/Flipper1) using a Button and a ViewFlipper:

```
<?xml version="1.0" encoding="utf-8"?>
<LinearLayout xmlns:android="http://schemas.android.com/apk/res/android"
    android:orientation="vertical"
    android:layout_width="fill_parent"
    android:layout_height="fill_parent"
    >
  <Button android:id="@+id/flip_me"
      android:layout_width="fill_parent"
      android:layout_height="wrap_content"
      android:text="Flip Me!"
      android:onClick="flip"
      />
  <ViewFlipper android:id="@+id/details"
      android:layout_width="fill_parent"
```

```
      android:layout_height="fill_parent"
      >
      <TextView
        android:layout_width="fill_parent"
        android:layout_height="wrap_content"
        android:textStyle="bold"
        android:textColor="#FF00FF00"
        android:text="This is the first panel"
      />
      <TextView
        android:layout_width="fill_parent"
        android:layout_height="wrap_content"
        android:textStyle="bold"
        android:textColor="#FFFF0000"
        android:text="This is the second panel"
      />
      <TextView
        android:layout_width="fill_parent"
        android:layout_height="wrap_content"
        android:textStyle="bold"
        android:textColor="#FFFFFF00"
        android:text="This is the third panel"
      />
  </ViewFlipper>
</LinearLayout>
```

Notice that the layout defines three child views for the ViewFlipper, each a TextView with a simple message. Of course, you could have very complicated child views, if you so choose.

To manually flip the views, we need to hook into the Button and flip them ourselves when the button is clicked:

```
package com.commonsware.android.flipper1;

import android.app.Activity;
import android.os.Bundle;
import android.view.View;
import android.widget.ViewFlipper;

public class FlipperDemo extends Activity {
  ViewFlipper flipper;

  @Override
  public void onCreate(Bundle icicle) {
    super.onCreate(icicle);
    setContentView(R.layout.main);

    flipper=(ViewFlipper)findViewById(R.id.details);
  }

  public void flip(View v) {
    flipper.showNext();
  }
}
```

This is just a matter of calling showNext() on the ViewFlipper, as you can on any ViewAnimator class. The result is a trivial activity: click the button, and the next TextView in sequence is displayed, wrapping around to the first after viewing the last, as shown in Figures 14–13 and 14–14.

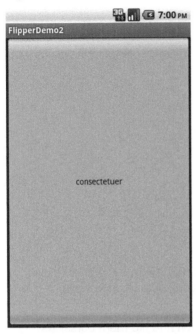

Figure 14–13. *The FlipperDemo application, showing the first panel*

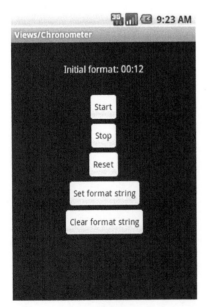

Figure 14–14. *The same application, after switching to the second panel*

Of course, this could be handled more simply by having a single TextView and changing the text and color on each click. However, you can imagine that the ViewFlipper contents could be much more complicated, like the contents you might put into a TabView.

As with the TabWidget, sometimes your ViewFlipper contents may not be known at compile time. And as with TabWidget, you can add new contents on-the-fly with ease.

For example, let's look at another sample activity (Fancy/Flipper2), using this layout:

```xml
<?xml version="1.0" encoding="utf-8"?>
<LinearLayout xmlns:android="http://schemas.android.com/apk/res/android"
    android:orientation="vertical"
    android:layout_width="fill_parent"
    android:layout_height="fill_parent"
    >
  <ViewFlipper android:id="@+id/details"
    android:layout_width="fill_parent"
    android:layout_height="fill_parent"
    >
  </ViewFlipper>
</LinearLayout>
```

Notice that the ViewFlipper has no contents at compile time. Also notice that there is no Button for flipping between the contents—more on this in a moment.

For the ViewFlipper contents, we will create large Button widgets, each containing one of the random words used in many chapters in this book. And, we will set up the ViewFlipper to automatically rotate between the Button widgets.

```java
package com.commonsware.android.flipper2;

import android.app.Activity;
import android.os.Bundle;
import android.view.View;
import android.view.ViewGroup;
import android.widget.Button;
import android.widget.ViewFlipper;

public class FlipperDemo2 extends Activity {
  static String[] items={"lorem", "ipsum", "dolor", "sit", "amet",
                          "consectetuer", "adipiscing", "elit",
                          "morbi", "vel", "ligula", "vitae",
                          "arcu", "aliquet", "mollis", "etiam",
                          "vel", "erat", "placerat", "ante",
                          "porttitor", "sodales", "pellentesque",
                          "augue", "purus"};
  ViewFlipper flipper;

  @Override
  public void onCreate(Bundle icicle) {
    super.onCreate(icicle);
    setContentView(R.layout.main);

    flipper=(ViewFlipper)findViewById(R.id.details);

    for (String item : items) {
```

```
        Button btn=new Button(this);

        btn.setText(item);

        flipper.addView(btn,
                    new ViewGroup.LayoutParams(
                            ViewGroup.LayoutParams.FILL_PARENT,
                            ViewGroup.LayoutParams.FILL_PARENT));
      }

      flipper.setFlipInterval(2000);
      flipper.startFlipping();
    }
}
```

After iterating over the funky words, turning each into a Button, and adding the Button as a child of the ViewFlipper, we set up the flipper to automatically flip between children (flipper.setFlipInterval(2000);) and to start flipping (flipper.startFlipping(.

The result is an endless series of buttons, each of which appears, as shown in Figure 14–15, and then is replaced by the next button in sequence after 2 seconds, wrapping around to the first after the last has been shown.

Figure 14–15. *The FlipperDemo2 application*

The autoflipping ViewFlipper is useful for status panels or other situations where you have a lot of information to display but not much room to display it. However, since it automatically flips between views, expecting users to interact with individual views is dicey, because the view might switch away partway through their interaction.

Getting in Somebody's Drawer

For a long time, Android developers yearned for a sliding-drawer container that worked like the one on the home screen, containing the icons for launching applications. The official implementation was in the open source code but was not part of the SDK, until Android 1.5, when the developers released SlidingDrawer for others to use.

Unlike most other Android containers, SlidingDrawer moves, switching from a closed to an open position. This puts some restrictions on which container can hold the SlidingDrawer. It needs to be in a container that allows multiple widgets to sit atop each other. RelativeLayout and FrameLayout satisfy this requirement. FrameLayout is a container purely for stacking widgets atop one another. On the flip side, LinearLayout does not allow widgets to stack (they fall one after another in a row or column), and so you should not have a SlidingDrawer as an immediate child of a LinearLayout.

Here is a layout showing a SlidingDrawer in a FrameLayout, from the Fancy/DrawerDemo project:

```xml
<?xml version="1.0" encoding="utf-8"?>
<FrameLayout xmlns:android="http://schemas.android.com/apk/res/android"
    android:layout_width="fill_parent"
    android:layout_height="fill_parent"
    android:background="#FF4444CC"
    >
  <SlidingDrawer
    android:id="@+id/drawer"
    android:layout_width="fill_parent"
    android:layout_height="fill_parent"
    android:handle="@+id/handle"
    android:content="@+id/content">
    <ImageView
      android:id="@id/handle"
      android:layout_width="wrap_content"
      android:layout_height="wrap_content"
      android:src="@drawable/tray_handle_normal"
    />
    <Button
      android:id="@id/content"
      android:layout_width="fill_parent"
      android:layout_height="fill_parent"
      android:text="I'm in here!"
    />
  </SlidingDrawer>
</FrameLayout>
```

The SlidingDrawer should contain two things:

- A handle, frequently an ImageView or something along those lines, such as the one used here, pulled from the Android open source project

- The contents of the drawer itself, usually some sort of container, but a Button in this example

Moreover, SlidingDrawer needs to know the android:id values of the handle and contents, via the android:handle and android:content attributes, respectively. These tell the drawer how to animate itself as it slides open and closed.

Figure 14–16 shows what the SlidingDrawer looks like closed, using the supplied handle, and Figure 14–17 shows what it looks like open.

Figure 14–16. *A SlidingDrawer, closed*

Figure 14–17. *A SlidingDrawer, open*

As you might expect, you can open and close the drawer from Java code, as well as via user touch events. However, you have two sets of these methods: ones that take place instantaneously (open(),close(), and toggle()) and ones that use the animation (animateOpen(), animateClose(), and animateToggle()). You can also lock() and unlock() the drawer; while locked, the drawer will not respond to touch events.

You can also register three types of callbacks if you wish:

- A listener to be invoked when the drawer is opened

- A listener to be invoked when the drawer is closed

- A listener to be invoked when the drawer is "scrolled" (i.e., the user drags or flings the handle)

For example, the Android launcher's SlidingDrawer toggles the icon on the handle from open to closed to "delete" (if you long-tap something on the desktop). It accomplishes this, in part, through callbacks like these.

SlidingDrawer can be vertical or horizontal. Note, though, that it keeps its orientation despite the screen orientation. In other words, if you rotate the Android device or emulator running DrawerDemo, the drawer always opens from the bottom—it does not always "stick" to the original side it opened from. This means that if you want the drawer to always open from the same side, like the launcher does, you will need separate layouts for portrait versus landscape, a topic discussed in Chapter 23.

Other Good Stuff

Android offers AbsoluteLayout, where the contents are laid out based on specific coordinate positions. You tell AbsoluteLayout where to place a child in precise x and y coordinates, and Android puts it there, no questions asked. On the plus side, this gives you precise positioning. On the minus side, it means your views will look right only on screens of a certain dimension, or you will need to write a bunch of code to adjust the coordinates based on screen size. Since Android screens might run the gamut of sizes, with new sizes cropping up periodically, using AbsoluteLayout could get quite annoying. Also, note that AbsoluteLayout is officially deprecated, meaning that although it is available to you, its use is discouraged.

Android also has the ExpandableListView. This provides a simplified tree representation, supporting two levels of depth: groups and children. Groups contain children; children are "leaves" of the tree. This requires a new set of adapters, since the ListAdapter family does not provide any sort of group information for the items in the list.

Here are some other widgets available in Android beyond those covered so far in this book:

- CheckedTextView: A TextView that can have either a check box or a radio button next to it, used with single- and multiple-choice lists

- Chronometer: A stopwatch-style countdown timer

- `Gallery`: A horizontal scrolling selection widget, designed for thumbnail previews of images (e.g., camera photos and album covers)

- `MultiAutoCompleteTextView`: Like an `AutoCompleteTextView`, except that the user can make multiple choices from the drop-down list, rather than just one

- `QuickContactBadge`: Given the identity of a contact from the user's contacts database, displays a roster of icons representing actions to be performed on that contact (place a call, send a text message, send an e-mail, etc.)

- `ToggleButton`: A two-state button where the states are indicated by a "light" and prose ("ON", "OFF") instead of a check mark

- `ViewSwitcher` (and the `ImageSwitcher` and `TextSwitcher` subclasses): Like a simplified `ViewFlipper` for toggling between two views

Chapter 15

Embedding the WebKit Browser

Other GUI toolkits let you use HTML for presenting information, from limited HTML renderers (e.g., Java/Swing and wxWidgets) to embedding Internet Explorer into .NET applications. Android is much the same, in that you can embed the built-in web browser as a widget in your own activities, for displaying HTML or full-fledged browsing. The Android browser is based on WebKit, the same engine that powers web browsers such as Apple's Safari and Google's Chrome.

The Android browser is sufficiently complex that it gets its own Java package (android.webkit). Using the WebView widget itself can be simple or powerful, based on your requirements.

A Browser, Writ Small

For simple stuff, WebView is not significantly different from any other widget in Android—pop it into a layout, tell it which URL to navigate to via Java code, and you are finished.

For example, here is a simple layout with a WebView (from WebKit/Browser1):

```
<?xml version="1.0" encoding="utf-8"?>
<WebView xmlns:android="http://schemas.android.com/apk/res/android"
  android:id="@+id/webkit"
  android:layout_width="fill_parent"
  android:layout_height="fill_parent"
/>
```

As with any other widget, you need to tell it how it should fill up the space in the layout (in this case, it fills all remaining space).

The Java code is equally simple:

```
package com.commonsware.android.browser1;

import android.app.Activity;
```

```
import android.os.Bundle;
import android.webkit.WebView;

public class BrowserDemo1 extends Activity {
  WebView browser;

  @Override
  public void onCreate(Bundle icicle) {
    super.onCreate(icicle);
    setContentView(R.layout.main);
    browser=(WebView)findViewById(R.id.webkit);

    browser.loadUrl("http://commonsware.com");
  }
}
```

The only thing unusual with this edition of onCreate() is that we invoke loadUrl() on the WebView widget, to tell it to load a web page (in this case, the home page of some random firm).

However, we also need to make one change to AndroidManifest.xml, requesting permission to access the Internet:

```
<?xml version="1.0"?>
<manifest xmlns:android="http://schemas.android.com/apk/res/android"
package="com.commonsware.android.browser1">
  <uses-permission android:name="android.permission.INTERNET"/>
  <application android:icon="@drawable/cw">
    <activity android:name=".BrowserDemo1" android:label="BrowserDemo1">
      <intent-filter>
        <action android:name="android.intent.action.MAIN"/>
        <category android:name="android.intent.category.LAUNCHER"/>
      </intent-filter>
    </activity>
  </application>
  <supports-screens android:largeScreens="true" android:normalScreens="true"
android:smallScreens="true" android:anyDensity="true"/>
</manifest>
```

If we fail to add this permission, the browser will refuse to load pages. Permissions will be covered in greater detail in Chapter 38.

The resulting activity looks like a web browser, but with hidden scrollbars, as shown in Figure 15–1.

Figure 15–1. *The BrowserDemo1 sample application*

As with the regular Android browser, you can pan around the page by dragging it, while the D-pad moves you around all the focusable elements on the page. What is missing is all the extra stuff that make up a web browser, such as a navigational toolbar.

Now, you may be tempted to replace the URL in that source code with something that relies on JavaScript, such as Google's home page. By default, JavaScript is turned off in WebView widgets. If you want to enable JavaScript, call getSettings().setJavaScriptEnabled(true); on the WebView instance. This option is covered in a bit more detail later in this chapter.

Loading It Up

There are two main ways to get content into the WebView. One, described in the previous section, is to provide the browser with a URL and have the browser display that page via loadUrl(). The browser will access the Internet through whatever means are available to that specific device at the present time (Wi-Fi, 2G, 3G, 4G, WiMAX, EDGE, HSDPA, HSPA, well-trained tiny carrier pigeons, etc.).

The alternative is to use loadData(). Here, you supply the HTML for the browser to view. You might use this to do the following:

- Display a manual that was installed as a file with your application package

- Display snippets of HTML you retrieved as part of other processing, such as the description of an entry in an Atom feed

■   Generate a whole user interface using HTML, instead of using the Android widget set

There are two flavors of loadData(). The simpler one allows you to provide the content, the MIME type, and the encoding, all as strings. Typically, your MIME type will be text/html and your encoding will be UTF-8 for ordinary HTML.

For example, you could replace the loadUrl() invocation in the previous example with the following:

```
browser.loadData("<html><body>Hello, world!</body></html>",
                "text/html", "UTF-8");
```

You would get the result shown in Figure 15–2.

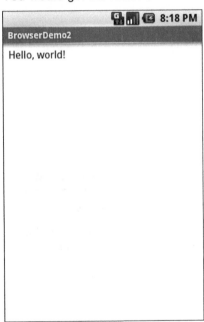

Figure 15–2. *The BrowserDemo2 sample application*

This is also available as a fully buildable sample, as WebKit/Browser2.

Navigating the Waters

As previously mentioned, the WebView widget doesn't have a navigation toolbar. This allows you to use it in places where such a toolbar would be pointless and a waste of screen real estate. That being said, if you want to offer navigational capabilities, you can, but you have to supply the UI.

WebView offers ways to perform garden-variety browser navigation, including the following methods:

- `reload()`: Refreshes the currently viewed web page

- `goBack()`: Goes back one step in the browser history

- `canGoBack()`: Determines if there is any history to go back to

- `goForward()`: Goes forward one step in the browser history

- `canGoForward()`: Determines if there is any history to go forward to

- `goBackOrForward()`: Goes backward or forward in the browser history, where a negative number as an argument represents how many steps to go backward, and a positive number represents how many steps to go forward

- `canGoBackOrForward()`: Determines if the browser can go backward or forward the stated number of steps (following the same positive/negative convention as `goBackOrForward()`)

- `clearCache()`: Clears the browser resource cache

- `clearHistory()`: Clears the browsing history

Entertaining the Client

If you are going to use the `WebView` as a local UI (versus browsing the Web), you will want to be able to get control at key times, particularly when users click links. You will want to make sure those links are handled properly, either by loading your own content back into the `WebView`, by submitting an `Intent` to Android to open the URL in a full browser, or by some other means (see Chapter 22).

Your hook into the `WebView` activity is via `setWebViewClient()`, which takes an instance of a `WebViewClient` implementation as a parameter. The supplied callback object will be notified of a wide range of events, from when parts of a page have been retrieved (`onPageStarted()`, etc.) to when you, as the host application, need to handle certain user- or circumstance-initiated events, such as `onTooManyRedirects()` or `onReceivedHttpAuthRequest()`.

A common hook will be `shouldOverrideUrlLoading()`, where your callback is passed a URL (plus the `WebView` itself), and you return `true` if you will handle the request or `false` if you want default handling (e.g., actually fetch the web page referenced by the URL). In the case of a feed reader application, for example, you will probably not have a full browser with navigation built into your reader. In this case, if the user clicks a URL, you probably want to use an `Intent` to ask Android to load that page in a full browser. But if you have inserted a "fake" URL into the HTML, representing a link to some activity-provided content, you can update the `WebView` yourself.

As an example, let's amend the first browser demo to make it an application that, upon a click, shows the current time. From WebKit/Browser3, here is the revised Java:

```java
public class BrowserDemo3 extends Activity {
  WebView browser;

  @Override
  public void onCreate(Bundle icicle) {
    super.onCreate(icicle);
    setContentView(R.layout.main);
    browser=(WebView)findViewById(R.id.webkit);
    browser.setWebViewClient(new Callback());

    loadTime();
  }

  void loadTime() {
    String page="<html><body><a href=\"clock\">"
            +new Date().toString()
            +"</a></body></html>";

    browser.loadData(page, "text/html", "UTF-8");
  }

  private class Callback extends WebViewClient {
    public boolean shouldOverrideUrlLoading(WebView view, String url) {
      loadTime();

      return(true);
    }
  }
}
```

Here, we load into the browser (loadTime()) a simple web page that consists of the current time, made into a hyperlink to the /clock URL. We also attach an instance of a WebViewClient subclass, providing our implementation of shouldOverrideUrlLoading(). In this case, no matter what the URL, we want to just reload the WebView via loadTime().

Running this activity gives the result shown in Figure 15–3.

Figure 15–3. *The BrowserDemo3 sample application*

Selecting the link and clicking the D-pad center button will "click" the link, causing the page to be rebuilt with the new time.

Settings, Preferences, and Options (Oh, My!)

With your favorite desktop web browser, you have some sort of settings, preferences, or options window. Between that and the toolbar controls, you can tweak and twiddle the behavior of your browser, from preferred fonts to the behavior of JavaScript. Similarly, you can adjust the settings of your WebView widget as you see fit, via the WebSettings instance returned from calling the widget's getSettings() method.

There are lots of options on WebSettings to play with. Most appear fairly esoteric (e.g., setFantasyFontFamily()). However, here are some that you may find more useful:

- Control the font sizing via setDefaultFontSize() (to use a point size) or setTextZoom() (to use constants indicating relative sizes like LARGER and SMALLEST)

- Control JavaScript via setJavaScriptEnabled() (to disable it outright) and setJavaScriptCanOpenWindowsAutomatically() (to merely stop it from opening pop-up windows)

- Control web site rendering via setUserAgent(), so you can supply your own user agent string to make the web server think you are a desktop browser, another mobile device (e.g., an iPhone), or whatever

■ The settings you change are not persistent, so you should store them
somewhere (such as via the Android preferences engine) if you are
allowing your users to determine the settings, versus hard-wiring the
settings in your application.

Chapter 16

Applying Menus

Like applications for the desktop and some mobile operating systems, Android supports activities with application menus. Most Android phones have a dedicated menu key for popping up the menu; other devices offer alternate means for triggering the menu to appear, such as the onscreen button used by the Archos 5 Android tablet.

Also, as with many GUI toolkits, you can create context menus for your Android applications. On a traditional GUI, a context menu might be triggered by the user clicking with the right-mouse button. On mobile devices, context menus typically appear when the user taps and holds over a particular widget. For example, if a TextView has a context menu, and the device is designed for finger-based touch input, you could push the TextView with your finger, hold it for a second or two, and a pop-up menu would appear.

Flavors of Menu

Android refers to the two types of menu described in the preceding section as options menus and context menus. The options menu is triggered by pressing the hardware Menu button on the device, while the context menu is raised by a tap-and-hold on the widget sporting the menu.

In addition, the options menu operates in one of two modes: icon or expanded. When the user first presses the Menu button, the icon mode will appear, showing up to the first six menu choices as large, finger-friendly buttons in a grid at the bottom of the screen. If the menu has more than six choices, the sixth button will be labeled More. Tapping the More option will bring up the expanded mode, showing the remaining choices not visible in the regular menu. The menu is scrollable, so the user can scroll to any of the menu choices.

Menus of Options

Instead of building your activity's options menu during onCreate(), the way you wire up the rest of your UI, you need to implement onCreateOptionsMenu(). This callback receives an instance of Menu.

The first thing you should do is chain upward to the superclass (super.onCreateOptionsMenu(menu)), so the Android framework can add in any menu choices it feels are necessary. Then you can go about adding your own options, as described in this section.

If you will need to adjust the menu during your activity's use (e.g., disable a now-invalid menu choice), just hold onto the Menu instance you receive in onCreateOptionsMenu(). Alternatively, you can implement onPrepareOptionsMenu(), which is called just before displaying the menu each time it is requested.

Given that you have received a Menu object via onCreateOptionsMenu(), you add menu choices by calling add(). There are many flavors of this method, which require some combination of the following parameters:

- A group identifier (int), which should be NONE unless you are creating a specific grouped set of menu choices for use with setGroupCheckable() (described shortly)

- A choice identifier (also an int), for use in identifying this choice in the onOptionsItemSelected() callback when a menu choice is chosen

- An order identifier (yet another int), for indicating where this menu choice should be slotted if the menu has Android-supplied choices alongside your own; for now, just use NONE

- The text of the menu choice, as a String or a resource ID

The add() family of methods all return an instance of MenuItem, where you can adjust any of the menu item settings you have already set (e.g., the text of the menu choice).

You can also set the shortcuts for the menu choice, which are single-character mnemonics that choose that menu item when the menu is visible. Android supports both an alphabetic (or QWERTY) set of shortcuts and a numeric set of shortcuts. These are set individually by calling setAlphabeticShortcut() and setNumericShortcut(), respectively. The menu is placed into alphabetic shortcut mode by calling setQwertyMode() on the menu with a true parameter.

The choice and group identifiers are keys used to unlock additional menu features, such as the following:

- Calling MenuItem#setCheckable() with a choice identifier, to control if the menu choice has a two-state check box alongside the title, where the check box value is toggled when the user chooses that menu item

- Calling Menu#setGroupCheckable() with a group identifier, to turn a set of menu choices into ones with a mutual-exclusion radio button between them, so that only one item in the group can be in the checked state at any time

You can create fly-out submenus by calling addSubMenu(), supplying the same parameters as addMenu(). Android will eventually call onCreatePanelMenu(), passing it the choice identifier of your submenu, along with another Menu instance representing the submenu itself. As with onCreateOptionsMenu(), you should chain upward to the superclass, and then add menu choices to the submenu. One limitation is that you cannot indefinitely nest submenus—a menu can have a submenu, but a submenu cannot have a sub-submenu.

Finally, you can even push your menu items up into the action bar, which makes your options more discoverable by your users and, more importantly, better utilizes all the available screen space on tablets and larger devices. We'll explore this capability in more depth in Chapter 27 when we focus on the action bar itself.

If the user makes a menu choice, your activity will be notified via the onOptionsItemSelected() callback that a menu choice was selected. You are given the MenuItem object corresponding to the selected menu choice. A typical pattern is to switch() on the menu ID (item.getItemId()) and take appropriate behavior. Note that onOptionsItemSelected() is used regardless of whether the chosen menu item was in the base menu or a submenu.

Menus in Context

By and large, context menus use the same guts as options menus. The two main differences are how you populate the menu and how you are informed of menu choices.

First, you need to indicate which widget or widgets on your activity have context menus. To do this, call registerForContextMenu() from your activity, supplying the View that is the widget needing a context menu.

Next, you need to implement onCreateContextMenu(), which, among other things, is passed the View you supplied in registerForContextMenu(). You can use that to determine which menu to build, assuming your activity has more than one.

The onCreateContextMenu() method gets the ContextMenu itself, the View the context menu is associated with, and a ContextMenu.ContextMenuInfo, which tells you which item in the list the user did the tap-and-hold over, in case you want to customize the context menu based on that information. For example, you could toggle a checkable menu choice based on the current state of the item.

It is also important to note that onCreateContextMenu() gets called each time the context menu is requested. Unlike the options menu (which is built only once per activity), context menus are discarded after they are used or dismissed. Hence, you do not want to hold onto the supplied ContextMenu object; just rely on getting the chance to rebuild the menu to suit your activity's needs on an on-demand basis based on user actions.

To find out when a context menu choice was chosen, implement onContextItemSelected() on the activity. Note that you get only the MenuItem instance that was chosen in this callback. As a result, if your activity has two or more context menus, you may want to ensure they have unique menu item identifiers for all their choices, so you can distinguish between them in this callback. Also, you can call getMenuInfo() on the MenuItem to get the ContextMenu.ContextMenuInfo you received in onCreateContextMenu(). Otherwise, this callback behaves the same as onOptionsItemSelected(), as described in the previous section.

Taking a Peek

In the sample project Menus/Menus, you will find an amended version of the ListView sample (List) with associated menus. Since the menus do not affect the layout, the XML layout file does not need to be changed and thus is not reprinted here. However, the Java code has a few new behaviors:

```
package com.commonsware.android.menus;

import android.app.AlertDialog;
import android.app.ListActivity;
import android.content.DialogInterface;
import android.os.Bundle;
import android.view.ContextMenu;
import android.view.Menu;
import android.view.MenuItem;
import android.view.View;
import android.widget.AdapterView;
import android.widget.ArrayAdapter;
import android.widget.EditText;
import android.widget.ListView;
import android.widget.TextView;
import java.util.ArrayList;

public class MenuDemo extends ListActivity {
  private static final String[] items={"lorem", "ipsum", "dolor",
          "sit", "amet", "consectetuer", "adipiscing", "elit",
          "morbi", "vel", "ligula", "vitae", "arcu", "aliquet",
          "mollis", "etiam", "vel", "erat", "placerat", "ante",
          "porttitor", "sodales", "pellentesque", "augue", "purus"};
  public static final int MENU_ADD = Menu.FIRST+1;
  public static final int MENU_RESET = Menu.FIRST+2;
  public static final int MENU_CAP = Menu.FIRST+3;
  public static final int MENU_REMOVE = Menu.FIRST+4 ;
  private ArrayList<String> words=null;

  @Override
  public void onCreate(Bundle icicle) {
    super.onCreate(icicle);

    initAdapter();
    registerForContextMenu(getListView());
  }
```

```java
@Override
public boolean onCreateOptionsMenu(Menu menu) {
  menu
    .add(Menu.NONE, MENU_ADD, Menu.NONE, "Add")
    .setIcon(R.drawable.ic_menu_add);
  menu
    .add(Menu.NONE, MENU_RESET, Menu.NONE, "Reset")
    .setIcon(R.drawable.ic_menu_refresh);

  return(super.onCreateOptionsMenu(menu));
}

@Override
public void onCreateContextMenu(ContextMenu menu, View v,
                                ContextMenu.ContextMenuInfo menuInfo) {
  menu.add(Menu.NONE, MENU_CAP, Menu.NONE, "Capitalize");
  menu.add(Menu.NONE, MENU_REMOVE, Menu.NONE, "Remove");
}

@Override
public boolean onOptionsItemSelected(MenuItem item) {
  switch (item.getItemId()) {
    case MENU_ADD:
      add();
      return(true);

    case MENU_RESET:
      initAdapter();
      return(true);
  }

  return(super.onOptionsItemSelected(item));
}

@Override
public boolean onContextItemSelected(MenuItem item) {
  AdapterView.AdapterContextMenuInfo info=
    (AdapterView.AdapterContextMenuInfo)item.getMenuInfo();
  ArrayAdapter<String> adapter=(ArrayAdapter<String>)getListAdapter();

  switch (item.getItemId()) {
    case MENU_CAP:
      String word=words.get(info.position);

      word=word.toUpperCase();

      adapter.remove(words.get(info.position));
      adapter.insert(word, info.position);

      return(true);

    case MENU_REMOVE:
      adapter.remove(words.get(info.position));

      return(true);
  }
```

```
      return(super.onContextItemSelected(item));
    }

    private void initAdapter() {
      words=new ArrayList<String>();

      for (String s : items) {
        words.add(s);
      }

      setListAdapter(new ArrayAdapter<String>(this,
                     android.R.layout.simple_list_item_1, words));
    }

    private void add() {
      final View addView=getLayoutInflater().inflate(R.layout.add, null);

      new AlertDialog.Builder(this)
        .setTitle("Add a Word")
        .setView(addView)
        .setPositiveButton("OK",
                        new DialogInterface.OnClickListener() {
          public void onClick(DialogInterface dialog,
                             int whichButton) {
            ArrayAdapter<String> adapter=(ArrayAdapter<String>)getListAdapter();
            EditText title=(EditText)addView.findViewById(R.id.title);

            adapter.add(title.getText().toString());
          }
        })
        .setNegativeButton("Cancel", null)
        .show();
    }
  }
```

In onCreate(), we register our ListView widget as having a context menu. We also delegate loading the adapter to an initAdapter() private method, one that copies the data out of our static String array and pours it into an ArrayList, using the ArrayList for the ArrayAdapter. The reason we do this is that we want to be able to change the contents of the list on-the-fly, and that is much easier if we use an ArrayList rather than an ordinary String array.

For the options menu, we override onCreateOptionsMenu() and add two menu items, one to add a new word to the list and one to reset the words to their initial state. These menu items have IDs defined locally as static data members (MENU_ADD and MENU_RESET), and they also sport icons copied from the Android open source project. If the user displays the menu, it looks as shown in Figure 16–1.

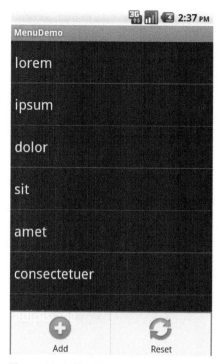

Figure 16–1. *The MenuDemo sample application and its options menu*

We also override onOptionsItemSelected(), which will be called if the user makes a choice from the menu. The supplied MenuItem has a getItemId() method that should map to either MENU_ADD or MENU_RESET. In the case of MENU_ADD, we call a private add() method that displays an AlertDialog with a custom View as its contents, inflated from res/layout/add.xml:

```xml
<?xml version="1.0" encoding="utf-8"?>
<LinearLayout xmlns:android="http://schemas.android.com/apk/res/android"
    android:orientation="horizontal"
    android:layout_width="fill_parent"
    android:layout_height="wrap_content"
    >
  <TextView
      android:text="Word:"
      android:layout_width="wrap_content"
      android:layout_height="wrap_content"
      />
  <EditText
      android:id="@+id/title"
      android:layout_width="fill_parent"
      android:layout_height="wrap_content"
      android:layout_marginLeft="4dip"
      />
</LinearLayout>
```

That produces a dialog box like the one shown in Figure 16–2.

Figure 16–2. *The same application, showing the Add a Word dialog box*

If the user taps the OK button, we get our ArrayAdapter and call add() on it, adding the entered word to the end of the list.

If the user chooses MENU_RESET, we call initAdapter() again, setting up a new ArrayAdapter and attaching it to our ListActivity.

For the context menu, we override onCreateContextMenu(). Once again, we define a pair of menu items with local IDs, MENU_CAP (to capitalize the long-tapped-upon word) and MENU_REMOVE (to remove the word). Since context menus have no icons, we can skip that part. That gives the user the context menu shown in Figure 16–3 if they long-tap on a word.

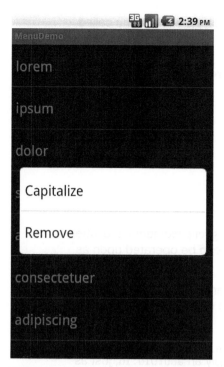

Figure 16–3. *The same application, showing the context menu*

We also override onContextMenuSelected(). Since this is a context menu for a ListView, our MenuItem has some extra information for us—specifically, which item was long-tapped upon in the list. To do that, we call getMenuInfo() on the MenuItem and cast the result to be an AdapterView.AdapterContextMenuInfo. That object, in turn, has a position data member, which is the index into our array of the word the user chose. From there, we work with our ArrayAdapter to capitalize or remove the word, as requested.

Yet More Inflation

Chapter 13 explained how you can describe Views via XML files and "inflate" them into actual View objects at runtime. Android also allows you to describe menus via XML files and inflate them when a menu is needed. This helps you keep your menu structure separate from the implementation of menu-handling logic, and it provides easier ways to develop menu-authoring tools.

Menu XML Structure

Menu XML goes in res/menu/ in your project tree, alongside the other types of resources that your project might employ. As with layouts, you can have several menu XML files in your project, each with its own filename and the .xml extension.

For example, from the `Menus/Inflation` sample project, here is a menu called `option.xml`:

```xml
<?xml version="1.0" encoding="utf-8"?>
<menu xmlns:android="http://schemas.android.com/apk/res/android">
  <item android:id="@+id/add"
    android:title="Add"
    android:icon="@drawable/ic_menu_add" />
  <item android:id="@+id/reset"
    android:title="Reset"
    android:icon="@drawable/ic_menu_refresh" />
</menu>
```

Note the following:

- You must start with a `menu` root element.

- Inside a `menu` element are `item` elements and `group` elements, the latter representing a collection of menu items that can be operated upon as a group.

- Submenus are specified by adding a `menu` element as a child of an `item` element, using this new menu element to describe the contents of the submenu.

- If you want to detect when an item is chosen, or to reference an item or group from your Java code, be sure to apply an `android:id`, just as you do with `View` layout XML.

Menu Options and XML

Inside the `item` and `group` elements, you can specify various options, matching up with corresponding methods on `Menu` or `MenuItem`, as follows:

- *Title*: The title of a menu item is provided via the `android:title` attribute on an `item` element. This can be either a literal string or a reference to a string resource (e.g., `@string/foo`).

- *Icon*: Menu items optionally have icons. To provide an icon, in the form of a reference to a drawable resource (e.g., `@drawable/eject`), use the `android:icon` attribute on the `item` element.

- *Order*: By default, the order of the items in the menu is determined by the order in which they appear in the menu XML. You can change that order by specifying the `android:orderInCategory` attribute on the `item` element. This is a 0-based index of the order for the items associated with the current category. There is an implicit default category; groups can provide an `android:menuCategory` attribute to specify a different category to use for items in that group. Generally, though, it is simplest just to put the items in the XML in the order in which you want them to appear.

- *Enabled*: Items and groups can be enabled or disabled, controlled in the XML via the android:enabled attribute on the item or group element. By default, items and groups are enabled. Disabled items and groups appear in the menu but cannot be selected. You can change an item's status at runtime via the setEnabled() method on MenuItem, or change a group's status via setGroupEnabled() on Menu.

- *Visible*: Items and groups can be visible or invisible, controlled in the XML via the android:visible attribute on the item or group element. By default, items and groups are visible. Invisible items and groups do not appear in the menu. You can change an item's status at runtime via the setVisible() method on MenuItem, or change a group's status via setGroupVisible() on Menu.

- *Shortcut*: Items can have shortcuts—single letters (android:alphabeticShortcut) or numbers (android:numericShortcut) that can be pressed to choose the item without having to use the touchscreen, D-pad, or trackball to navigate the full menu.

Inflating the Menu

Actually using the menu, once it's defined in XML, is easy. Just create a MenuInflater and tell it to inflate your menu.

The Menus/Inflation project is a clone of the Menus/Menus project, with the menu creation converted to use menu XML resources and MenuInflater. The options menu was converted to the XML shown previously in this section; here is the context menu:

```xml
<?xml version="1.0" encoding="utf-8"?>
<menu xmlns:android="http://schemas.android.com/apk/res/android">
  <item android:id="@+id/cap"
    android:title="Capitalize" />
  <item android:id="@+id/remove"
    android:title="Remove" />
</menu>
```

The Java code is nearly identical, changing mostly in the implementation of onCreateOptionsMenu() and onCreateContextMenu():

```java
@Override
public boolean onCreateOptionsMenu(Menu menu) {
  new MenuInflater(this).inflate(R.menu.option, menu);

  return(super.onCreateOptionsMenu(menu));
}

@Override
public void onCreateContextMenu(ContextMenu menu, View v,
                                ContextMenu.ContextMenuInfo menuInfo) {
  new MenuInflater(this).inflate(R.menu.context, menu);
}
```

Here, we see how MenuInflater "pours" the menu items specified in the menu resource (e.g., R.menu.option) into the supplied Menu or ContextMenu object.

We also need to change onOptionsItemSelected() and onContextItemSelected() to use the android:id values specified in the XML:

```
@Override
public boolean onOptionsItemSelected(MenuItem item) {
  switch (item.getItemId()) {
    case R.id.add:
      add();
      return(true);

    case R.id.reset:
      initAdapter();
      return(true);
  }

  return(super.onOptionsItemSelected(item));
}

@Override
public boolean onContextItemSelected(MenuItem item) {
  AdapterView.AdapterContextMenuInfo info=
    (AdapterView.AdapterContextMenuInfo)item.getMenuInfo();
  ArrayAdapter<String> adapter=(ArrayAdapter<String>)getListAdapter();

  switch (item.getItemId()) {
    case R.id.cap:
      String word=words.get(info.position);

      word=word.toUpperCase();

      adapter.remove(words.get(info.position));
      adapter.insert(word, info.position);

      return(true);

    case R.id.remove:
      adapter.remove(words.get(info.position));

      return(true);
  }

  return(super.onContextItemSelected(item));
}
```

When Giant Menus Walk the Earth

With Android 3.x and 4.0, new ways of dealing with tablets and large displays have been introduced and folded into the core of the platform. Options menus in particular change from being something triggered by a Menu button to a drop-down menu from the action bar. Fortunately, this is backward-compatible, so your existing menus will not need to change to adopt this new look. We'll cover the overall implications of using larger devices in Chapter 26, and the action bar itself is covered in Chapter 27.

Chapter 17

Showing Pop-Up Messages

Sometimes, your activity (or other piece of Android code) will need to speak up.

Not every interaction with Android users will be tidy and containable in fragments or activities composed of views. Errors will crop up. Background tasks may take much longer than expected. Something asynchronous may occur, such as an incoming message. In these and other cases, you may need to communicate with the user outside the bounds of the traditional user interface.

Of course, this is nothing new. Error messages in the form of dialog boxes have been around for a long time. More subtle indicators also exist, from task tray icons to bouncing dock icons to vibrating cell phones.

Android has quite a few systems for letting you alert your users outside the bounds of an Activity-based UI. One, notifications, is tied heavily into intents and services and, as such, is covered Chapter 37. In this chapter, you will learn about two means of raising pop-up messages: toasts and alerts.

Raising Toasts

A Toast is a transient message, meaning that it displays and disappears on its own without user interaction. Moreover, it does not take focus away from the currently active Activity, so if the user is busy writing the next Great Programming Guide, keystrokes will not be "eaten" by the message.

Since a Toast is transient, you have no way of knowing if the user even notices it. You get no acknowledgment from the user, nor does the message stick around for a long time to pester the user. Hence, the Toast is mostly for advisory messages, such as indicating a long-running background task is completed, the battery has dropped to a low level, and so on.

Making a Toast is fairly easy. The Toast class offers a static makeText() method that accepts a String (or string resource ID) and returns a Toast instance. The makeText() method also needs the Activity (or other Context) plus a duration. The duration is expressed in the form of the LENGTH_SHORT constant or LENGTH_LONG constant to indicate, on a relative basis, how long the message should remain visible.

If you would prefer your Toast be made out of some other View, rather than be a boring old piece of text, simply create a new Toast instance via the constructor (which takes a Context), and then call setView() to supply it with the view to use and setDuration() to set the duration.

Once your Toast is configured, call its show() method, and the message will be displayed. You will see an example of this in action later in this chapter.

Alert! Alert!

If you would prefer something in the more classic dialog box style, what you want is an AlertDialog. As with any other modal dialog box, an AlertDialog pops up, grabs the focus, and stays there until closed by the user. You might use this for a critical error, a validation message that cannot be effectively displayed in the base activity UI, or some other situation where you are sure that the user needs to see the message immediately.

The simplest way to construct an AlertDialog is to use the Builder class. Following in true builder style, Builder offers a series of methods to configure an AlertDialog, each method returning the Builder for easy chaining. At the end, you call show() on the builder to display the dialog box.

Commonly used configuration methods on Builder include the following:

- setMessage(): Sets the "body" of the dialog box to be a simple textual message, from either a supplied String or a supplied string resource ID

- setTitle() and setIcon(): Configure the text and/or icon to appear in the title bar of the dialog box

- setPositiveButton() and setNegativeButton(): Indicate which button(s) should appear across the bottom of the dialog box, where they should be positioned (left, center, or right, respectively), what their captions should be, and what logic should be invoked when the button is clicked (besides dismissing the dialog box).

If you need to configure the AlertDialog beyond what the builder allows, instead of calling show(), call create() to get the partially built AlertDialog instance, configure it the rest of the way, and then call one of the flavors of show() on the AlertDialog itself. Once show() is called, the dialog box will appear and await user input.

Note that pressing any of the buttons will close the dialog box, even if you have registered a listener for the button in question. Hence, if all you need a button to do is close the dialog box, give it a caption and a null listener. There is no option, with AlertDialog, to have a button at the bottom invoke a listener yet not close the dialog box.

Checking Them Out

To see how these work in practice, take a peek at `Messages/Message`, containing the following layout:

```
<?xml version="1.0" encoding="utf-8"?>
<Button xmlns:android="http://schemas.android.com/apk/res/android"
  android:id="@+id/alert"
  android:text="Raise an alert"
  android:layout_width="fill_parent"
  android:layout_height="fill_parent"
  android:onClick="showAlert"
/>
```

The following is the Java code:

```
public void onCreate(Bundle icicle) {
   super.onCreate(icicle);

   setContentView(R.layout.main);
}

public void showAlert(View view) {
   new AlertDialog.Builder(this)
     .setTitle("MessageDemo")
     .setMessage("Let's raise a toast!")
     .setNeutralButton("Here, here!", new DialogInterface.OnClickListener() {
       public void onClick(DialogInterface dlg, int sumthin) {
         Toast
           .makeText(MessageDemo.this, "<clink, clink>",
                 Toast.LENGTH_SHORT)
           .show();
       }
     })
     .show();
}
```

The layout is unremarkable—just a really large `Button` to show the `AlertDialog`. However, Ice Cream Sandwich adds two new options to the `AlertDialog(context, int)` form of invocation. These options support device-wide "light" and "dark" backgrounds for alerts via the `THEME_DEVICE_DEFAULT_LIGHT` and `THEME_DEVICE_DEFAULT_DARK` values. These options aid in promoting the notion of seamless experience across the whole Android device.

When you click the `Button`, we use a builder (`new Builder(this)`) to set the title (`setTitle("MessageDemo")`), message (`setMessage("Let's raise a toast!")`), and neutral button (`setNeutralButton("Here, here!", new OnClickListener() ...)`) before showing the dialog box. When the button is clicked, the `OnClickListener` callback triggers the `Toast` class to make us a text-based toast (`makeText(this, "<clink, clink>", LENGTH_SHORT)`), which we then `show()`. The result is a typical dialog box, as shown in Figure 17–1.

Figure 17–1. *The MessageDemo sample application, after clicking the Raise an alert button*

When you close the dialog box via the button, it raises the toast, as shown in Figure 17–2.

Figure 17–2. *The same application, after clicking the Make a toast button*

Chapter 18

Handling Activity Lifecycle Events

As you know, Android devices, by and large, are phones. As such, some activities are more important than others—taking a call is probably more important to users than playing Sudoku. And, since it is a phone, it probably has less RAM than your current desktop or notebook.

As a result of the phone's limited RAM, your activity may find itself being killed off because other activities are going on and the system needs your activity's memory. Think of it as the Android equivalent of the circle of life—your activity dies so others may live, and so on. You cannot assume that your activity will run until you think it is complete, or even until the user thinks it is complete. This is one example, perhaps the most important, of how an activity's life cycle will affect your own application logic.

This chapter covers the various states and callbacks that make up an activity's life cycle, and how you can hook into them appropriately.

Schrödinger's Activity

An activity, generally speaking, is in one of four states at any point in time:

- *Active*: The activity was started by the user, is running, and is in the foreground. This is what you are used to thinking of in terms of your activity's operation.

- *Paused*: The activity was started by the user, is running, and is visible, but a notification or something is overlaying part of the screen. During this time, the user can see your activity but may not be able to interact with it. Examples include the user being prompted to accept an incoming call, or being warned of a battery low or critically low state.

■ *Stopped*: The activity was started by the user, is running, but is hidden by other activities that have been launched or switched to. Your application will not be able to present anything meaningful to the user directly, but may communicate by way of a Notification.

■ *Dead*: Either the activity was never started (e.g., just after a phone reset) or the activity was terminated, perhaps due to lack of available memory.

Life, Death, and Your Activity

Android uses the methods described in this section to call into your activity as the activity transitions between the four states listed in the previous section. Some transitions may result in multiple calls to your activity, and sometimes Android will kill your application without calling it. This whole area is rather murky and probably subject to change, so pay close attention to the official Android documentation as well as this section when deciding which events deserve attention and which you can safely ignore.

Note that for all of these methods, you should chain upward and invoke the superclass's edition of the method, or Android may raise an exception.

onCreate() and onDestroy()

We have been implementing onCreate() in all of our Activity subclasses in all the examples. This method will be called in three situations:

■ When the activity is first started (e.g., since a system restart), onCreate() will be invoked with a null parameter.

■ If the activity had been running, then sometime later was killed off, onCreate() will be invoked with the Bundle from onSaveInstanceState() as a parameter (as described in the next section).

■ If the activity had been running and you have set up your activity to have different resources based on different device states (e.g., landscape versus portrait), your activity will be re-created and onCreate() will be called. Working with resources is covered in Chapter 23.

Here is where you initialize your UI and set up anything that needs to be done once, regardless of how the activity is used.

On the other end of the life cycle, onDestroy() may be called when the activity is shutting down, either because the activity called finish() (which "finishes" the activity) or because Android needs RAM and is closing the activity prematurely. Note that onDestroy() may not be called if the need for RAM is urgent (e.g., an incoming phone call), but the activity will still be shut down. Hence, onDestroy() is mostly for cleanly releasing resources you obtained in onCreate() (if any).

Take care when dealing with an activity that includes a view populated with an adapter from a database such as SQLite. It's prudent to call `close()` on your database and/or adapter objects, but also remember that you can't rely on these being called in `onDestroy()` if your shutdown is of the abrupt kind. We'll discuss this further in Chapter 32.

onStart(), onRestart(), and onStop()

An activity can come to the foreground either because it is first being launched or because it is being brought back to the foreground after having been hidden (e.g., by another activity or by an incoming phone call). The `onStart()` method is called in either of those cases.

The `onRestart()` method is called in the case where the activity had been stopped and is now restarting.

Conversely, `onStop()` is called when the activity is about to be stopped.

onPause() and onResume()

The `onResume()` method is called just before your activity comes to the foreground, either after being initially launched, after being restarted from a stopped state, or after a pop-up dialog box (e.g., an incoming call) is cleared. This is a great place to refresh the UI based on things that may have occurred since the user was last looking at your activity. For example, if you are polling a service for changes to some information (e.g., new entries for a feed), `onResume()` is a fine time to both refresh the current view and, if applicable, kick off a background thread to update the view (e.g., via a `Handler`).

Conversely, anything that steals your user away from your activity—typically, the activation of another activity—will result in your `onPause()` method being called. Here, you should undo anything you did in `onResume()`, such as stopping background threads, releasing any exclusive-access resources you may have acquired (e.g., camera), and the like.

Once `onPause()` is called, Android reserves the right to kill off your activity's process at any point. Hence, you should not be relying on receiving any further events.

The Grace of State

Mostly, the aforementioned methods are for dealing with things at the application-general level (e.g., wiring together the last pieces of your UI in `onCreate()` or closing down background threads in `onPause()`).

However, a large part of the goal of Android is to have a patina of seamlessness. Activities may come and go as dictated by memory requirements, but ideally, users are unaware that this is going on. If, for example, a user was using a calculator, took a lunch break, and returned to that calculator, he should see whatever number he was working on before the break, unless he took some action to close down the calculator (e.g., pressed the Back button to exit it).

To make all this work, activities need to be able to save their application-instance state, and to do so quickly and cheaply. Since activities could be killed off at any time, activities may need to save their state more frequently than you might expect. Then, when the activity restarts, the activity should get its former state back, so it can restore the activity to the way it appeared previously. Think of it as establishing a bookmark, such that when the user returns to that bookmark, you can restore the application to the same state that it was in when the user left it.

Saving instance state is handled by onSaveInstanceState(). This supplies a Bundle, into which activities can pour whatever data they need (e.g., the number showing on the calculator's display). This method implementation needs to be speedy, so do not try to be fancy—just put your data in the Bundle and exit the method.

That instance state is provided to you again in two places: in onCreate() and in onRestoreInstanceState(). It is your choice when you wish to reapply the state data to your activity—either callback is a reasonable option.

The built-in implementation of onSaveInstanceState() will save likely mutable state from a subset of widgets. For example, it will save the text in an EditText, but it will not save the status of whether a Button is enabled or disabled. This works as long as the widgets are uniquely identified via their android:id attributes.

Hence, if you implement onSaveInstanceState(), you can either chain upward and leverage the inherited implementation or not chain upward and override the inherited implementation. Similarly, some activities may not need onSaveInstanceState() to be implemented at all, as the built-in one handles everything that is needed.

Chapter **19**

Handling Rotation

Some Android devices offer a slide-out keyboard that triggers rotating the screen from portrait to landscape orientation. Other devices use accelerometers to determine when the screen rotates. As a result, it is reasonable to assume that switching from portrait to landscape orientation and back again may be something that users of your application will want to do.

As this chapter describes, Android has a number of ways for you to handle screen rotation so that your application can properly handle either orientation. Keep in mind, though, that these facilities only help you to detect and manage the rotation process — you still must make sure your layouts and fragments look decent in each orientation.

A Philosophy of Destruction

By default, when there is a change in the device configuration that might affect resource selection, Android will destroy and re-create any running or paused activities the next time they are to be viewed. This could happen for a variety of different configuration changes, including these:

- Rotating the screen (i.e., orientation change)
- Extending or hiding a physical keyboard on devices that have a sliding keyboard
- Putting the device in a car or desk dock, or removing it from a dock
- Changing the locale, and thereby changing the preferred language

Screen rotation is the change most likely to trip you up, since a change in orientation can cause your application to load a different set of resources (e.g., layouts).

The key here is that Android's default behavior of destroying and re-creating any running or paused activities is probably the behavior that is best for most of your activities. You do have some control over the matter, though, and can tailor how your activities respond to orientation changes or similar configuration switches.

It's All the Same, Just Different

Since, by default, Android destroys and re-creates your activity on a rotation, you may only need to hook into the same onSaveInstanceState() that you would if your activity were destroyed for any other reason (e.g., low memory or other reasons we discussed in chapter 18). Implement that method in your activity and fill in the supplied Bundle with enough information to get you back to your current state. Then, in onCreate() (or onRestoreInstanceState(), if you prefer), pick the data out of the Bundle and use it to restore your activity to the way it was.

To demonstrate this, let's take a look at the Rotation/RotationOne project. This and the other sample projects in this chapter use a pair of main.xml layouts, one in res/layout/ for use in portrait mode and one in res/layout-land/ for use in landscape mode. Here is the portrait layout:

```xml
<?xml version="1.0" encoding="utf-8"?>
<LinearLayout xmlns:android="http://schemas.android.com/apk/res/android"
  android:orientation="vertical"
  android:layout_width="fill_parent"
  android:layout_height="fill_parent"
  >
  <Button android:id="@+id/pick"
    android:layout_width="fill_parent"
    android:layout_height="fill_parent"
    android:layout_weight="1"
    android:text="Pick"
    android:enabled="true"
    android:onClick="pickContact"
  />
  <Button android:id="@+id/view"
    android:layout_width="fill_parent"
    android:layout_height="fill_parent"
    android:layout_weight="1"
    android:text="View"
    android:enabled="false"
    android:onClick="viewContact"
  />
</LinearLayout>
```

Here is the similar landscape layout:

```xml
<?xml version="1.0" encoding="utf-8"?>
<LinearLayout xmlns:android="http://schemas.android.com/apk/res/android"
  android:orientation="horizontal"
  android:layout_width="fill_parent"
  android:layout_height="fill_parent"
  >
  <Button android:id="@+id/pick"
    android:layout_width="fill_parent"
    android:layout_height="fill_parent"
    android:layout_weight="1"
    android:text="Pick"
    android:enabled="true"
    android:onClick="pickContact"
```

```
    />
    <Button android:id="@+id/view"
      android:layout_width="fill_parent"
      android:layout_height="fill_parent"
      android:layout_weight="1"
      android:text="View"
      android:enabled="false"
      android:onClick="viewContact"
    />
</LinearLayout>
```

Basically, both layouts contain a pair of buttons, each taking up half the screen. In portrait mode, the buttons are stacked; in landscape mode, they are side by side.

If you were to simply create a project, put in those two layouts, and compile it, the application would appear to work just fine—a rotation (Ctrl+F12 in the emulator) will cause the layout to change. And while buttons lack state, if you were using other widgets (e.g., EditText), you would even find that Android hangs onto some of the widget state for you (e.g., the text entered in the EditText).

What Android cannot help you with automatically is anything held outside the widgets.

Picking and Viewing a Contact

This application lets users pick a contact and then view the contact, via separate buttons. The View button is enabled only after the user picks a contact via the Pick button. Let's take a closer look at how this feat is accomplished.

When the user clicks the Pick button, we call startActivityForResult(). This is a variation on startActivity(), designed for activities that are set up to return some sort of result—a user's choice of file, contact, or whatever. Relatively few activities are set up this way, so you cannot expect to call startActivityForResult() and get answers from any activity you choose.

In this case, we want to pick a contact. There is an ACTION_PICK Intent action available in Android that is designed for this sort of scenario. An ACTION_PICK Intent indicates to Android that we want to pick...something. That "something" is determined by the Uri we put in the Intent.

In our case, it turns out that we can use an ACTION_PICK Intent for certain system-defined Uri values to let the user pick a contact from the device's list of contacts. In particular, on Android 2.0 and higher, we can use android.provider.ContactsContract.Contacts.CONTENT_URI for this purpose:

```
public void pickContact(View v) {
  Intent i=new Intent(Intent.ACTION_PICK,
                      Contacts.CONTENT_URI);

  startActivityForResult(i, PICK_REQUEST);
}
```

For Android 1.6 and earlier, there is a separate android.provider.Contacts.CONTENT_URI that we could use.

The second parameter to startActivityForResult() is an identifying number, to help us distinguish this call to startActivityForResult() from any others we might make. Calling startActivityForResult() with an ACTION_PICK Intent for the Contacts.CONTENT_URI will bring up a contact-picker activity, supplied by Android.

When the user taps a contact, the picker activity ends (e.g., via finish()), and control returns to our activity. At that point, our activity is called with onActivityResult(). Android supplies us with three pieces of information:

- The identifying number we supplied to startActivityForResult(), so we can match this result to its original request

- A result status, either RESULT_OK or RESULT_CANCELED, to indicate whether the user made a positive selection or abandoned the picker (e.g., by pressing the Back button)

- An Intent that represents the result data itself, for a RESULT_OK response

The details of what is in the Intent will need to be documented by the activity that you called. In the case of an ACTION_PICK Intent for the Contacts.CONTENT_URI, the returned Intent has its own Uri (via getData()) that represents the chosen contact. In the RotationOne example, we stick that in a data member of the activity and enable the View button:

```
@Override
protected void onActivityResult(int requestCode, int resultCode,
                                Intent data) {
  if (requestCode==PICK_REQUEST) {
    if (resultCode==RESULT_OK) {
      contact=data.getData();
      viewButton.setEnabled(true);
    }
  }
}
```

If the user clicks the now-enabled View button, we create an ACTION_VIEW Intent on the contact's Uri, and call startActivity() on that Intent:

```
public void viewContact(View v) {
  startActivity(new Intent(Intent.ACTION_VIEW, contact));
}
```

This will bring up an Android-supplied activity to view details of that contact.

Saving Your State

Given that we have used startActivityForResult() to pick a contact, now we need to hang onto that contact when the screen orientation changes. In the RotationOne example, we do this via onSaveInstanceState():

```
package com.commonsware.android.rotation.one;

import android.app.Activity;
```

```
import android.content.Intent;
import android.net.Uri;
import android.os.Bundle;
import android.provider.ContactsContract.Contacts;
import android.view.View;
import android.widget.Button;
import android.util.Log;

public class RotationOneDemo extends Activity {
  static final int PICK_REQUEST=1337;
  Button viewButton=null;
  Uri contact=null;

  @Override
  public void onCreate(Bundle savedInstanceState) {
    super.onCreate(savedInstanceState);
    setContentView(R.layout.main);

    viewButton=(Button)findViewById(R.id.view);
    restoreMe(savedInstanceState);

    viewButton.setEnabled(contact!=null);
  }

  @Override
  protected void onActivityResult(int requestCode, int resultCode,
                                  Intent data) {
    if (requestCode==PICK_REQUEST) {
      if (resultCode==RESULT_OK) {
        contact=data.getData();
        viewButton.setEnabled(true);
      }
    }
  }

  public void pickContact(View v) {
    Intent i=new Intent(Intent.ACTION_PICK,
                    Contacts.CONTENT_URI);

    startActivityForResult(i, PICK_REQUEST);
  }

  public void viewContact(View v) {
    startActivity(new Intent(Intent.ACTION_VIEW, contact));
  }

  @Override
  protected void onSaveInstanceState(Bundle outState) {
    super.onSaveInstanceState(outState);

    if (contact!=null) {
      outState.putString("contact", contact.toString());
    }
  }

  private void restoreMe(Bundle state) {
```

```
        contact=null;

    if (state!=null) {
      String contactUri=state.getString("contact");

      if (contactUri!=null) {
        contact=Uri.parse(contactUri);
      }
    }
  }
}
```

By and large, it looks like a normal activity...because it is. Initially, the "model"—a Uri named contact—is null. It is set as the result of spawning the ACTION_PICK subactivity. Its string representation is saved in onSaveInstanceState() and restored in restoreMe() (called from onCreate()). If the contact is not null, the View button is enabled and can be used to view the chosen contact.

Visually, it looks pretty much as you would expect, as shown in Figures 19–1 and 19–2.

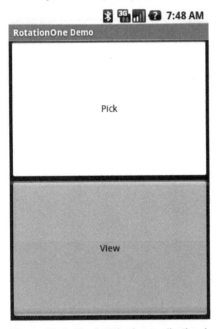

Figure 19–1. *The RotationOne application, in portrait mode*

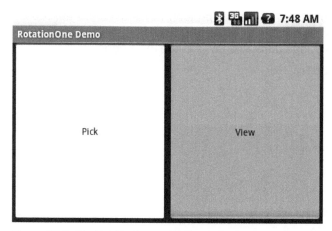

Figure 19–2. *The RotationOne application, in landscape mode*

The benefit to this implementation is that it handles a number of system events beyond mere rotation, such as being closed by Android due to low memory.

For fun, comment out the restoreMe() call in onCreate() and try running the application. You will see that the application "forgets" a contact selected in one orientation when you rotate the emulator or device.

Now with More Savings!

The problem with onSaveInstanceState() is that you are limited to a Bundle. That's because this callback is also used in cases where your whole process might be terminated (e.g., low memory), so the data to be saved must be something that can be serialized and has no dependencies on your running process.

For some activities, that limitation is not a problem. For others, it is more annoying. Take an online chat, for example. You have no means of storing a socket in a Bundle, so by default, you have to drop your connection to the chat server and reestablish it. That not only may be a performance hit, but it might also affect the chat itself, such as showing in the chat logs that you are disconnecting and reconnecting.

One way to get past this is to use onRetainNonConfigurationInstance() instead of onSaveInstanceState() for "light" changes like a rotation. Your activity's onRetainNonConfigurationInstance() callback can return an Object, which you can retrieve later via getLastNonConfigurationInstance(). The Object can be just about anything you want. Typically, it will be some kind of "context" object holding activity state, such as running threads, open sockets, and the like. Your activity's onCreate() can call getLastNonConfigurationInstance(), and if you get a non-null response, you now have your sockets and threads and whatnot. The biggest limitation is that you do not want to put in the saved context anything that might reference a resource that will get swapped out, such as a Drawable loaded from a resource.

Let's take a look at the Rotation/RotationTwo sample project, which uses this approach to handling rotations. The layouts, and hence the visual appearance, are the same as with Rotation/RotationOne. Where things differ slightly is in the Java code:

```java
package com.commonsware.android.rotation.two;

import android.app.Activity;
import android.content.Intent;
import android.net.Uri;
import android.os.Bundle;
import android.provider.ContactsContract.Contacts;
import android.view.View;
import android.widget.Button;
import android.util.Log;

public class RotationTwoDemo extends Activity {
  static final int PICK_REQUEST=1337;
  Button viewButton=null;
  Uri contact=null;

  @Override
  public void onCreate(Bundle savedInstanceState) {
    super.onCreate(savedInstanceState);
    setContentView(R.layout.main);

    viewButton=(Button)findViewById(R.id.view);
    restoreMe();

    viewButton.setEnabled(contact!=null);
  }

  @Override
  protected void onActivityResult(int requestCode, int resultCode,
                                  Intent data) {
    if (requestCode==PICK_REQUEST) {
      if (resultCode==RESULT_OK) {
        contact=data.getData();
        viewButton.setEnabled(true);
      }
    }
  }

  public void pickContact(View v) {
    Intent i=new Intent(Intent.ACTION_PICK,
                        Contacts.CONTENT_URI);

    startActivityForResult(i, PICK_REQUEST);
  }

  public void viewContact(View v) {
    startActivity(new Intent(Intent.ACTION_VIEW, contact));
  }

  @Override
  public Object onRetainNonConfigurationInstance() {
    return(contact);
```

```
  }

  private void restoreMe() {
    contact=null;

    if (getLastNonConfigurationInstance()!=null) {
      contact=(Uri)getLastNonConfigurationInstance();
    }
  }
}
```

In this case, we override onRetainNonConfigurationInstance(), returning the actual Uri for our contact, rather than a string representation of it. In turn, restoreMe() calls getLastNonConfigurationInstance(), and if it is not null, we hold onto it as our contact and enable the View button.

The advantage here is that we are passing around the Uri rather than a string representation. In this case, that is not a big saving. But our state could be much more complicated, including threads, sockets, and other things we cannot pack into a Bundle.

However, even the onRetainNonConfigurationInstance() approach to handling rotations may be too intrusive to your application. Suppose, for example, you are creating a real-time game, such as a first-person shooter. The "hiccup" your users experience as your activity is destroyed and re-created might be enough to get them shot, which they may not appreciate. While this would be less of an issue on the T-Mobile G1, since a rotation requires sliding open the keyboard and therefore is unlikely to be done mid-game, other devices might rotate based solely on the device's position as determined by accelerometers. For applications such as this, there is a third possibility for handling rotations, which is to tell Android that you will handle them yourself, without any assistance from the framework.

DIY Rotation

To handle rotations without Android's assistance, do the following:

1. Put an android:configChanges entry in your AndroidManifest.xml file, listing the configuration changes you want to handle yourself versus allowing Android to handle them for you.

2. Implement onConfigurationChanged() in your Activity, which will be called when one of the configuration changes you listed in android:configChanges occurs.

Now, for any configuration change you want, you can bypass the whole activity-destruction process and simply get a callback letting you know of the change.

To see this in action, turn to the Rotation/RotationThree sample application. Once again, our layouts are the same, so the application looks the same as the preceding two samples. However, the Java code is significantly different, because we are no longer concerned with saving our state, but rather with updating our UI to deal with the layout.

But first, we need to make a small change to our manifest:

```xml
<?xml version="1.0" encoding="utf-8"?>
<manifest xmlns:android="http://schemas.android.com/apk/res/android"
 package="com.commonsware.android.rotation.three" android:versionCode="1"
 android:versionName="1.0.0">
  <uses-sdk android:minSdkVersion="5" android:targetSdkVersion="6"/>
    <application android:label="@string/app_name" android:icon="@drawable/cw">
        <activity android:name=".RotationThreeDemo" android:label="@string/app_name"
 android:configChanges="keyboardHidden|orientation">
            <intent-filter>
                <action android:name="android.intent.action.MAIN"/>
                <category android:name="android.intent.category.LAUNCHER"/>
            </intent-filter>
        </activity>
    </application>
  <supports-screens android:largeScreens="true" android:normalScreens="true"
 android:smallScreens="true" android:anyDensity="true"/>
</manifest>
```

Here, we state that we will handle keyboardHidden and orientation configuration changes ourselves. This covers us for any cause of the rotation, whether it is a sliding keyboard or a physical rotation. Note that this is set on the activity, not the application. If you have several activities, you will need to decide for each which of the tactics outlined in this chapter you wish to use.

In addition, we need to add an android:id to our LinearLayout containers, such as follows:

```xml
<?xml version="1.0" encoding="utf-8"?>
<LinearLayout xmlns:android="http://schemas.android.com/apk/res/android"
  android:id="@+id/container"
  android:orientation="vertical"
  android:layout_width="fill_parent"
  android:layout_height="fill_parent"
  >
  <Button android:id="@+id/pick"
    android:layout_width="fill_parent"
    android:layout_height="fill_parent"
    android:layout_weight="1"
    android:text="Pick"
    android:enabled="true"
    android:onClick="pickContact"
  />
  <Button android:id="@+id/view"
    android:layout_width="fill_parent"
    android:layout_height="fill_parent"
    android:layout_weight="1"
    android:text="View"
    android:enabled="false"
    android:onClick="viewContact"
  />
</LinearLayout>
```

The Java code for this project is shown here:

```java
package com.commonsware.android.rotation.three;
```

```java
import android.app.Activity;
import android.content.Intent;
import android.content.res.Configuration;
import android.net.Uri;
import android.os.Bundle;
import android.provider.ContactsContract.Contacts;
import android.view.View;
import android.widget.Button;
import android.widget.LinearLayout;

public class RotationThreeDemo extends Activity {
  static final int PICK_REQUEST=1337;
  Button viewButton=null;
  Uri contact=null;

  @Override
  public void onCreate(Bundle savedInstanceState) {
    super.onCreate(savedInstanceState);

    setContentView(R.layout.main);
    viewButton=(Button)findViewById(R.id.view);
    viewButton.setEnabled(contact!=null);
  }

  @Override
  protected void onActivityResult(int requestCode, int resultCode,
                                  Intent data) {
    if (requestCode==PICK_REQUEST) {
      if (resultCode==RESULT_OK) {
        contact=data.getData();
        viewButton.setEnabled(true);
      }
    }
  }

  public void pickContact(View v) {
    Intent i=new Intent(Intent.ACTION_PICK,
                        Contacts.CONTENT_URI);

    startActivityForResult(i, PICK_REQUEST);
  }

  public void viewContact(View v) {
    startActivity(new Intent(Intent.ACTION_VIEW, contact));
  }

  public void onConfigurationChanged(Configuration newConfig) {
    super.onConfigurationChanged(newConfig);

    LinearLayout container=(LinearLayout)findViewById(R.id.container);

    if (newConfig.orientation==Configuration.ORIENTATION_LANDSCAPE) {
      container.setOrientation(LinearLayout.HORIZONTAL);
    }
    else {
```

```
        container.setOrientation(LinearLayout.VERTICAL);
      }
    }
  }
}
```

Our onConfigurationChanged() needs to update the UI to reflect the orientation change. Here, we find our LinearLayout and tell it to change its orientation to match that of the device. The orientation field on the Configuration object will tell us how the device is oriented.

...BUT GOOGLE DOES NOT RECOMMEND THIS

You might think that onConfigurationChanged() and android:configChanges would be the ultimate solution for handling rotation. After all, we no longer have to worry about all that messy passing of data to the new activity as the old one is being destroyed. The onConfigurationChanged() approach is very sexy.

However, Google does not recommend it.

The primary concern is forgetting about resources. With the onConfigurationChanged() approach, you must ensure that every resource that might possibly have changed as a result of this configuration change gets updated. That includes strings, layouts, drawables, menus, animations, preferences, dimensions, colors, and all the others. If you fail to ensure that everything is updated completely, your app will have a whole series of little (or not so little) bugs as a result.

Allowing Android to destroy and re-create your activity guarantees you will get the proper resources. All you need to do is arrange to pass the proper data from the old activity to the new activity.

The onConfigurationChanged() approach is appropriate only where the user would be directly affected by a destroy-and-create cycle. For example, imagine a video-player application that is playing a streaming video. Destroying and re-creating the activity would necessarily cause the application to have to reconnect to the stream, losing buffered data in the process. Users will get frustrated if an accidental movement causes the device to change orientation and interrupt their video playback. In this case, since the user will perceive problems with a destroy-and-create cycle, onConfigurationChanged() is an appropriate choice.

Forcing the Issue

Some activities simply are not meant to change orientation. Games, camera previews, video players, and the like may make sense only in landscape orientation, for example. While most activities should allow the user to work in any desired orientation, for activities where only one orientation makes sense, you can control it.

To block Android from rotating your activity, all you need to do is add android:screenOrientation = "portrait" (or "landscape", as you prefer) to your AndroidManifest.xml file, as follows (from the Rotation/RotationFour sample project):

```
<?xml version="1.0" encoding="utf-8"?>
<manifest xmlns:android="http://schemas.android.com/apk/res/android"↵
  package="com.commonsware.android.rotation.four" android:versionCode="1"↵
```

```
android:versionName="1.0.0">
  <uses-sdk android:minSdkVersion="5" android:targetSdkVersion="6"/>
    <application android:label="@string/app_name" android:icon="@drawable/cw">
        <activity android:name=".RotationFourDemo" android:screenOrientation=↵
"portrait" android:label="@string/app_name">
            <intent-filter>
                <action android:name="android.intent.action.MAIN"/>
                <category android:name="android.intent.category.LAUNCHER"/>
            </intent-filter>
        </activity>
    </application>
    <supports-screens android:largeScreens="true" android:normalScreens="true"↵
 android:smallScreens="true" android:anyDensity="true"/>
</manifest>
```

Since this is applied on a per-activity basis, you will need to decide which of your activities may need this turned on.

At this point, your activity is locked into whatever orientation you specified, regardless of what you do. Figures 19–3 and 19–4 show the same activity as in the previous three sections, but using the preceding manifest and with the emulator set for both portrait and landscape orientation. Note that the UI does not move a bit, but remains in portrait mode.

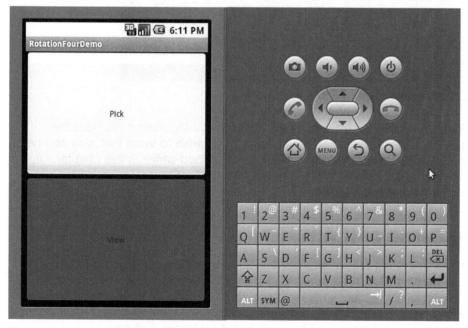

Figure 19–3. *The RotationFour application, in portrait mode*

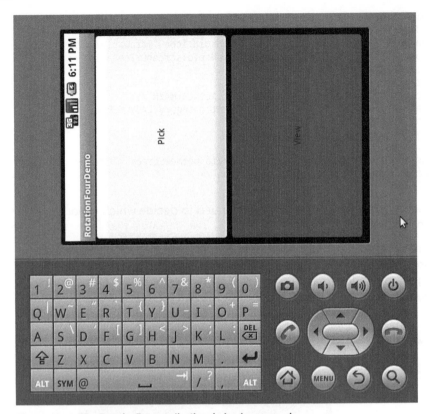

Figure 19–4. *The RotationFour application, in landscape mode*

Note that Android will still destroy and re-create your activity, even if you have the orientation set to a specific value as shown here. If you wish to avoid that, you also need to set android:configChanges in the manifest, as described earlier in this chapter. Or, you can still use onSaveInstanceState() or onRetainNonConfigurationInstance() to save your activity's mutable state.

Making Sense of It All

As noted at the beginning of this chapter, devices with a slide-out keyboard (such as T-Mobile G1, Motorola DROID/Milestone, etc.) change screen orientation when the keyboard is exposed or hidden, whereas other devices change screen orientation based on the accelerometer. If you have an activity that should change orientation based on the accelerometer, even if the device has a slide-out keyboard, just add android:screenOrientation = "sensor" to your AndroidManifest.xml file as follows (from the Rotation/RotationFive sample project):

```
<?xml version="1.0" encoding="utf-8"?>
<manifest xmlns:android="http://schemas.android.com/apk/res/android"↵
  package="com.commonsware.android.rotation.five" android:versionCode="1"↵
  android:versionName="1.0.0">
```

```
<uses-sdk android:minSdkVersion="5" android:targetSdkVersion="6"/>
    <application android:label="@string/app_name" android:icon="@drawable/cw">
        <activity android:name=".RotationFiveDemo" android:screenOrientation="sensor"↩
android:label="@string/app_name">
            <intent-filter>
                <action android:name="android.intent.action.MAIN"/>
                <category android:name="android.intent.category.LAUNCHER"/>
            </intent-filter>
        </activity>
    </application>
    <supports-screens android:largeScreens="true" android:normalScreens="true"↩
android:smallScreens="true" android:anyDensity="true"/>
</manifest>
```

The sensor, in this case, tells Android you want the accelerometers to control the screen orientation, so the physical shift in the device orientation controls the screen orientation.

Android 2.3 added a number of other possible values for android:screenOrientation:

- reverseLandscape and reversePortrait: Indicate that you want the screen to be in landscape or portrait orientation, respectively, but upside down compared to the normal landscape and portrait orientations

- sensorLandscape and sensorPortrait: Indicate that you want the screen to be locked in landscape or portrait orientation, respectively, but the sensors can be used to determine which side is "up"

- fullSensor: Allows the sensors to put the screen in any of the four possible orientations (portrait, reverse portrait, landscape, reverse landscape), whereas sensor toggles only between portrait and landscape

Later versions of Android added even more possibilities:

- behind: Matches the orientation of whatever is behind this activity

- user: Adopts the user's handset-wide preference for orientation behavior (this is obviously dependent on using a device that offers a global setting as an option)

Your preferences and options are expanded further by using fragments, which are discussed in their own dedicated section in Chapter 28.

Chapter 20

Dealing with Threads

Users like snappy applications. Users do not like applications that feel sluggish. The way to help make your application feel snappy to users is to use the standard threading capabilities built into Android. This chapter will walk you through the issues involved with thread management in Android and some of the options for keeping the UI crisp and responsive.

The Main Application Thread

You might think that when you call setText() on a TextView, the screen is updated with the text you supply, right then and there. That is not how it works. Rather, everything that modifies the widget-based UI goes through a message queue. Calls to setText() do not update the screen; they just pop a message on a queue telling the operating system to update the screen. The operating system pops these messages off of this queue and does what the messages require.

The queue is processed by one thread, variously called the *main application thread* and the *UI thread*. As long as that thread can keep processing messages, the screen will update, user input will be handled, and so on.

However, the main application thread is also used for nearly all callbacks into your activity. Your onCreate(),onClick(),onListItemClick(), and similar methods are all called on the main application thread. While your code is executing in these methods, Android is not processing messages on the queue, meaning the screen does not update, user input is not handled, and so on.

This, of course, is bad. So bad, in fact, that if you take more than a few seconds to do work on the main application thread, Android may display the dreaded "application not responding" (ANR) error, and your activity may be killed off. Hence, you want to make sure that all of your work on the main application thread happens quickly. This means that anything slow should be done in a background thread, so as not to tie up the main application thread. This includes activities such as the following:

- Internet access, such as sending data to a web service or downloading an image

■ Significant file operations, since flash storage can be remarkably slow at times

■ Any sort of complex calculations

Fortunately, Android supports threads using the standard Thread class from Java, plus all the wrappers and control structures you would expect, such as the java.util.concurrent class package.

However, there is one big limitation: you cannot modify the UI from a background thread. You can modify the UI only from the main application thread. Hence, you need to move long-running work into background threads, but those threads need to do something to arrange to update the UI using the main application thread. Android provides a wide range of tools to do just that, and these tools are the primary focus of this chapter.

Making Progress with ProgressBars

If you are going to fork background threads to do work on behalf of the user, you should consider keeping the user informed that work is going on. This is particularly true if the user is effectively waiting for that background work to complete.

The typical approach to keeping users informed of progress is some form of progress bar, like you see when you copy a bunch of files from place to place in many desktop operating systems. Android supports this through the ProgressBar widget.

A ProgressBar keeps track of progress, defined as an integer, with 0 indicating no progress has been made. You can define the maximum end of the range—which value indicates progress is complete—via setMax(). By default, a ProgressBar starts with a progress of 0, though you can start from some other position via setProgress(). If you prefer your progress bar to be indeterminate, use setIndeterminate() and set it to true.

In your Java code, you can either positively set the amount of progress that has been made (via setProgress()) or increment the progress from its current amount (via incrementProgressBy()). You can find out how much progress has been made via getProgress().

There are other alternatives for displaying progress—ProgressDialog, a progress indicator in the activity's title bar, and so on—but a ProgressBar is a good place to start.

Getting Through the Handlers

The most flexible means of making an Android-friendly background thread is to create an instance of a Handler subclass. You need only one Handler object per activity, and you do not need to manually register it. Merely creating the instance is sufficient to register it with the Android threading subsystem.

Your background thread can communicate with the Handler, which will do all of its work on the activity's UI thread. This is important, as UI changes, such as updating widgets, should occur only on the activity's UI thread.

You have two options for communicating with the Handler: messages and Runnable objects.

Messages

To send a Message to a Handler, first invoke obtainMessage() to get the Message object out of the pool. There are a few flavors of obtainMessage(), allowing you to create empty Message objects or ones populated with message identifiers and arguments. The more complicated your Handler processing needs to be, the more likely it is you will need to put data into the Message to help the Handler distinguish different events.

Then, you send the Message to the Handler via its message queue, using one of the sendMessage...() family of methods, such as the following:

- sendMessage(): Puts the message on the queue immediately

- sendMessageAtFrontOfQueue(): Puts the message on the queue immediately and places it at the front of the message queue (versus the back, which is the default), so your message takes priority over all others

- sendMessageAtTime(): Puts the message on the queue at the stated time, expressed in the form of milliseconds based on system uptime (SystemClock.uptimeMillis())

- sendMessageDelayed(): Puts the message on the queue after a delay, expressed in milliseconds

- sendEmptyMessage(): Sends an empty Message object to the queue, allowing you to skip the obtainMessage() step if you were planning on leaving it empty anyway

To process these messages, your Handler needs to implement handleMessage(), which will be called with each message that appears on the message queue. There, the Handler can update the UI as needed. However, it should still do that work quickly, as other UI work is suspended until the Handler is finished.

For example, let's create a ProgressBar and update it via a Handler. Here is the layout from the Threads/Handler sample project:

```xml
<?xml version="1.0" encoding="utf-8"?>
<LinearLayout xmlns:android="http://schemas.android.com/apk/res/android"
  android:orientation="vertical"
  android:layout_width="fill_parent"
  android:layout_height="fill_parent"
  >
  <ProgressBar android:id="@+id/progress"
    style="?android:attr/progressBarStyleHorizontal"
```

```
    android:layout_width="fill_parent"
    android:layout_height="wrap_content" />
</LinearLayout>
```

The ProgressBar, in addition to setting the width and height as normal, also employs the style property. This particular style indicates the ProgressBar should be drawn as the traditional horizontal bar showing the amount of work that has been completed.

And here is the Java:

```java
package com.commonsware.android.threads;

import android.app.Activity;
import android.os.Bundle;
import android.os.Handler;
import android.os.Message;
import android.widget.ProgressBar;
import java.util.concurrent.atomic.AtomicBoolean;

public class HandlerDemo extends Activity {
  ProgressBar bar;
  Handler handler=new Handler() {
    @Override
    public void handleMessage(Message msg) {
      bar.incrementProgressBy(5);
    }
  };
  AtomicBoolean isRunning=new AtomicBoolean(false);

  @Override
  public void onCreate(Bundle icicle) {
    super.onCreate(icicle);
    setContentView(R.layout.main);
    bar=(ProgressBar)findViewById(R.id.progress);
  }

  public void onStart() {
    super.onStart();
    bar.setProgress(0);

    Thread background=new Thread(new Runnable() {
      public void run() {
        try {
          for (int i=0;i<20 && isRunning.get();i++) {
            Thread.sleep(1000);
            handler.sendMessage(handler.obtainMessage());
          }
        }
        catch (Throwable t) {
          // just end the background thread
        }
      }
    });

    isRunning.set(true);
    background.start();
```

```
  }
  public void onStop() {
    super.onStop();
    isRunning.set(false);
  }
}
```

As part of constructing the Activity, we create an instance of Handler, with our implementation of handleMessage(). Basically, for any message received, we update the ProgressBar by 5 points, and then exit the message handler.

We then take advantage of onStart() and onStop(). In onStart(), we set up a background thread. In a real system, this thread would do something meaningful. Here, we just sleep 1 second, post a Message to the Handler, and repeat for a total of 20 passes. This, combined with the 5-point increase in the ProgressBar position, will march the bar clear across the screen, as the default maximum value for ProgressBar is 100. You can adjust that maximum via setMax(). For example, you might set the maximum to be the number of database rows you are processing, and update once per row.

Note that we then *leave* onStart(). This is crucial. The onStart() method is invoked on the activity UI thread, so it can update widgets and such. However, that means we need to get out of onStart(), both to let the Handler get its work done and to inform Android that our activity is not stuck.

The resulting activity is simply a horizontal progress bar, as shown in Figure 20–1.

Figure 20–1. *The HandlerDemo sample application*

Note, though, that while `ProgressBar` samples like this one show your code arranging to update the progress on the UI thread, for this specific widget, that is not necessary. At least as of Android 1.5, `ProgressBar` is now UI thread safe, in that you can update it from any thread, and it will handle the details of performing the actual UI update on the UI thread.

Runnables

If you would rather not fuss with `Message` objects, you can also pass `Runnable` objects to the `Handler`, which will run those `Runnable` objects on the activity UI thread. `Handler` offers a set of `post...()` methods for passing `Runnable` objects in for eventual processing.

Just as `Handler` supports `post()` and `postDelayed()` to add `Runnable` objects to the event queue, you can use those same methods on any `View` (i.e., any widget or container). This slightly simplifies your code, in that you can then skip the `Handler` object.

Where Oh Where Has My UI Thread Gone?

Sometimes, you may not know if you are currently executing on the UI thread of your application. For example, if you package some of your code in a JAR for others to reuse, you might not know whether your code is being executed on the UI thread or from a background thread.

To help combat this problem, `Activity` offers `runOnUiThread()`. This works similarly to the `post()` methods on `Handler` and `View`, in that it queues up a `Runnable` to run on the UI thread, if you are not on the UI thread right now. If you already are on the UI thread, it invokes the `Runnable` immediately. This gives you the best of both worlds: no delay if you are on the UI thread, yet safety in case you are not.

Asyncing Feeling

Android 1.5 introduced a new way of thinking about background operations: `AsyncTask`. In one (reasonably) convenient class, Android handles all of the chores of doing work on the UI thread versus on a background thread. Moreover, Android itself allocates and removes that background thread. And, it maintains a small work queue, further accentuating the fire-and-forget feel to `AsyncTask`.

The Theory

There is a saying, popular in marketing circles, "When a man buys a 1/4-inch drill bit at a hardware store, he does not want a 1/4-inch drill bit—he wants 1/4-inch holes." Hardware stores cannot sell holes, so they sell the next-best thing: devices (drills and drill bits) that make creating holes easy.

Similarly, Android developers who have struggled with background thread management do not strictly want background threads. Rather, they want work to be done off the UI thread, so users are not stuck waiting and activities do not get the dreaded ANR error. And while Android cannot magically cause work to not consume UI thread time, it can offer things that make such background operations easier and more transparent. AsyncTask is one such example.

To use AsyncTask, you must do the following:

- Create a subclass of AsyncTask, commonly as a private inner class of something that uses the task (e.g., an activity)

- Override one or more AsyncTask methods to accomplish the background work, plus whatever work associated with the task that needs to be done on the UI thread (e.g., update progress)

- When needed, create an instance of the AsyncTask subclass and call execute() to have it begin doing its work

What you do *not* have to do is

- Create your own background thread

- Terminate that background thread at an appropriate time

- Call all sorts of methods to arrange for bits of processing to be done on the UI thread

AsyncTask, Generics, and Varargs

Creating a subclass of AsyncTask is not quite as easy as, say, implementing the Runnable interface. AsyncTask uses generics, and so you need to specify three data types:

- The type of information that is needed to process the task (e.g., URLs to download)

- The type of information that is passed within the task to indicate progress

- The type of information that is passed to the post-task code when the task is completed

What makes this all the more confusing is that the first two data types are actually used as varargs, meaning that an array of these types is used within your AsyncTask subclass.

This should become clearer as we work our way toward an example.

The Stages of AsyncTask

There are four methods you can override in AsyncTask to accomplish your ends.

The one you must override, for the task class to be useful, is doInBackground(). This will be called by AsyncTask on a background thread. It can run as long as is necessary to accomplish whatever work needs to be done for this specific task. Note, though, that tasks are meant to be finite; using AsyncTask for an infinite loop is not recommended.

The doInBackground() method will receive, as parameters, a varargs array of the first of the three data types listed in the preceding section—the data needed to process the task. So, if your task's mission is to download a collection of URLs, doInBackground() will receive those URLs to process. The doInBackground() method must return a value of the third data type listed in the preceding section—the result of the background work.

You may wish to override onPreExecute(). This method is called, from the UI thread, before the background thread executes doInBackground(). Here, you might initialize a ProgressBar or otherwise indicate that background work is commencing.

Also, you may wish to override onPostExecute(). This method is called, from the UI thread, after doInBackground() completes. It receives, as a parameter, the value returned by doInBackground() (e.g., success or failure flag). Here, you might dismiss the ProgressBar and make use of the work done in the background, such as updating the contents of a list.

In addition, you may wish to override onProgressUpdate(). If doInBackground() calls the task's publishProgress() method, the object(s) passed to that method are provided to onProgressUpdate(), but in the UI thread. That way, onProgressUpdate() can alert the user as to the progress that has been made on the background work, such as updating a ProgressBar or continuing an animation. The onProgressUpdate() method will receive a varargs of the second data type from the preceding list—the data published by doInBackground() via publishProgress().

A Sample Task

As mentioned earlier, implementing an AsyncTask is not quite as easy as implementing a Runnable. However, once you get past the generics and varargs, it is not too bad.

For example, the following is an implementation of a ListActivity that uses an AsyncTask, from the Threads/Asyncer sample project:

```
package com.commonsware.android.async;

import android.app.ListActivity;
import android.os.AsyncTask;
import android.os.Bundle;
import android.os.SystemClock;
import android.widget.ArrayAdapter;
import android.widget.Toast;
import java.util.ArrayList;
```

```
public class AsyncDemo extends ListActivity {
  private static final String[] items={"lorem", "ipsum", "dolor",
                                  "sit", "amet", "consectetuer",
                                  "adipiscing", "elit", "morbi",
                                  "vel", "ligula", "vitae",
                                  "arcu", "aliquet", "mollis",
                                  "etiam", "vel", "erat",
                                  "placerat", "ante",
                                  "porttitor", "sodales",
                                  "pellentesque", "augue",
                                  "purus"};
  @Override
  public void onCreate(Bundle savedInstanceState) {
    super.onCreate(savedInstanceState);
    setContentView(R.layout.main);

    setListAdapter(new ArrayAdapter<String>(this,
                    android.R.layout.simple_list_item_1,
                    new ArrayList()));

    new AddStringTask().execute();
  }

  class AddStringTask extends AsyncTask<Void, String, Void> {
    @Override
    protected Void doInBackground(Void... unused) {
      for (String item : items) {
        publishProgress(item);
        SystemClock.sleep(200);
      }

      return(null);
    }

    @Override
    protected void onProgressUpdate(String... item) {
      ((ArrayAdapter)getListAdapter()).add(item[0]);
    }

    @Override
    protected void onPostExecute(Void unused) {
      Toast
        .makeText(AsyncDemo.this, "Done!", Toast.LENGTH_SHORT)
        .show();
    }
  }
}
```

This is another variation on the *lorem ipsum* list of words, used frequently throughout this book. This time, rather than simply hand the list of words to an ArrayAdapter, we simulate having to work to create these words in the background using AddStringTask, our AsyncTask implementation.

Let's examine this project's code piece by piece.

The AddStringTask Declaration

The AddStringTask declaration is as follows:

```
class AddStringTask extends AsyncTask<Void, String, Void> {
```

Here, we use the generics to set up the specific types of data we are going to leverage in AddStringTask:

- We do not need any configuration information in this case, so our first type is Void.

- We want to pass each string generated by our background task to onProgressUpdate(), to allow us to add it to our list, so our second type is String.

- We do not have any results, strictly speaking (beyond the updates), so our third type is Void.

The doInBackground() Method

The doInBackground() method is next in the code:

```
@Override
protected Void doInBackground(Void... unused) {
  for (String item : items) {
    publishProgress(item);
    SystemClock.sleep(200);
  }

  return(null);
}
```

The doInBackground() method is invoked in a background thread. Hence, we can take as long as we like. In a production application, we might be doing something like iterating over a list of URLs and downloading each. Here, we iterate over our static list of *lorem ipsum* words, call publishProgress() for each, and then sleep 200 milliseconds to simulate real work being done.

Since we elected to have no configuration information, we should not need parameters to doInBackground(). However, the contract with AsyncTask says we must accept a varargs of the first data type, which is why our method parameter is Void... unused.

Since we elected to have no results, we should not need to return anything. Again, though, the contract with AsyncTask says we must return an object of the third data type. Since that data type is Void, our returned object is null.

The onProgressUpdate() Method

Next up is the onProgressUpdate() method:

```
@Override
protected void onProgressUpdate(String... item) {
  ((ArrayAdapter)getListAdapter()).add(item[0]);
}
```

The onProgressUpdate() method is called on the UI thread, and we want to do something to let the user know we are making progress on loading these strings. In this case, we simply add the string to the ArrayAdapter, so it is appended to the end of the list.

The onProgressUpdate() method receives a String... varargs because that is the second data type in our class declaration. Since we are passing only one string per call to publishProgress(), we need to examine only the first entry in the varargs array.

The onPostExecute() Method

The next method is onPostExecute():

```
@Override
protected void onPostExecute(Void unused) {
  Toast
    .makeText(AsyncDemo.this, "Done!", Toast.LENGTH_SHORT)
    .show();
}
```

The onPostExecute() method is called on the UI thread, and we want to do something to indicate that the background work is complete. In a real system, there may be some ProgressBar to dismiss or some animation to stop. Here, we simply raise a Toast.

Since we elected to have no results, we should not need any parameters. The contract with AsyncTask says we must accept a single value of the third data type. Since that data type is Void, our method parameter is Void unused.

The Activity

The activity is as follows:

```
new AddStringTask().execute();
```

To use AddStringTask, we simply create an instance and call execute() on it. That starts the chain of events eventually leading to the background thread doing its work.

If AddStringTask required configuration parameters, we would have not used Void as our first data type, and the constructor would accept zero or more parameters of the defined type. Those values would eventually be passed to doInBackground().

The Results

If you build, install, and run this project, you will see the list being populated in real time over a few seconds, followed by a Toast indicating completion, as shown in Figure 20–2.

Figure 20–2. *The AsyncDemo, partway through loading the list of words*

Threads and Rotation

One problem with the default destroy-and-create cycle that activities go through on an orientation change comes from background threads. If the activity has started some background work—through an AsyncTask, for example—and then the activity is destroyed and re-created, the AsyncTask needs to know about this somehow. Otherwise, the AsyncTask might well send updates and final results to the *old* activity, with the new activity none the wiser. In fact, the new activity might start the background work *again*, wasting resources.

One way to deal with this is to disable the destroy-and-create cycle, by taking over configuration changes, as described in a previous section. Another alternative is to have a smarter activity and AsyncTask. You can see an example of that in the Rotation/RotationAsync sample project. As shown next, this project uses a ProgressBar, much like the Handler demo from earlier in this chapter. It also has a TextView to indicate when the background work is completed, initially invisible.

```
<?xml version="1.0" encoding="utf-8"?>
<LinearLayout xmlns:android="http://schemas.android.com/apk/res/android"
    android:orientation="vertical"
```

```
    android:layout_width="fill_parent"
    android:layout_height="fill_parent"
    >
  <ProgressBar android:id="@+id/progress"
    style="?android:attr/progressBarStyleHorizontal"
    android:layout_width="fill_parent"
    android:layout_height="wrap_content"
  />
  <TextView android:id="@+id/completed"
      android:layout_width="fill_parent"
      android:layout_height="wrap_content"
      android:text="Work completed!"
      android:visibility="invisible"
  />
</LinearLayout>
```

The "business logic" is for an AsyncTask to do some (fake) work in the background, updating the ProgressBar along the way, and making the TextView visible when it is finished. More importantly, it needs to do this in such a way as to behave properly if the screen is rotated. This means the following:

- We cannot "lose" our AsyncTask, having it continue doing work and updating the wrong activity.

- We cannot start a second AsyncTask, thereby doubling our workload.

- We need to have the UI correctly reflect our work's progress or completion.

Manual Activity Association

Earlier, this chapter showed the use of an AsyncTask that was implemented as a regular inner class of the Activity class. That works well when you are not concerned about rotation. For example, if the AsyncTask is not affecting the UI—such as uploading a photo—rotation will not be an issue for you. Having the AsyncTask as an inner class of the Activity means you get ready access to the Activity for any place where you need a Context.

However, for the rotation scenario, a regular inner class will work poorly. The AsyncTask will think it knows which Activity it is supposed to work with, but in reality it will be holding onto an implicit reference to the old activity, not one after an orientation change.

So, in RotationAsync, the RotationAwareTask class is a static inner class. This means RotationAwareTask does not have any implicit reference to any RotationAsync Activity (old or new):

```
import android.app.Activity;
import android.os.AsyncTask;
import android.os.Bundle;
import android.os.SystemClock;
import android.util.Log;
import android.view.View;
import android.widget.ProgressBar;
```

```java
public class RotationAsync extends Activity {
  private ProgressBar bar=null;
  private RotationAwareTask task=null;

  @Override
  public void onCreate(Bundle savedInstanceState) {
    super.onCreate(savedInstanceState);
    setContentView(R.layout.main);

    bar=(ProgressBar)findViewById(R.id.progress);

    task=(RotationAwareTask)getLastNonConfigurationInstance();

    if (task==null) {
      task=new RotationAwareTask(this);
      task.execute();
    }
    else {
      task.attach(this);
      updateProgress(task.getProgress());

      if (task.getProgress()>=100) {
        markAsDone();
      }
    }
  }

  @Override
  public Object onRetainNonConfigurationInstance() {
    task.detach();

    return(task);
  }

  void updateProgress(int progress) {
    bar.setProgress(progress);
  }

  void markAsDone() {
    findViewById(R.id.completed).setVisibility(View.VISIBLE);
  }

  static class RotationAwareTask extends AsyncTask<Void, Void, Void> {
    RotationAsync activity=null;
    int progress=0;

    RotationAwareTask(RotationAsync activity) {
      attach(activity);
    }

    @Override
    protected Void doInBackground(Void... unused) {
      for (int i=0;i<20;i++) {
        SystemClock.sleep(500);
        publishProgress();
      }
```

```
      return(null);
    }

    @Override
    protected void onProgressUpdate(Void... unused) {
      if (activity==null) {
        Log.w("RotationAsync", "onProgressUpdate() skipped - no activity");
      }
      else {
        progress+=5;
        activity.updateProgress(progress);
      }
    }

    @Override
    protected void onPostExecute(Void unused) {
      if (activity==null) {
        Log.w("RotationAsync", "onPostExecute() skipped - no activity");
      }
      else {
        activity.markAsDone();
      }
    }

    void detach() {
      activity=null;
    }

    void attach(RotationAsync activity) {
      this.activity=activity;
    }

    int getProgress() {
      return(progress);
    }
  }
}
```

Since we want RotationAwareTask to update the current RotationAsync Activity, we
supply that Activity when we create the task, via the constructor. RotationAwareTask
also has attach() and detach() methods to change which Activity the task knows
about, as we will see shortly.

Flow of Events

When RotationAsync starts up for the first time, it creates a new instance of the
RotationAwareTask class and executes it. At this point, the task has a reference to the
RotationAsync Activity and can do its (fake) work, telling RotationAsync to update the
progress along the way.

Now, suppose that during the middle of the doInBackground() processing, the user
rotates the screen. Our Activity will be called with
onRetainNonConfigurationInstance(). Here, we want to do two things:

- Since this `Activity` instance is being destroyed, we need to make sure the task no longer holds onto a reference to it. Hence, we call `detach()`, causing the task to set its `RotationAsync` data member (`activity`) to `null`.

- We return the `RotationAwareTask` object, so that our new `RotationAsync` instance can get access to it.

Eventually, the new `RotationAsync` instance will be created. In `onCreate()`, we try to get access to any current `RotationAwareTask` instance via `getLastNonConfigurationInstance()`. If that was `null`, then we know that this is a newly created activity, and so we create a new task. If, however, `getLastNonConfigurationInstance()` returned the task object from the old `RotationAsync` instance, we hold onto it and update our UI to reflect the current progress that has been made. We also `attach()` the new `RotationAsync` to the `RotationAwareTask`, so as further progress is made, the task can notify the proper activity.

The net result is that our `ProgressBar` smoothly progresses from 0 to 100, even while rotations are going on.

Why This Works

Most callback methods in Android are driven by messages on the message queue being processed by the main application thread. Normally, this queue is being processed whenever the main application thread is not otherwise busy, such as running our code. However, when a configuration change occurs, like a screen rotation, that no longer holds true. In between the call to the `onRetainNonConfigurationInstance()` instance of the old activity and the completion of `onCreate()` of the new activity, the message queue is left alone.

So, let's suppose that, in between `onRetainNonConfigurationInstance()` activity and the subsequent `onCreate()`, our `AsyncTask`'s background work completes. This will trigger `onPostExecute()` to be called...eventually. However, since `onPostExecute()` is actually launched from a message on the message queue, `onPostExecute()` will not be called until after our `onCreate()` has completed. Hence, our `AsyncTask` can keep running during the configuration change, as long as we do two things:

- In `onCreate()` of the new activity instance, we update the `AsyncTask` to have it work with our new activity, rather than the old one.

- We do not attempt to use the activity from `doInBackground()`.

And Now, the Caveats

Background threads, while eminently possible using the Android `Handler` system, are not all happiness and warm puppies. Background threads not only add complexity, but also have real-world costs in terms of available memory, CPU, and battery life. Hence, you need to account for a wide range of scenarios with your background thread, including the following:

- The possibility that users will interact with your activity's UI while the background thread is chugging along. If the work that the background thread is doing is altered or invalidated by the user input, you will need to communicate this to the background thread. Android includes many classes in the `java.util.concurrent` package that will help you communicate safely with your background thread.

- The possibility that the activity will be killed off while background work is going on. For example, after starting your activity, the user might have a call come in, followed by a text message, followed by a need to look up a contact—all of which might be sufficient to kick your activity out of memory. Chapter 18 covers the various events Android will take your activity through; hook to the proper ones, and be sure to shut down your background thread cleanly when you have the chance.

- The possibility that users will get irritated if you chew up a lot of CPU time and battery life without giving any payback. Tactically, this means using `ProgressBar` or other means of letting users know that something is happening. Strategically, this means you still need to be efficient at what you do—background threads are no panacea for sluggish or pointless code.

- The possibility that you will encounter an error during background processing. For example, if you are gathering information from the Internet, the device might lose connectivity. Alerting the user of the problem via a notification (covered in Chapter 37) and shutting down the background thread may be your best option.

Chapter 21

Creating Intent Filters

Up to now, the focus of this book has been on activities opened directly by the user from the device's launcher. This is the most obvious case for getting your activity up and running and making it visible to the user. And, in many cases, it is the primary way the user will start using your application.

However, remember that the Android system is based on many loosely coupled components. The things that you might accomplish in a desktop GUI via dialog boxes, child windows, and the like are mostly supposed to be independent activities. While one activity will be "special," in that it shows up in the launcher, the other activities all need to be reached...somehow.

The "somehow" is via intents.

An intent is basically a message that you pass to Android saying, "Yo! I want to do...er...something! Yeah!" How specific the "something" is depends on the situation — sometimes you know exactly what you want to do (e.g., open one of your other activities), and sometimes you do not.

In the abstract, Android is all about intents and receivers of those intents. So, now that you are well versed in creating activities, let's dive into intents, so we can create more complex applications while simultaneously being "good Android citizens."

What's Your Intent?

When Sir Tim Berners-Lee cooked up the Hypertext Transfer Protocol (HTTP), he set up a system of verbs plus addresses in the form of URLs. The address indicates a resource, such as a web page, graphic, or server-side program. The verb indicates what should be done: GET to retrieve it, POST to send form data to it for processing, and so on.

Intents are similar, in that they represent an action plus context. There are more actions and more components to the context with Android intents than there are with HTTP verbs and resources, but the concept is still the same. Just as a web browser knows how to process a verb+URL pair, Android knows how to find activities or other application logic that will handle a given intent.

Pieces of Intents

The two most important pieces of an intent are the action and what Android refers to as the *data*. These are almost exactly analogous to HTTP verbs and URLs: the action is the verb, and the data is a `Uri`, such as `content://contacts/people/1`, representing a contact in the contacts database. Actions are constants, such as `ACTION_VIEW` (to bring up a viewer for the resource), `ACTION_EDIT` (to edit the resource), or `ACTION_PICK` (to choose an available item given a `Uri` representing a collection, such as `content://contacts/people`).

If you were to create an intent combining `ACTION_VIEW` with a content `Uri` of `content://contacts/people/1`, and pass that intent to Android, Android would know to find and open an activity capable of viewing that resource.

There are other criteria you can place inside an intent (represented as an `Intent` object), besides the action and data `Uri`, such as the following:

- *Category*: Your "main" activity will be in the `LAUNCHER` category, indicating it should appear on the launcher menu. Other activities will probably be in the `DEFAULT` category or the `ALTERNATIVE` category.

- *MIME type*: This indicates the type of resource you want to operate on, if you do not know a collection `Uri`.

- *Component*: This is the class of the activity that is supposed to receive this intent. Using components this way obviates the need for the other properties of the intent. However, it does make the intent more fragile, as it assumes specific implementations.

- *Extras*: This refers to a `Bundle` of other information you want to pass along to the receiver with the intent, typically information that the receiver might want to take advantage of. Which pieces of information a given receiver can use is up to the receiver and (hopefully) is well documented.

You will find rosters of the standard actions and categories in the Android SDK documentation for the `Intent` class.

Intent Routing

As noted in the previous section, if you specify the target component in your intent, Android has no doubt where the intent is supposed to be routed to, and it will launch the named activity. This might be fine if the target intent is in your application. It definitely is not recommended for sending intents to other applications. Component names, by and large, are considered private to the application and are subject to change. Content `Uri` templates and MIME types are the preferred ways of identifying services you wish third-party code to supply.

If you do not specify the target component, then Android has to figure out which activities (or other receivers) are eligible to receive the intent. Note the use of the plural *activities*, as a broadly written intent might well resolve to several activities. That is the...ummm...intent (pardon the pun), as you will see later in this chapter. This routing approach is referred to as *implicit routing*.

Basically, there are three rules, all of which must be true for a given activity to be eligible for a given intent:

- The activity must support the specified action.

- The activity must support the stated MIME type (if supplied).

- The activity must support all of the categories named in the intent.

The upshot is that you want to make your intents specific enough to find the right receiver(s), and no more specific than that. This will become clearer as we work through some examples later in this chapter.

Stating Your Intent(ions)

All Android components that wish to be notified via intents must declare intent filters, so Android knows which intents should go to that component. To do this, you need to add intent-filter elements to your AndroidManifest.xml file.

All of the example projects have intent filters defined, courtesy of the Android application-building script (android create project or the IDE equivalent). They look something like this:

```
<?xml version="1.0"?>
<manifest xmlns:android="http://schemas.android.com/apk/res/android"
package="com.commonsware.android.skeleton">
    <application>
        <activity android:name=".Now" android:label="Now">
            <intent-filter>
                <action android:name="android.intent.action.MAIN"/>
                <category android:name="android.intent.category.LAUNCHER"/>
            </intent-filter>
        </activity>
    </application>
</manifest>
```

Note the intent-filter element under the activity element. Here, we declare that this activity:

- Is the main activity for this application

- Is in the LAUNCHER category, meaning it gets an icon in the Android main menu

Because this activity is the main one for the application, Android knows this is the component it should launch when somebody chooses the application from the main menu.

You are welcome to have more than one action or more than one category in your intent filters. That indicates that the associated component (e.g., activity) handles multiple different sorts of intents.

More than likely, you will also want to have your secondary (non-MAIN) activities specify the MIME type of data they work on. Then, if an intent is targeted for that MIME type—either directly, or indirectly by the Uri referencing something of that type—Android will know that the component handles such data.

For example, you could have an activity declared like this:

```
<activity android:name=".TourViewActivity">
  <intent-filter>
    <action android:name="android.intent.action.VIEW" />
    <category android:name="android.intent.category.DEFAULT" />
    <data android:mimeType="vnd.android.cursor.item/vnd.commonsware.tour" />
  </intent-filter>
</activity>
```

This activity will be launched by an intent requesting to view a Uri representing a vnd.android.cursor.item/vnd.commonsware.tour piece of content. That Intent could come from another activity in the same application (e.g., the MAIN activity for this application) or from another activity in another Android application that happens to know a Uri that this activity handles.

Narrow Receivers

In the preceding examples, the intent filters were set up on activities. Sometimes, tying intents to activities is not exactly what you want, as in the following cases:

- Some system events might cause you to want to trigger something in a service rather than an activity.

- Some events might need to launch different activities in different circumstances, where the criteria are not solely based on the intent itself, but some other state (e.g., if we get intent X and the database has a Y, then launch activity M; if the database does not have a Y, then launch activity N).

For these cases, Android offers the receiver, defined as a class implementing the BroadcastReceiver interface. Broadcast receivers are disposable objects designed to receive intents—specifically, broadcast intents—and take action.

The BroadcastReceiver interface has only one method: onReceive(). Receivers implement that method, where they do whatever it is they wish to do upon an incoming intent. To declare a receiver, add a receiver element to your AndroidManifest.xml file:

```
<receiver android:name=".MyIntentReceiverClassName" />
```

A receiver is alive for only as long as it takes to process onReceive()—as soon as that method returns, the receiver instance is subject to garbage collection and will not be reused. This means receivers are somewhat limited in what they can do, mostly to avoid anything that involves any sort of callback. For example, they cannot bind to a service, and they cannot open a dialog box.

The exception is if the `BroadcastReceiver` is implemented on some longer-lived component, such as an activity or service. In that case, the receiver lives as long as its "host" does (e.g., until the activity is frozen). However, in this case, you cannot declare the receiver via `AndroidManifest.xml`. Instead, you need to call `registerReceiver()` on your `Activity`'s `onResume()` callback to declare interest in an intent, and then call `unregisterReceiver()` from your `Activity`'s `onPause()` when you no longer need those intents.

Intents for Every Occasion

The number of actions encompassed by the `Intent` class steadily grows with each new version of Android. With the release of Ice Cream Sandwich (ICS), version 4.0, Google has added a further six actions and deprecated three that are no longer required. The Android SDK documentation covers all 97 intent actions available in ICS, which you can read at your leisure. Here are some highlights to get you thinking about the possibilities:

- `ACTION_AIRPLANE_MODE_CHANGED`: The device has entered or exited airplane mode.

- `ACTION_CAMERA_BUTTON`: The camera button was pressed.

- `ACTION_DATE_CHANGED`: The date has changed. This could be important for applications like reminder lists, calendars, and so forth.

- `ACTION_HEADSET_PLUG`: Headphones were attached or removed. This is quite important for music-playing apps and similar apps.

You can start to see the possibilities as well as the complexities.

The Pause Caveat

There is one hiccup with using `Intent` objects to pass arbitrary messages around: it works only when the receiver is active. To quote from the documentation for `BroadcastReceiver`:

> If registering a receiver in your `Activity.onResume()` implementation, you should unregister it in `Activity.onPause()`. (You won't receive intents when paused, and this will cut down on unnecessary system overhead). Do not unregister in `Activity.onSaveInstanceState()`, because this won't be called if the user moves back in the history stack.

Hence, you can use the `Intent` framework as an arbitrary message bus only in the following situations:

- Your receiver does not care if it misses messages because it was not active.

- You provide some means of getting the receiver "caught up" on messages it missed while it was inactive.

- Your receiver is registered in the manifest.

Chapter 22

Launching Activities and Subactivities

The theory behind the Android UI architecture is that developers should decompose their application into distinct activities. For example, a calendar application could have activities for viewing the calendar, viewing a single event, editing an event (including adding a new one), viewing and editing events on the same screen for larger displays, and so forth. This implies that one of your activities has the means to start up another activity. For example, if a user selects an event from the view-calendar activity, you might want to show the view-event activity for that event. This means that you need to be able to cause the view-event activity to launch and show a specific event (the one the user chose).

This can be further broken down into two scenarios:

- You know which activity you want to launch, probably because it is another activity in your own application.

- You have a content Uri to do something, and you want your users to be able to do something with it, but you do not know up front what the options are.

This chapter covers the first scenario; the second is beyond the scope of this book.

Peers and Subs

One key question you need to answer when you decide to launch an activity is this: does your activity need to know when the launched activity ends?

For example, suppose you want to spawn an activity to collect authentication information for some web service you are connecting to—maybe you need to authenticate with OpenID in order to use an OAuth service. In this case, your main activity will need to know when the authentication is complete so it can start to use the web service.

On the other hand, imagine an e-mail application in Android. When the user elects to view an attachment, neither you nor the user necessarily expects the main activity to know when the user is done viewing that attachment.

In the first scenario, the launched activity is clearly subordinate to the launching activity. In that case, you probably want to launch the child as a subactivity, which means your activity will be notified when the child activity is complete.

In the second scenario, the launched activity is more a peer of your activity, so you probably want to launch the child just as a regular activity. Your activity will not be informed when the child is done, but, then again, your activity really does not need to know.

Start 'Em Up

The two pieces for starting an activity are an intent and your choice of how to start it up.

Make an Intent

As discussed in the previous chapter, intents encapsulate a request, made to Android, for some activity or other receiver to do something. If the activity you intend to launch is one of your own, you may find it simplest to create an explicit intent, naming the component you wish to launch. For example, from within your activity, you could create an intent like this:

```
new Intent(this, HelpActivity.class);
```

This stipulates that you want to launch the HelpActivity. This activity would need to be named in your AndroidManifest.xml file, though not necessarily with any intent filter, since you are trying to request it directly.

Or, you could put together an intent for some Uri, requesting a particular action:

```
Uri uri=Uri.parse("geo:"+lat.toString()+","+lon.toString());
Intent i=new Intent(Intent.ACTION_VIEW, uri);
```

Here, given that you have the latitude and longitude of some position (lat and lon, respectively) of type Double, you construct a geo scheme Uri and create an intent requesting to view this Uri (ACTION_VIEW).

Make the Call

Once you have your intent, you need to pass it to Android and get the child activity to launch. You have two main options (with a few more advanced/specialized variants):

- The simplest option is to call startActivity() with the Intent. This will cause Android to find the best-match activity and pass the intent to it for handling. Your activity will not be informed when the child activity is complete.

- You can call startActivityForResult(), passing it the Intent and a number (unique to the calling activity). Android will find the best-match activity and pass the intent to it for handling. Your activity will be notified when the child activity is complete, via the onActivityResult() callback.

- In some cases, you may want or need conditional launching, batch launching, etc. of activities. Additional methods like startActivities(), startActivityFromFragment(), and startActivityIfNeeded() can help with these cases.

With startActivityForResult(), as noted, you can implement the onActivityResult() callback to be notified when the child activity has completed its work. The callback receives the unique number supplied to startActivityForResult(), so you can determine which child activity is the one that has completed. You also get the following:

- A result code, from the child activity calling setResult(). Typically, this is RESULT_OK or RESULT_CANCELED, though you can create your own return codes (pick a number starting with RESULT_FIRST_USER).

- An optional String containing some result data, possibly a URL to some internal or external resource. For example, an ACTION_PICK intent typically returns the selected bit of content via this data string.

- An optional Bundle containing additional information beyond the result code and data string.

To demonstrate launching a peer activity, take a peek at the Activities/Launch sample application. The XML layout is fairly straightforward: two fields for the latitude and longitude, plus a button.

```xml
<?xml version="1.0" encoding="utf-8"?>
<LinearLayout xmlns:android="http://schemas.android.com/apk/res/android"
  android:orientation="vertical"
  android:layout_width="fill_parent"
  android:layout_height="fill_parent"
  >
  <TableLayout
    android:layout_width="fill_parent"
    android:layout_height="wrap_content"
    android:stretchColumns="1,2"
  >
    <TableRow>
      <TextView
        android:layout_width="wrap_content"
        android:layout_height="wrap_content"
        android:paddingLeft="2dip"
        android:paddingRight="4dip"
        android:text="Location:"
      />
      <EditText android:id="@+id/lat"
        android:layout_width="fill_parent"
        android:layout_height="wrap_content"
        android:cursorVisible="true"
        android:editable="true"
        android:singleLine="true"
```

```
        android:layout_weight="1"
      />
      <EditText android:id="@+id/lon"
        android:layout_width="fill_parent"
        android:layout_height="wrap_content"
        android:cursorVisible="true"
        android:editable="true"
        android:singleLine="true"
        android:layout_weight="1"
      />
    </TableRow>
  </TableLayout>
  <Button android:id="@+id/map"
    android:layout_width="fill_parent"
    android:layout_height="wrap_content"
    android:text="Show Me!"
    android:onClick="showMe"
  />
</LinearLayout>
```

The button's showMe() callback method simply takes the latitude and longitude, pours them into a geo scheme Uri, and then starts the activity:

```java
package com.commonsware.android.activities;

import android.app.Activity;
import android.content.Intent;
import android.net.Uri;
import android.os.Bundle;
import android.view.View;
import android.widget.EditText;

public class LaunchDemo extends Activity {
  private EditText lat;
  private EditText lon;

  @Override
  public void onCreate(Bundle icicle) {
    super.onCreate(icicle);
    setContentView(R.layout.main);

    lat=(EditText)findViewById(R.id.lat);
    lon=(EditText)findViewById(R.id.lon);
  }

  public void showMe(View v) {
    String _lat=lat.getText().toString();
    String _lon=lon.getText().toString();
    Uri uri=Uri.parse("geo:"+_lat+","+_lon);

    startActivity(new Intent(Intent.ACTION_VIEW, uri));
  }
}
```

We've kept the activity very basic so as to focus on our topic of handling the geo intent. We start as shown in Figure 22–1.

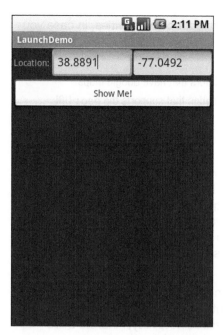

Figure 22–1. *The LaunchDemo sample application, with a location filled in*

If you fill in a location (e.g., 38.8891 latitude and -77.0492 longitude) and click the button, the resulting map is more interesting, as shown in Figure 22–2. Note that this is the built-in Android map activity—we did not create our own activity to display this map.

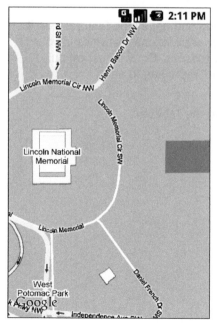

Figure 22–2. *The map launched by LaunchDemo, showing the Lincoln Memorial in Washington DC*

In Chapter 40, you will see how you can create maps in your own activities, in case you need greater control over how the map is displayed.

> **NOTE:** This geo: Intent will work only on devices or emulators that have Google Maps installed, or on devices that have some other mapping application that supports the geo: URL.

Tabbed Browsing, Sort Of

One of the main features of the modern desktop web browser is tabbed browsing, where a single browser window can show several pages split across a series of tabs. On a mobile device, this may not make a lot of sense, given that you lose screen real estate for the tabs themselves. In this book, however, we do not let little things like sensibility stop us, so this section demonstrates a tabbed browser, using TabActivity and Intent objects.

As you may recall from the Chapter 14 section "Putting It on My Tab," a tab can have either a View or an Activity as its content. If you want to use an Activity as the content of a tab, you provide an Intent that will launch the desired Activity; Android's tab-management framework will then pour the Activity's UI into the tab.

Your natural instinct might be to use an http: Uri the way we used a geo: Uri in the previous example:

```
Intent i=new Intent(Intent.ACTION_VIEW);
i.setData(Uri.parse("http://commonsware.com"));
```

That way, you could use the built-in browser application and get all the features that it offers. Alas, this does not work. You cannot host other applications' activities in your tabs; only your own activities are allowed, for security reasons. So, we dust off our WebView demos from Chapter 15 and use those instead, repackaged as Activities/IntentTab.

Here is the source to the main activity, the one hosting the TabView:

```
package com.commonsware.android.intenttab;

import android.app.Activity;
import android.app.TabActivity;
import android.content.Intent;
import android.net.Uri;
import android.os.Bundle;
import android.webkit.WebView;
import android.widget.TabHost;

public class IntentTabDemo extends TabActivity {
  @Override
  public void onCreate(Bundle savedInstanceState) {
    super.onCreate(savedInstanceState);

    TabHost host=getTabHost();
```

```
    Intent i=new Intent(this, CWBrowser.class);

    i.putExtra(CWBrowser.URL, "http://commonsware.com");
    host.addTab(host.newTabSpec("one")
            .setIndicator("CW")
            .setContent(i));

    i=new Intent(i);
    i.putExtra(CWBrowser.URL, "http://www.android.com");
    host.addTab(host.newTabSpec("two")
            .setIndicator("Android")
            .setContent(i));
  }
}
```

As you can see, we are using TabActivity as the base class, and so we do not need our own layout XML—TabActivity supplies it for us. All we do is get access to the TabHost and add two tabs, each specifying an Intent that directly refers to another class. In this case, our two tabs will each host a CWBrowser, with a URL to load supplied via an Intent extra.

The CWBrowser activity is a simple modification to the earlier browser demos:

```
package com.commonsware.android.intenttab;

import android.app.Activity;
import android.content.Intent;
import android.net.Uri;
import android.os.Bundle;
import android.webkit.WebView;

public class CWBrowser extends Activity {
  public static final String URL="com.commonsware.android.intenttab.URL";
  private WebView browser;

  @Override
  public void onCreate(Bundle icicle) {
    super.onCreate(icicle);

    browser=new WebView(this);
    setContentView(browser);
    browser.loadUrl(getIntent().getStringExtra(URL));
  }
}
```

They simply load a different URL into the browser: the CommonsWare home page in one, the Android home page in the other.

The resulting UI shows what tabbed browsing could look like on Android, as shown in Figures 22–3 and 22–4.

Figure 22–3. *The IntentTabDemo sample application, showing the first tab*

Figure 22–4. *The IntentTabDemo sample application, showing the second tab*

However, this approach is rather wasteful. There is a fair bit of overhead in creating an activity that you do not need just to populate tabs in a TabHost. In particular, it increases the amount of stack space needed by your application, and running out of stack space is a significant problem in Android, as will be described in a later chapter.

Chapter 23

Working with Resources

Resources are static bits of information held outside the Java source code. You have seen one type of resource—the layout—frequently in the examples in this book. There are many other types of resources, such as images and strings, that you can take advantage of in your Android applications.

The Resource Lineup

Resources are stored as files under the `res/` directory in your Android project layout. With the exception of raw resources (`res/raw/`), all the other types of resources are parsed for you, either by the Android packaging system or by the Android system on the device or emulator. So, for example, when you lay out an activity's UI via a layout resource (`res/layout/`), you do not have to parse the layout XML yourself because Android handles that for you.

In addition to layout resources (introduced in Chapter 8), there are several other types of resource available to you, including the following:

- Images (`res/drawable-mdpi/`, `res/drawable-ldpi`, etc.), for putting static icons, images, photos, or other pictures in a user interface

- Raw (`res/raw/`), for arbitrary files that have meaning to your application but not necessarily to Android frameworks

- Strings, colors, arrays, and dimensions (`res/values/`), for both giving these sorts of constants symbolic names and keeping them separate from the rest of the code (e.g., for internationalization and localization)

- XML (`res/xml/`), for static XML files containing your own data and structure

String Theory

Keeping your labels and other bits of text outside the main source code of your application is generally considered to be a very good idea. In particular, it helps with internationalization and localization, covered in the "Different Strokes for Different Folks" section later in this chapter. Even if you are not going to translate your strings to other languages, it is easier to make corrections if all the strings are in one spot instead of scattered throughout your source code.

Android supports regular externalized strings, along with *string formats*, where the string has placeholders for dynamically inserted information. On top of that, Android supports simple text formatting, called *styled text*, so you can make your words be bold or italic intermingled with normal text.

Plain Strings

Generally speaking, all you need for plain strings is an XML file in the `res/values` directory (typically named `res/values/strings.xml`), with a `resources` root element, and one child `string` element for each string you wish to encode as a resource. The `string` element takes a name attribute, which is the unique name for this string, and a single text element containing the text of the string, as shown in this example:

```
<resources>
  <string name="quick">The quick brown fox...</string>
  <string name="laughs">He who laughs last...</string>
</resources>
```

The only tricky part is if the string value contains a quote mark (") or an apostrophe ('). In those cases, you will want to escape those values, by preceding them with a backslash (e.g., `These are the times that try men\'s souls.`). Or, if it is just an apostrophe, you could enclose the value in quote marks (e.g., `"These are the times that try men's souls."`).

You can then reference this string from a layout file (as `@string/...`, where the ellipsis is the unique name, such as `@string/laughs`). Or you can get the string from your Java code by calling `getString()` with the resource ID of the string resource, which is the unique name prefixed with `R.string.` (e.g., `getString(R.string.quick)`).

String Formats

As with other implementations of the Java language, Android's Dalvik virtual machine supports string formats. Here, the string contains placeholders representing data to be replaced at runtime by variable information (e.g., `My name is %1$s`). Plain strings stored as resources can be used as string formats:

```
String strFormat=getString(R.string.my_name);
String strResult=String.format(strFormat, "Tim");
((TextView)findViewById(R.id.some_label)).setText(strResult);
```

There is also a flavor of getString() that does the String.format() call for you:

```
String strResult=getString(R.string.my_name, "Tim");
((TextView)findViewById(R.id.some_label)).setText(strResult);
```

It is very important that you use the version of the placeholders that takes an index—
%1$s instead of just %s. Strategically, translations of your string resources may cause you
to apply the variable data in a different order than did your original translation, and using
nonindexed placeholders locks you into a particular order. Tactically, your project will fail
to compile, as the Android build tools reject nonindexed placeholders nowadays.

Styled Text

If you want really rich text, you should have raw resources containing HTML, and then
pour those into a WebKit widget. However, for light HTML formatting, using inline
elements such as <b>, <i>, and <u>, you can just use them in a string resource:

```
<resources>
  <string name="b">This has <b>bold</b> in it.</string>
  <string name="i">Whereas this has <i>italics</i>!</string>
</resources>
```

You can access these via getText(), which gives you back an object supporting the
android.text.Spanned interface and therefore has all of the formatting applied:

```
((TextView)findViewById(R.id.another_label))
          .setText(getText(R.string.b));
```

Styled Text and Formats

Where styled text gets tricky is with styled string formats, as String.format() works on
String objects, not Spanned objects with formatting instructions. If you really want to
have styled string formats, here is the workaround:

1. Entity-escape the angle brackets in the string resource (e.g., this is
    <b>%1$s</b>).

2. Retrieve the string resource as normal, though it will not be styled at this
    point (e.g., getString(R.string.funky_format)).

3. Generate the format results, being sure to escape any string values you
    substitute, in case they contain angle brackets or ampersands:

```
String.format(getString(R.string.funky_format),
          TextUtils.htmlEncode(strName));
```

4. Convert the entity-escaped HTML into a Spanned object via
    Html.fromHtml():

```
someTextView.setText(Html
                  .fromHtml(resultFromStringFormat));
```

To see this in action, let's look at the Resources/Strings demo. Here is the layout file:

```xml
<?xml version="1.0" encoding="utf-8"?>
<LinearLayout xmlns:android="http://schemas.android.com/apk/res/android"
  android:orientation="vertical"
  android:layout_width="fill_parent"
  android:layout_height="fill_parent"
  >
  <LinearLayout
    android:orientation="horizontal"
    android:layout_width="fill_parent"
    android:layout_height="wrap_content"
    >
    <Button android:id="@+id/format"
      android:layout_width="wrap_content"
      android:layout_height="wrap_content"
      android:text="@string/btn_name"
      android:onClick="applyFormat"
      />
    <EditText android:id="@+id/name"
      android:layout_width="fill_parent"
      android:layout_height="wrap_content"
      />
  </LinearLayout>
  <TextView android:id="@+id/result"
    android:layout_width="fill_parent"
    android:layout_height="wrap_content"
    />
</LinearLayout>
```

As you can see, it is just a button, a field, and a label. The idea is for users to enter their name in the field, and then click the button to cause the label to be updated with a formatted message containing their name.

The Button in the layout file references a string resource (@string/btn_name), so we need a string resource file (res/values/strings.xml):

```xml
<?xml version="1.0" encoding="utf-8"?>
<resources>
  <string name="app_name">StringsDemo</string>
  <string name="btn_name">Name:</string>
  <string name="funky_format">My name is &lt;b&gt;%1$s&lt;/b&gt;</string>
</resources>
```

The app_name resource is automatically created by the android create project command. The btn_name string is the caption of the Button, while our styled string format is in funky_format.

Finally, to hook all this together, we need a pinch of Java:

```java
package com.commonsware.android.strings;

import android.app.Activity;
import android.os.Bundle;
import android.text.TextUtils;
import android.text.Html;
import android.view.View;
import android.widget.EditText;
```

```
import android.widget.TextView;

public class StringsDemo extends Activity {
  EditText name;
  TextView result;

  @Override
  public void onCreate(Bundle icicle) {
    super.onCreate(icicle);
    setContentView(R.layout.main);

    name=(EditText)findViewById(R.id.name);
    result=(TextView)findViewById(R.id.result);
  }

  public void applyFormat(View v) {
    String format=getString(R.string.funky_format);
    String simpleResult=String.format(format,
                  TextUtils.htmlEncode(name.getText().toString()));
    result.setText(Html.fromHtml(simpleResult));
  }
}
```

The string resource manipulation can be found in `applyFormat()`, which is called when the button is clicked. First, we get our format via `getString()`—something we could have done at `onCreate()` time for efficiency. Next, we format the value in the field using this format, getting a `String` back, since the string resource is in entity-encoded HTML. Note the use of `TextUtils.htmlEncode()` to entity-encode the entered name, in case somebody decides to use an ampersand or something. Finally, we convert the simple HTML into a styled text object via `Html.fromHtml()` and update our label.

When the activity is first launched, we have an empty label, as shown in Figure 23–1.

Figure 23–1. *The StringsDemo sample application, as initially launched*

If we fill in a name and click the button, we get the result shown in Figure 23–2.

Figure 23–2. *The same application, after filling in some heroic figure's name*

Got the Picture?

Android supports images in the PNG, JPEG, BMP, WEBP, and GIF formats. GIF is officially discouraged, however. PNG is the most common format given its preference in earlier versions of Android, and growing popularity on the Web in general. WEBP is newly supported in Ice Cream Sandwich. It's a codec built on the VP8 technology acquired by Google in its purchase of On2 Technologies in 2010. WEBP (usually pronounced "weppy") provides approximately 40 percent better compression than JPEG for the same image quality. Images can be used anywhere that you require a Drawable, such as the image and background of an ImageView.

Using images is simply a matter of putting your image files in res/drawable/ and then referencing them as a resource. Within layout files, images are referenced as @drawable/..., where the ellipsis is the base name of the file (e.g., for res/drawable/foo.png, the resource name is @drawable/foo). In Java, where you need an image resource ID, use R.drawable. plus the base name (e.g., R.drawable.foo).

So, let's update the previous example to use an icon for the button instead of the string resource. This can be found as Resources/Images. We slightly adjust the layout file, using an ImageButton and referencing a drawable named @drawable/icon, which refers to an image file in res/drawable with a base name of icon. In this case, we use a 32×32-pixel PNG file from the Nuvola icon set.

```xml
<?xml version="1.0" encoding="utf-8"?>
<LinearLayout xmlns:android="http://schemas.android.com/apk/res/android"
  android:orientation="vertical"
  android:layout_width="fill_parent"
  android:layout_height="fill_parent"
  >
  <LinearLayout
    android:orientation="horizontal"
    android:layout_width="fill_parent"
    android:layout_height="wrap_content"
    >
    <ImageButton android:id="@+id/format"
      android:layout_width="wrap_content"
      android:layout_height="wrap_content"
      android:src="@drawable/icon"
      android:onClick="applyFormat"
      />
    <EditText android:id="@+id/name"
      android:layout_width="fill_parent"
      android:layout_height="wrap_content"
      />
  </LinearLayout>
  <TextView android:id="@+id/result"
    android:layout_width="fill_parent"
    android:layout_height="wrap_content"
    />
</LinearLayout>
```

Now, our button has the desired icon, as shown in Figure 23–3.

Figure 23–3. *The ImagesDemo sample application*

XML: The Resource Way

If you wish to package static XML with your application, you can use an XML resource. Simply put the XML file in res/xml/, and you can access it by getXml() on a Resources object, supplying it a resource ID of R.xml. plus the base name of your XML file. For example, in an activity, with an XML file of words.xml, you could call getResources().getXml(R.xml.words). This returns an instance of an XmlPullParser, found in the org.xmlpull.v1 Java namespace.

An XML pull parser is event-driven: you keep calling next() on the parser to get the next event, which could be START_TAG, END_TAG, END_DOCUMENT, and so on. On a START_TAG event, you can access the tag's name and attributes; a single TEXT event represents the concatenation of all text nodes that are direct children of this element. By looping, testing, and invoking per-element logic, you parse the file.

To see this in action, let's rewrite the Java code for the Files/Static sample project to use an XML resource. This new project, Resources/XML, requires that you place the words.xml file from Static not in res/raw/, but in res/xml/. The layout stays the same, so all that needs to be replaced is the Java source:

```
package com.commonsware.android.resources;

import android.app.Activity;
import android.os.Bundle;
import android.app.ListActivity;
import android.view.View;
import android.widget.AdapterView;
```

```java
import android.widget.ArrayAdapter;
import android.widget.ListView;
import android.widget.TextView;
import android.widget.Toast;
import java.io.InputStream;
import java.util.ArrayList;
import org.xmlpull.v1.XmlPullParser;
import org.xmlpull.v1.XmlPullParserException;

public class XMLResourceDemo extends ListActivity {
  TextView selection;
  ArrayList<String> items=new ArrayList<String>();

  @Override
  public void onCreate(Bundle icicle) {
    super.onCreate(icicle);
    setContentView(R.layout.main);
    selection=(TextView)findViewById(R.id.selection);

    try {
      XmlPullParser xpp=getResources().getXml(R.xml.words);

      while (xpp.getEventType()!=XmlPullParser.END_DOCUMENT) {
        if (xpp.getEventType()==XmlPullParser.START_TAG) {
          if (xpp.getName().equals("word")) {
            items.add(xpp.getAttributeValue(0));
          }
        }

        xpp.next();
      }
    }
    catch (Throwable t) {
      Toast
        .makeText(this, "Request failed: "+t.toString(), Toast.LENGTH_LONG)
        .show();
    }

    setListAdapter(new ArrayAdapter<String>(this,
                        android.R.layout.simple_list_item_1,
                        items));
  }

  public void onListItemClick(ListView parent, View v, int position,
                  long id) {
    selection.setText(items.get(position).toString());
  }
}
```

Now, inside our try...catch block, we get our XmlPullParser and loop until the end of the document. If the current event is START_TAG and the name of the element is word (xpp.getName().equals("word")), then we get the one and only attribute and pop that into our list of items for the selection widget. Since we have complete control over the XML file, it is safe enough to assume there is exactly one attribute. In other cases, if you are not sure that the XML is properly defined, you might consider checking the attribute count (getAttributeCount()) and the name of the attribute (getAttributeName()), instead of assuming the 0-index attribute is what you think it is.

The result looks the same as before, albeit with a different name in the title bar, as shown in Figure 23–4.

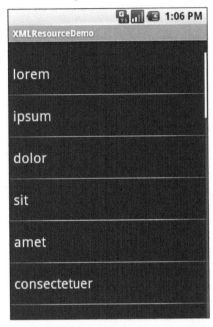

Figure 23–4. *The XMLResourceDemo sample application*

Miscellaneous Values

In the res/values/ directory, in addition to string resources, you can place one or more XML files describing other simple resources, such as dimensions, colors, and arrays. You have already seen uses of dimensions and colors in previous examples, where they were passed as simple strings (e.g., "10dip") as parameters to calls. You could set these up as Java static final objects and use their symbolic names, but that works only inside Java source, not in layout XML files. By putting these values in resource XML files, you can reference them from both Java and layouts, plus have them centrally located for easy editing.

Resource XML files have a root element of resources; everything else is a child of that root.

Dimensions

Dimensions are used in several places in Android to describe distances, such as a widget's padding. There are several different units of measurement available to you:

- in and mm for inches and millimeters, respectively. These are based on the actual size of the screen.

- pt for points. In publishing terms, a point is 1/72 inch (again, based on the actual physical size of the screen)

- dip and sp for device-independent pixels and scale-independent pixels, respectively. One pixel equals one dip for a 160-dpi resolution screen, with the ratio scaling based on the actual screen pixel density. Scale-independent pixels also take into account the user's preferred font size.

To encode a dimension as a resource, add a dimen element, with a name attribute for your unique name for this resource, and a single child text element representing the value:

```
<resources>
  <dimen name="thin">10px</dimen>
  <dimen name="fat">1in</dimen>
</resources>
```

In a layout, you can reference dimensions as @dimen/..., where the ellipsis is a placeholder for your unique name for the resource (e.g., thin and fat from the preceding sample). In Java, you reference dimension resources by the unique name prefixed with R.dimen. (e.g., Resources.getDimen(R.dimen.thin)).

Colors

Colors in Android are hexadecimal RGB values, with the option to also specify an alpha channel. You have your choice of single-character hex values or double-character hex values, providing four styles:

- #RGB

- #ARGB

- #RRGGBB

- #AARRGGBB

These work similarly to their counterparts in Cascading Style Sheets (CSS).

You can, of course, put these RGB values as string literals in Java source or layout resources. If you wish to turn them into resources, though, all you need to do is add color elements to the resource file, with a name attribute for your unique name for this color, and a single text element containing the RGB value itself:

```
<resources>
  <color name="yellow_orange">#FFD555</color>
  <color name="forest_green">#005500</color>
  <color name="burnt_umber">#8A3324</color>
</resources>
```

In a layout, you can reference colors as @color/..., replacing the ellipsis with your unique name for the color (e.g., burnt_umber). In Java, you reference color resources by the unique name prefixed with R.color. (e.g., Resources.getColor(R.color.forest_green)).

Arrays

Array resources are designed to hold lists of simple strings, such as a list of honorifics (Mr., Mrs., Ms., Dr., etc.).

In the resource file, you need one string-array element per array, with a name attribute for the unique name you are giving the array. Then, add one or more child item elements, each with a single text element containing the value for that entry in the array:

```
<?xml version="1.0" encoding="utf-8"?>
<resources>
  <string-array name="cities">
    <item>Philadelphia</item>
    <item>Pittsburgh</item>
    <item>Allentown/Bethlehem</item>
    <item>Erie</item>
    <item>Reading</item>
    <item>Scranton</item>
    <item>Lancaster</item>
    <item>Altoona</item>
    <item>Harrisburg</item>
  </string-array>
  <string-array name="airport_codes">
    <item>PHL</item>
    <item>PIT</item>
    <item>ABE</item>
    <item>ERI</item>
    <item>RDG</item>
    <item>AVP</item>
    <item>LNS</item>
    <item>AOO</item>
    <item>MDT</item>
  </string-array>
</resources>
```

From your Java code, you can then use Resources.getStringArray() to get a String[] of the items in the list. The parameter to getStringArray() is your unique name for the array, prefixed with R.array. (e.g., Resources.getStringArray(R.array.honorifics)).

Different Strokes for Different Folks

One set of resources may not fit all situations where your application may be used. One obvious area comes with string resources and dealing with internationalization (I18N) and localization (L10N). Putting strings all in one language works fine—at least for the developer—but covers only one language.

That is not the only scenario where resources might need to differ, though. Here are others:

- *Screen orientation*: Is the screen in a portrait or landscape orientation? Or is the screen square and, therefore, without an orientation?

- *Screen size*: How many pixels does the screen have, so you can size your resources accordingly (e.g., large versus small icons)?

- *Touchscreen*: Does the device have a touchscreen? If so, is the touchscreen set up to be used with a stylus or a finger?

- *Keyboard*: Which keyboard does the user have (QWERTY, numeric, neither), either now or as an option?

- *Other input*: Does the device have some other form of input, like a D-pad or click-wheel?

The way Android currently handles this is by having multiple resource directories, with the criteria for each embedded in its name.

Suppose, for example, you want to support strings in both English and Spanish. Normally, for a single-language setup, you would put your strings in a file named `res/values/strings.xml`. To support both English and Spanish, you would create two folders, `res/values-en/` and `res/values-es/`, where the value after the hyphen is the ISO 639-1 two-letter code for the language. Your English strings would go in `res/values-en/strings.xml` and the Spanish ones would go in `res/values-es/strings.xml`. Android will choose the proper file based on the user's device settings.

An even better approach is for you to consider some language to be your default, and put those strings in `res/values/strings.xml`. Then, create other resource directories for your translations (e.g., `res/values-es/strings.xml` for Spanish). Android will try to match a specific language set of resources; failing that, it will fall back to the default of `res/values/strings.xml`.

Seems easy, right?

Where things start to get complicated is when you need to use multiple disparate criteria for your resources. For example, suppose you want to develop for the following devices:

- HTC Nexus 1, which has a normal-size, high-density screen and no hardware keyboard

- Samsung Galaxy Tab, which has a large-size, high-density screen and no hardware keyboard

- Motorola Charm, which has a small-size, medium-density screen and a hardware keyboard

You may want to have somewhat different layouts for these devices, to take advantage of different screen real estate and different input options. Specifically, you may want the following:

- Different layouts for each combination of size, orientation, and keyboard
- Different drawables for each density

Once you get into these sorts of situations, though, all sorts of rules come into play, such as the following:

- The configuration options (e.g., -en) have a particular order of precedence, and they must appear in the directory name in that order. The Android documentation outlines the specific order in which these options can appear. For the purposes of this example, screen size is more important than screen orientation, which is more important than screen density, which is more important than whether or not the device has a keyboard.

- There can be only one value of each configuration option category per directory.

- Options are case sensitive.

So, for the sample scenario, in theory, we would need the following directories, representing the possible combinations:

- `res/layout-large-port-mdpi-qwerty`
- `res/layout-large-port-mdpi-nokeys`
- `res/layout-large-port-hdpi-qwerty`
- `res/layout-large-port-hdpi-nokeys`
- `res/layout-large-land-mdpi-qwerty`
- `res/layout-large-land-mdpi-nokeys`
- `res/layout-large-land-hdpi-qwerty`
- `res/layout-large-land-hdpi-nokeys`
- `res/layout-normal-port-mdpi-qwerty`
- `res/layout-normal-port-mdpi-nokeys`
- `res/layout-normal-port-finger-qwerty`
- `res/layout-normal-port-hdpi-nokeys`
- `res/layout-normal-land-mdpi-qwerty`
- `res/layout-normal-land-mdpi-nokeys`
- `res/layout-normal-land-hdpi-qwerty`

- `res/layout-normal-land-hdpi-nokeys`
- `res/drawable-large-port-mdpi-qwerty`
- `res/drawable-large-port-mdpi-nokeys`
- `res/drawable-large-port-hdpi-qwerty`
- `res/drawable-large-port-hdpi-nokeys`
- `res/drawable-large-land-mdpi-qwerty`
- `res/drawable-large-land-mdpi-nokeys`
- `res/drawable-large-land-hdpi-qwerty`
- `res/drawable-large-land-hdpi-nokeys`
- `res/drawable-normal-port-mdpi-qwerty`
- `res/drawable-normal-port-mdpi-nokeys`
- `res/drawable-normal-port-finger-qwerty`
- `res/drawable-normal-port-hdpi-nokeys`
- `res/drawable-normal-land-mdpi-qwerty`
- `res/drawable-normal-land-mdpi-nokeys`
- `res/drawable-normal-land-hdpi-qwerty`
- `res/drawable-normal-land-hdpi-nokeys`

Don't panic! We will shorten this list in just a moment!

Note that there is nothing preventing you from also having a directory with the unadorned base name (`res/layout`). In fact, this is really a good idea, in case future editions of the Android runtime introduce other configuration options you did not consider—having a default layout might make the difference between your application working or failing on that new device.

As promised, we can cut the number of required directories substantially. We do so by decoding the rules Android uses for determining which, among a set of candidates, is the correct resource directory to use:

1. Android tosses out directories that are specifically invalid. So, for example, if the screen size of the device is `normal`, Android drops the -large directories as candidates, since they call for some other size.

2. Android counts the number of matches for each folder, and pays attention to only those with the most matches.

3. Android goes in the order of precedence of the options; in other words, it goes from left to right in the directory name.

Also, our drawables vary only by density, and our layouts do not vary by density, so we can clear out a lot of combinations by focusing on only the relevant platform differences.

So, we could skate by with only the following configurations:

- res/layout-large-land-qwerty
- res/layout-large-qwerty
- res/layout-large-land
- res/layout-large
- res/layout-normal-land-qwerty
- res/layout-normal-qwerty
- res/layout-normal-land
- res/layout
- res/drawable-hdpi
- res/drawable

Here, we take advantage of the fact that specific matches take precedence over unspecified values. So, a device with a QWERTY keyboard will choose a resource with qwerty in the directory over a resource that does not specify its keyboard type.

We could refine this even further, to cover only the specific devices we are targeting (e.g., there is no large device with qwerty):

- res/layout-large-land
- res/layout-large
- res/layout-land-qwerty
- res/layout-qwerty
- res/layout-land
- res/layout
- res/drawable-hdpi
- res/drawable

If we did not care about having different layouts depending on whether the device had a hardware keyboard, we could drop the two -qwerty resource sets.

We will see these resource sets again in Chapter 25, which describes how to support multiple screen sizes.

RTL Languages: Going Both Ways

Android 2.3 added support for many more languages than it supported in previous versions of the platform. As such, you now have greater opportunity to localize your application where it is needed.

In particular, Android 2.3 added support for right-to-left (RTL) languages, notably Hebrew and Arabic. Previously, Android supported only languages written horizontally from left to right, such as English. This means you may create localized versions for RTL languages, but first you need to consider whether your UI in general will work properly for RTL languages. For example:

- Are your TextView widgets aligned on the left side with other widgets or containers? If so, is that the right configuration for your RTL users?

- Will there be any issues with your EditText widgets when users start entering RTL text, such as inappropriate scrolling because you have not properly constrained the EditText widget's width?

- If you created your own forms of text input, outside of EditText and the input method framework (e.g., custom onscreen virtual keyboards), will they support RTL languages?

Chapter 24

Defining and Using Styles

Every now and then, you will find some code with a cryptic style attribute in a layout element. For example, in the chapter on threading, the following ProgressBar was presented:

```xml
<?xml version="1.0" encoding="utf-8"?>
<LinearLayout xmlns:android="http://schemas.android.com/apk/res/android"
  android:orientation="vertical"
  android:layout_width="fill_parent"
  android:layout_height="fill_parent"
  >
  <ProgressBar android:id="@+id/progress"
    style="?android:attr/progressBarStyleHorizontal"
    android:layout_width="fill_parent"
    android:layout_height="wrap_content" />
</LinearLayout>
```

Something about that magic style attribute changed our ProgressBar from a normal circle to a horizontal bar.

This chapter briefly explores the concept of styles, including how you create them and how you apply them to your own widgets.

Styles: DIY DRY

The purpose of styles is to encapsulate a set of attributes that you intend to use repeatedly, conditionally, or otherwise keep separate from your layouts proper. The primary use case is "don't repeat yourself" (DRY)—if you have a bunch of widgets that look the same, use a style to use a single definition for "look the same," rather than copying the look from widget to widget.

That paragraph will make a bit more sense if we look at an example, specifically the Styles/NowStyled sample project. This is the same project we examined in an earlier chapter, with a full-screen button that shows the date and time at which the activity was launched or the button was pushed. In this example, we want to change the appearance of the text on the face of the button, which we will accomplish by using a style.

The res/layout/main.xml file in this project is the same as it was in Chapter 20, but with the addition of a style attribute:

```
<?xml version="1.0" encoding="utf-8"?>
<Button xmlns:android="http://schemas.android.com/apk/res/android"
  android:id="@+id/button"
  android:text=""
  android:layout_width="fill_parent"
  android:layout_height="fill_parent"
  style="@style/bigred"
/>
```

> **NOTE:** Because the style attribute is part of stock XML, and therefore is not in the android namespace, it does not get the android: prefix.

The value, @style/bigred, points to a style resource. Style resources are values resources and can be found in the res/values/ directory in your project, or in other resource sets (e.g., res/values-v11/ for values resources to be used only on API level 11 or higher). The convention is to keep style resources in a styles.xml file, such as the following from the NowStyled project:

```
<?xml version="1.0" encoding="utf-8"?>
<resources>
  <style name="bigred">
    <item name="android:textSize">30sp</item>
    <item name="android:textColor">#FFFF0000</item>
  </style>
</resources>
```

The <style> element supplies the name of the style, which is what we use when referring to the style from a layout. The <item> children of the <style> element represent values of attributes to be applied to whatever the style is applied to—in our example, our Button widget. So, our Button will have a comparatively large font (android:textSize set to 30sp) and its text will appear in red (android:textColor set to #FFFF0000).

No changes are needed elsewhere in the project—nothing needs to be adjusted in the manifest, in the Java code of the activity, and so on. Just defining the style and applying it to the widget gives us the result shown in Figure 24–1.

Figure 24–1. *The Styles/NowStyled sample application*

Elements of Style

There are four questions to consider when applying a style:

- Where do you put the style attributes to say you want to apply a style?
- Which attributes can you define via a style?
- How do you inherit from a previously defined style (your own or one from Android)?
- What values can the attributes have in a style definition?

Where to Apply a Style

The style attribute can be applied to a widget, which affects only that widget.

The style attribute can also be applied to a container, which affects only that container. However, doing this does not automatically style its children. For example, suppose res/layout/main.xml looked instead like this:

```
<?xml version="1.0" encoding="utf-8"?>
<LinearLayout xmlns:android="http://schemas.android.com/apk/res/android"
    android:layout_width="fill_parent"
    android:layout_height="fill_parent"
```

```
        style="@style/bigred"
  >
    <Button
      android:id="@+id/button"
      android:text=""
      android:layout_width="fill_parent"
      android:layout_height="fill_parent"
    />
</LinearLayout>
```

The resulting UI would not have the Button text in a big red font, despite the style attribute. The style affects only the container, not the contents of the container.

You can also apply a style to an activity or an application as a whole, in which case it is referred to as a *theme*, as covered a bit later in this chapter.

The Available Attributes

When styling a widget or container, you can apply any of that widget's or container's attributes in the style itself. So, if it appears in the "XML Attributes" or "Inherited XML Attributes" section of the Android JavaDocs, you can put it in a style.

Note that Android will ignore invalid styles. So, had we applied the bigred style to the LinearLayout as shown above, everything would run fine, just with no visible results. Despite the fact that LinearLayout has no android:textSize or android:textColor attribute, no compile-time failure or runtime exception occurs.

Also, layout directives, such as android:layout_width, can be put in a style.

Inheriting a Style

You can also indicate that you want to inherit style attributes from another style, by specifying a parent attribute on the <style> element. For example, take a look at this style resource (which you will see again in Chapter 28, which covers UI design using the fragment framework):

```
<?xml version="1.0" encoding="utf-8"?>
<resources>
  <style name="activated" parent="android:Theme.Holo">
    <item name="android:background">?android:attr/activatedBackgroundIndicator</item>
  </style>
</resources>
```

Here, we are indicating that we want to inherit the Theme.Holo style from within Android. Hence, in addition to specifying all of our own attribute definitions, we are specifying that we want all the attribute definitions from Theme.Holo as well.

In many cases, this will not be necessary. If you do not specify a parent, your attribute definitions will be blended into whatever default style is being applied to the widget or container.

The Possible Values

Typically, the value that you will give the attributes in the style will be some constant, like 30sp or #FFFF0000. Sometimes, though, you may want to perform a bit of indirection, by applying some other attribute value from the theme from which you are inheriting. In that case, you need to use the somewhat cryptic ?android:attr/ syntax, along with a few related magic incantations.

For example, let's look again at this style resource:

```xml
<?xml version="1.0" encoding="utf-8"?>
<resources>
  <style name="activated" parent="android:Theme.Holo">
    <item name="android:background">?android:attr/activatedBackgroundIndicator</item>
  </style>
</resources>
```

Here, we are indicating that the value of android:background is not some constant value, or even a reference to a drawable resource (e.g., @drawable/my_background). Instead, we are referring to the value of some other attribute—activatedBackgroundIndicator—from our inherited theme. Whatever the theme defines as being the activatedBackgroundIndicator is what our background should be.

Sometimes this is applied to a style as a whole. For example, let's look again at the ProgressBar:

```xml
<?xml version="1.0" encoding="utf-8"?>
<LinearLayout xmlns:android="http://schemas.android.com/apk/res/android"
  android:orientation="vertical"
  android:layout_width="fill_parent"
  android:layout_height="fill_parent"
  >
  <ProgressBar android:id="@+id/progress"
    style="?android:attr/progressBarStyleHorizontal"
    android:layout_width="fill_parent"
    android:layout_height="wrap_content" />
</LinearLayout>
```

Here, our style attribute—not a style resource—is pointing to a theme-supplied attribute (progressBarStyleHorizontal). If you poke through the Android source code, you will see that this is defined as being a style resource, specifically @android:style/Widget.ProgressBar.Horizontal. Hence, we are saying to Android that we want our ProgressBar styled as @android:style/Widget.ProgressBar.Horizontal, via the indirection of ?android:attr/progressBarStyleHorizontal.

This portion of the Android style system is still very underdocumented, even with the latest release of Android 4.0 Ice Cream Sandwich—the entire inheritance topic is three short paragraphs. Google itself recommends that you look at the Android source code listing the various styles to see what is possible.

This is one place where inheriting a style becomes important. In the first example shown in this section, we inherited from Theme.Holo, because we specifically wanted the activatedBackgroundIndicator value from Theme.Holo. That value might not exist in other styles, or it might not have the value we want.

Themes: A Style by Any Other Name...

Themes are styles applied to an activity or application via an android:theme attribute on the <activity> or <application> element. If the theme you are applying is your own, simply reference it as @style/..., just as you would in a style attribute of a widget. If the theme you are applying comes from Android, though, typically you will use a value with @android:style/ as the prefix, such as @android:style/Theme.Dialog or @android:style/Theme.Light.

In a theme, your focus is not so much on styling widgets, but styling the activity itself. For example, here is the definition of @android:style/Theme.NoTitleBar.Fullscreen:

```
<!-- Variant of the default (dark) theme that has no title bar and
  fills the entire screen -->
<style name="Theme.NoTitleBar.Fullscreen">
  <item name="android:windowFullscreen">true</item>
  <item name="android:windowContentOverlay">@null</item>
</style>
```

It specifies that the activity should take over the entire screen, removing the status bar on Android 1.x and 2.x devices (android:windowFullscreen set to true), and the action bar on Android 3.x and 4.x devices. It also specifies that the content overlay—a layout that wraps around your activity's content view—should be set to nothing (android:windowContentOverlay set to @null), having the effect of removing the title bar.

A theme might also specify other styles that are applied to specific widgets. For example, we see the following in the root theme (Theme):

```
<item name="progressBarStyleHorizontal">@android:style/Widget.ProgressBar↩
.Horizontal</item>
```

Here, progressBarStyleHorizontal is pointing to @android:style/ Widget.ProgressBar.Horizontal. This is how we are able to reference ?android:attr/progressBarStyleHorizontal in our ProgressBar widget, and we could create our own theme that redefines progressBarStyleHorizontal to point to some other style (e.g., if we want to change the rounded rectangle used for the actual progress bar image itself).

Honeycomb and Tablets

Chapter 25

Handling Multiple Screen Sizes

For the first year or so after Android 1.0 was released, all production Android devices had the same screen resolution (HVGA, 320×480 pixels) and size (around 3.5 inches, or 9 centimeters). Starting in late 2009, though, devices started arriving with widely disparate screen sizes and resolutions, from tiny QVGA (240×320) screens to much larger WVGA (480×800) screens. In late 2010, tablets and Google TV devices appeared, offering yet more screen sizes, and with the release of Honeycomb and Ice Cream Sandwich, tablet and larger screen sizes exploded.

Of course, users will expect your application to be functional on all of these screens, and perhaps take advantage of larger screen sizes to add greater value. To that end, Android 1.6 added new capabilities to help better support these differing screen sizes and resolutions, and these capabilities have been extended in subsequent Android releases. With the release of Android 3.0, the optional fragment system was introduced as a more capable—though more complex—way of handling differing screen sizes. The Android documentation has extensive coverage of the mechanics of handling multiple screen sizes using both the traditional and fragment approaches. You are encouraged to read that documentation along with this chapter (and Chapter 28) to understand fully how best to cope with, and perhaps take advantage of, multiple screen sizes.

This chapter will deal with the more theoretical and abstract design ideas, with a number of sections discussing the screen size options and theory. We'll then move on to provide an in-depth look at how to make a fairly simple application handle multiple screen sizes well. This chapter will eschew the added complexity of fragments, but don't fear: we'll return to the topic and fragments in Chapter 28.

Taking the Default

Let's suppose that you start off by totally ignoring the issue of screen sizes and resolutions. What happens?

If your application is compiled for Android 1.5 or lower, Android will assume your application was designed to look good on the classic screen size and resolution. Android will then automatically do the following:

- If your application is installed on a device with a larger screen, Android will run your application in compatibility mode, scaling everything based on the actual screen size. So, suppose you have a 24-pixel square PNG file, and Android installs and runs your application on a device with the standard physical size but a WVGA resolution (a so-called high-density screen). Android might scale your PNG file to be 36 pixels when it displays it, so it will take up the same visible space on the screen. On the plus side, Android handles this automatically; on the minus side, bitmap-scaling algorithms tend to make the images a bit fuzzy.

- If your application is installed on a device with a smaller screen, Android will block your application from running. Hence, QVGA devices, like the HTC Tattoo, will be unable to get your application, even if it is available on the Android Market.

To give you an example of how this affects your app, Figure 25–1 shows the `Containers/Table` sample application as viewed on an HTC Tattoo, with its QVGA screen.

Figure 25–1. *Table sample in QVGA via compatibility mode*

If your application is compiled for Android 1.6 or higher, Android assumes that you are properly handling all screen sizes, and therefore will not run your application in compatibility mode. Given the huge improvements in successive releases, especially Android 2.2, 3.0, and 4.0, few if any developers will be targeting pre-1.6 releases. That means you'll almost invariably take this approach of handling screen size management yourself. You will see how to tailor this in a later section.

Whole in One

The simplest approach to handling multiple screen sizes in Android is to design your user interface (UI) so that it automatically scales for the screen size, without any size-specific code or resources. In other words, "it just works."

This implies, though, that everything you use in your UI can be gracefully scaled by Android and that everything will fit, even on a QVGA screen.

The following sections provide some tips for achieving this all-in-one solution.

Think About Rules, Not Positions

Some developers, perhaps those coming from the drag-and-drop school of UI development, think first and foremost about the positions of widgets. They think that they want certain widgets to be certain fixed sizes at certain fixed locations. They get frustrated with Android layout managers (containers) and gravitate to the deprecated `AbsoluteLayout` as a way to design UIs in the way they are used to doing it.

That approach rarely works well, even on desktops, as can be seen in applications that do not handle window resizing very well. Similarly, that approach will not work on mobile devices, particularly Android, with their wide range of screen sizes and resolutions.

Instead of thinking about positions, think about rules. You need to teach Android the "business rules" about where widgets should be sized and placed, and then Android will interpret those rules based on what the device's screen actually supports in terms of resolution.

The simplest rules are the `fill_parent` and `wrap_content` values for `android:layout_width` and `android:layout_height`. They do not specify specific sizes, but rather adapt to the space available.

The richest environment for easily specifying rules is `RelativeLayout`. While complicated on the surface, `RelativeLayout` does an excellent job of letting you control your layout while still adapting it to other screen sizes. For example, you can do the following:

- Explicitly anchor widgets to the bottom or right side of the screen, rather than hoping they will wind up there courtesy of some other layout

- Control the distances between widgets that are connected (e.g., a label for a field should be to the left of the field) without having to rely on padding or margins

The greatest control for specifying rules is to create your own layout class. For example, suppose you are creating a series of applications that implement card games. You may want to have a layout class that knows the following about playing cards: how they overlap, which are face up versus face down, how big it should be to handle varying numbers of cards, and so forth. While you could achieve the desired look with, say, a `RelativeLayout`, you may be better served implementing a `PlayingCardLayout` or a `HandOfCardsLayout` or something that is more explicitly tailored for your application. Unfortunately, creating custom layout classes is underdocumented at this point in time.

Consider Physical Dimensions

Android offers a wide range of available units of measure for dimensions. The most popular has been the pixel (px), because it is easy to wrap your head around the concept. After all, every Android device has a screen with a certain number of pixels in each direction.

However, pixels start to become troublesome as screen density changes. As the number of pixels in a given screen size increases, the pixels effectively shrink. A 32-pixel icon on a traditional Android device might be finger-friendly, but on a high-density device (say, WVGA in a mobile phone form factor), 32 pixels may be a bit small for use with a finger.

If you have something intrinsically scalable (e.g., a `Button`) for which you had been specifying a size in pixels, you might consider switching to using millimeters (mm) or inches (in) as the unit of measure. 10 millimeters is 10 millimeters regardless of the screen resolution or the screen size. This way, you can ensure that your widget is sized to be finger-friendly, regardless of the number of pixels that might take.

Avoid "Real" Pixels

In some circumstances, using millimeters for dimensions does not make sense. In such cases, you may want to consider using other units of measure while still avoiding "real" pixels.

Android offers dimensions measured in density-independent pixels (dip). These map 1:1 to pixels for a 160-dpi screen (e.g., a classic HVGA Android device) and scale from there. For example, on a 240-dpi device (e.g., a phone-sized WVGA device), the ratio is 2:3, so 50dip = 50px at 160 dpi and = 75px at 240 dpi. The advantage to the user of going with dip is that the actual size of the dimension stays the same, so visibly there is no difference between 50dip at 160 dpi and 50dip at 240 dpi.

Android also offers dimensions measured in scaled pixels (sp). Scaled pixels, in theory, are scaled based on the user's choice of font size (FONT_SCALE value in `System.Settings`).

Choose Scalable Drawables

Classic bitmaps—PNG, JPG, BMP, and GIF—are not intrinsically scalable, nor is the latest image format supported in Android 4.0—WEBP. If you are not running in compatibility mode, Android will not even try to scale these for you based on screen resolution and size. Whatever size of bitmap you supply is the size it will be, even if that makes the image too large or too small on some screens.

One way to address this is to try to avoid static bitmaps, using nine-patch bitmaps and XML-defined drawables (e.g., GradientDrawable) as alternatives. A nine-patch bitmap is a PNG file specially encoded to have rules indicating how that image can be stretched to take up more space. XML-defined drawables use a quasi-SVG XML language to define shapes, their strokes and fills, and so on.

Tailor-Made, Just for You (and You, and You, and...)

There will be times when you want to have different looks or behaviors based on screen size or density. Android has techniques that you can use to switch out resources or code blocks based on the environment in which your application runs. When these techniques are properly used in combination with the techniques described in the preceding section, achieving screen size- and density-independence is eminently possible, at least for devices running Android 1.6 and newer.

Adding the <supports-screens> Element

The first step to proactively supporting different screen sizes is to add the <supports-screens> element to your AndroidManifest.xml file. This specifies which screen sizes your application explicitly supports and which it does not support. Those that it does not explicitly support will be handled by the automatic compatibility mode, described previously.

Here is a manifest containing a <supports-screens> element:

```xml
<?xml version="1.0" encoding="utf-8"?>
<manifest xmlns:android="http://schemas.android.com/apk/res/android"
  package="com.commonsware.android.eu4you"
  android:versionCode="1"
  android:versionName="1.0">
  <supports-screens
    android:largeScreens="true"
    android:normalScreens="true"
    android:smallScreens="true"
    android:anyDensity="true"
  />
  <application android:label="@string/app_name"
    android:icon="@drawable/cw">
    <activity android:name=".EU4You"
              android:label="@string/app_name">
      <intent-filter>
        <action android:name="android.intent.action.MAIN" />
        <category android:name="android.intent.category.LAUNCHER" />
      </intent-filter>
    </activity>
  </application>
</manifest>
```

The android:smallScreens, android:normalScreens, and android:largeScreens attributes are fairly self-explanatory: each takes a Boolean value that indicates whether your application explicitly supports screens of that size (true) or requires compatibility mode assistance (false). Android 2.3 has also added android:xlargeScreens for larger tablets, televisions, and more (theatres, anyone?).

The android:anyDensity attribute indicates whether you are taking density into account in your calculations (true) or not (false). If false, Android will treat all of your dimensions (e.g., 4px) as if they were for a normal-density (160-dpi) screen. If your application is running on a screen with lower or higher density, Android will scale your dimensions accordingly. If you indicate that android:anyDensity = "true", you are telling Android not to do that, putting the onus on you to use density-independent units, such as dip, mm, or in.

Resources and Resource Sets

The primary way to toggle different things based on screen size or density is to create resource sets. By creating resource sets that are specific to different device characteristics, you teach Android how to render each, and Android then switches among those sets automatically.

Default Scaling

By default, Android scales all drawable resources. Those that are intrinsically scalable, as previously described, will scale nicely. Ordinary bitmaps are scaled using a normal scaling algorithm, which may or may not give you great results. It also may slow down your application a bit. To avoid this, you need to set up separate resource sets containing your nonscalable bitmaps.

Density-Based Sets

If you wish to have different layouts, dimensions, or the like based on different screen densities, you can use the -ldpi, -mdpi, -hdpi, and -xhdpi resource set labels. For example, res/values-hdpi/dimens.xml would contain dimensions used in high-density devices.

Note that there is a bug in Android 1.5 (API level 3) when it comes to working with these screen-density resource sets. Even though all Android 1.5 devices are medium density, Android 1.5 might pick one of the other densities by accident. If you intend to support Android 1.5 and use screen-density resource sets, you need to clone the contents of your -mdpi set, with the clone named -mdpi-v3. This version-based set is described in greater detail a bit later in this section.

Size-Based Sets

Similarly, if you wish to have different resource sets based on screen size, Android offers
-small, -normal, -large, and -xlarge resource set labels. Creating res/layout-large-
land/ would indicate layouts to use on large screens (e.g., WVGA) in landscape
orientation.

Version-Based Sets

There may be times when earlier versions of Android get confused by newer resource
set labels. To help with that, you can add a version label to your resource set, of the
form -vN, where N is an API level. Hence, res/drawable-large-v4/ indicates these
drawables should be used on large screens at API level 4 (Android 1.6) and newer.

So, if you find that Android 1.5 emulators or devices are grabbing the wrong resource
sets, consider adding -v4 to their resource set names to filter them out.

Finding Your Size

If you need to take different actions in your Java code based on screen size or density,
you have a few options.

If there is something distinctive in your resource sets, you can "sniff" based on that and
branch accordingly in your code. For example, as you will see in the code sample later
in this chapter, you can have extra widgets in some layouts (e.g., res/layout-
large/main.xml); simply seeing if an extra widget exists will tell you if you are running a
large screen or not.

You can also find out your screen size class via a Configuration object, typically obtained
by an Activity via getResources().getConfiguration(). A Configuration object has a
public field named screenLayout that is a bitmask indicating the type of screen the
application is running on. You can test to see if your screen is small, normal, or large, or if
it is long (where "long" indicates a 16:9 or similar aspect ratio, compared to 4:3). For
example, here we test to see if we are running on a large screen:

```
if (getResources().getConfiguration().screenLayout
      & Configuration.SCREENLAYOUT_SIZE_LARGE)
    ==Configuration.SCREENLAYOUT_SIZE_LARGE) {
 // yes, we are large
}
else {
 // no, we are not
}
```

Similarly, you can find out your screen density, or the exact number of pixels in your
screen size, using the DisplayMetrics class.

Ain't Nothing Like the Real Thing

The Android emulators will help you test your application on different screen sizes. However, that will only get you so far, because mobile device LCDs have different characteristics from those of your desktop or notebook, such as the following:

- Mobile device LCDs may have a much higher density than that of your development machine.

- A mouse allows for much more precise touchscreen input than does an actual fingertip.

Where possible, you are going to need to either use the emulator in new and exciting ways or try to get your hands on actual devices with alternative screen resolutions.

Density Differs

The Motorola DROID has a 240-dpi, 3.7-inch, 480×854-pixel screen (an FWVGA display). To emulate a DROID screen, based on pixel count, takes up one-third of a 19-inch, 1280×1024-pixel LCD monitor, because the LCD monitor's density is much lower than that of the DROID—around 96 dpi. So, when you fire up your Android emulator for an FWVGA display like that of the DROID, you will get a massive emulator window.

This is still perfectly fine for determining the overall look of your application in an FWVGA environment. Regardless of density, widgets will still align the same, sizes will have the same relationships (e.g., widget A might be twice as tall as widget B, and that will be true regardless of density), and so on.

However, keep the following in mind:

- Things that might appear to be a suitable size when viewed on a 19-inch LCD may be entirely too small on a mobile device screen of the same resolution.

- Things that you can easily click with a mouse in the emulator may be much too small to pick out on a physically smaller and denser screen when used with a finger.

Adjusting the Density

By default, the emulator keeps the pixel count accurate at the expense of density, which is why you get the really big emulator window. You do have an option, though, of having the emulator keep the density accurate at the expense of pixel count.

The easiest way to do this is to use the Android AVD Manager, introduced in Android 1.6. The Android 2.0 edition of this tool has a Launch Options dialog box that pops up when you start an emulator instance via the Start button, as shown in Figure 25–2.

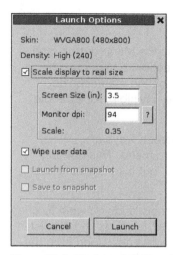

Figure 25–2. *The Launch Options dialog box*

By default, the "Scale display to real size" check box is unchecked, and Android will open the emulator window normally. You can check that check box and then provide two bits of scaling information:

- The screen size of the device you wish to emulate, in inches (e.g., 3.7 inches for the Motorola DROID)

- The dpi of your monitor (click the ? button to open a calculator that helps you determine what your dpi value is)

This gives you an emulator window that more accurately depicts what your user interface will look like on a physical device, at least in terms of sizes. However, since the emulator is using far fewer pixels than will a device, fonts may be difficult to read, images may be blocky, and so forth.

Ruthlessly Exploiting the Situation

So far, we have focused on how you can ensure that your layouts look decent on other screen sizes. For screens that are smaller than the norm (e.g., QVGA), that is perhaps all you can hope to achieve.

Once you get into larger screens, though, another possibility emerges: using different layouts designed to take advantage of the extra screen space. This is particularly useful when the physical screen size is larger (e.g., a 5-inch LCD like that on the Dell Streak Android tablet, or a 7-inch LCD like that on the Samsung Galaxy Tab), rather than simply having more pixels in the same physical space.

The following sections describe some ways you might take advantage of additional space.

Replace Menus with Buttons

An options menu selection requires two physical actions: press the Menu button, and then tap on the appropriate menu choice. A context menu selection requires two physical actions as well: long-tap on the widget, and then tap on the menu choice. Context menus have the additional problem of being effectively invisible; for example, users may not realize that your ListView has a context menu.

You might consider augmenting your UI to provide direct onscreen ways of accomplishing things that might otherwise be hidden away on a menu. This not only reduces the number of steps a user needs to take to do things, but also makes those options more obvious.

For example, suppose you are creating a media player application, and you want to offer manual playlist management. You have an activity that displays the songs in a playlist in a ListView. On an options menu, you have an Add choice, to add a new song from the ones on the device to the playlist. On a context menu on the ListView, you have a Remove choice, plus Move Up and Move Down choices to reorder the songs in the list. For large screens, though, you might consider adding four ImageButton widgets to your UI for these four options, with the three from the context menu enabled only when a row is selected by the D-pad or trackball. On regular or small screens, you would stick with just using the menus.

Replace Tabs with a Simple Activity

You may have introduced a TabHost into your UI to allow you to display more widgets in the available screen space. As long as the widget space you save by moving them to a separate tab is larger than the space taken up by the tabs themselves, you win. However, having multiple tabs means more user steps to navigate your UI, particularly if the user needs to flip back and forth between tabs frequently.

If you have only two tabs, consider changing your UI to offer a large-screen layout that removes the tabs and puts all the widgets on one screen (or again, wait for the discussion on fragments in Chapter 28). This enables the user to see everything without having to switch tabs all the time.

If you have three or more tabs, you probably lack screen space to put all those tabs' contents on one activity. However, you might consider going half and half: have popular widgets be on the activity all of the time, leaving your TabHost to handle the rest on (roughly) half of the screen.

Consolidate Multiple Activities

The most powerful technique is to use a larger screen to get rid of activity transitions outright. For example, if you have a ListActivity where clicking on an item brings up that item's details in a separate activity, consider supporting a large-screen layout where the details are on the same activity as the ListView (e.g., ListView on the left, details on the right, in a landscape layout). This eliminates the user having to constantly press the Back button to leave one set of details before viewing another.

You will see this technique applied in the sample code presented in the following section.

Example: EU4You

To examine how to use some of the techniques introduced in the previous sections, let's look at the ScreenSizes/EU4You sample application. This application has one activity (EU4You) that contains a ListView with the roster of European Union members and their respective flags. Clicking on one of the countries brings up the mobile Wikipedia page for that country.

In the source code to this book, you will find four versions of this application. We start with an application that is ignorant of screen size and slowly add in more screen-related features.

The First Cut

First, here is our AndroidManifest.xml file, which looks distinctly like the one shown earlier in this chapter:

```
<?xml version="1.0" encoding="utf-8"?>
<manifest xmlns:android="http://schemas.android.com/apk/res/android"
  package="com.commonsware.android.eu4you"
  android:versionCode="1"
  android:versionName="1.0">
  <supports-screens
    android:xlargeScreens="true"
    android:largeScreens="true"
    android:normalScreens="true"
    android:smallScreens="true"
    android:anyDensity="true"
  />
  <application android:label="@string/app_name"
    android:icon="@drawable/cw">
    <activity android:name=".EU4You"
              android:label="@string/app_name">
      <intent-filter>
        <action android:name="android.intent.action.MAIN" />
        <category android:name="android.intent.category.LAUNCHER" />
      </intent-filter>
    </activity>
  </application>
</manifest>
```

Note that we have included the <supports-screens> element, which indicates that we do indeed support all screen sizes. This blocks most of the automatic scaling that Android would do if we did not specify that we support certain screen sizes.

Our main layout is size-independent, as it is just a full-screen ListView:

```xml
<?xml version="1.0" encoding="utf-8"?>
<ListView xmlns:android="http://schemas.android.com/apk/res/android"
  android:id="@android:id/list"
  android:layout_width="fill_parent"
  android:layout_height="fill_parent"
/>
```

Our row, though, will eventually need some tweaking:

```xml
<?xml version="1.0" encoding="utf-8"?>
<LinearLayout xmlns:android="http://schemas.android.com/apk/res/android"
  android:layout_width="fill_parent"
  android:layout_height="wrap_content"
  android:padding="2dip"
  android:minHeight="?android:attr/listPreferredItemHeight"
>
  <ImageView android:id="@+id/flag"
    android:layout_width="wrap_content"
    android:layout_height="wrap_content"
    android:layout_gravity="center_vertical|left"
    android:paddingRight="4dip"
  />
  <TextView android:id="@+id/name"
    android:layout_width="wrap_content"
    android:layout_height="wrap_content"
    android:layout_gravity="center_vertical|right"
    android:textSize="20dip"
  />
</LinearLayout>
```

For example, right now, our font size is set to 20dip, which will not vary by screen size or density.

Our EU4You activity is a bit verbose, mostly because there are a lot of EU members, so we need to have the smarts to display the flag and the text in the row:

```java
package com.commonsware.android.eu4you;

import android.app.ListActivity;
import android.content.Intent;
import android.net.Uri;
import android.os.Bundle;
import android.view.View;
import android.view.ViewGroup;
import android.widget.ArrayAdapter;
import android.widget.ImageView;
import android.widget.ListView;
import android.widget.TextView;
import java.util.ArrayList;

public class EU4You extends ListActivity {
  static private ArrayList<Country> EU=new ArrayList<Country>();

  static {
    EU.add(new Country(R.string.austria, R.drawable.austria,
                       R.string.austria_url));
    EU.add(new Country(R.string.belgium, R.drawable.belgium,
                       R.string.belgium_url));
```

```java
        EU.add(new Country(R.string.bulgaria, R.drawable.bulgaria,
                    R.string.bulgaria_url));
        EU.add(new Country(R.string.cyprus, R.drawable.cyprus,
                    R.string.cyprus_url));
        EU.add(new Country(R.string.czech_republic,
                    R.drawable.czech_republic,
                    R.string.czech_republic_url));
        EU.add(new Country(R.string.denmark, R.drawable.denmark,
                    R.string.denmark_url));
        EU.add(new Country(R.string.estonia, R.drawable.estonia,
                    R.string.estonia_url));
        EU.add(new Country(R.string.finland, R.drawable.finland,
                    R.string.finland_url));
        EU.add(new Country(R.string.france, R.drawable.france,
                    R.string.france_url));
        EU.add(new Country(R.string.germany, R.drawable.germany,
                    R.string.germany_url));
        EU.add(new Country(R.string.greece, R.drawable.greece,
                    R.string.greece_url));
        EU.add(new Country(R.string.hungary, R.drawable.hungary,
                    R.string.hungary_url));
        EU.add(new Country(R.string.ireland, R.drawable.ireland,
                    R.string.ireland_url));
        EU.add(new Country(R.string.italy, R.drawable.italy,
                    R.string.italy_url));
        EU.add(new Country(R.string.latvia, R.drawable.latvia,
                    R.string.latvia_url));
        EU.add(new Country(R.string.lithuania, R.drawable.lithuania,
                    R.string.lithuania_url));
        EU.add(new Country(R.string.luxembourg, R.drawable.luxembourg,
                    R.string.luxembourg_url));
        EU.add(new Country(R.string.malta, R.drawable.malta,
                    R.string.malta_url));
        EU.add(new Country(R.string.netherlands, R.drawable.netherlands,
                    R.string.netherlands_url));
        EU.add(new Country(R.string.poland, R.drawable.poland,
                    R.string.poland_url));
        EU.add(new Country(R.string.portugal, R.drawable.portugal,
                    R.string.portugal_url));
        EU.add(new Country(R.string.romania, R.drawable.romania,
                    R.string.romania_url));
        EU.add(new Country(R.string.slovakia, R.drawable.slovakia,
                    R.string.slovakia_url));
        EU.add(new Country(R.string.slovenia, R.drawable.slovenia,
                    R.string.slovenia_url));
        EU.add(new Country(R.string.spain, R.drawable.spain,
                    R.string.spain_url));
        EU.add(new Country(R.string.sweden, R.drawable.sweden,
                    R.string.sweden_url));
        EU.add(new Country(R.string.united_kingdom,
                    R.drawable.united_kingdom,
                    R.string.united_kingdom_url));
    }

    @Override
    public void onCreate(Bundle savedInstanceState) {
```

```java
    super.onCreate(savedInstanceState);
    setContentView(R.layout.main);
    setListAdapter(new CountryAdapter());
}

@Override
protected void onListItemClick(ListView l, View v,
                               int position, long id) {
    startActivity(new Intent(Intent.ACTION_VIEW,
                       Uri.parse(getString(EU.get(position).url))));
}

static class Country {
    int name;
    int flag;
    int url;

    Country(int name, int flag, int url) {
        this.name=name;
        this.flag=flag;
        this.url=url;
    }
}

class CountryAdapter extends ArrayAdapter<Country> {
    CountryAdapter() {
        super(EU4You.this, R.layout.row, R.id.name, EU);
    }

    @Override
    public View getView(int position, View convertView,
                        ViewGroup parent) {
        CountryWrapper wrapper=null;

        if (convertView==null) {
            convertView=getLayoutInflater().inflate(R.layout.row, null);
            wrapper=new CountryWrapper(convertView);
            convertView.setTag(wrapper);
        }
        else {
            wrapper=(CountryWrapper)convertView.getTag();
        }

        wrapper.populateFrom(getItem(position));

        return(convertView);
    }
}

class CountryWrapper {
    private TextView name=null;
    private ImageView flag=null;
    private View row=null;

    CountryWrapper(View row) {
        this.row=row;
```

```
      }

    TextView getName() {
      if (name==null) {
        name=(TextView)row.findViewById(R.id.name);
      }

      return(name);
    }

    ImageView getFlag() {
      if (flag==null) {
        flag=(ImageView)row.findViewById(R.id.flag);
      }

      return(flag);
    }

    void populateFrom(Country nation) {
      getName().setText(nation.name);
      getFlag().setImageResource(nation.flag);
    }
  }
}
```

Figures 25–3, 25–4, and 25–5 show what the activity looks like in an ordinary HVGA emulator, a WVGA emulator, and a QVGA screen, respectively.

Figure 25–3. *EU4You, original version, HVGA*

Figure 25–4. *EU4You, original version, WVGA (800×480 pixels)*

Figure 25–5. *EU4You, original version, QVGA*

Fixing the Fonts

The first problem that should be fixed is the font size. As you can see, with a fixed 20-pixel size, the font ranges from big to tiny, depending on screen size and density. For a WVGA screen, the font may be rather difficult to read.

We could put the dimension as a resource (res/values/dimens.xml) and have different versions of that resource based on screen size or density. However, it is simpler to just specify a density-independent size, such as 5mm, as seen in the ScreenSizes/EU4You_2 project:

```xml
<?xml version="1.0" encoding="utf-8"?>
<LinearLayout xmlns:android="http://schemas.android.com/apk/res/android"
  android:layout_width="fill_parent"
  android:layout_height="wrap_content"
  android:padding="2dip"
  android:minHeight="?android:attr/listPreferredItemHeight"
>
  <ImageView android:id="@+id/flag"
    android:layout_width="wrap_content"
    android:layout_height="wrap_content"
    android:layout_gravity="center_vertical|left"
    android:paddingRight="4dip"
  />
  <TextView android:id="@+id/name"
    android:layout_width="wrap_content"
    android:layout_height="wrap_content"
    android:layout_gravity="center_vertical|right"
    android:textSize="5mm"
  />
</LinearLayout>
```

Figures 25–6, 25–7, and 25–8 show what the new activity looks like on HVGA, WVGA, and QVGA screens, respectively.

Figure 25–6. *EU4You, 5mm font version, HVGA*

Figure 25–7. *EU4You, 5mm font version, WVGA (800×480 pixels)*

Figure 25–8. *EU4You, 5mm font version, QVGA*

Now our font is a consistent size and large enough to match the flags.

Fixing the Icons

So, what about those icons? They should vary in size as well, since they are the same for all three emulators.

However, Android automatically scales bitmap resources, even with `<supports-screens>` and its attributes set to `true`. On the plus side, this means you may not have to do anything with these bitmaps. However, you are relying on a device to do the scaling, which definitely costs CPU time (and, hence, battery life). Also, the scaling algorithms that the device uses may not be optimal, compared to what you can do with graphics tools on your development machine.

The `ScreenSizes/EU4You_3` project creates `res/drawable-ldpi` and `res/drawable-hdpi`, putting in smaller and larger renditions of the flags, respectively. This project also renames `res/drawable` to `res/drawable-mdpi`. Android will use the flags for the appropriate screen density, depending on what the device or emulator needs.

Because this effect is subtle and will not show up well in this book, screenshots aren't provided.

Using the Space

While the activity looks fine on WVGA in portrait mode, it really wastes a lot of space in landscape mode, as shown in Figure 25–9.

Figure 25–9. *EU4You, landscape WVGA (800×480 pixels)*

We can put that space to better use by having the Wikipedia content appear directly on the main activity when in large-screen landscape mode; that saves having to spawn a separate browser activity.

To do this, we first must clone the main.xml layout into a res/layout-large-land rendition that incorporates a WebView widget, as seen in ScreenSizes/EU4You_4:

```xml
<?xml version="1.0" encoding="utf-8"?>
<LinearLayout xmlns:android="http://schemas.android.com/apk/res/android"
  android:layout_width="fill_parent"
  android:layout_height="fill_parent"
>
  <ListView
    android:id="@android:id/list"
    android:layout_width="fill_parent"
    android:layout_height="fill_parent"
    android:layout_weight="1"
  />
  <WebView
    android:id="@+id/browser"
    android:layout_width="fill_parent"
    android:layout_height="fill_parent"
    android:layout_weight="1"
  />
</LinearLayout>
```

Then, we need to adjust our activity to look for that WebView and use it if found, and otherwise to default to launching a browser activity:

```java
@Override
public void onCreate(Bundle savedInstanceState) {
  super.onCreate(savedInstanceState);
  setContentView(R.layout.main);

  browser=(WebView)findViewById(R.id.browser);

  setListAdapter(new CountryAdapter());
```

```
}

@Override
protected void onListItemClick(ListView l, View v,
                               int position, long id) {
  String url=getString(EU.get(position).url);

  if (browser==null) {
    startActivity(new Intent(Intent.ACTION_VIEW,
                             Uri.parse(url)));
  }
  else {
    browser.loadUrl(url);
  }
}
}
```

This gives us a more space-efficient edition of the activity, as shown in Figure 25–10.

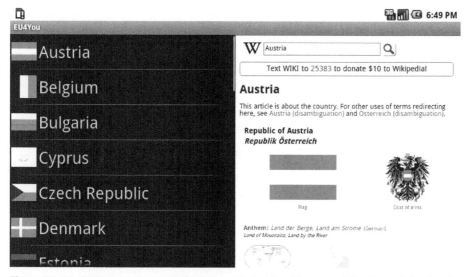

Figure 25–10. *EU4You, landscape WVGA (800×480 pixels), set for normal density, and showing the embedded WebView*

If the user clicks a link in the Wikipedia page, the full browser opens, for easier surfing. We could repeat the exercise to add even more data to the activity for an xlarge screen.

Note that testing this version of the activity, to see this behavior, requires a bit of extra emulator work. By default, Android sets up WVGA devices as being high-density, meaning WVGA is not large in terms of resource sets, but rather normal. You will need to create a different emulator AVD that is set for normal (medium) density, which will result in a large screen size.

What If It Is Not a Browser?

Of course, EU4You does cheat a bit. The second activity is a browser (or `WebView` in the embedded form), not some activity of your own creation. Things get slightly more complicated if the second activity is some activity of yours, with many widgets in a layout, and you want to both use it as an activity (for smaller screens) and have it embedded in your main activity UI (for larger screens).

The best way to approach this problem, for Android 1.6 and newer, is to employ the new fragments system. Although this was introduced with Android 3.0, the Android Compatibility Library makes fragments available in earlier versions of Android. The basic use of fragments—complete with another edition of the EU4You sample—will be covered in Chapter 28.

Chapter 26

Focusing on Tablets and Larger UIs

February 2011 saw the introduction of Android 3.0 and a UI paradigm that embraced screens of radically larger size than the traditional phones for which earlier versions of Android had been designed. Fast-forward to October 2011, and Android 4.0 Ice Cream Sandwich (ICS) has been released, unifying the tablet-specific Honeycomb UI system from Android 3.0 with the mainstream Android code base. The move to embrace tablets, and indeed larger devices such as televisions, cinema displays, and so forth, presents the biggest single change in Android since Android 0.9, before the first phones were available.

Whether to consider tablet devices when designing and building Android applications is a matter of your own preference, but knowing the ways in which the platform has adapted to large formats will allow you to design your code to easily accommodate tablets in the future and, most importantly, deal with the core tenets of the APIs that must be addressed regardless of your feelings toward tablets. This chapter is focused more on the big picture of the current state of the APIs for tablet-sized devices and their place within Android.

Why the Drive to Tablets?

In principle, Android's original phone-centric UI can run on tablets. After all, a few tablets have shipped with Android 2.2 support, such as the Samsung Galaxy Tab and ZTE V9. Clearly, those manufacturers thought the Android of the time was strong enough for their tablet devices.

That being said, as you get into larger tablets (e.g., the Motorola XOOM with its 10-inch diagonal screen), the older Android phone UI starts to become clunkier. Although applications can scale up to use the larger screen, the default way to scale up is just to make everything bigger, frequently resulting in a lot of wasted space. Whereas an e-mail client on a phone might dedicate an activity to showing the list of e-mails in the inbox, an e-mail client on a tablet really ought to show the list of e-mails plus something else, such as the content of a selected e-mail. We have the room, so we may as well use it.

Similarly, the dependence on menus, while reasonable on a phone, makes less sense on a tablet. We have the space to show more of those functions right on the screen. Hiding them in menus makes them less discoverable to users and requires extra taps to access.

So, "modern" Android is designed to retain the essence of the Android user experience, while allowing applications to (relatively) gracefully take advantage of the space that is available.

What the User Sees

A tablet screen looks a bit different from an Android 2.x screen on a traditional phone, as shown in Figure 26–1.

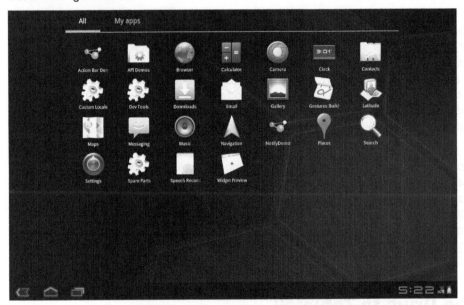

Figure 26–1. *The Android app launcher, as seen on the emulator configured as a tablet*

With all that additional real estate, various stock components can be placed in more varied locations. In this example, we see the system bar located on the bottom of the screen. On the left end of the system bar are onscreen buttons for Back, Home, and recent tasks (obviating the need to remember the long-press of the Home button to achieve the same effect). Notification icons appear on the right of the system bar, along with the clock and the signal and battery strength indicators (the concept of notifications will be covered in Chapter 37).

The UI of an application that has not been optimized for Android 3.x/4.0 appears much the same, as shown in Figure 26–2.

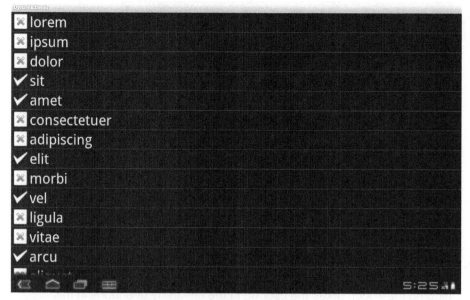

Figure 26–2. *The FancyLists/Dynamic sample project, on Android 3.0*

The only substantive difference is the new icon forth from the left in the system bar, which will open an Android 2.x options menu, if the application has one.

Tablet-optimized applications will look a bit different, as shown in Figure 26–3.

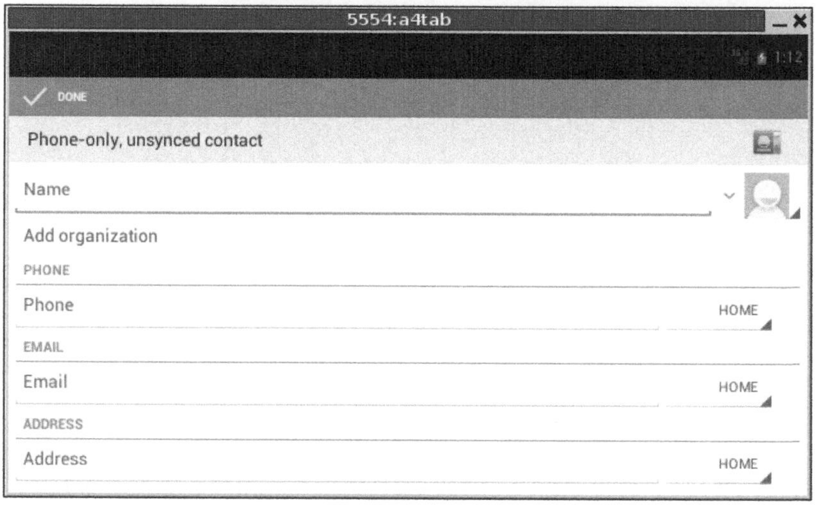

Figure 26–3. *Adding a contact on Android 4.0*

At the top of the screen is the action bar, taking over the space where pre-Android 3.0 apps would use menus. In Figure 26–3, the Done option appears as a menu choice. Other menu behaviors to note are things such as the < icon on the left end of the action bar, as shown in Figure 26–4.

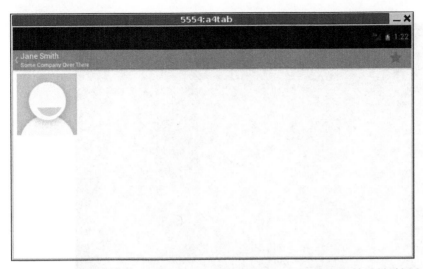

Figure 26–4. *The < icon for moving up in the hierarchy of actions, displayed in Android 4.0*

In this case, tapping the < icon takes the user up in the hierarchy of actions in this application, going "up" from viewing a new contact to viewing the list of existing contacts, as shown in Figure 26–5.

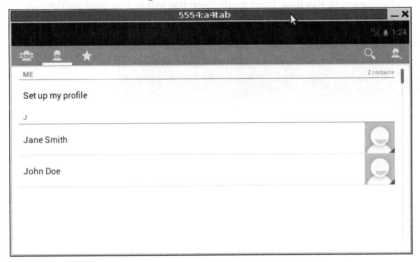

Figure 26–5. *The roster of available contacts as displayed in Android 4.0*

Our UI has come almost full-circle over the life of several Android versions. In Android 2.x, the contacts UI would have one activity with the list of contacts, and a separate activity to view the details of that contact. In Android 3.0, these are combined into a single activity. With Android 4.0, we've reverted to the one-activity-per-operation mode.

The right side of the action bar includes a "Find contacts" search icon (magnifying glass) and an icon for adding a new contact. Adjacent to these would be icons representing any other available options menu items and context menu items.

Dealing with the Rest of the Devices

Of course, all the Android phones in the world haven't up and vanished just because Android 4.0 has been released. The goal is for you to create an application that supports both phones and tablets from a single code base.

Your phone-centric app will run just fine on a tablet, though you may wish to do some things to take advantage of larger screen sizes, as was discussed in the previous chapter. If you want to adopt the general look and feel of the Ice Cream Sandwich UI, you will need to include android:targetSdkVersion="14" in your <uses-sdk> element in the manifest. If you previously developed for Honeycomb and became accustomed to explicitly turning on hardware accelerations using the android:hardwareAccelerated="true" attribute, the good news is that you no longer need to explicitly set such acceleration in Android 4.0. Hardware acceleration is now the default. This excerpt from the ScreenSizes/EU4You_5 sample project's AndroidManifest.xml file shows the SDK change:

```
<?xml version="1.0" encoding="utf-8"?>
<manifest xmlns:android="http://schemas.android.com/apk/res/android"
  package="com.commonsware.android.eu4you"
  android:versionCode="1"
  android:versionName="1.0">
  <uses-permission android:name="android.permission.INTERNET" />
  <supports-screens
    android:largeScreens="true"
    android:normalScreens="true"
    android:smallScreens="true"
    android:anyDensity="true"
  />
  <uses-sdk android:minSdkVersion="4" android:targetSdkVersion="14" />
  <application android:label="@string/app_name"
    android:icon="@drawable/cw"
    <activity android:name=".EU4You"
              android:label="@string/app_name">
      <intent-filter>
        <action android:name="android.intent.action.MAIN" />
        <category android:name="android.intent.category.LAUNCHER" />
      </intent-filter>
    </activity>
  </application>
</manifest>
```

The resulting application works fine on older devices, but with no other changes, we get the result shown in Figure 26–6 on a Motorola XOOM.

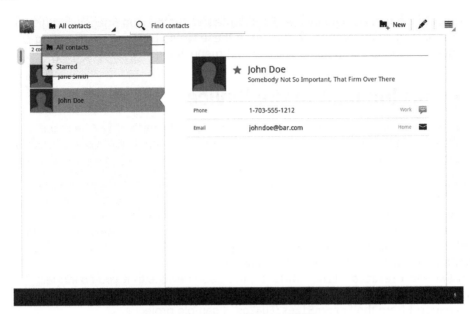

Figure 26–6. *The EU4You sample application, on a Motorola XOOM*

If you want to take advantage of some of the newer features of Ice Cream Sandwich, you will also need to think about backward compatibility, to make sure that what you implement in your application will work successfully on both newer and older versions of Android. This topic is covered later in this book.

If you have resources, such as styles, that need to be version-specific, you can use the -v*NN* resource set suffix syntax, where *NN* denotes the version you are targeting. For example, you could have a res/values/styles.xml and a res/values-v14/styles.xml— the latter would be used on Ice Cream Sandwich, and the former would be used on older versions of Android. But first, you need to explore all the tablet UI features that you can take advantage of, which is the point of the next few chapters.

Chapter 27

Using the Action Bar

One of the easiest ways to make your application blend in better with the latest and greatest Android UI is to enable the action bar, introduced in Chapter 26. What makes it "easy" is that most of the basic functionality of the action bar is backward compatible — the Android 4.0 settings will not cause the application to crash on earlier versions of Android.

The sample project shown in this chapter is Menus/ActionBar, which extends the Menus/Inflation project shown in a previous chapter.

Enabling the Action Bar

By default, your Android application will not use the action bar. In fact, it will not even be displayed on the screen. If you want the action bar to appear on the screen, you need to include android:targetSdkVersion="11" or later in your <uses-sdk> element in the manifest, such as the manifest for the Menus/ActionBar project:

```
<?xml version="1.0" encoding="utf-8"?>
<manifest xmlns:android="http://schemas.android.com/apk/res/android"
package="com.commonsware.android.inflation">
    <application android:label="@string/app_name"
                android:icon="@drawable/cw"
                android:hardwareAccelerated="true">
        <activity android:name=".InflationDemo" android:label="@string/app_name">
            <intent-filter>
                <action android:name="android.intent.action.MAIN"/>
                <category android:name="android.intent.category.LAUNCHER"/>
            </intent-filter>
        </activity>
    </application>
    <uses-sdk android:minSdkVersion="4" android:targetSdkVersion="11" />
    <supports-screens android:xlargeScreens="true"
                android:largeScreens="true"
                android:normalScreens="true"
                android:smallScreens="true"
                android:anyDensity="true"/>
</manifest>
```

This will cause your options menu to appear in the upper-right corner of the screen, under a menu icon in the action bar, as shown in Chapter 26. Also, your activity's icon will appear in the upper-left corner, with your activity's name (from the android:label attribute in the manifest) alongside of it.

While this gives you the basic contemporary look and feel—including the Ice Cream Sandwich–themed widgets—it does not really change the user experience all that much.

Promoting Menu Items to the Action Bar

The next step for integrating with the action bar is to promote certain options menu items from being part of the options menu to being always visible on the action bar itself. This makes them easier to find and saves the user a tap when the time comes to use them.

To do this, in your menu XML resource, you can add the android:showAsAction attribute to an <item> element. A value of ifRoom means that the menu item will appear in the action bar if there is space for it, while a value of always means that the menu item will always be put in the action bar. All else being equal, ifRoom is the better choice, as it will adapt better to smaller screens, once the Honeycomb UI moves onto phones. You can also combine this with the withText value (e.g., ifRoom|withText) to make the title of the menu item appear adjacent to the item's icon (otherwise, only the icon appears in the action bar).

For example, the Menus/ActionBar project's options.xml menu resource has android:showAsAction on the first two menu items:

```
<?xml version="1.0" encoding="utf-8"?>
<menu xmlns:android="http://schemas.android.com/apk/res/android">
  <item android:id="@+id/add"
    android:title="Add"
    android:icon="@drawable/ic_menu_add"
    android:actionLayout="@layout/add"
    android:showAsAction="ifRoom"/>
  <item android:id="@+id/reset"
    android:title="Reset"
    android:icon="@drawable/ic_menu_refresh"
    android:showAsAction="ifRoom|withText"/>
  <item android:id="@+id/about"
    android:title="About"
    android:icon="@drawable/ic_menu_info_details" />
</menu>
```

The second menu item, Reset—for resetting the contents of the list—is a normal "with text" action bar button. The first menu item, Add, does something a bit different, which we will examine later in this chapter. The fact that the third menu item, About, does not have android:showAsAction means that it will remain in the menu, even if there is room in the action bar.

Note that the Java code does not change—onCreateOptionsMenu() and onOptionsItemSelected() for our InflationDemo activity do not need to be adjusted because menu items are promoted into the action bar via the menu XML resource alone.

Responding to the Logo

The activity icon in the upper-left corner of the screen is tappable. If the user taps it, it triggers onOptionsItemSelected()...but not for one of the options menu items you may have defined yourself. Rather, the magic value of android.R.id.home is used. In the Menus/ActionBar project, we wire it to the same code that is invoked if the user chooses the About options menu item—displaying a Toast:

```
@Override
public boolean onOptionsItemSelected(MenuItem item) {
  switch (item.getItemId()) {
    case R.id.add:
      add();
      return(true);

    case R.id.reset:
      initAdapter();
      return(true);

    case R.id.about:
    case android.R.id.home:
      Toast
        .makeText(this,
                  "Action Bar Sample App",
                  Toast.LENGTH_LONG)
        .show();
      return(true);
  }

  return(super.onOptionsItemSelected(item));
}
```

In a project with multiple activities, though, the expectation is that tapping the logo will take you to the "home" activity for the application, whatever that might mean.

Adding Custom Views to the Action Bar

You can do more with the action bar than simply convert options menu items into what amount to toolbar buttons. You can add your own custom UI to the action bar. In the case of Menus/ActionBar, we'll replace the Add menu choice and resulting dialog box with an Add field right in the action bar itself.

This, however, is a bit tricky to implement, as described next.

Defining the Layout

To put something custom in the action bar, we need to define what the "something custom" is, in the form of a layout XML file. Fortunately, we already have a layout XML file for adding a word to the list—it is the one that the Menus/Inflation sample wrapped in a custom AlertDialog for when the Add options menu item was tapped. That original layout looked like this:

```xml
<?xml version="1.0" encoding="utf-8"?>
<LinearLayout xmlns:android="http://schemas.android.com/apk/res/android"
    android:orientation="horizontal"
    android:layout_width="fill_parent"
    android:layout_height="wrap_content"
    >
  <TextView
      android:text="Word:"
      android:layout_width="wrap_content"
      android:layout_height="wrap_content"
      />
  <EditText
      android:id="@+id/title"
      android:layout_width="fill_parent"
      android:layout_height="wrap_content"
      android:layout_marginLeft="4dip"
      />
</LinearLayout>
```

We need to make some minor adjustments to this layout to use it for the action bar:

```xml
<?xml version="1.0" encoding="utf-8"?>
<LinearLayout xmlns:android="http://schemas.android.com/apk/res/android"
    android:orientation="horizontal"
    android:layout_width="fill_parent"
    android:layout_height="wrap_content"
    >
  <TextView
      android:text="Word:"
      android:layout_width="wrap_content"
      android:layout_height="wrap_content"
      android:textAppearance="@android:style/TextAppearance.Medium"
      />
  <EditText
      android:id="@+id/title"
      android:layout_width="fill_parent"
      android:layout_height="wrap_content"
      android:layout_marginLeft="4dip"
      android:width="160sp"
      android:inputType="text"
      android:imeActionId="1337"
      android:imeOptions="actionDone"
      />
</LinearLayout>
```

Specifically, we made these minor adjustments:

- We added an `android:textAppearance` attribute to the TextView representing our Add caption. The `android:textAppearance` attribute allows us to define the font type, size, color, and weight (e.g., bold) in one shot. We specifically used a magic value of `@android:style/TextAppearance.Medium` so that the caption matches the styling of the Reset label on the other menu item we promoted to the action bar.

- We specified `android:width="160sp"` for the `EditText` widget, because `android:layout_width="fill_parent"` is ignored in the action bar—otherwise, we would take up the rest of the bar.

- We specified `android:inputType="text"` on the `EditText` widget, which, among other things, restricts us to a single line of text.

- We `android:imeActionId` and `android:imeOptions` on the `EditText` widget to control the action button of the soft keyboard, so we get control when the user presses the Enter key on the soft keyboard.

Putting the Layout in the Menu

Next, we need to teach Android to use this layout for our Add options menu item if we are running on up-to-date releases of Android, such as Ice Cream Sandwich or Honeycomb. To do this, we use the `android:actionLayout` attribute on our `<item>` element, referencing our layout resource (`@layout/add`), as was shown earlier in this chapter. This attribute will be ignored on earlier versions of Android, so it is safe to use.

If we did nothing else, we would get the desired UI, shown in Figure 27–1.

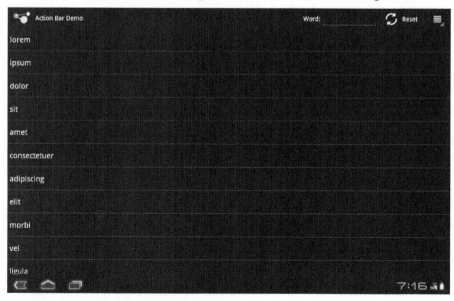

Figure 27–1. *The Menus/ActionBar sample application*

However, while the user could type something in, we have no way to find out what they type in, when they are done, and so forth.

Getting Control of User Input

Given our soft keyboard settings we put on the EditText widget, we can arrange to find out when the user presses the Enter key either on the soft keyboard or on a hardware keyboard. To do that, though, we need to get our hands on the EditText widget itself. You might think it is added when the UI is inflated in onCreate()...but you would be mistaken.

With an action bar, onCreateOptionsMenu() is called after onCreate() as part of setting up the UI. On classic versions of Android, onCreateOptionsMenu() would not be called until the user pressed the Menu button. But, since some of the options menu items might be promoted into the action bar, Android calls onCreateOptionsMenu() automatically now. The EditText will exist after we inflate our options.xml menu resource.

However, the best way to get the EditText is not to use findViewById() on the activity. Rather, we should call getActionView() on the MenuItem associated with our Add option. This will return the root of the view hierarchy inflated from the layout resource we defined in the android:actionLayout attribute in the menu resource. In this case, that is the LinearLayout from res/layout/add.xml, so we need to call findViewById() on it to get the EditText:

```
@Override
public boolean onCreateOptionsMenu(Menu menu) {
  new MenuInflater(this).inflate(R.menu.option, menu);

  EditText add=(EditText)menu
                    .findItem(R.id.add)
                    .getActionView()
                    .findViewById(R.id.title);

  add.setOnEditorActionListener(onSearch);

  return(super.onCreateOptionsMenu(menu));
}
```

Then, we can call setOnEditorActionListener() on the EditText, to register an OnEditorActionListener object that will get control when the user presses Enter on the hard or soft keyboard:

```
private TextView.OnEditorActionListener onSearch=
  new TextView.OnEditorActionListener() {
  public boolean onEditorAction(TextView v, int actionId,
                         KeyEvent event) {
    if (event==null || event.getAction()==KeyEvent.ACTION_UP) {
      addWord(v);

      InputMethodManager imm=(InputMethodManager)getSystemService(INPUT_METHOD_SERVICE);
```

```
    imm.hideSoftInputFromWindow(v.getWindowToken(), 0);
  }

  return(true);
  }
};
```

That in turn calls an `addWord()` method, supplying the `EditText`, which adds the word to the list via the `ArrayAdapter`:

```
private void addWord(TextView title) {
  ArrayAdapter<String> adapter=(ArrayAdapter<String>)getListAdapter();

  adapter.add(title.getText().toString());
}
```

That same `addWord()` method can also be used from the `add()` method that displays the `AlertDialog`, even though that will not be used on a tablet, since the Add menu choice no longer exists as a menu choice:

```
private void add() {
  final View addView=getLayoutInflater().inflate(R.layout.add, null);

  new AlertDialog.Builder(this)
    .setTitle("Add a Word")
    .setView(addView)
    .setPositiveButton("OK",
                      new DialogInterface.OnClickListener() {
      public void onClick(DialogInterface dialog,
                          int whichButton) {
        addWord((TextView)addView.findViewById(R.id.title));
      }
    })
    .setNegativeButton("Cancel", null)
    .show();
}
```

The net result is that when the user types something in the Add field and presses the Enter key, the word is added to the bottom of the list. This saves some taps over the traditional phone UI, as the user does not have to open the options menu, does not have to tap the options menu item, and does not have to tap a button on the dialog box.

Note that our `OnEditorActionListener` does something more than simply add the word to the list: it hides the soft keyboard. It does this using the `InputMethodManager`, as was seen in a previous chapter.

Don't Forget the Phones!

With the exception of the custom view feature described in the preceding section, everything shown in this chapter regarding the action bar is automatically backward compatible. The code and resources that work on Ice Cream Sandwich–flavored versions of Android will work on classic versions of Android unmodified.

If, however, you want to use the custom view feature, you have a problem—the getActionView() method was new to API Level 11 and will be unavailable on older versions of Android. This means you will need to compile for at least API Level 11 (e.g., set your Eclipse target or Ant default.properties to reference android-11) or higher, and you will need to take steps to avoid calling getActionView() on older devices. We will explore how to pull off this feat in a later chapter.

Chapter 28

Fragments

Perhaps the largest change facing Android developers in 2011 was the introduction of the fragment system with Android 3.0, and the recent merging of the fragment system into the main code base with Android 4.0 Ice Cream Sandwich. Fragments are an optional layer you can put between your activities and your widgets, designed to help you reconfigure your activities to support screens both large (e.g., tablets) and small (e.g., phones). However, the fragment system also adds an extra layer of complexity, one that will take the Android developer community some time to adjust to. Hence, the public comments, blog posts, and sample apps using fragments are a little rarer, because fragments were introduced so long after Android itself was.

This chapter covers basic uses of fragments, including supporting fragments on pre–Android 3.0 devices.

Introducing Fragments

Fragments are not widgets, like `Button` or `EditText`. Fragments are not containers, like `LinearLayout` or `RelativeLayout`. Fragments are not activities.

Rather, fragments aggregate widgets and containers. Fragments then can be placed into activities—sometimes several fragments for one activity, sometimes one fragment per activity. And the reason for this is the variation in Android screen sizes.

The Problem Addressed by Fragments

A tablet has a larger screen than does a phone. A TV has a larger screen than does a tablet. Taking advantage of that extra screen space makes sense, as outlined in Chapter 25, which explained how to handle multiple screen sizes. In that chapter, we profiled an `EU4You` sample application, eventually winding up with an activity that would load in a different layout for larger-sized screens, one that had an embedded `WebView` widget. The activity would detect that widget's existence and use it to load web content related to a selected country, rather than launching a separate browser activity or some activity containing only a `WebView`.

However, the scenario outlined in Chapter 25 was fairly trivial. Imagine that, instead of a `WebView`, we have a `TableLayout` containing 28 widgets. On larger-sized screens, we want the `TableLayout` in the same activity as an adjacent `ListView`; on smaller screens, we want the `TableLayout` to be in a separate activity, since there would not be enough room otherwise. To do this using early Android technology, we would need to either duplicate all of the `TableLayout`-handling logic in both activities, create an activity base class and hope that both activities can inherit from it, or turn the `TableLayout` and its contents into a custom `ViewGroup`...or do something else. And that would just be for *one* such scenario—multiply that by many activities in a larger application, and the complexity mounts.

The Fragments Solution

Fragments reduce, but do not eliminate, that complexity.

With fragments, each discrete chunk of user interface that could be used in multiple activities (based on screen size) goes in a fragment. The activities in question determine, based on screen size, who gets the fragment.

In the case of EU4You, we have two fragments. One fragment represents the list of countries. The other fragment represents the details for that country (in our case, a `WebView`). On a larger-screen device, we want both fragments to be in one activity, while on a smaller-screen device, we will house those fragments in two separate activities. This provides to users with larger screens the same benefits they got with the last version of EU4You: getting more information in fewer clicks. Yet the techniques we demonstrate with fragments will be more scalable, able to handle more complex UI patterns than the simple `WebView`-or-not scenario of EU4You.

In this case, our entire UI will be inside of fragments. That is not necessary. Fragments are an opt-in technology—you need them only for the parts of your UI that could appear in different activities in different scenarios. In fact, your activities that do not change at all (say, a help screen) might not use fragments whatsoever.

Fragments also give us a few other bells and whistles, including the following:

- *Capability to add fragments dynamically based on user interaction*: For example, the Gmail application initially shows a `ListFragment` of the user's mail folders. Tapping a folder adds a second `ListFragment` to the screen, showing the conversations in that folder. Tapping a conversation adds a third `Fragment` to the screen, showing the messages in that conversation.

- *Capability to animate dynamic fragments as they move on and off the screen*: For example, when the user taps a conversation in Gmail, the folders `ListFragment` slides off the screen to the left, the conversations `ListFragment` slides left and shrinks to take up less room, and the messages `Fragment` slides in from the right.

- *Automatic Back button management for dynamic fragments*: For example, when the user presses Back while viewing the messages Fragment, that Fragment slides off to the right, the conversations ListFragment slides right and expands to fill more of the screen, and the folders ListFragment slides back in from the left. None of that has to be managed by developers—simply adding the dynamic fragment via a FragmentTransaction allows Android to automatically handle the Back button, including reversing all animations.

- *Capability to add options to the options menu, and therefore to the action bar*: Call setHasOptionsMenu() in onCreate() of your fragment to register an interest in this, and then override onCreateOptionsMenu() and onOptionsItemSelected() in the fragment the same way you might in an activity. A fragment can also register widgets to have context menus, and handle those context menus the same way as an activity would.

- *Capability to add tabs to the action bar*: The action bar can have tabs, replacing a TabHost, where each tab's content is a fragment. Similarly, the action bar can have a navigation mode, with a Spinner to switch between modes, where each mode is represented by a fragment.

If you have access to any recent device running Honeycomb or Ice Cream Sandwich, fire up the Gmail application to see all the fragment bells and whistles in action.

The Android Compatibility Library

If fragments were available only for Android 3.0 and higher, we would be right back where we started, as not all Android devices today run Android 3.0 and higher.

Fortunately, this is not the case, because Google has released the Android Compatibility Library (ACL), which is available via the Android SDK and AVD Manager (where you install the other SDK support files, create and start your emulator AVDs, and so forth). The ACL gives you access to the fragment system on versions of Android going back to Android 1.6. Because the vast majority of Android devices are running 1.6 or higher, this allows you to start using fragments while maintaining backward compatibility. Over time, this library may add other features to help with backward compatibility, for applications that wish to use it.

The material in this chapter focuses on using the ACL when employing fragments. Generally speaking, using the ACL for fragments is almost identical to using the native Android 3.0 fragment classes directly.

Since the ACL only supports versions back to Android 1.6, Android 1.5 devices will not be able to use fragment-based applications. This is a very small percentage of the Android device spectrum at this time—around 1 percent as of the time of this writing.

Creating Fragment Classes

The first step toward setting up a fragment-based application is to create fragment classes for each of your fragments. Just as you inherit from Activity (or a subclass) for your activities, you inherit from Fragment (or a subclass) for your fragments.

Here, we will examine the Fragments/EU4You_6 sample project and the fragments that it defines.

> **NOTE:** The convention of this book will be to use "fragment" as a generic noun and Fragment to refer to the actual Fragment class.

General Fragments

Besides inheriting from Fragment, the only thing required of a fragment is to override onCreateView(). This will be called as part of putting the fragment on the screen. You need to return a View that represents the body of the fragment. Most likely, you will create your fragment's UI via an XML layout file, and onCreateView() will inflate that fragment layout file.

For example, here is DetailsFragment from EU4You_6, which will wrap around our WebView to show the web content for a given country:

```
import android.support.v4.app.Fragment;
import android.os.Bundle;
import android.view.LayoutInflater;
import android.view.View;
import android.view.ViewGroup;
import android.webkit.WebView;

public class DetailsFragment extends Fragment {
  @Override
  public View onCreateView(LayoutInflater inflater, ViewGroup container,
                           Bundle savedInstanceState) {
    return(inflater.inflate(R.layout.details_fragment, container, false));
  }

  public void loadUrl(String url) {
    ((WebView)(getView().findViewById(R.id.browser))).loadUrl(url);
  }
}
```

Note that we are inheriting not from android.app.Fragment but from android.support.v4.app.Fragment. The latter is the Fragment implementation from the ACL, so it can be used across Android versions.

The onCreateView() implementation inflates a layout that happens to have a WebView in it:

```
<?xml version="1.0" encoding="utf-8"?>
<WebView
```

```
    xmlns:android="http://schemas.android.com/apk/res/android"
    android:id="@+id/browser"
    android:layout_width="fill_parent"
    android:layout_height="fill_parent"
/>
```

It also exposes a loadUrl() method, to be used by a hosting activity both to tell the fragment that it is time to display some web content and to supply the URL for doing the same. The implementation of loadUrl() in DetailsFragment uses getView() to retrieve the View created in onCreateView(), finds the WebView in it, and delegates the loadUrl() call to the WebView.

There are a myriad of other lifecycle methods available on Fragment. The more important ones include mirrors of the standard onCreate(), onStart(), onResume(), onPause(), onStop(), and onDestroy() methods of an activity. Since the fragment is the one with the widgets, it will implement more of the business logic that formerly might have resided in the activity for these methods. For example, in onPause() or onStop(), since the user may not be returning to your application, you may wish to save any unsaved edits to some temporary storage. In the case of DetailsFragment, there was nothing that really qualified here, so those lifecycle methods were left alone.

ListFragment

One Fragment subclass that is sure to be popular is ListFragment. This wraps a ListView in a Fragment, designed to simplify setting up lists of things such as countries, mail folders, mail conversations, and so forth. Similar to a ListActivity, all you need to do is call setListAdapter() with your chosen and configured ListAdapter, plus override onListItemClick() to respond to when the user clicks on a row in the list.

In EU4You_6, we have a CountriesFragment that represents the list of available countries. It initializes the ListAdapter in onActivityCreated(), which is called after onCreate() has wrapped up in the activity that holds the fragment:

```
@Override
public void onActivityCreated(Bundle state) {
  super.onActivityCreated(state);

  setListAdapter(new CountryAdapter());

  if (state!=null) {
    int position=state.getInt(STATE_CHECKED, -1);

    if (position>-1) {
      getListView().setItemChecked(position, true);
    }
  }
}
```

The code dealing with the Bundle supplied to onCreate() will be explained a bit later in this chapter.

The CountryAdapter is nearly identical to the one from previous EU4You samples, except that there is no getLayoutInflater() method on a Fragment, so we have to use the static from() method on LayoutInflater and supply our activity via getActivity():

```
class CountryAdapter extends ArrayAdapter<Country> {
  CountryAdapter() {
    super(getActivity(), R.layout.row, R.id.name, EU);
  }

  @Override
  public View getView(int position, View convertView,
                      ViewGroup parent) {
    CountryWrapper wrapper=null;

    if (convertView==null) {
      convertView=LayoutInflater
                    .from(getActivity())
                    .inflate(R.layout.row, null);
      wrapper=new CountryWrapper(convertView);
      convertView.setTag(wrapper);
    }
    else {
      wrapper=(CountryWrapper)convertView.getTag();
    }

    wrapper.populateFrom(getItem(position));

    return(convertView);
  }
}
```

Similarly, the CountryWrapper is no different from previous EU4You samples:

```
static class CountryWrapper {
  private TextView name=null;
  private ImageView flag=null;
  private View row=null;

  CountryWrapper(View row) {
    this.row=row;
    name=(TextView)row.findViewById(R.id.name);
    flag=(ImageView)row.findViewById(R.id.flag);
  }

  TextView getName() {
    return(name);
  }

  ImageView getFlag() {
    return(flag);
  }

  void populateFrom(Country nation) {
    getName().setText(nation.name);
    getFlag().setImageResource(nation.flag);
  }
```

```
}
```

The list of countries is the same as well:

```
static {
  EU.add(new Country(R.string.austria, R.drawable.austria,
                  R.string.austria_url));
  EU.add(new Country(R.string.belgium, R.drawable.belgium,
                  R.string.belgium_url));
  EU.add(new Country(R.string.bulgaria, R.drawable.bulgaria,
                  R.string.bulgaria_url));
  EU.add(new Country(R.string.cyprus, R.drawable.cyprus,
                  R.string.cyprus_url));
  EU.add(new Country(R.string.czech_republic,
                  R.drawable.czech_republic,
                  R.string.czech_republic_url));
  EU.add(new Country(R.string.denmark, R.drawable.denmark,
                  R.string.denmark_url));
  EU.add(new Country(R.string.estonia, R.drawable.estonia,
                  R.string.estonia_url));
  EU.add(new Country(R.string.finland, R.drawable.finland,
                  R.string.finland_url));
  EU.add(new Country(R.string.france, R.drawable.france,
                  R.string.france_url));
  EU.add(new Country(R.string.germany, R.drawable.germany,
                  R.string.germany_url));
  EU.add(new Country(R.string.greece, R.drawable.greece,
                  R.string.greece_url));
  EU.add(new Country(R.string.hungary, R.drawable.hungary,
                  R.string.hungary_url));
  EU.add(new Country(R.string.ireland, R.drawable.ireland,
                  R.string.ireland_url));
  EU.add(new Country(R.string.italy, R.drawable.italy,
                  R.string.italy_url));
  EU.add(new Country(R.string.latvia, R.drawable.latvia,
                  R.string.latvia_url));
  EU.add(new Country(R.string.lithuania, R.drawable.lithuania,
                  R.string.lithuania_url));
  EU.add(new Country(R.string.luxembourg, R.drawable.luxembourg,
                  R.string.luxembourg_url));
  EU.add(new Country(R.string.malta, R.drawable.malta,
                  R.string.malta_url));
  EU.add(new Country(R.string.netherlands, R.drawable.netherlands,
                  R.string.netherlands_url));
  EU.add(new Country(R.string.poland, R.drawable.poland,
                  R.string.poland_url));
  EU.add(new Country(R.string.portugal, R.drawable.portugal,
                  R.string.portugal_url));
  EU.add(new Country(R.string.romania, R.drawable.romania,
                  R.string.romania_url));
  EU.add(new Country(R.string.slovakia, R.drawable.slovakia,
                  R.string.slovakia_url));
  EU.add(new Country(R.string.slovenia, R.drawable.slovenia,
                  R.string.slovenia_url));
  EU.add(new Country(R.string.spain, R.drawable.spain,
                  R.string.spain_url));
```

```
    EU.add(new Country(R.string.sweden, R.drawable.sweden,
                        R.string.sweden_url));
    EU.add(new Country(R.string.united_kingdom,
                        R.drawable.united_kingdom,
                        R.string.united_kingdom_url));
}
```

...as is the definition of a Country, from a separate public class:

```
public class Country {
    int name;
    int flag;
    int url;

    Country(int name, int flag, int url) {
        this.name=name;
        this.flag=flag;
        this.url=url;
    }
}
```

Persistent Highlight

One thing leaps out at you when you use fragment-based applications like Gmail. When you tap on a row in a list, and another fragment is shown (or updated) within the same activity, the row you tapped remains highlighted. This runs counter to the traditional use of a ListView, where the list selector is present only when using a D-pad, trackball, or similar pointing device. The purpose is to show the user the context of the adjacent fragment.

The actual implementation differs from what you might expect. These ListView widgets are actually implementing CHOICE_MODE_SINGLE, what normally would be rendered using a RadioButton along the right side of the rows. In a ListFragment, though, the typical styling for a single-choice ListFragment is via an "activated" background.

In EU4You_6, this is handled via the row layout (res/layout/row.xml) used by our CountryAdapter:

```
<?xml version="1.0" encoding="utf-8"?>
<LinearLayout xmlns:android="http://schemas.android.com/apk/res/android"
  android:layout_width="fill_parent"
  android:layout_height="wrap_content"
  android:padding="2dip"
  android:minHeight="?android:attr/listPreferredItemHeight"
  style="@style/activated"
>
  <ImageView android:id="@+id/flag"
    android:layout_width="wrap_content"
    android:layout_height="wrap_content"
    android:layout_gravity="center_vertical|left"
    android:paddingRight="4dip"
  />
  <TextView android:id="@+id/name"
    android:layout_width="wrap_content"
    android:layout_height="wrap_content"
```

```
    android:layout_gravity="center_vertical|right"
    android:textSize="5mm"
  />
</LinearLayout>
```

Notice the `style` attribute, pointing to an `activated` style. That is defined by EU4You_6 as a local style, versus one provided by the operating system. In fact, it has to have two implementations of the style, because the "activated" concept is new to Android 3.0 and cannot be used in previous versions of Android.

So, EU4You_6 has `res/values/styles.xml` with a backward-compatible empty style:

```
<?xml version="1.0" encoding="utf-8"?>
<resources>
  <style name="activated">
  </style>
</resources>
```

It also has `res/values-v11/styles.xml`. The `-v11` resource set suffix means that this will be used only on API Level 11 (Android 3.0) and higher. Here, the style inherits from the standard Android Holographic theme and uses the standard activated background color:

```
<?xml version="1.0" encoding="utf-8"?>
<resources>
  <style name="activated" parent="android:Theme.Holo">
    <item name="android:background">?android:attr/activatedBackgroundIndicator</item>
  </style>
</resources>
```

In `CountriesFragment`, the activity will let us know if `CountriesFragment` appears alongside `DetailsFragment` — thus requiring single-choice mode — via an `enablePersistentSelection()` method:

```
public void enablePersistentSelection() {
  getListView().setChoiceMode(ListView.CHOICE_MODE_SINGLE);
}
```

Also, in `onListItemClick()`, `CountriesFragment` "checks" the row the user clicked on, thereby enabling the persistent highlight:

```
@Override
public void onListItemClick(ListView l, View v, int position,
                            long id) {
  l.setItemChecked(position, true);

  if (listener!=null) {
    listener.onCountrySelected(EU.get(position));
  }
}
```

The `listener` object and call to `onCountrySelected()` will be explained later in this chapter.

Other Fragment Base Classes

The ACL has one other subclass of `Fragment`: `DialogFragment`. This is used to help coordinate between a modal `Dialog` and a fragment-based UI.

Android 3.0 itself has two more subclasses of `Fragment`, which are not available in the ACL as of the time of this writing:

- `PreferenceFragment`: For use in the new Honeycomb-style `PreferenceActivity` (covered in Chapter 31)

- `WebViewFragment`: A `Fragment` wrapped around a `WebView`

Fragments, Layouts, Activities, and Multiple Screen Sizes

Having some fragment classes and their accompanying layouts is all well and good, but we need to hook them up to activities and get them on the screen. Along the way, we have to think about dealing with multiple screen sizes, much like we went with the `WebView`-or-browser approach with the previous version of the EU4You sample.

In Android 3.0 and higher, any activity can host a fragment. However, for the ACL, you need to inherit from `FragmentActivity` to use fragments. This limitation of the ACL definitely causes challenges, particularly if you were aiming to put a map in a fragment, a topic we will discuss later in this book. Other activity base classes pose less of an issue—`ListActivity` would be replaced by `ListFragment`, for example.

Fragments can be added in either of two ways to an activity:

- You can define them via `<fragment>` elements in the activity's layout. These fragments are fixed and will always exist for the lifetime of this activity instance.

- You can add them on-the-fly via `FragmentManager` and a `FragmentTransaction`. This gives you more flexibility, but adds a degree of complexity. This technique is not covered in this book.

One big limitation of dealing with multiple screen sizes is that the layouts need to have the same starting fragments for any configuration change. So, a small-screen version of an activity and a large-screen version of an activity can have different mixes of fragments, but a portrait layout and a landscape layout for the same screen size must have the same fragments defined. Otherwise, when the screen is rotated, Android will have problems, trying to work with a fragment that does not exist, for example.

We also need to work out communications between our fragments and our activities. The activities define what fragments they hold, so they typically know which classes implement those fragments and can call methods on them directly. The fragments, though, only know that they are hosted by *some* activity, and that activity may differ from case to case. Hence, the typical pattern is to use interfaces for fragment-to-activity communication:

- Define an interface for the methods that the fragment will want to call on its activity (or some other object supplied by that activity).

- The activity provides an implementation of that interface via some setter method on the fragment when the fragment is created.

- The fragment uses that interface implementation as needed.

We will see all of this as we work through the EU4You_6 activities and their corresponding layouts.

In the earlier versions of the EU4You project, we had only one activity, also named EU4You. In EU4You_6, though, we have two activities:

- EU4You: Handles displaying the CountriesFragment in all screen sizes, plus the DetailsFragment on larger screens

- DetailsActivity: Hosts the DetailsFragment on smaller screens

While we could probably get away with having EU4You launch the browser activity for smaller screens, rather than have a DetailsActivity host a WebView-only DetailsFragment, the latter approach is more realistic for more fragment-based applications.

EU4You

First we'll take a look at the pieces of the EU4You activity.

The Layout

For normal-screen devices, we want to display only the CountriesFragment. That is accomplished via res/layout/main.xml just having the appropriate <fragment> element:

```
<?xml version="1.0" encoding="utf-8"?>
<fragment xmlns:android="http://schemas.android.com/apk/res/android"
  class="com.commonsware.android.eu4you.CountriesFragment"
  android:id="@+id/countries"
  android:layout_width="fill_parent"
  android:layout_height="fill_parent"
/>
```

The class attribute indicates which Java class implements the fragment. Otherwise, this layout is unremarkable.

Note that fragments do not get listed in the manifest file the way activities do.

The Other Layout

For large-screen devices, in the landscape mode, we want to have both the CountriesFragment and the DetailsFragment, side by side. That way, users can tap on a country and view the details without flipping back and forth between activities. It also enables us to take advantage of the screen space better.

However, there is a catch. If we want to predefine those two fragments in our layout file, we have to use that same pair of fragments for *both* landscape and portrait modes— despite the fact that we do not want to use the DetailsFragment in EU4You in portrait mode (having a list vertically stacked over the WebView would be odd looking, at best). As a workaround, we will use the same layout file for both orientations and then make adjustments in our Java code. Another approach to the problem would be to have the layout file only have the CountriesFragment and to use FragmentManager and a FragmentTransaction to add in the DetailsFragment. Here, though, we will use other tricks.

Hence, in res/layout-large/ (not res/layout-large-land/), we have this layout:

```
<?xml version="1.0" encoding="utf-8"?>
<LinearLayout
  xmlns:android="http://schemas.android.com/apk/res/android"
  android:orientation="horizontal"
  android:layout_width="fill_parent"
  android:layout_height="fill_parent">
  <fragment class="com.commonsware.android.eu4you.CountriesFragment"
    android:id="@+id/countries"
    android:layout_weight="30"
    android:layout_width="0px"
    android:layout_height="fill_parent"
  />
  <fragment class="com.commonsware.android.eu4you.DetailsFragment"
    android:id="@+id/details"
    android:layout_weight="70"
    android:layout_width="0px"
    android:layout_height="fill_parent"
  />
</LinearLayout>
```

Note that we are responsible for the positioning of the fragments, so here we use a horizontal LinearLayout to wrap around the two <fragment> elements.

The Listener Interface

When the user chooses a country in the CountriesFragment, we want to let our containing activity know about that. In this case, it so happens that the only activity that will ever host CountriesFragment is EU4You. However, perhaps in the future that will not be the case. So, we should abstract out the communications from CountriesFragment to its hosting activity via a listener interface.

Hence, the EU4You_6 project has a CountryListener interface:

```
package com.commonsware.android.eu4you;

public interface CountryListener {
  void onCountrySelected(Country c);
}
```

The CountriesFragment holds onto an instance of CountryListener, supplied by the hosting activity:

```
public void setCountryListener(CountryListener listener) {
  this.listener=listener;
}
```

And, when the user clicks on a country and triggers onListItemClick(), CountriesFragment calls the onCountrySelected() method on the interface:

```
@Override
public void onListItemClick(ListView l, View v, int position,
                            long id) {
  l.setItemChecked(position, true);

  if (listener!=null) {
    listener.onCountrySelected(EU.get(position));
  }
}
```

The Activity

The EU4You activity is not long, though it is a bit tricky:

```
package com.commonsware.android.eu4you;

import android.content.Intent;
import android.content.res.Configuration;
import android.net.Uri;
import android.os.Bundle;
import android.support.v4.app.Fragment;
import android.support.v4.app.FragmentActivity;
import android.view.View;

public class EU4You extends FragmentActivity implements CountryListener {
  private boolean detailsInline=false;

  @Override
  public void onCreate(Bundle savedInstanceState) {
    super.onCreate(savedInstanceState);
    setContentView(R.layout.main);

    CountriesFragment countries
      =(CountriesFragment)getSupportFragmentManager()
                      .findFragmentById(R.id.countries);

    countries.setCountryListener(this);

    Fragment f=getSupportFragmentManager().findFragmentById(R.id.details);

    detailsInline=(f!=null &&
                   (getResources().getConfiguration().orientation==
                    Configuration.ORIENTATION_LANDSCAPE));

    if (detailsInline) {
      countries.enablePersistentSelection();
```

```
        }
        else if (f!=null) {
          f.getView().setVisibility(View.GONE);
        }
      }

      @Override
      public void onCountrySelected(Country c) {
        String url=getString(c.url);

        if (detailsInline) {
          ((DetailsFragment)getSupportFragmentManager()
                              .findFragmentById(R.id.details))
                              .loadUrl(url);
        }
        else {
          Intent i=new Intent(this, DetailsActivity.class);

          i.putExtra(DetailsActivity.EXTRA_URL, url);
          startActivity(i);
        }
      }
    }
```

Our mission in onCreate() is to wire up our fragments. The fragments themselves are created by our call to setContentView(), inflating our layout and the fragments defined therein. In addition, though, EU4You does the following:

- Finds the CountriesFragment and registers itself as the CountryListener, since EU4You implements that interface.

- Finds the DetailsFragment, if it exists. If it exists and we are in landscape mode, we tell the CountriesFragment to enable the persistent highlight, to remind the user what details are being loaded on the right. If it exists and we are in portrait mode, we actually do not want DetailsFragment but need it to be consistent with the layout mode, so we mark the fragment's contents as being GONE. If the DetailsFragment does not exist, we do not have to do anything special.

Getting the FragmentManager for calls like findFragmentById() is accomplished via getFragmentManager(). The ACL, however, defines a separate getSupportFragmentManager(), to ensure you are working with the ACL's implementation of FragmentManager and to work across the wider range of Android versions.

In addition, since EU4You implements the CountryListener interface, it must implement onCountrySelected(). Here, EU4You notes whether or not we should be routing to an inline edition of DetailsFragment. If we should be, then onCountrySelected() passes the Country to the DetailsFragment, so it loads that country's web page. Otherwise, we launch the DetailsActivity, supplying the URL as an extra.

DetailsActivity

The DetailsActivity will be used where the DetailsFragment is not being shown in the EU4You activity, including in the following cases:

- When the device has a normal screen size and therefore does not have the DetailsFragment in the layout

- When the device has a large screen in the portrait size and therefore EU4You is hiding its own DetailsFragment

The Layout

The layout just has our <fragment> element in it, since there is nothing else to show:

```xml
<?xml version="1.0" encoding="utf-8"?>
<fragment xmlns:android="http://schemas.android.com/apk/res/android"
  class="com.commonsware.android.eu4you.DetailsFragment"
  android:id="@+id/details"
  android:layout_width="fill_parent"
  android:layout_height="fill_parent"
/>
```

The Activity

DetailsActivity simply passes the URL from the Intent extra on to the DetailsFragment, telling it what web content to display:

```java
package com.commonsware.android.eu4you;

import android.support.v4.app.FragmentActivity;
import android.content.Intent;
import android.net.Uri;
import android.os.Bundle;

public class DetailsActivity extends FragmentActivity {
  public static final String EXTRA_URL="com.commonsware.android.eu4you.EXTRA_URL";

  @Override
  public void onCreate(Bundle savedInstanceState) {
    super.onCreate(savedInstanceState);
    setContentView(R.layout.details);

    DetailsFragment details
      =(DetailsFragment)getSupportFragmentManager()
                        .findFragmentById(R.id.details);

    details.loadUrl(getIntent().getStringExtra(EXTRA_URL));
  }
}
```

Fragments and Configuration Changes

In Chapter 19, we reviewed how activities can deal with configuration changes, such as screen rotations. How does this translate into a world of fragments?

Well, as is typical, there is good news, and there is other news.

The good news is that fragments have onSaveInstanceState() methods that they can override, behaving much like their activity counterparts. The Bundle then is made available in a variety of places, such as onCreate() and onActivityCreated(), though there is no dedicated onRestoreInstanceState().

The other news is that not only do fragments lack onRetainNonConfigurationInstance(), but the ACL's FragmentActivity does not allow you to extend onRetainNonConfigurationInstance(), as that is used internally. Applications using the direct Android implementation of fragments do not suffer from this problem. This limitation is substantial, and the developer community is still collectively working out ways to get past the limitation.

Designing for Fragments

The overall design approach for fragments favors having business logic in the fragment, with activities serving as an orchestration layer for interfragment navigation and things that fragments are incapable of (e.g., onRetainNonConfigurationInstance()). For example, the Gmail application originally probably had much of its business logic implemented in each activity (e.g., an activity for folders, an activity for a list of conversations, an activity for a single conversation). Nowadays, that application is probably built around having that business logic delegated to fragments, with the activities merely choosing which fragments to display based upon available screen size.

This has caused quite a bit of restructuring of existing applications since fragments debuted at the start of 2011. For example, a ListActivity might have launched another activity from onListItemClick(). The first-cut refactoring of that would have the fragment's onListItemClick() launch an activity. However, the fragment does not know whether or not the content requested by the user should be shown in another activity—it might go to another fragment within the current activity. Hence, the fragment should not blindly call startActivity() but rather should call a method on its container activity (or, more likely, a listener interface implemented by that activity), telling it of the click event and letting it decide the right course of action.

Chapter 29

Handling Platform Changes

Android has been rapidly evolving since its initial release, and will continue to do so over the next few years. Perhaps, in time, the rate of change will decline some. However, for the present, you should assume that there will be significant Android releases every 6 to 12 months, and changes to the lineup of possible Android hardware on an ongoing basis. So, while right now the focus of Android is phones and tablets, soon you will see Android netbooks, Android TVs, Android media players, and so on.

Many of these changes will have little impact on your existing code. Some, though, will necessitate at least new rounds of testing for your applications, and perhaps changes to those applications based upon the test results.

This chapter covers several issues that may cause you trouble in the future as Android evolves, and provides some recommendations on how to deal with them.

Things That Make You Go Boom

Android *will* change, not only in terms of what Google introduces, but also in how device manufacturers tweak Android for their own hardware. This section points out a couple of places where these changes can affect your application if you're not prepared for them.

View Hierarchy

Android is not designed to handle arbitrarily complicated view hierarchies. Here, *view hierarchy* means containers holding containers holding containers holding widgets. The `hierarchyviewer` program, described in a later chapter, depicts such view hierarchies well.

Android has always had limits as to how deep the view hierarchy can be. In Android 1.5, though, the limit was reduced, so some applications that worked fine on Android 1.1 would crash with a `StackOverflowException` in the newer Android. This, of course, was frustrating to developers who never realized there was an issue with view hierarchy depth and then got caught by this change.

The lessons to take from this are as follows:

- Keep your view hierarchies shallow. Once you drift into double-digit depth, you are increasingly likely to run out of stack space.

- If you encounter a StackOverflowException and the stack trace looks like it is somewhere in the middle of drawing your widgets, your view hierarchy is probably too complex.

Changing Resources

The core Android team may change resources with an Android upgrade, and those may have unexpected effects in your application. For example, in Android 1.5, the Android team changed the stock Button background, to allow for smaller buttons. However, applications that implicitly relied on the former larger minimum size wound up breaking and needing some UI adjustment.

Similarly, applications can reuse public resources, such as icons, available inside of Android proper. While doing so saves some storage space, many of these resources are public by necessity and are not considered part of the SDK. For example, hardware manufacturers may change the icons to fit some alternative UI look and feel. Relying on the existing ones to always look as they do is a bit dangerous. You are better served by copying those resources out of the Android open source project into your own code base.

Handling API Changes

The core Android team has generally done a good job of keeping APIs stable, and supporting a deprecation model when they do change APIs. In Android, when a feature is *deprecated*, that does not mean the feature is going away, just that its continued use is discouraged. And, of course, new APIs are released with every new Android update. Changes to the APIs are well documented with each release via an API differences report.

Unfortunately, the Android Market—the primary distribution channel for Android applications—allows you to upload only one Android package (APK) file for each application. Hence, you need that one APK file to deal with as many Android versions as possible. Many times, your code will "just work" and not require changing. Other times, though, you will need to make adjustments, particularly if you want to support new APIs on new versions while not breaking on old versions. Let's examine some techniques for handling these cases.

Minimum, Maximum, Target, and Build Versions

Android goes to great lengths to help you deal with the fact that at any point in time, there will be many Android OS versions out on the market. Unfortunately, the tools supplied by Android have given us a somewhat confusing set of overlapping concepts, such as targets and SDK versions. This section attempts to clarify those concepts.

Targets vs. SDK Versions vs. OS Versions

The concept of targets was introduced toward the beginning of this book. Targets are used when defining AVDs, to determine what sort of device those AVDs support. Targets are also used when creating new projects, primarily to determine what version of the SDK build tools will be used to build your project.

A target combines an API level with an indicator of whether or not the target includes Google APIs (e.g., Google Maps support).

An API level is an integer representing a version of the Android API. Each Android OS release that makes changes to the Android API triggers a new API level. Following are the API levels:

- 3: Android 1.5r1, 1.5r2, and 1.5r3

- 4: Android 1.6r1 and 1.6r2

- 5: Android 2.0

- 6: Android 2.0.1

- 7: Android 2.1.x

- 8: Android 2.2.x

- 9: Android 2.3, 2.3.1, and 2.3.2

- 10: Android 2.3.3 and 2.3.4

- 11: Android 3.0.x

- 12: Android 3.1.x

- 13: Android 3.2

- 14: Android 4.0

Google maintains a web page that outlines which versions of Android are in use today, based on requests made to the Android Market.

Minimum SDK Version

In your `AndroidManifest.xml` file, you should add a `<uses-sdk>` element. This element describes how your application relates to the various SDK versions.

The most critical attribute to have in `<uses-sdk>` is `android:minSdkVersion`. This indicates what the lowest API level is that your application supports. Devices running Android OS versions associated with lower API levels will not be able to install your application. Your application may not even appear to those devices in the Android Market listings, should you elect to publish via that distributor.

If you skip this attribute, Android assumes your application works on *all* Android API versions. That may be true, but it is rather dangerous to assume if you have not tested it. Hence, set `android:minSdkVersion` to the lowest level you are testing and are willing to support.

Target SDK Version

Another `<uses-sdk>` attribute is `android:targetSdkVersion`. This represents the version of the Android API that you are primarily developing for. Any Android device running a newer version of the OS may elect to apply some compatibility settings that will help apps such as yours, targeting an older API, to run on the newer version.

Most of the time, you should set this to be the current Android API version, as of the time you are publishing your application.

In particular, with Ice Cream Sandwich, you need to specify a target of 14 or 15 to get the new look and feel.

Maximum SDK Version

The third `<uses-sdk>` attribute is `android:maxSdkVersion`. Any Android device running a newer Android OS than is indicated by this API level will be prohibited from running your application.

On the plus side, this ensures that your application will not be used on API levels you have not tested, particularly if you set this to be the current Android API version as of your publication date.

However, bear in mind that your application will be filtered out of the Android Market for these newer devices. Over time, this will limit the reach of your application, if you do not release an update with a higher maximum SDK version.

The core Android team recommends that you not use this option and instead rely on Android's intrinsic backward compatibility—particularly leveraging your `android:targetSdkVersion` value—to allow your application to continue to run on new Android OS versions.

Detecting the Version

If you simply want to take different branches in your code based on version, the easiest thing to do is inspect android.os.Build.VERSION.SDK_INT. This public static integer value will reflect the same API level as you use when creating AVDs and specifying API levels in the manifest. So, you can compare that value to, say, android.os.Build.VERSION_CODES.DONUT to see whether you are running on Android 1.6 or newer.

Wrapping the API

So long as the APIs you try to use exist across all Android versions you are supporting, just branching may be sufficient. Where things get troublesome is when the APIs change, such as when there are new parameters to methods, new methods, or even new classes. You need code that will work regardless of Android version, while also letting you take advantage of new APIs where available.

The challenge is that if you try loading into the virtual machine code that refers to classes, methods, and such that do not exist in the version of Android that the device is running on, your application will crash with a VerifyError. You need to *compile* against the version of Android that contains the latest APIs you are trying to use—you just cannot load that code into an older Android device.

Note that the key phrase here is "load that code." You don't necessarily have a problem just because a class exists in your application that uses a newer-than-available API. It is only if you execute code that triggers Android to load that class into your running process that you will encounter the VerifyError.

With that in mind, there are three primary tricks to deal with this situation, outlined in the following sections.

Detecting Classes

Perhaps all you need to do is disable some features in your app that lead to things that are not possible on a given device. For example, suppose you have an activity that uses the fragments feature. You cannot successfully start that activity on a pre-3.0 device. Stopping that activity may just be a matter of disabling a menu choice or Button or something.

To see if a certain class (say, ListFragment) is available to you, you can call Class.forName(). This will either return a Class object representing the requested class or throw an Exception if it is not available. You can use the exception handler as the spot to disable the UI paths that would cause your application to try to start an activity that uses the unavailable class.

Reflection

If you need limited access to a class that will not exist on older versions of Android, you can use a bit of reflection.

For example, in the chapter on rotation, we used a series of sample applications that allowed the user to pick a contact. That relied on an ACTION_PICK Intent, using a specific Uri for the contact's content provider. In those samples, we specifically used ContactsContract, the revised contacts API offered in Android 2.0 and beyond. That means those projects will not work on older versions of Android.

However, all we really need is this magic Uri value. If we can devise a way to get the right Uri for older versions of Android, as well as the right Uri for newer versions of Android, without causing problems, we can be more backward compatible.

Fortunately, this is fairly easy to do with some reflection:

```
static {
  int sdk=new Integer(Build.VERSION.SDK).intValue();

  if (sdk>=5) {
    try {
      Class clazz=Class.forName("android.provider.ContactsContract$Contacts");

      CONTENT_URI=(Uri)clazz.getField("CONTENT_URI").get(clazz);
    }
    catch (Throwable t) {
      Log.e("PickDemo", "Exception when determining CONTENT_URI", t);
    }
  }
  else {
    CONTENT_URI=android.provider.Contacts.People.CONTENT_URI;
  }
}
```

Here, we examine the API level of the device by looking at Build.VERSION.SDK (we could use Build.VERSION.SDK_INT, but that wasn't added until Android 1.6—the code shown here works on Android 1.5 as well). If we are at Android 2.0 (API level 5) or higher, we use Class.forName() to get at the new ContactsContract.Contacts class, and then use reflection to get at the CONTENT_URI static data member on that class. If we are on an older version of Android, we simply use the Uri published by the older Contacts.People class.

Since we are not directly referencing ContactsContract.Contacts in our code, we can safely execute this, even on older versions of Android.

Conditional Class Loading

Reflection works but is a pain for anything complex. Also, it is slower than calling code directly.

The most powerful technique, therefore, is simply to organize your code such that you have regular classes using newer APIs, but you do not load those classes on older devices. We will examine this technique later in this book.

Patterns for Ice Cream Sandwich and Honeycomb

With the advent of Honeycomb (Android 3.0), and now Ice Cream Sandwich (Android 4.0), supporting multiple Android versions is now a significant challenge. The UI changes required to support differing UIs will, in many cases, require you to take steps to make sure that your application still works successfully on older versions of Android. This section outlines some patterns for dealing with this area of backward compatibility.

The Action Bar

As noted in Chapter 27, many of the action bar's basic features will work in a backward-compatible fashion. For example, indicating than an options menu item can be shown in the action bar requires just an attribute in the menu resource XML, an attribute that will be ignored on older versions of Android. Honeycomb-capable devices will put the item in the action bar, while devices running previous Android versions will not.

However, not all of the action bar's features are backward compatible. In the `Menus/ActionBar` sample application in Chapter 27, we added a custom `View` to the action bar, to allow people to add words to our list without dealing with menus and dialog boxes. However, this required some code that works only on API level 11 (Android 3.0) and higher. More advanced action bar capabilities—ones beyond the scope of this book—will have similar requirements.

You need to arrange to use those action bar methods only on devices that run API level 11 or higher. Conditional class loading, outlined earlier in this chapter, is one such technique, and is the technique used in the `Menus/ActionBarBC` sample application. Let's take a look at how this works.

Checking the API Level

Our original`onCreateOptionsMenu()` looked like this:

```
@Override
public boolean onCreateOptionsMenu(Menu menu) {
  new MenuInflater(this).inflate(R.menu.option, menu);

  EditText add=(EditText)menu
                        .findItem(R.id.add)
                        .getActionView()
                        .findViewById(R.id.title);

  add.setOnEditorActionListener(onSearch);

  return(super.onCreateOptionsMenu(menu));
}
```

This is fine, but it will work only on API level 11 and higher, as getActionView() only exists from that API level onward. Hence, we cannot run this code, or even load this class, on older versions of Android without getting a VerifyError.

The new version of onCreateOptionsMenu() hides the offending code and checks the API level:

```
@Override
public boolean onCreateOptionsMenu(Menu menu) {
  new MenuInflater(this).inflate(R.menu.option, menu);

  EditText add=null;

  if (Build.VERSION.SDK_INT>=Build.VERSION_CODES.HONEYCOMB) {
    View v=ICSHCHelper.getAddActionView(menu);

    if (v!=null) {
      add=(EditText)v.findViewById(R.id.title);
    }
  }

  if (add!=null) {
    add.setOnEditorActionListener(onSearch);
  }

  return(super.onCreateOptionsMenu(menu));
}
```

We hide only the code that retrieves the View that we theoretically have put in the action bar. If we are on an older version of Android, the HONEYCOMB check will fail, and we will wind up with a null View, so we skip adding the OnEditorActionListener to the EditText inside of that View.

This has another benefit: it works if the Android device runs API level 11 or higher but does not have room for our custom View. Android tablets will have an action bar and sufficient room, but future Honeycomb-capable phones might have an action bar but lack sufficient room. In that case, the phone would leave the Add options menu item in place, and we still would wind up with a null View. This code handles that scenario; the original code did not.

Isolating the Ice Cream Sandwich/Honeycomb Code

Our Honeycomb-specific code is held in a separate ICSHCHelper class (ICS for Ice Cream Sandwich, HC for Honeycomb), one that will only be used on API level 11 (or higher) devices:

```
package com.commonsware.android.inflation;

import android.view.Menu;
import android.view.View;

class ICSHCHelper {
  static View getAddActionView(Menu menu) {
```

```
    return(menu.findItem(R.id.add).getActionView());
  }
}
```

ICSHCHelper has a single getAddActionView() static method that finds the View for the Add action bar entry, if there is one.

Since we do not try to execute any code on this class except for inside the HONEYCOMB check, it is safe to have this class on older versions of Android. The Menus/ActionBarHC app works on Android 1.6 and newer.

Writing Tablet-Only Apps

Ideally, your Android applications work on all form factors: phones, tablets, and so forth. However, you may want to create an app that simply would be unusable on phones. Ideally, you would want to keep your app off of small-screen devices, so that users are not disappointed.

To do this, you can take advantage of the fact that Android will scale apps up but will not scale apps down. In other words, if you specify that your application does not support some larger screen sizes (e.g., android:xlargeScreens="false" appears in your <supports-screens> element in your AndroidManifest.xml file), Android still allows your app to run on such screens and takes steps to help your app run with the additional screen space. However, if you specify that your application does not support some smaller screen sizes (e.g., android:smallScreens="false" appears in your <supports-screens> element), Android will not run your app, and you will be filtered out of the Android Market for such devices.

Hence, if your application will work well only on larger-screen devices, use a <supports-screens> element like this:

```
<supports-screens android:xlargeScreens="true"
                  android:largeScreens="true"
                  android:normalScreens="false"
                  android:smallScreens="false"
                  android:anyDensity="true"/>
```

Data Stores, Network Services, and APIs

Chapter 30

Accessing Files

While Android offers structured storage, via preferences and databases, sometimes a simple file will suffice. Android offers two models for accessing files: one for files prepackaged with your application and one for files created on-device by your application.

You and the Horse You Rode in On

Let's suppose you have some static data you want to ship with the application, such as a list of words for a spell checker. The easiest way to deploy that is to put the file in the res/raw directory, so that it will be put in the Android application APK file as part of the packaging process as a raw resource.

To access this file, you need to get yourself a Resources object. From an activity, that is as simple as calling getResources(). A Resources object offers openRawResource() to get an InputStream on the file you specify. Rather than a path, openRawResource() expects an integer identifier for the file as packaged. This works just like accessing widgets via findViewById(); for example, if you put a file named words.xml in res/raw, the identifier is accessible in Java as R.raw.words.

Since you can get only an InputStream, you have no means of modifying this file. Hence, it is useful really only for static reference data. Moreover, since it doesn't change until the user installs an updated version of your application package, either the reference data must be valid for the foreseeable future or you must provide some means of updating the data. The simplest way to handle that is to use the reference data to bootstrap some other modifiable form of storage (e.g., a database), but that results in two copies of the data in storage. An alternative is to keep the reference data as is and keep modifications in a file or database, and then merge them together when you need a complete picture of the information. For example, if your application ships a file of URLs, you could have a second file that tracks URLs added by the user or references URLs that were deleted by the user.

In the Files/Static sample project, you will find a reworking of the list box example from earlier, this time using a static XML file instead of a hardwired array in Java. The layout is the same:

```xml
<?xml version="1.0" encoding="utf-8"?>
<LinearLayout xmlns:android="http://schemas.android.com/apk/res/android"
  android:orientation="vertical"
  android:layout_width="fill_parent"
  android:layout_height="fill_parent" >
  <TextView
    android:id="@+id/selection"
    android:layout_width="fill_parent"
    android:layout_height="wrap_content"
  />
  <ListView
    android:id="@android:id/list"
    android:layout_width="fill_parent"
    android:layout_height="fill_parent"
    android:drawSelectorOnTop="false"
  />
</LinearLayout>
```

In addition to that XML file, you also need an XML file with the words to show in the list:

```xml
<words>
  <word value="lorem" />
  <word value="ipsum" />
  <word value="dolor" />
  <word value="sit" />
  <word value="amet" />
  <word value="consectetuer" />
  <word value="adipiscing" />
  <word value="elit" />
  <word value="morbi" />
  <word value="vel" />
  <word value="ligula" />
  <word value="vitae" />
  <word value="arcu" />
  <word value="aliquet" />
  <word value="mollis" />
  <word value="etiam" />
  <word value="vel" />
  <word value="erat" />
  <word value="placerat" />
  <word value="ante" />
  <word value="porttitor" />
  <word value="sodales" />
  <word value="pellentesque" />
  <word value="augue" />
  <word value="purus" />
</words>
```

While this XML structure is not exactly a model of space efficiency, it will suffice for a demo.

The Java code now must read in that XML file, parse out the words, and put them someplace for the list to pick up:

```java
public class StaticFileDemo extends ListActivity {
  TextView selection;
```

```
ArrayList<String> items=new ArrayList<String>();

@Override
public void onCreate(Bundle icicle) {
  super.onCreate(icicle);
  setContentView(R.layout.main);
  selection=(TextView)findViewById(R.id.selection);

  try {
    InputStream in=getResources().openRawResource(R.raw.words);
    DocumentBuilder builder=DocumentBuilderFactory
                            .newInstance()
                            .newDocumentBuilder();
    Document doc=builder.parse(in, null);
    NodeList words=doc.getElementsByTagName("word");

    for (int i=0;i<words.getLength();i++) {
      items.add(((Element)words.item(i)).getAttribute("value"));
    }

    in.close();
  }
  catch (Throwable t) {
    Toast
      .makeText(this, "Exception: "+t.toString(), Toast.LENGTH_LONG)
      .show();
  }

  setListAdapter(new ArrayAdapter<String>(this,
                        android.R.layout.simple_list_item_1,
                        items));
}

public void onListItemClick(ListView parent, View v, int position,
                  long id) {
  selection.setText(items.get(position).toString());
}
}
```

> **NOTE:** Our call to openRawResource() references R.raw.words as previously described. From Ice Cream Sandwich onward—and more specifically, SDK and ADT releases 14 and 15—Google has moved to disallow some references to resource fields in this fashion, to allow for library projects to be compiled only once and then reused across applications. Normally, this wouldn't warrant a mention. However, in Eclipse, the ADT plug-in released with SDK 14 mistakenly flags as an error our usage, as an attempt to use R.raw.words in a switch statement. Until this glitch is ironed out, you'll need to either build from the command line or tweak your ADT plug-in level.

The differences mostly lie within onCreate(). We get an InputStream for the XML file (getResources().openRawResource(R.raw.words)), then use the built-in XML parsing logic to parse the file into a DOM Document, pick out the word elements, and then pour the value attributes into an ArrayList for use by the ArrayAdapter.

The resulting activity looks the same as before, as shown in Figure 30–1, since the list of words is the same, just relocated.

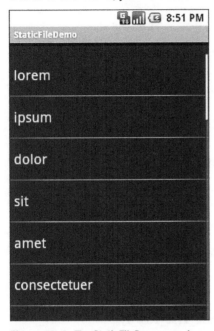

Figure 30–1. *The StaticFileDemo sample application*

Of course, there are even easier ways to have XML files available to you as prepackaged files, such as by using an XML resource. That is covered in Chapter 31. However, while this example used XML, the file could just as easily have been a simple one-word-per-line list, or in some other format not handled natively by the Android resource system.

Readin' 'n Writin'

Reading and writing your own, application-specific data files is nearly identical to what you might do in a desktop Java application. The key is to use op enFileInput() and openFileOutput() on your Activity or other Context to get an InputStream and OutputStream, respectively. From that point forward, it is not much different from regular Java I/O logic:

- Wrap those streams as needed, such as by using an InputStreamReader or OutputStreamWriter for text-based I/O.

- Read or write the data.

- Use close() to release the stream when done.

If two applications both try to read a notes.txt file via openFileInput(), each will access its own edition of the file. If you need to have one file accessible from many places, you probably want to create a content provider, as will be described in an upcoming chapter.

Note that openFileInput() and openFileOutput() do not accept file paths (e.g., path/to/file.txt), just simple file names.

Following is the layout for the world's most trivial text editor, pulled from the Files/ReadWrite sample application:

```xml
<?xml version="1.0" encoding="utf-8"?>
<EditText xmlns:android="http://schemas.android.com/apk/res/android"
  android:id="@+id/editor"
  android:layout_width="fill_parent"
  android:layout_height="fill_parent"
  android:singleLine="false"
  android:gravity="top"
  />
```

All we have here is a large text-editing widget...which is pretty boring.

The Java is only slightly more complicated:

```java
package com.commonsware.android.readwrite;

import android.app.Activity;
import android.os.Bundle;
import android.view.View;
import android.widget.Button;
import android.widget.EditText;
import android.widget.Toast;
import java.io.BufferedReader;
import java.io.File;
import java.io.InputStream;
import java.io.InputStreamReader;
import java.io.OutputStream;
import java.io.OutputStreamWriter;

public class ReadWriteFileDemo extends Activity {
  private final static String NOTES="notes.txt";
  private EditText editor;

  @Override
  public void onCreate(Bundle icicle) {
    super.onCreate(icicle);
    setContentView(R.layout.main);
    editor=(EditText)findViewById(R.id.editor);
  }

  public void onResume() {
    super.onResume();

    try {
      InputStream in=openFileInput(NOTES);

      if (in!=null) {
```

```
          InputStreamReader tmp=new InputStreamReader(in);
          BufferedReader reader=new BufferedReader(tmp);
          String str;
          StringBuilder buf=new StringBuilder();

          while ((str = reader.readLine()) != null) {
            buf.append(str+"\n");
          }

          in.close();
          editor.setText(buf.toString());
        }
      }
      catch (java.io.FileNotFoundException e) {
        // that's OK, we probably haven't created it yet
      }
      catch (Throwable t) {
        Toast
          .makeText(this, "Exception: "+t.toString(), Toast.LENGTH_LONG)
          .show();
      }
    }

    public void onPause() {
      super.onPause();

      try {
        OutputStreamWriter out=
            new OutputStreamWriter(openFileOutput(NOTES, 0));

        out.write(editor.getText().toString());
        out.close();
      }
      catch (Throwable t) {
        Toast
          .makeText(this, "Exception: "+t.toString(), Toast.LENGTH_LONG)
          .show();
      }
    }
  }
```

First, we hook into onResume(), so we get control when our editor is coming back to life, from a fresh launch or after having been frozen. We use openFileInput() to read in notes.txt and pour the contents into the text editor. If the file is not found, we assume this is the first time the activity was run (or the file was deleted by other means), and we just leave the editor empty.

Next, we hook into onPause(), so we get control as our activity gets hidden by another activity or is closed, such as via the device's Back button. Here, we use openFileOutput() to open notes.txt, into which we pour the contents of the text editor.

The net result is that we have a persistent notepad, as shown in Figures 30–2 and 30–3. Whatever is typed in will remain until deleted, surviving our activity being closed (e.g., via the Back button), the phone being turned off, or similar situations.

Figure 30–2. *The ReadWriteFileDemo sample application, as initially launched*

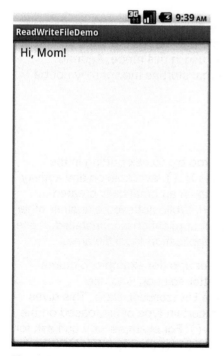

Figure 30–3. *The same application, after entering some text*

Another approach for working with application-local files is to use getFilesDir(). This returns a File object pointing to a place in the onboard flash where an application can store files. This directory is where openFileInput() and openFileOutput() work. However, while openFileInput() and openFileOutput() do not support subdirectories, the File from getFilesDir() can be used to create and navigate subdirectories if desired.

The files stored here are accessible only to your application, by default. Other applications on the device have no rights to read, let alone write, to this space. However, bear in mind that some users "root" their Android phones, gaining superuser access. These users will be able to read and write whatever files they wish. As a result, please do not consider application-local files to be secure against interested users.

External Storage: Giant Economy-Size Space

In addition to application-local storage, you also have access to external storage. This may be in the form of a removable media card, like an SD card or microSD card, or in the form of additional onboard flash set aside to serve in the "external storage" role.

On the plus side, external storage tends to have more space available than onboard storage. Onboard storage can be rather limited; for example, the original T-Mobile G1 (HTC Dream) had a total of 70MB for all applications combined. Although newer phones offer more onboard space, external storage is usually at least 2GB and can be as big as 32GB.

On the minus side, all applications can, if they wish, read and write external storage, so these files are not very secure. Furthermore, external storage can be mounted on a host computer as a USB mass storage device—when it is in use in this mode, Android applications cannot access it. As a result, files on external storage may or may not be available to you at any given moment.

Where to Write

If you have files tied to your application that are simply too big to risk putting in the application-local file area, you can use getExternalFilesDir(), available on any activity or other Context. This gives you a File object pointing to an automatically created directory on external storage, unique for your application. While not secure against other applications, it does have one big advantage: when your application is uninstalled, these files are automatically deleted, just like the ones in the application-local file area.

If you have files that belong more to the user than to your app (for example, pictures taken by the camera, downloaded MP3 files, etc.), a better solution is to use getExternalStoragePublicDirectory(), available on the Environment class. This gives you a File object pointing to a directory set aside for a certain type of file, based on the type you pass into getExternalStoragePublicDirectory(). For example, you can ask for DIRECTORY_MOVIES, DIRECTORY_MUSIC, or DIRECTORY_PICTURES for storing MP4, MP3, or

JPEG files, respectively. These files will be left behind when your application is uninstalled.

You will also find a `getExternalStorageDirectory()` method on `Environment`, pointing to the root of the external storage. This is no longer the preferred approach—the methods previously described help keep the user's files better organized. However, if you are supporting older Android devices, you may need to use `getExternalStorageDirectory()`, simply because the newer options may not be available to you.

When to Write

Starting with Android 1.6, you also need to hold permissions to work with external storage (e.g., `WRITE_EXTERNAL_STORAGE`). The concept of permissions will be covered in a later chapter.

Also, external storage may be tied up if the user has mounted it as a USB storage device. You can use `getExternalStorageState()` (a static method on `Environment`) to determine whether or not the external storage is presently available.

StrictMode: Avoiding Janky Code

Users are more likely to like your application if, to them, it feels responsive. By "responsive," we mean that it reacts swiftly and accurately to user operations, like taps and swipes.

Conversely, users are less likely to be happy with your application if they perceive that your UI is "janky"—sluggish to respond to their requests. For example, perhaps your lists do not scroll as smoothly as users would like, or tapping a button does not yield the immediate results they seek.

While threads and `AsyncTask` and the like can help, it may not always be obvious where you should apply them. A full-scale performance analysis, using Traceview or similar Android tools, is certainly possible. However, there are a few standard sorts of things that developers do, sometimes quite by accident, on the main application thread that tend to cause sluggishness:

- Flash I/O, both for the onboard storage and for external storage (e.g., the SD card)
- Network I/O

However, even here, it may not be obvious that you are performing these operations on the main application thread. This is particularly true when the operations are really being done by Android's code that you are simply calling.

That is where `StrictMode` comes in. Its mission is to help you determine when you are doing things on the main application thread that might cause a janky user experience.

Setting Up StrictMode

StrictMode works on a set of policies. There are presently two categories of policies: VM policies and thread policies. VM policies represent bad coding practices that pertain to your entire application, notably leaking SQLite Cursor objects and kin. Thread policies represent things that are bad when performed on the main application thread, notably flash I/O and network I/O.

Each policy dictates what StrictMode should watch for (e.g., flash reads are OK but flash writes are not) and how StrictMode should react when you violate the rules, such as

- Log a message to LogCat

- Display a dialog box

- Crash your application (seriously!)

The simplest thing to do is call the static enableDefaults() method on StrictMode from onCreate() of your first activity. This will set up normal operation, reporting all violations by simply logging to LogCat. However, you can set your own custom policies via Builder objects if you so choose.

Seeing StrictMode in Action

The Threads/ReadWriteStrict sample application is a reworking of the Files/ReadWrite sample application shown earlier in this chapter. All it adds is a custom StrictMode thread policy:

```
StrictMode.setThreadPolicy(new StrictMode.ThreadPolicy.Builder()
                         .detectAll()
                         .penaltyLog()
                         .build());
```

If you run the application, the user will see no difference. However, you will have a debug-level log message in LogCat with the following stack trace:

```
12-28 17:19:40.009: DEBUG/StrictMode(480): StrictMode policy violation; ~duration=169↵
 ms: android.os.StrictMode$StrictModeDiskReadViolation: policy=23 violation=2
12-28 17:19:40.009: DEBUG/StrictMode(480): at↵
 android.os.StrictMode$AndroidBlockGuardPolicy.onReadFromDisk(StrictMode.java:745)
12-28 17:19:40.009: DEBUG/StrictMode(480): at↵
 dalvik.system.BlockGuard$WrappedFileSystem.open(BlockGuard.java:228)
12-28 17:19:40.009: DEBUG/StrictMode(480): at↵
 android.app.ContextImpl.openFileOutput(ContextImpl.java:410)
12-28 17:19:40.009: DEBUG/StrictMode(480): at↵
 android.content.ContextWrapper.openFileOutput(ContextWrapper.java:158)
12-28 17:19:40.009: DEBUG/StrictMode(480): at↵
 com.commonsware.android.readwrite.ReadWriteFileDemo.onPause(ReadWriteFileDemo.java:82)
...
```

Here, StrictMode is warning us that we attempted a flash write on the main application thread (the thread on which we set the StrictMode policy). Ideally, we would rewrite this project to use an AsyncTask or something for writing out the data.

Development Only, Please!

Do not use StrictMode in production code. It is designed for use when you are building, testing, and debugging your application. It is not designed to be used in the field.

To deal with this, you could

- Simply comment out or remove the StrictMode setup code when you prepare your production builds

- Use some sort of production flag to skip the StrictMode setup code when needed

Conditionally Being Strict

StrictMode is only for Android 2.3 and higher. Hence, if we have it in our code, even in development mode, it might interfere when we try testing on older emulators or devices. As we saw in an earlier chapter, there are techniques for dealing with this, but using reflection for configuring StrictMode would be rather painful.

The right approach, therefore, is simply to organize your code such that you have regular classes using newer APIs, but you do not load those classes on older devices. The APIVersions/ReadWriteStrict project demonstrates this, allowing an application to use Android 2.3's StrictMode where available and skip it where it is not available.

When we examined StrictMode earlier in this section, we configured StrictMode right in the onCreate() method of our sample activity. This works, but only on Android 2.3 and newer.

To allow this to work on older versions of Android, we use StrictWrapper:

```
package com.commonsware.android.readwrite;

import android.os.Build;

abstract class StrictWrapper {
  static private StrictWrapper INSTANCE=null;

  static public void init() {
    if (Build.VERSION.SDK_INT>=Build.VERSION_CODES.GINGERBREAD) {
      INSTANCE=new StrictForRealz();
    }
    else {
      INSTANCE=new NotAllThatStrict();
    }
  }

  static class NotAllThatStrict extends StrictWrapper {
    // no methods needed
  }
}
```

This odd-looking class encapsulates our "do-we-or-don't-we" logic for dealing with StrictMode. It contains an init() method that, when called, checks to see which version of Android the application is running on, and creates a singleton instance of a StrictWrapper subclass based upon it—StrictForRealz for Android 2.3 and higher, NotAllThatStrict for older versions of Android. The latter class, a static inner class of StrictWrapper, does nothing, reflecting that there is no StrictMode in newer versions of Android.

StrictForRealz contains the StrictMode initialization logic:

```
package com.commonsware.android.readwrite;

import android.os.StrictMode;

class StrictForRealz extends StrictWrapper {
  StrictForRealz() {
    StrictMode.setThreadPolicy(new StrictMode.ThreadPolicy.Builder()
                       .detectAll()
                       .penaltyLog()
                       .build());
  }
}
```

And, our onCreate() method of our activity calls init() on StrictWrapper, to trigger creating the proper object:

```
@Override
public void onCreate(Bundle icicle) {
  super.onCreate(icicle);
  setContentView(R.layout.main);

  StrictWrapper.init();

  editor=(EditText)findViewById(R.id.editor);
}
```

When the activity first starts up, neither StrictWrapper nor StrictForRealz is loaded in the process. As soon as we reach the init() statement in onCreate(), Android loads StrictWrapper into the process, but this is safe, as it does not refer to any potentially nonexistent classes. The init() method on StrictWrapper then executes a statement involving StrictForRealz only if we are safely on a supported version of Android. Hence, StrictForRealz will be loaded into the process only if we are on a newer Android release, so our use of StrictMode in StrictForRealz will not trigger a VerifyError.

Here, all we needed was a bit of initialization. The singleton pattern is used to demonstrate that you could expose a version-dependent API implementation if you desired. Simply define the API as abstract methods on the abstract class (StrictWrapper) and have version-dependent concrete implementations of those abstract methods on the concrete subclasses (StrictForRealz, NotAllThatStrict).

Linux File Systems: You Sync, You Win

Android is built atop a Linux kernel and uses Linux file systems for holding its files. Classically, Android used YAFFS (Yet Another Flash File System), optimized for use on low-power devices for storing data to flash memory. Many devices still use YAFFS today.

YAFFS has one big problem: only one process can write to the file system at a time. Rather than offering file-level locking, YAFFS has partition-level locking. This can become a bit of a bottleneck, particularly as Android devices grow in power and start wanting to do more things at the same time, like their desktop and notebook brethren.

Android is starting to move toward ext4, another Linux file system aimed more at desktops/notebooks. Your applications will not directly perceive the difference. However, ext4 does a fair bit of buffering, and it can cause problems for applications that do not take this buffering into account. Linux application developers ran headlong into this in 2008 and 2009, when ext4 started to become popular. As an Android developer, you will need to think about it now...for your own file storage.

If you are using SQLite or SharedPreferences, you do not need to worry about this problem. Android (and SQLite, if you are using it) handles all the buffering issues for you. If, however, you write your own files, you may wish to contemplate an extra step as you flush your data to disk. Specifically, you need to trigger a Linux system call known as fsync(), which tells the file system to ensure all buffers are written to disk.

If you are using java.io.RandomAccessFile in a synchronous mode, this step is handled for you as well, so you will not need to worry about it. However, Java developers tend to use FileOutputStream, which does not trigger an fsync(), even when you call close() on the stream. Instead, you call getFD().sync() on the FileOutputStream to trigger the fsync(). Note that this may be time consuming, and so disk writes should be done off the main application thread wherever practical, such as via an AsyncTask.

Chapter 31

Using Preferences

Android has many different ways for you to store data for long-term use by your activity. The simplest to use is the preferences system, which is the focus of this chapter.

Android allows activities and applications to keep preferences, in the form of key/value pairs (akin to a Map), that will hang around between invocations of an activity. As the name suggests, the primary purpose of preferences is to enable you to store user-specified configuration details, such as the last feed the user looked at in your feed reader, the sort order to use by default on a list, or whatever. Of course, you can store in the preferences whatever you like, as long as it is keyed by a String and has a primitive value (boolean, String, etc.)

Preferences can be either for a single activity or shared among all activities in an application. Other components, such as services, also can work with shared preferences.

Getting What You Want

To get access to the preferences, you have three APIs to choose from:

- getPreferences() from within your Activity, to access activity-specific preferences

- getSharedPreferences() from within your Activity (or other application Context), to access application-level preferences

- getDefaultSharedPreferences(), on PreferenceManager, to get the shared preferences that work in concert with Android's overall preference framework

The first two methods take a security mode parameter—the right choice is MODE_PRIVATE, so that no other applications can access the file. The getSharedPreferences() method also takes a name of a set of preferences. getPreferences() effectively calls getSharedPreferences() with the activity's class name as the preference set name. The getDefaultSharedPreferences() method takes the Context for the preferences (e.g., your Activity).

All of these methods return an instance of SharedPreferences, which offers a series of getters to access named preferences, returning a suitably typed result (e.g., getBoolean() to return a Boolean preference). The getters also take a default value, which is returned if there is no preference set under the specified key.

Unless you have a good reason to do otherwise, you are best served using the third option—getDefaultSharedPreferences()—as that will give you the SharedPreferences object that works with a PreferenceActivity by default, as will be described later in this chapter.

Stating Your Preference

Given the appropriate SharedPreferences object, you can use edit() to get an editor for the preferences. This object has a set of setters that mirror the getters on the parent SharedPreferences object. It also has the following methods:

- remove(): Deletes a single named preference
- clear(): Deletes all preferences
- commit(): Persists your changes made via the editor

The commit() method is important, because if you modify preferences via the editor and fail to commit() the changes, those changes will evaporate once the editor goes out of scope. Note that Android 2.3 has an apply() method, which works like commit() but runs faster.

Conversely, since the preferences object supports live changes, if one part of your application (say, an activity) modifies shared preferences, another part of your application (say, a service) will have access to the changed value immediately.

Introducing PreferenceFragment and PreferenceActivity

You could roll your own activity to collect preferences from the user. On the whole, this is a bad idea. Instead, use preference XML resources and a PreferenceFragment or a PreferenceActivity, depending on your targeted version of Android. Why? One of the common complaints about Android developers is that they lack discipline, not following any standards or conventions inherent in the platform. For other operating systems, the device manufacturer might prevent you from distributing apps that violate their human interface guidelines. With Android, that is not the case—but this is not a blanket permission to do whatever you want. Where there is a standard or convention, please follow it, so that users will feel more comfortable with your app and their device. Using a PreferenceFragment in Android 3.0 or later, or a PreferenceActivity in earlier versions, for collecting preferences is one such convention. The behavior of PreferenceActivity was revamped with Android 3.0 and 4.0, so we'll introduce the new way of working with preferences first, and then illustrate the original model—useful for the many existing Android 1.x and 2.x devices with which your code may need to be compatible.

Preferences via Fragments

Android 3.0 and beyond introduce a new and improved `PreferenceScreen` and `PreferenceActivity`. This allows preference selection on larger screens to look great, providing rapid access to a large number of settings, as shown in Figure 31–1.

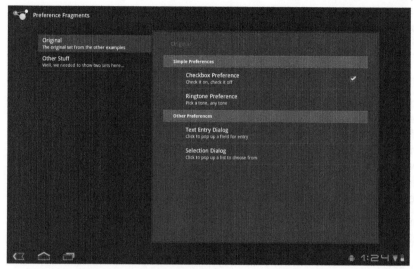

Figure 31–1. *PreferenceActivity using fragments*

On the minus side, the new system is not part of the Android Compatibility Library, and as such cannot be used directly on pre-3.0 versions of Android. That being said, it is possible to work out a backward-compatible solution, though it may require some effort if you have a lot of preferences.

Preferences the New and Improved Way

In pre-Honeycomb versions of Android, a `PreferenceActivity` subclass loads preferences from resource files, to indicate what should go on the screen. In Honeycomb and Ice Cream Sandwich, a `PreferenceActivity` subclass loads preference *headers* from resource files, to indicate what should go on the screen.

Preference Headers

Visually, preference headers are not preference categories (placing a header over a set of preferences). Rather, preference headers are the major clusters of preferences. The headers are listed on the left, with the preferences for the selected header shown on the right, as depicted in Figure 31–1. Ice Cream Sandwich or Honeycomb PreferenceActivity calls loadHeadersFromResource(), pointing to another XML resource that describes the preference headers. For example, here is res/xml/preference_headers.xml from the Prefs/Fragments sample project:

```
<preference-headers xmlns:android="http://schemas.android.com/apk/res/android">
    <header android:fragment="com.commonsware.android.preffrags.StockPreferenceFragment"
            android:title="Original"
            android:summary="The original set from the other examples">
      <extra android:name="resource" android:value="preferences" />
    </header>
    <header android:fragment="com.commonsware.android.preffrags.StockPreferenceFragment"
            android:title="Other Stuff"
            android:summary="Well, we needed to show two sets here...">
      <extra android:name="resource" android:value="preferences2" />
    </header>
</preference-headers>
```

Each <header> element indicates the PreferenceFragment subclass that will describe the preferences that belong to the header. In addition, the <header> element describes the title and summary for the header, along with an optional icon (android:icon attribute). A <header> element may also have one or more <extra> child elements, providing a key/value pair of extra data that a PreferenceFragment can use for configuration. In the preceding example, each <header> element has one <extra> element defining the name of an XML resource that will hold the preferences for that header.

Hence, the PreferenceActivity is a very short structure:

```
package com.commonsware.android.preffrags;

import android.os.Bundle;
import android.preference.PreferenceActivity;
import java.util.List;

public class EditPreferences extends PreferenceActivity {
  @Override
  public void onBuildHeaders(List<Header> target) {
    loadHeadersFromResource(R.xml.preference_headers, target);
  }
}
```

You override an onLoadHeaders() method and call loadHeadersFromResource() there.

PreferenceFragment and StockPreferenceFragment

As previously mentioned, the preference headers point to subclasses of PreferenceFragment. The job of PreferenceFragment is to do what PreferenceActivity does in older versions of Android (which we'll cover shortly)—call addPreferencesFromResource() to define the preferences to be displayed on the right when the associated header is tapped on the left.

What is odd about PreferenceFragment is that it requires subclasses. Considering that the vast majority of such fragments would simply call addPreferencesFromResource()

once on a single resource, it would seem logical to have that built into Android, allowing subclasses of PreferenceFragment for more complicated cases. Yet, that is not presently supported. Official Android samples would have you create one PreferenceFragment subclass for each preference header, which seems wasteful.

Another approach is to use StockPreferenceFragment, a PreferenceFragment subclass that is implemented in the Prefs/Fragments project but can be used wherever. It assumes that you have added an <extra> to the <header> identifying the name of the preference XML resource to load, and it loads it. No extra subclasses are required. That is how both headers shown in the previous section can point to the single StockPreferenceFragment implementation.

StockPreferenceFragment is not especially long, but it does employ one trick:

```
package com.commonsware.android.preffrags;

import android.os.Bundle;
import android.preference.PreferenceFragment;

public class StockPreferenceFragment extends PreferenceFragment {
  @Override
  public void onCreate(Bundle savedInstanceState) {
    super.onCreate(savedInstanceState);

    int res=getActivity()
              .getResources()
              .getIdentifier(getArguments().getString("resource"),
                        "xml",
                        getActivity().getPackageName());

    addPreferencesFromResource(res);
  }
}
```

To get at the extras, a PreferenceFragment can call getArguments(), which returns a Bundle. In our case, we can get the resources extra value via getArguments().getString("resource"). The problem is, this is a String, not a resource ID. In order to call addPreferencesFromResource(), we need the resource ID of the preference that we know only by name.

The trick is to use getIdentifier(). The getIdentifier() method on the Resources object—itself obtained by calling getResources() on an Activity—will use reflection to find the resource ID when given three pieces of information:

- The name of the resource (in this case, the value from the arguments)

- The type of the resource (in this case, xml)

- The package where this ID should reside (typically, your own package, obtained by calling getPackageName() on an Activity)

So, StockPreferenceFragment uses getIdentifier() to convert the resource extra into a resource ID, which it then uses with addPreferencesFromResource().

Note that getIdentifier() is not particularly fast, since it uses reflection. Do not use this in a tight loop, in getView() of an Adapter, or any place where it may be called thousands of times.

Avoiding Nested PreferenceScreen Elements

In pre-Honeycomb Android, if you have a lot of preferences, you might consider turning them into nested PreferenceScreen elements. It is better to break them out into separate preference headers. Partly, this is to provide a better user experience—users can directly see and access the various headers, versus having to wade through your preferences to find ones that lead to nested PreferenceScreens. It is also partly because the nested PreferenceScreen UI does not adopt the contemporary Android look and feel (e.g., there are no nested preference headers), so there will be a visual clash.

Intents for Headers or Preferences

If you need to collect some preferences that are beyond what the standard preferences can handle, you have some choices.

One choice is to create a custom Preference. Extending DialogPreference to create your own Preference implementation is not especially hard. However, it does constrain you to something that can fit in a dialog box.

Another option is to specify an <intent> element as a child of a <header> element. When the user taps this header, your specified Intent is used with startActivity(), giving you a gateway to your own activity for collecting things that are beyond what the preference UI can handle. For example, you could have the following <header>:

```
<header android:icon="@drawable/something"
        android:title="Fancy Stuff"
        android:summary="Click here to transcend your plane of existence">
  <intent android:action="com.commonsware.android.MY_CUSTOM_ACTION" />
</header>
```

Then, as long as you have an activity with an <intent-filter> specifying your desired action (com.commonsware.android.MY_CUSTOM_ACTION), that activity will get control when the user taps the associated header.

Adding Backward Compatibility

Of course, everything described in this section works only on Android 3.0 through 4.0 and higher. What about the millions of other Android devices? Are they chopped liver? No. For one thing, chopped liver has notoriously bad cellular reception. However, they will have to retreat to the original PreferenceActivity approach. Since older versions of Android cannot load classes that refer to other classes or methods that are from newer versions of Android, the simplest approach is to have two PreferenceActivity classes, one new and one old.

For example, the `Prefs/FragmentsBC` sample project has all the code from `Prefs/Fragments`, with a few alterations. First, the specific version of the `EditPreferences` class that targets Ice Cream Sandwich and Honeycomb is renamed `EditPreferencesNew`. Another `EditPreferences` class, based on our original prefragment implementation, is added:

```
package com.commonsware.android.preffrags;

import android.os.Bundle;
import android.preference.PreferenceActivity;

public class EditPreferences extends PreferenceActivity {
  @Override
  public void onCreate(Bundle savedInstanceState) {
    super.onCreate(savedInstanceState);

    addPreferencesFromResource(R.xml.preferences);
    addPreferencesFromResource(R.xml.preferences2);
  }
}
```

Here, we take advantage of the fact that addPreferencesFromResource() can be called multiple times to simply chain together our two preference headers' worth of preferences. And, the options menu choice for opening our PreferenceActivity changes to choose the right one, based on our Build.VERSION.SDK_INT value:

```
  @Override
  public boolean onOptionsItemSelected(MenuItem item) {
    switch (item.getItemId()) {
      case EDIT_ID:
        if (Build.VERSION.SDK_INT<Build.VERSION_CODES.HONEYCOMB) {
                                                        startActivity(new
Intent(this, EditPreferences.class));
        }
        else {
                                                        startActivity(new
Intent(this, EditPreferencesNew.class));
        }

        return(true);
    }

    return(super.onOptionsItemSelected(item));
  }
```

Hence, we use the `EditPreferencesNew` class only when that is known to be safe. Otherwise, we use the older one.

The Older Model of Preference Handling

In older versions of Android, pre 3.x, the linchpin to the preferences framework and `PreferenceActivity` is yet another XML data structure. You can describe your application's preferences in an XML file stored in your project's `res/xml/` directory. Given that, Android can present a pleasant UI for manipulating those preferences, which

are then stored in the SharedPreferences you get back from
getDefaultSharedPreferences(). Even if you plan to target Android 3.0 and later, the
examples that follow are useful to you because they show how the basic preference
elements such as check boxes and entry fields behave—basic elements that are
common to both old and new approaches.

The following is the preference XML for the Prefs/Simple preferences sample project:

```
<PreferenceScreen
  xmlns:android="http://schemas.android.com/apk/res/android">
  <CheckBoxPreference
    android:key="checkbox"
    android:title="Checkbox Preference"
    android:summary="Check it on, check it off" />
  <RingtonePreference
    android:key="ringtone"
    android:title="Ringtone Preference"
    android:showDefault="true"
    android:showSilent="true"
    android:summary="Pick a tone, any tone" />
</PreferenceScreen>
```

The root of the preference XML is a PreferenceScreen element. Some of the things you
can have inside a PreferenceScreen element, not surprisingly, are preference definitions.
These are subclasses of Preference, such as CheckBoxPreference or
RingtonePreference, as shown in the preceding XML. As you might expect, these allow
you to check a check box or choose a ringtone, respectively. In the case of
RingtonePreference, you have the option of allowing users to choose the system default
ringtone or choose Silent as a ringtone.

Letting Users Have Their Say

Given that you have set up the preference XML, you can use a nearly built-in activity for
allowing your users to set their preferences. The activity is "nearly built-in" because you
merely need to subclass it and point it to your preference XML, plus hook the activity
into the rest of your application.

For example, here is the EditPreferences activity of the Prefs/Simple project:

```
package com.commonsware.android.simple;

import android.app.Activity;
import android.os.Bundle;
import android.preference.PreferenceActivity;


public class EditPreferences extends PreferenceActivity {
  @Override
  public void onCreate(Bundle savedInstanceState) {
    super.onCreate(savedInstanceState);

    addPreferencesFromResource(R.xml.preferences);
  }
```

```
}
```

As you can see, there is not much *to* see. All you need to do is call addPreferencesFromResource() and specify the XML resource containing your preferences.

You will also need to add this as an activity to your AndroidManifest.xml file:

```xml
<?xml version="1.0" encoding="utf-8"?>
<manifest xmlns:android="http://schemas.android.com/apk/res/android"
package="com.commonsware.android.simple">
    <application android:label="@string/app_name" android:icon="@drawable/cw">
        <activity android:name=".SimplePrefsDemo" android:label="@string/app_name">
            <intent-filter>
                <action android:name="android.intent.action.MAIN"/>
                <category android:name="android.intent.category.LAUNCHER"/>
            </intent-filter>
        </activity>
        <activity android:name=".EditPreferences" android:label="@string/app_name">
        </activity>
    </application>
    <supports-screens android:largeScreens="true" android:normalScreens="true"
android:smallScreens="true" android:anyDensity="true"/>
</manifest>
```

And you will need to arrange to invoke the activity, such as from a menu option. The following is pulled from SimplePrefsDemo:

```java
public boolean onCreateOptionsMenu(Menu menu) {
    menu.add(Menu.NONE, EDIT_ID, Menu.NONE, "Edit Prefs")
        .setIcon(R.drawable.misc)
        .setAlphabeticShortcut('e');

    return(super.onCreateOptionsMenu(menu));
}

@Override
public boolean onOptionsItemSelected(MenuItem item) {
    switch (item.getItemId()) {
      case EDIT_ID:
        startActivity(new Intent(this, EditPreferences.class));
        return(true);
    }

    return(super.onOptionsItemSelected(item));
}
```

That is all that is required, and it really is not that much code outside of the preferences XML. What you get for your effort is an Android-supplied preference UI, as shown in Figure 31–2.

Figure 31–2. *The Simple project's preferences UI*

The check box can be directly checked or unchecked. To change the ringtone preference, just select the entry in the preference list to bring up a selection dialog box, as shown in Figure 31–3.

Figure 31–3. *Choosing a ringtone preference*

Note that there is no explicit save or commit button or menu on the
PreferenceActivity—changes are persisted automatically.

The SimplePrefsDemo activity, beyond having the aforementioned menu, also displays
the current preferences via a TableLayout:

```xml
<?xml version="1.0" encoding="utf-8"?>
<TableLayout
  xmlns:android="http://schemas.android.com/apk/res/android"
  android:layout_width="fill_parent"
  android:layout_height="fill_parent"
>
  <TableRow>
    <TextView
        android:text="Checkbox:"
        android:paddingRight="5dip"
    />
    <TextView android:id="@+id/checkbox"
    />
  </TableRow>
  <TableRow>
    <TextView
        android:text="Ringtone:"
        android:paddingRight="5dip"
    />
    <TextView android:id="@+id/ringtone"
    />
  </TableRow>
</TableLayout>
```

The fields for the table are found in onCreate():

```java
public void onCreate(Bundle savedInstanceState) {
  super.onCreate(savedInstanceState);
  setContentView(R.layout.main);

  checkbox=(TextView)findViewById(R.id.checkbox);
  ringtone=(TextView)findViewById(R.id.ringtone);
}
```

The fields are updated on each onResume():

```java
public void onResume() {
  super.onResume();

  SharedPreferences prefs=PreferenceManager
                        .getDefaultSharedPreferences(this);

  checkbox.setText(new Boolean(prefs
                              .getBoolean("checkbox", false))
                      .toString());
  ringtone.setText(prefs.getString("ringtone", "<unset>"));
}
```

This means the fields will be updated when the activity is opened and after the
preferences activity is left (e.g., via the Back button), as shown in Figure 31–4.

Figure 31–4. *The Simple project's list of saved preferences*

Adding a Wee Bit o' Structure

If you have a lot of preferences for users to set, having them all in one big list may become troublesome. Android's preference UI gives you a few ways to impose a bit of structure on your bag of preferences, including categories and screens.

Categories are added via a `PreferenceCategory` element in your preference XML and are used to group together related preferences. Rather than have your preferences all as children of the root `PreferenceScreen`, you can put a few `PreferenceCategory` elements in the `PreferenceScreen`, and then put your preferences in their appropriate categories. Visually, this adds a divider with the category title between groups of preferences.

If you have lots and lots of preferences—more than are convenient for users to scroll through—you can also put them on separate "screens" by introducing the `PreferenceScreen` element. Yes, *that* `PreferenceScreen` element.

Any children of `PreferenceScreen` go on their own screen. If you nest `PreferenceScreen` elements, the parent screen displays the screen as a placeholder entry, and tapping that entry brings up the child screen.

For example, from the `Prefs/Structured` sample project, here is a preference XML file that contains both `PreferenceCategory` and nested `PreferenceScreen` elements:

```
<PreferenceScreen
  xmlns:android="http://schemas.android.com/apk/res/android">
  <PreferenceCategory android:title="Simple Preferences">
    <CheckBoxPreference
```

```
      android:key="checkbox"
      android:title="Checkbox Preference"
      android:summary="Check it on, check it off"
    />
    <RingtonePreference
      android:key="ringtone"
      android:title="Ringtone Preference"
      android:showDefault="true"
      android:showSilent="true"
      android:summary="Pick a tone, any tone"
    />
  </PreferenceCategory>
  <PreferenceCategory android:title="Detail Screens">
    <PreferenceScreen
      android:key="detail"
      android:title="Detail Screen"
      android:summary="Additional preferences held in another page">
      <CheckBoxPreference
        android:key="checkbox2"
        android:title="Another Checkbox"
        android:summary="On. Off. It really doesn't matter."
      />
    </PreferenceScreen>
  </PreferenceCategory>
</PreferenceScreen>
```

The result, when you use this preference XML with your `PreferenceActivity` implementation, is a categorized list of elements, as shown in Figure 31–5.

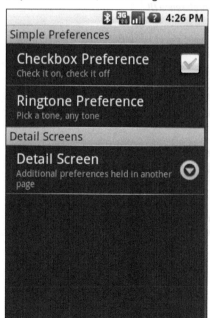

Figure 31–5. *The Structured project's preference UI, showing categories and a screen placeholder*

If you tap the Detail Screen entry, you are taken to the child preference screen, as shown in Figure 31–6.

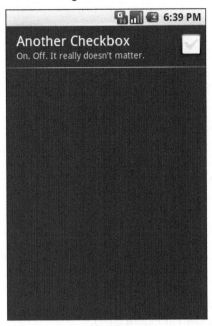

Figure 31–6. *The child preference screen of the Structured project's preference UI*

The Kind of Pop-Ups You Like

Of course, not all preferences are check boxes and ringtones. For others, like entry fields and lists, Android uses pop-up dialog boxes. Users do not enter their preference directly in the preference UI activity, but rather tap a preference, fill in a value, and tap OK to commit the change.

Structurally, in the preference XML, fields and lists are not significantly different from other preference types, as seen in this preference XML from the `Prefs/Dialogs` sample project:

```
<PreferenceScreen
  xmlns:android="http://schemas.android.com/apk/res/android">
  <PreferenceCategory android:title="Simple Preferences">
    <CheckBoxPreference
      android:key="checkbox"
      android:title="Checkbox Preference"
      android:summary="Check it on, check it off"
    />
    <RingtonePreference
      android:key="ringtone"
      android:title="Ringtone Preference"
      android:showDefault="true"
      android:showSilent="true"
      android:summary="Pick a tone, any tone"
```

```
      />
   </PreferenceCategory>
   <PreferenceCategory android:title="Detail Screens">
     <PreferenceScreen
       android:key="detail"
       android:title="Detail Screen"
       android:summary="Additional preferences held in another page">
       <CheckBoxPreference
         android:key="checkbox2"
         android:title="Another Checkbox"
         android:summary="On. Off. It really doesn't matter."
       />
     </PreferenceScreen>
   </PreferenceCategory>
   <PreferenceCategory android:title="Other Preferences">
     <EditTextPreference
       android:key="text"
       android:title="Text Entry Dialog"
       android:summary="Click to pop up a field for entry"
       android:dialogTitle="Enter something useful"
     />
     <ListPreference
       android:key="list"
       android:title="Selection Dialog"
       android:summary="Click to pop up a list to choose from"
       android:entries="@array/cities"
       android:entryValues="@array/airport_codes"
       android:dialogTitle="Choose a Pennsylvania city" />
   </PreferenceCategory>
</PreferenceScreen>
```

With the field (EditTextPreference), in addition to the title and summary you put on the preference itself, you can also supply the title to use for the dialog box.

With the list (ListPreference), you supply both a dialog box title and two string-array resources: one for the display names and one for the values. These need to be in the same order and have the same number of elements, because the index of the chosen display name determines which value is stored as the preference in the SharedPreferences. For example, here are the arrays for use by the ListPreference shown in the preceding example:

```
<?xml version="1.0" encoding="utf-8"?>
<resources>
  <string-array name="cities">
    <item>Philadelphia</item>
    <item>Pittsburgh</item>
    <item>Allentown/Bethlehem</item>
    <item>Erie</item>
    <item>Reading</item>
    <item>Scranton</item>
    <item>Lancaster</item>
    <item>Altoona</item>
    <item>Harrisburg</item>
  </string-array>
  <string-array name="airport_codes">
    <item>PHL</item>
    <item>PIT</item>
```

```
      <item>ABE</item>
      <item>ERI</item>
      <item>RDG</item>
      <item>AVP</item>
      <item>LNS</item>
      <item>AOO</item>
      <item>MDT</item>
   </string-array>
</resources>
```

When you bring up the preference UI, you start with another category with another pair of preference entries, as shown in Figure 31–7.

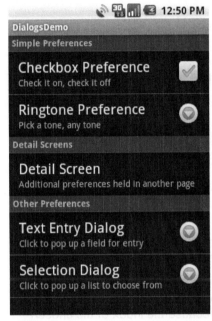

Figure 31–7. *The preference screen of the Dialogs project's preference UI*

Tapping Text Entry Dialog brings up a text entry dialog box—in this case, with the prior preference entry filled in, as shown in Figure 31–8.

Figure 31–8. *Editing a text preference*

Tapping Selection Dialog brings up a selection dialog box showing the display names from the one array, as shown in Figure 31–9.

Figure 31–9. *Editing a list preference*

Chapter 32

Managing and Accessing Local Databases

SQLite is a very popular embedded database, as it combines a clean SQL interface with a very small memory footprint and decent speed. Moreover, it is public domain, so everyone can use it. Many firms (e.g., Adobe, Apple, Google, Sun, and Symbian) and open source projects (e.g., Mozilla, PHP, and Python) ship products with SQLite.

For Android, SQLite is "baked into" the Android runtime, so every Android application can create SQLite databases. Since SQLite uses a SQL interface, it is fairly straightforward to use for people with experience in other SQL-based databases. However, its native API is written in C, and while Java libraries such as JDBC are available for it, JDBC might be too much overhead for a memory-limited device like a phone, anyway. Hence, Android programmers have a different API to learn. The good news is that it is not very difficult.

This chapter will cover the basics of SQLite use in the context of working on Android. It by no means is a thorough coverage of SQLite as a whole. If you want to learn more about SQLite and how to use it in environments other than Android, a fine book is *The Definitive Guide to SQLite, Second Edition*, by Grant Allen (your present author) and Michael Owens (Apress, 2010). This also covers other complementary topics such as security of SQLite databases and more.

Much of the sample code shown in this chapter comes from the `Database/Constants` application. This application presents a list of physical constants, with names and values culled from Android's `SensorManager`, as shown in Figure 32–1.

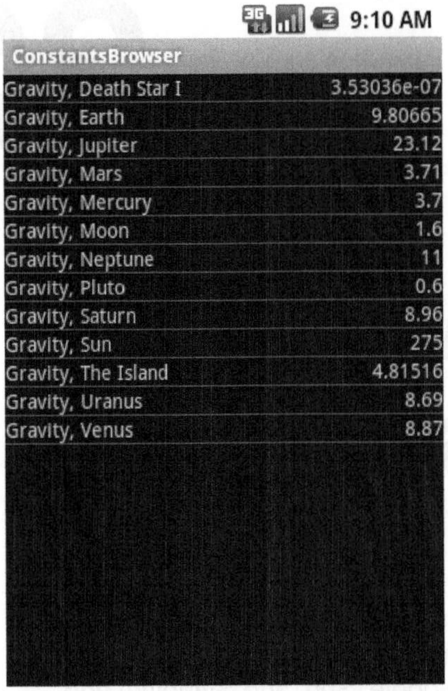

Figure 32–1. *The Constants sample application, as initially launched*

You can pop up a menu to add a new constant, which brings up a dialog box in which to fill in the name and value of the constant, as shown in Figure 32–2.

Figure 32–2. *The Constants sample application's Add Constant dialog box*

The constant is then added to the list. A long-tap on an existing constant will bring up a context menu with a Delete option, which, after confirmation, will delete the constant.

And, of course, all of this is stored in a SQLite database.

A Quick SQLite Primer

SQLite, as the name suggests, uses a dialect of SQL for data manipulation queries (SELECT, INSERT, et al.), and data definition (CREATE TABLE, et al.). SQLite has a few places where it deviates from the SQL-92 and SQL-99 standards, which is no different from most relational databases. The good news is that SQLite is so space-efficient that the Android runtime can include all of SQLite, not some arbitrary subset to trim it down to size.

The biggest difference between SQLite and other relational databases is the data typing. While you can specify the data types for columns in a CREATE TABLE statement, and SQLite will use those as a hint, that is as far as it goes. You can put whatever data you want in whatever column you want. Put a string in an INTEGER column? Sure, no problem! Vice versa? That works, too! SQLite refers to this as *manifest typing*, as described in the documentation:

> In manifest typing, the datatype is a property of the value itself, not of the column in which the value is stored. SQLite thus allows the user to store any value of any datatype into any column regardless of the declared type of that column.

Start at the Beginning

No databases are automatically supplied to you by Android. If you want to use SQLite, you will need to create your own database, and then populate it with your own tables, indexes, and data.

To create and open a database, your best option is to craft a subclass of SQLiteOpenHelper. This class wraps up the logic to create and upgrade a database, per your specifications, as needed by your application. Your subclass of SQLiteOpenHelper will need three methods:

- The constructor, chaining upward to the SQLiteOpenHelper constructor. This takes the Context (e.g., an Activity), the name of the database, an optional cursor factory (typically, just pass null), and an integer representing the version of the database schema you are using.

- onCreate(), which passes you a SQLiteDatabase object that you populate with tables and initial data, as appropriate.

- onUpgrade(), which passes you a SQLiteDatabase object and the old and new version numbers, so you can figure out how best to convert the database from the old schema to the new one. If you don't care for the existing data or database, the simplest, albeit least friendly, approach is to drop the old tables and create new ones. A better approach would be to use the appropriate CREATE or ALTER TABLE statements to upgrade your schema (though be sure to check out the conditions on using ALTER TABLE, discussed later in this chapter).

For example, here is a DatabaseHelper class from Database/Constants that, in onCreate(), creates a table and adds a number of rows, and in onUpgrade() cheats by dropping the existing table and executing onCreate():

```
package com.commonsware.android.constants;

import android.content.ContentValues;
import android.content.Context;
import android.database.Cursor;
import android.database.SQLException;
import android.database.sqlite.SQLiteOpenHelper;
import android.database.sqlite.SQLiteDatabase;
import android.hardware.SensorManager;

public class DatabaseHelper extends SQLiteOpenHelper {
  private static final String DATABASE_NAME="db";
  static final String TITLE="title";
  static final String VALUE="value";

  public DatabaseHelper(Context context) {
    super(context, DATABASE_NAME, null, 1);
  }

  @Override
  public void onCreate(SQLiteDatabase db) {
    db.execSQL("create table constants (_id integer primary key autoincrement, title↵
text, value real);");

    ContentValues cv=new ContentValues();

    cv.put(TITLE, "Gravity, Death Star I");
    cv.put(VALUE, SensorManager.GRAVITY_DEATH_STAR_I);
    db.insert("constants", TITLE, cv);

    cv.put(TITLE, "Gravity, Earth");
    cv.put(VALUE, SensorManager.GRAVITY_EARTH);
    db.insert("constants", TITLE, cv);

    cv.put(TITLE, "Gravity, Jupiter");
    cv.put(VALUE, SensorManager.GRAVITY_JUPITER);
    db.insert("constants", TITLE, cv);

    cv.put(TITLE, "Gravity, Mars");
    cv.put(VALUE, SensorManager.GRAVITY_MARS);
    db.insert("constants", TITLE, cv);
```

```
    cv.put(TITLE, "Gravity, Mercury");
    cv.put(VALUE, SensorManager.GRAVITY_MERCURY);
    db.insert("constants", TITLE, cv);

    cv.put(TITLE, "Gravity, Moon");
    cv.put(VALUE, SensorManager.GRAVITY_MOON);
    db.insert("constants", TITLE, cv);

    cv.put(TITLE, "Gravity, Neptune");
    cv.put(VALUE, SensorManager.GRAVITY_NEPTUNE);
    db.insert("constants", TITLE, cv);

    cv.put(TITLE, "Gravity, Pluto");
    cv.put(VALUE, SensorManager.GRAVITY_PLUTO);
    db.insert("constants", TITLE, cv);

    cv.put(TITLE, "Gravity, Saturn");
    cv.put(VALUE, SensorManager.GRAVITY_SATURN);
    db.insert("constants", TITLE, cv);

    cv.put(TITLE, "Gravity, Sun");
    cv.put(VALUE, SensorManager.GRAVITY_SUN);
    db.insert("constants", TITLE, cv);

    cv.put(TITLE, "Gravity, The Island");
    cv.put(VALUE, SensorManager.GRAVITY_THE_ISLAND);
    db.insert("constants", TITLE, cv);

    cv.put(TITLE, "Gravity, Uranus");
    cv.put(VALUE, SensorManager.GRAVITY_URANUS);
    db.insert("constants", TITLE, cv);

    cv.put(TITLE, "Gravity, Venus");
    cv.put(VALUE, SensorManager.GRAVITY_VENUS);
    db.insert("constants", TITLE, cv);
  }

  @Override
  public void onUpgrade(SQLiteDatabase db, int oldVersion, int newVersion) {
    android.util.Log.w("Constants", "Upgrading database, which will destroy all↩
 old data");
    db.execSQL("drop table if exists constants");
    onCreate(db);
  }
}
```

We will take a closer look at what onCreate() is doing—in terms of execSQL() and insert() calls—later in this chapter.

To use your SQLiteOpenHelper subclass, create and hold onto an instance of it. Then, when you need a SQLiteDatabase object to do queries or data modifications, ask your SQLiteOpenHelper to getReadableDatabase() or getWriteableDatabase(), depending on whether or not you will be changing its contents. For example, our `ConstantsBrowser` activity opens the database in `onCreate()` as part of doing a query:

```
constantsCursor=db
                .getReadableDatabase()
                .rawQuery("select _id, title, value "+
                        "from constants order by title",
                        null);
```

When you are done with the database (e.g., your activity is being closed), simply call `close()` on your `SQLiteOpenHelper` to release your connection.

For `onUpgrade()` to work properly, your version numbers for your database schema must increase as you move forward. A typical pattern is to start with 1 and work your way up from there.

There are two other methods you can elect to override in your `SQLiteOpenHelper`, if you feel the need:

- `onOpen()`: You can override this to get control when somebody opens this database. Usually, this is not required.

- `onDowngrade()`: Introduced in Android 3.0, this method will be called if the code requests a schema that is older than what is in the database presently. This is the converse of `onUpgrade()`. If your version numbers differ, one of these two methods will be invoked. Since normally you are moving forward with updates, you can usually skip `onDowngrade()`.

Setting the Table

For creating your tables and indexes, you will need to call `execSQL()` on your `SQLiteDatabase`, providing the Data Definition Language (DDL) statement you wish to apply against the database. Barring a database error, this method returns nothing.

So, for example, you can call `execSQL()` to create the `constants` table, as shown in the `DatabaseHelper` `onCreate()` method:

```
db.execSQL("create table constants (_id integer primary key autoincrement, title text,
value real);");
```

This will create a table, named `constants`, with a primary key column named `_id` that is an autoincremented integer (i.e., SQLite will assign the value for you when you insert rows), plus two data columns: `title` (text) and `value` (a float, or *real* in SQLite terms). SQLite will automatically create an index for you on your primary key column. You could add other indexes here via some `CREATE INDEX` statements.

Most likely, you will create tables and indexes when you first create the database, or possibly when the database needs upgrading to accommodate a new release of your application. The exception may be if you decide to package a preconfigured SQLite database with your application—an option we'll explore later in this chapter. If you do not change your table schemas, you might never drop your tables or indexes, but if you do, just use `execSQL()` to invoke `DROP INDEX` and `DROP TABLE` statements as needed.

Makin' Data

Given that you have a database and one or more tables, you probably want to put some data in them. You have two major approaches for doing this:

- Use execSQL(), just as you did for creating the tables. The execSQL() method works for any SQL that does not return results, so it can handle INSERT, UPDATE, DELETE, and so forth just fine.

- Use the insert(),update(), and delete() methods on the SQLiteDatabase object, which eliminates much of the SQL syntax required to do basic operations.

For example, here we insert() a new row into our constants table:

```
private void processAdd(DialogWrapper wrapper) {
  ContentValues values=new ContentValues(2);

  values.put(DatabaseHelper.TITLE, wrapper.getTitle());
  values.put(DatabaseHelper.VALUE, wrapper.getValue());

  db.getWritableDatabase().insert("constants", DatabaseHelper.TITLE, values);
  constantsCursor.requery();
}
```

These methods make use of ContentValues objects, which implement a Map-esque interface, albeit one that has additional methods for working with SQLite types. For example, in addition to get() to retrieve a value by its key, you have getAsInteger(), getAsString(), and so forth.

The insert() method takes the name of the table, the name of one column as the "null column hack," and a ContentValues with the initial values you want put into this row. The null column hack is for the case where the ContentValues instance is empty—the column named as the null column hack will be explicitly assigned the value NULL in the SQL INSERT statement generated by insert(). This is required due to a quirk in SQLite's support for the SQL INSERT statement.

The update() method takes the name of the table, a ContentValues representing the columns and replacement values to use, an optional WHERE clause, and an optional list of parameters to fill into the WHERE clause, to replace any embedded question marks (?). Since update() replaces only columns with fixed values, versus ones computed based on other information, you may need to use execSQL() to accomplish some ends. The WHERE clause and parameter list work akin to the positional SQL parameters you may be used to from other SQL APIs.

The delete() method works akin to update(), taking the name of the table, the optional WHERE clause, and the corresponding parameters to fill into the WHERE clause. For example, here we delete() a row from our constants table, given its _ID:

```
private void processDelete(long rowId) {
  String[] args={String.valueOf(rowId)};
```

```
    db.getWritableDatabase().delete("constants", "_ID=?", args);
    constantsCursor.requery();
}
```

What Goes Around, Comes Around

As with INSERT, UPDATE, and DELETE, you have two main options for retrieving data from a SQLite database using SELECT:

- Use rawQuery() to invoke a SELECT statement directly
- Use query() to build up a query from its component parts

Confounding matters further is the SQLiteQueryBuilder class and the issue of cursors and cursor factories. Let's take all of this one piece at a time.

Raw Queries

The simplest solution, at least in terms of the API, is rawQuery(). Simply call it with your SQL SELECT statement. The SELECT statement can include positional parameters; the array of these forms your second parameter to rawQuery(). This parameter is null if your query contains no positional parameters. So, we wind up with this:

```
constantsCursor=db
                .getReadableDatabase()
                .rawQuery("SELECT _ID, title, value "+
                        "FROM constants ORDER BY title",
                        null);
```

The return value is a Cursor, which is the common structure most database APIs use in handling sets of results from database queries. Your Cursor contains methods for iterating over results (discussed shortly, in the "Using Cursors" section).

If your queries are pretty much "baked into" your application, this is a very straightforward way to use them. However, it gets complicated if parts of the query are dynamic, beyond what positional parameters can really handle. For example, if the set of columns you need to retrieve is not known at compile time, puttering around concatenating column names into a comma-delimited list can be annoying...which is where query() comes in.

Regular Queries

The query() method takes the discrete pieces of a SELECT statement and builds the query from them. The pieces, in the order they appear as parameters to query(), are as follows:The name of the table to query against

- The list of columns to retrieve
- The WHERE clause, optionally including positional parameters

- The list of values to substitute in for those positional parameters

- The GROUP BY clause, if any

- The HAVING clause, if any

- The ORDER BY clause, if any

These can be null when they are not needed (except the table name, of course):

```
String[] columns={"ID", "inventory"};
String[] parms={"snicklefritz"};
Cursor result=db.query("widgets", columns, "name=?",
                       parms, null, null, null);
```

The one large drawback of the query() method is right there in the first bullet point: only one table can be queried, and joining tables either implicitly or explicitly is beyond the method's scope.

Using Cursors

No matter how you execute the query, you get a Cursor back. This is the Android/SQLite edition of the database cursor, a concept used in many database systems. With the cursor, you can do the following:

- Find out how many rows are in the result set via getCount() (though be warned, counting rows this way implicitly retrieves all of the data in the result set)

- Iterate over the rows via moveToFirst(),moveToNext(), and isAfterLast()

- Find out the names of the columns via getColumnNames(), convert those into column numbers via getColumnIndex(), and get values for the current row for a given column via methods like getString(),getInt(), and so on

- Re-execute the query that created the cursor via requery()

- Release the cursor's resources via close()

For example, here we iterate over a widgets table entries:

```
Cursor result=
  db.rawQuery("select id, name, inventory from widgets", null);

while (!result.moveToNext()) {
 int id=result.getInt(0);
 String name=result.getString(1);
 int inventory=result.getInt(2);

 // do something useful with these
}
```

```
result.close();
```

You can also wrap a Cursor in a SimpleCursorAdapter or other implementation, and then hand the resulting adapter to a ListView or other selection widget. Note, though, that if you are going to use CursorAdapter or its subclasses (such as SimpleCursorAdapter), the result set of your query *must* contain an integer column named _ID that is unique for the result set. This "id" value is then supplied to methods such as onListItemClick(), to identify which item the user clicked on in the AdapterView.

For example, after retrieving the sorted list of constants, we pop those into the ListView for the ConstantsBrowser activity in just a few lines of code:

```
ListAdapter adapter=new SimpleCursorAdapter(this,
                    R.layout.row, constantsCursor,
                    new String[] {DatabaseHelper.TITLE,
                                  DatabaseHelper.VALUE},
                    new int[] {R.id.title, R.id.value});
```

Custom CursorAdapters

You may recall from an earlier chapter that you can override getView() in ArrayAdapter to provide more custom control over how rows are displayed. However, CursorAdapter and its subclasses have a default implementation of getView(), which inspects the supplied View to recycle. If it is null, getView() calls newView() and then bindView(). If it is not null, getView() just calls bindView(). If you are extending CursorAdapter—used for displaying results of a database or content provider query—you should override newView() and bindView() instead of getView().

All this does is remove your if() test you would have had in getView() and puts each branch of that test in an independent method, akin to the following:

```
public View newView(Context context, Cursor cursor,
                    ViewGroup parent) {
  LayoutInflater inflater=getLayoutInflater();
  View row=inflater.inflate(R.layout.row, null);
  ViewWrapper wrapper=new ViewWrapper(row);

  row.setTag(wrapper);

  return(row);
}

public void bindView(View row, Context context, Cursor cursor) {
  ViewWrapper wrapper=(ViewWrapper)row.getTag();

  // actual logic to populate row from Cursor goes here
}
```

Making Your Own Cursors

There may be circumstances in which you want to use your own Cursor subclass, rather than the stock implementation provided by Android. In those cases, you can use queryWithFactory() and rawQueryWithFactory(), which take a SQLiteDatabase.CursorFactory instance as a parameter. The factory, as you might expect, is responsible for creating new cursors via its newCursor() implementation.

Finding and implementing a valid use for this facility is left as an exercise for you. Suffice it to say that you should not need to create your own cursor classes much, if at all, in ordinary Android development.

SQLite and Android Versions

The underlying SQLite library included with Android has evolved as new versions of both continue to be released. The initial release of Android shipped with SQLite 3.5.9. Android 2.2 Froyo updated the SQLite library to 3.6.22. This was a relatively minor upgrade, dealing with bug fixes and the like. Android 3.0 Honeycomb again upgraded the SQLite library to 3.7.4, and this is still the version in use with Android 4.0 Ice Cream Sandwich. While you can treat this upgrade as just another point release fixing bugs and providing incremental improvements, the 3.7 release of SQLite includes a quite radical set of enhanced features around concurrency, logging, and locking.

You might never need to worry about these changes, particularly as your application is likely to be the only one concurrently accessing your SQLite database. There are however a few subtleties introduced.

First, the major internal version number of the SQLite database format was incremented for new databases created with SQLite version 3.7 and later, and older databases could be upgraded to this new format. If you plan on packaging your own SQLite database as part of your application (rather than creating it via onCreate()), you should consider which older devices and versions of Android you will support, and ensure you use the older SQLite database format. It can still be read and manipulated by SQLite 3.7.4 without any form of upgrade.

Second, some new features of SQLite are obviously only made available in later versions. This will mainly affect some of the more advanced queries you execute using rawQuery(), such as using SQL standard foreign key creation commands.

Flash: Sounds Faster Than It Is

Your database will be stored on flash memory, normally the onboard flash for the device. Reading data off of flash is relatively quick. While the memory is not especially fast, there is no seek time to move hard drive heads around, as you find with magnetic media, so performing a query against a SQLite database tends to be speedy.

Writing data to flash is another matter entirely. Sometimes, this may happen fairly quickly, on the order of a couple of milliseconds. Sometimes, though, it may take hundreds of milliseconds, even for writing small amounts of data. Moreover, flash tends to get slower the fuller it is, so the speed your users will see varies even more.

The net result is that you should seriously consider doing all database write operations off the main application thread, such as via an `AsyncTask`, as is described in Chapter 20. That way, the database write operations will not slow down your UI.

There are also situations in which writing to flash-based storage can be a risky move. When battery power is low, believing that writing to flash will complete before the battery is drained can be a bit too trusting on your part as a developer. Similarly, relying on the ability to write to flash during power-cycling of the device is not a good move. In these situations, you can add an `Intent` receiver to your application to watch out for `ACTION_BATTERY_CHANGED` broadcasts, and then examine the data provided to see what's happening to the battery, its current charge level, and so on.

Note that the emulator behaves differently, because it is typically using a file on your hard drive for storing data, rather than flash. While the emulator tends to be much slower than hardware for CPU and GPU operations, the emulator will tend to be much faster for writing data to flash. Hence, just because you are not seeing any UI slowdowns due to database I/O in the emulator, do not assume that will be the same when your code is running on a real Android device.

Ship Ahoy!

Many applications are shipped with an existing database in place, to support all manner of uses from a handy reference list, through to a complete offline cache. You can incorporate a database you've created elsewhere in your project for packaging with your compiled application.

First, include your SQLite database file in the `assets/` folder of your project. To use your bundled database in your code, you can pass its location and file name to the `openDatabase()` method. Calling `openDatabase()` can take as its first parameter the full path and file name. In practice, this full path and file name is constructed by concatenating the following:

- The path used to refer to all database assets,
  `/data/data/your.application.package/databases/`
- Then your desired database file name; e.g., `your-db-name`

Data, Data, Everywhere

If you are used to developing for other databases, you are also probably used to having tools to inspect and manipulate the contents of the database, beyond merely the database's API. With Android's emulator, you have two main options for this.

First, the emulator is supposed to bundle in the `sqlite3` console program and make it available from the `adb shell` command. Once you are in the emulator's shell, just execute `sqlite3`, providing it the path to your database file. Your database file can be found at the following location:

`/data/data/your.app.package/databases/your-db-name`

Here, `your.app.package` is the Java package for your application (e.g., `com.commonsware.android`) and `your-db-name` is the name of your database, as supplied to `createDatabase()`.

The `sqlite3` program works, and if you are used to poking around your tables using a console interface, you are welcome to use it. If you prefer something a little friendlier, you can always copy the SQLite database from the device onto your development machine, and then use a SQLite-aware client program to putter around. Note, though, that you are working off a copy of the database; if you want your changes to go back to the device, you will need to transfer the database back over.

To copy the database from the device, you can use the `adb pull` command (or the equivalent in your IDE, or the File Manager in the Dalvik Debug Monitor Service), which takes the path to the on-device database and the local destination as parameters. To store a modified database on the device, use `adb push`, which takes the local path to the database and the on-device destination as parameters.

One of the most-accessible SQLite clients is the SQLite Manager extension for Firefox, shown in Figure 32–3, as it works across all platforms.

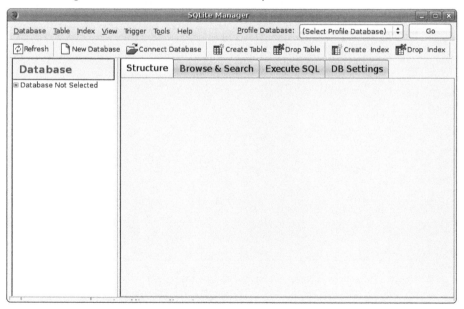

Figure 32–3. *SQLite Manager Firefox extension*

You can find other client tools on the SQLite web site.

Chapter **33**

Leveraging Java Libraries

Java has as many third-party libraries as any other modern programming language, if not more. These third-party libraries are the innumerable JARs that you can include in a server or desktop Java application—the things that the Java SDKs themselves do not provide.

In the case of Android, the Dalvik virtual machine (VM) at its heart is not precisely Java, and what it provides in its SDK is not precisely the same as what any traditional Java SDK provides. That being said, many Java third-party libraries provide capabilities that Android lacks natively, and therefore may be of use to you in your projects, if you can get them to work with Android's flavor of Java.

This chapter explains what it will take for you to leverage such libraries and describes the limitations of Android's support for arbitrary third-party code.

Ants and JARs

You have two choices for integrating third-party code into your project: use the source code or use prepackaged JARs.

If you choose to use the source code, all you need to do is copy it into your own source tree (under src/ in your project), so it can sit alongside your existing code, and then let the compiler perform its magic.

If you choose to use an existing JAR, perhaps one for which you do not have the source code, you will need to teach your build chain how to use the JAR. First, place the JAR in the libs/ directory in your Android project. Then, if you are using an IDE, you probably need to add the JAR to your build path (Ant will automatically pick up all JARs found in libs/). This is definitely required for Eclipse, where you will need to place a reference to your JARs under the Libraries tab of the Java Build Path page.

And that's it. Adding third-party code to your Android application is fairly easy. Getting it to actually *work* may be somewhat more complicated, however.

The Outer Limits

Not all available Java code will work well with Android. There are a number of factors to consider, including the following:

- *Expected platform APIs*: Does the code assume a newer JVM than the one Android is based on? Or, does the code assume the existence of Java APIs that ship with Java 2 Platform, Standard Edition (J2SE), but not with Android, such as Swing?

- *Size*: Existing Java code designed for use on desktops or servers does not need to be concerned much about on-disk size or, to some extent, even in-RAM size. Android, of course, is short on both. Using third-party Java code, particularly when prepackaged as JARs, may balloon the size of your application.

- *Performance*: Does the Java code effectively assume a much more powerful CPU than what you may find on many Android devices? Just because a desktop can run it without issue does not mean your average mobile phone will handle it well.

- *Interface*: Does the Java code assume a console interface? Or is it a pure API that you can wrap your own interface around?

- *Operating system*: Does the Java code assume the existence of certain console programs? Does the Java code assume it can use a Windows DLL?

- *Language version*: Was the JAR compiled with an older version of Java (1.4.2 or older)? Was the JAR compiled with a different compiler than the official one from Sun (e.g., GCJ)?

- *Dependencies*: Does the Java code depend on other third-party JARs that might have some of these problems as well? Does the Java code depend on third-party libraries (e.g., the JSON library from http://json.org) that are built into Android, but expect a different version of those libraries?

One trick for addressing some of these concerns is to use open source Java code and actually work with the code to make it more Android-friendly. For example, if you are using only 10 percent of the third-party library, maybe it's worthwhile to recompile the subset of the project to be only what you need, or at least to remove the unnecessary classes from the JAR. The former approach is safer, in that you get compiler help to make sure you are not discarding some essential piece of code, although it may be more tedious to do.

Following the Script

Unlike other mobile device operating systems, Android has no restrictions on what you can run on it, as long as you can do it in Java using the Dalvik VM. This includes incorporating your own scripting language into your application, something that is expressly prohibited on some other devices.

One possible Java scripting language is BeanShell (www.beanshell.org/). BeanShell gives you Java-compatible syntax with implicit typing and no compilation required.

To add BeanShell scripting, you need to put the BeanShell interpreter's JAR file in your libs/ directory. Unfortunately, the 2.0b4 JAR available for download from the BeanShell site does not work out of the box with the Android 0.9 and newer SDKs, perhaps due to the compiler that was used to build it. Instead, you should probably check out the source code from Apache Subversion and execute ant jarcore to build it, and then copy the resulting JAR (in BeanShell's dist/ directory) to your own project's libs/. Or, just use the BeanShell JAR that accompanies the source code for this book in the Java/AndShell project.

From there, using BeanShell on Android is no different from using BeanShell in any other Java environment:

1. Create an instance of the BeanShell Interpreter class.

2. Set any globals for the script's use via Interpreter#set().

3. Call Interpreter#eval() to run the script and, optionally, get the result of the last statement.

For example, here is the XML layout for the world's smallest BeanShell IDE:

```xml
<?xml version="1.0" encoding="utf-8"?>
<LinearLayout xmlns:android="http://schemas.android.com/apk/res/android"
    android:orientation="vertical"
    android:layout_width="fill_parent"
    android:layout_height="fill_parent"
    >
<Button
    android:id="@+id/eval"
    android:layout_width="fill_parent"
    android:layout_height="wrap_content"
    android:text="Go!"
    android:onClick="go"
    />
<EditText
    android:id="@+id/script"
    android:layout_width="fill_parent"
    android:layout_height="fill_parent"
    android:singleLine="false"
    android:gravity="top"
    />
</LinearLayout>
```

Couple that with the following activity implementation:

```
package com.commonsware.android.andshell;

import android.app.Activity;
import android.app.AlertDialog;
import android.os.Bundle;
import android.view.View;
import android.widget.EditText;
import android.widget.Toast;
import bsh.Interpreter;

public class MainActivity extends Activity {
  private Interpreter i=new Interpreter();

  @Override
  public void onCreate(Bundle icicle) {
    super.onCreate(icicle);
    setContentView(R.layout.main);
  }

  public void go(View v) {
    EditText script=(EditText)findViewById(R.id.script);
    String src=script.getText().toString();

    try {
      i.set("context", MainActivity.this);
      i.eval(src);
    }
    catch (bsh.EvalError e) {
      AlertDialog.Builder builder=
                new AlertDialog.Builder(MainActivity.this);

      builder
        .setTitle("Exception!")
        .setMessage(e.toString())
        .setPositiveButton("OK", null)
        .show();
    }
  }
}
```

Compile and run it (including incorporating the BeanShell JAR as previously mentioned), and install it on the emulator. Fire it up, and you get a trivial IDE, with a large text area for your script and a big Go! button to execute it, as shown in Figure 33–1.

Figure 33–1. *The AndShell BeanShell IDE*

```
import android.widget.Toast;

Toast.makeText(context, "Hello, world!", Toast.LENGTH_LONG).show();
```

Note the use of `context` to refer to the activity when making the `Toast`. That is the global set by the activity to reference back to itself. You could call this global variable anything you want, as long as the `set()` call and the script code use the same name.

Click the Go! button, and you get the result shown in Figure 33–2.

Figure 33–2. *The AndShell BeanShell IDE, executing some code*

And now, some caveats:

- ■ Not all scripting languages will work. For example, those that implement their own form of just-in-time (JIT) compilation, generating Java bytecodes on-the-fly, would probably need to be augmented to generate Dalvik VM bytecodes instead of those for stock Java implementations. Simpler languages that execute from parsed scripts, calling Java reflection APIs to call back into compiled classes, will likely work better. Even there, though, not every feature of the language may work, if it relies on some facility in a traditional Java API that does not exist in Dalvik. For example, there could be stuff hidden inside BeanShell or the add-on JARs that does not work on today's Android.

- ■ Scripting languages without JIT will inevitably be slower than compiled Dalvik applications. Slower may mean users experience sluggishness. Slower definitely means more battery life is consumed for the same amount of work. So, building a whole Android application in BeanShell, simply because you feel it is easier to program in, may cause your users to be unhappy.

- ■ Scripting languages that expose the whole Java API, like BeanShell, can pretty much do anything the underlying Android security model allows. So, if your application has the READ_CONTACTS permission, expect any BeanShell scripts your application runs to have the same permission.

- ■ Last, but certainly not least, is that language interpreter JARs tend to be...portly. The BeanShell JAR used in this example is 200KB. That is not ridiculous, considering what it does, but it will make applications that use BeanShell that much bigger to download, take up that much more space on the device, and so on.

Reviewing the Script

Since this chapter covers scripting in Android, you may be interested to know that you have options beyond embedding BeanShell directly in your project.

Some experiments have been conducted with other JVM-based programming languages, such as JRuby and Jython. At present, their support for Android is not always 100 percent smooth, but progress is continually being made. Those interested in JRuby on Android, for instance, should investigate the Ruboto open source project, at http://ruboto.org.

Additionally, Scripting Layer for Android (SL4A), described at http://code.google.com/p/android-scripting/, allows you to write scripts in a wide range of scripting languages, beyond BeanShell, such as the following:

- Perl

- Python

- JRuby

- Lua

- JavaScript (implemented via Rhino, the Mozilla JavaScript interpreter written in Java)

- PHP

These scripts are not full-fledged applications, though the SL4A team is working on allowing you to turn them into APK files complete with basic UIs. For on-device development, SL4A is a fine choice. Notable projects developed with SL4A include the Nexus One sensor logging payload. If you're interested in further SL4A reading and development, an excellent book on the topic is *Pro Android Python with SL4A*, by Paul Ferrill (Apress, 2011).

Chapter 34

Communicating via the Internet

The expectation is that most, if not all, Android devices will have built-in Internet access. That could be Wi-Fi, cellular data services (EDGE, 3G, 4G, etc.), or possibly something else entirely. Regardless, most people—or at least those with a data plan or Wi-Fi access—will be able to get to the Internet from their Android phone.

Not surprisingly, the Android platform gives developers a wide range of ways to make use of this Internet access. Some offer high-level access, such as the integrated WebKit browser component. If you want, you can drop all the way down to using raw sockets. In between, you can leverage APIs—both on-device and from third-party JARs—that give you access to specific protocols: HTTP, XMPP, SMTP, and so on.

The emphasis of this book is on the higher-level forms of access: the WebKit component, discussed in Chapter 15, and Internet-access APIs, discussed in this chapter. As busy coders, we should be trying to reuse existing components wherever possible, versus rolling our own on-the-wire protocol.

REST and Relaxation

Android does not have built-in SOAP or XML-RPC client APIs. However, it does have the Apache HttpClient library baked in. You can either layer a SOAP/XML-RPC layer atop this library or use it "straight" for accessing REST-style web services. For the purposes of this book, REST-style web services are considered simple HTTP requests for ordinary URLs over the full range of HTTP verbs, with formatted payloads (XML, JSON, etc.) as responses.

More expansive tutorials, FAQs, and HOWTOs can be found at the HttpClient web site (http://hc.apache.org/). Here, we'll cover the basics, while checking the weather.

HTTP Operations via Apache HttpClient

The first step to using HttpClient is, not surprisingly, to create an HttpClient object. The client object handles all HTTP requests on your behalf. Since HttpClient is an interface, you will need to actually instantiate some implementation of that interface, such as DefaultHttpClient.

Those requests are bundled up into HttpRequest instances, with different HttpRequest implementations for each different HTTP verb (e.g., HttpGet for HTTP GET requests). You create an HttpRequest implementation instance, fill in the URL to retrieve and other configuration data (e.g., form values if you are doing an HTTP POST via HttpPost), and then pass the method to the client to actually make the HTTP request via execute().

What happens at this point can be as simple or as complicated as you want. You can get an HttpResponse object back, with a response code (e.g., 200 for OK), HTTP headers, and the like. Or, you can use a flavor of execute() that takes a ResponseHandler<String> as a parameter, with the net result being that execute() returns just the String representation of the response body. In practice, this is not a recommended approach, because you really should be checking your HTTP response codes for errors. However, for trivial applications, like book examples, the ResponseHandler<String> approach works just fine.

For example, let's take a look at the Internet/Weather sample project. This implements an activity that retrieves weather data for your current location from the National Weather Service. (Note that this probably works only for geographic locations in the United States.) That data is converted into an HTML page, which is poured into a WebKit widget for display. Rebuilding this demo using a ListView is left as an exercise for the reader. Also, since this sample is relatively long, we will show only relevant pieces of the Java code here in this chapter, though you can always download the full source from the CommonsWare web site.

To make this a bit more interesting, we use the Android location services to figure out where we are...sort of. The full details of how that works are provided in Chapter 39.

In the onResume() method, we toggle on location updates, so we will be informed where we are now and when we move a significant distance (10 kilometers). When a location is available—either at the start or based on movement—we retrieve the National Weather Service data via our updateForecast() method:

```java
private void updateForecast(Location loc) {
  String url=String.format(format, loc.getLatitude(),
                           loc.getLongitude());
  HttpGet getMethod=new HttpGet(url);

  try {
    ResponseHandler<String> responseHandler=new BasicResponseHandler();
    String responseBody=client.execute(getMethod,
                                       responseHandler);
    buildForecasts(responseBody);
```

```
    String page=generatePage();

    browser.loadDataWithBaseURL(null, page, "text/html",
                                "UTF-8", null);
  }
  catch (Throwable t) {
    android.util.Log.e("WeatherDemo", "Exception fetching data", t);
    Toast
      .makeText(this, "Request failed: "+t.toString(), Toast.LENGTH_LONG)
      .show();
  }
}
```

The updateForecast() method takes a Location as a parameter, obtained from the location update process. For now, all you need to know is that Location sports getLatitude() and getLongitude() methods that return the latitude and longitude of the device's position, respectively.

We hold the URL to the National Weather Service XML in a string resource, and pour in the latitude and longitude at runtime. Given our HttpClient object created in onCreate(), we populate an HttpGet with that customized URL, and then execute that method. Given the resulting XML from the REST service, we build the forecast HTML page, as described next, and pour that into the WebKit widget. If the HttpClient blows up with an exception, we provide that error as a Toast.

Note that we also shut down the HttpClient object in onDestroy().

Parsing Responses

The response you get will be formatted using some system—HTML, XML, JSON, or whatever. It is up to you, of course, to pick out the information you need and do something useful with it. In the case of the WeatherDemo, we need to extract the forecast time, temperature, and icon (indicating sky conditions and precipitation) and generate an HTML page from it.

Android includes the following parsers:

- Three XML parsers: the traditional W3C DOM (org.w3c.dom), a SAX parser (org.xml.sax), and the XML pull parser (discussed in Chapter 23)

- A JSON parser (org.json)

You are also welcome to use third-party Java code, where possible, to handle other formats, such as a dedicated RSS/Atom parser for a feed reader. The use of third-party Java code is discussed in Chapter 33.

For WeatherDemo, we use the W3C DOM parser in our buildForecasts() method:

```
void buildForecasts(String raw) throws Exception {
  DocumentBuilder builder=DocumentBuilderFactory
                            .newInstance()
                            .newDocumentBuilder();
  Document doc=builder.parse(new InputSource(new StringReader(raw)));
```

```
NodeList times=doc.getElementsByTagName("start-valid-time");

for (int i=0;i<times.getLength();i++) {
  Element time=(Element)times.item(i);
  Forecast forecast=new Forecast();

  forecasts.add(forecast);
  forecast.setTime(time.getFirstChild().getNodeValue());
}

NodeList temps=doc.getElementsByTagName("value");

for (int i=0;i<temps.getLength();i++) {
  Element temp=(Element)temps.item(i);
  Forecast forecast=forecasts.get(i);

  forecast.setTemp(new Integer(temp.getFirstChild().getNodeValue()));
}

NodeList icons=doc.getElementsByTagName("icon-link");

for (int i=0;i<icons.getLength();i++) {
  Element icon=(Element)icons.item(i);
  Forecast forecast=forecasts.get(i);

  forecast.setIcon(icon.getFirstChild().getNodeValue());
}
}
```

The National Weather Service XML format is curiously structured, relying heavily on sequential position in lists versus the more object-oriented style you find in formats like RSS or Atom. That being said, we can take a few liberties and simplify the parsing somewhat, taking advantage of the fact that the elements we want (start-valid-time for the forecast time, value for the temperature, and icon-link for the icon URL) are all unique within the document.

The HTML comes in as an InputStream and is fed into the DOM parser. From there, we scan for the start-valid-time elements and populate a set of Forecast models using those start times. Then, we find the temperature value elements and icon-link URLs and fill those in to the Forecast objects.

In turn, the generatePage() method creates a rudimentary HTML table with the forecasts:

```
String generatePage() {
  StringBuilder bufResult=new StringBuilder("<html><body><table>");

  bufResult.append("<tr><th width=\"50%\">Time</th>"+
                   "<th>Temperature</th><th>Forecast</th></tr>");

  for (Forecast forecast : forecasts) {
    bufResult.append("<tr><td align=\"center\">");
    bufResult.append(forecast.getTime());
    bufResult.append("</td><td align=\"center\">");
```

```
    bufResult.append(forecast.getTemp());
    bufResult.append("</td><td><img src=\"");
    bufResult.append(forecast.getIcon());
    bufResult.append("\"></td></tr>");
  }

  bufResult.append("</table></body></html>");

  return(bufResult.toString());
}
```

The result looks like Figure 34–1.

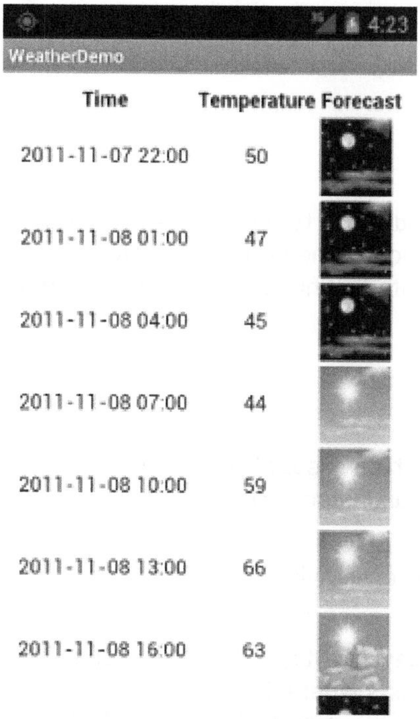

Figure 34–1. *The WeatherDemo sample application*

NOTE: You will have to set your location in Eclipse if you are using the emulator. Open the DDMS perspective with **Window ➤ Open Perspective ➤ Other ➤ DDMS**. Select your emulator in the **Devices ➤ Name** panel, and then set your emulator's location in the Emulator Control panel using the Longitude and Latitude boxes. When you are ready, click Send. You will need to do this each time the application is launched.

Stuff to Consider

If you need to use SSL, bear in mind that the default HttpClient setup does not include SSL support. Mostly, this is because you need to decide how to handle SSL certificate presentation: Do you blindly accept all certificates, even self-signed or expired ones? Or do you want to ask users if they really want to use some strange certificates?

Similarly, HttpClient, by default, is designed for single-threaded use. If you will be using HttpClient from some other place where multiple threads might be an issue, you can readily set up HttpClient to support multiple threads.

For these sorts of topics, you are best served by checking out the HttpClient web site for documentation and support.

AndroidHttpClient

Starting in Android 2.2 (API level 8), you can use the AndroidHttpClient class, found in the android.net.http package. This is an implementation of the HttpClient interface, like DefaultHttpClient. However, it is preconfigured with settings that the core Android team feels make sense for the platform.

What you gain are the following:

- SSL management

- A direct way to specify the user agent string, which is supplied in your call to the static newInstance() method to get an instance of AndroidHttpClient

- Utility methods for working with material compressed via GZIP, for parsing dates in HTTP headers, and so on

What you lose is automatic cookie storage. A regular DefaultHttpClient will cache cookies in memory and use them on subsequent requests where they are needed. AndroidHttpClient does not. There are ways to fix that, by using an HttpContext object, as is described in the AndroidHttpClient documentation.

Also, AndroidHttpClient prevents you from using it on the main application thread—requests can be made only on a background thread. This is a feature, even if some people might consider it to be a bug.

Since this class is available only in Android 2.2 and beyond, it may not make sense to do much with it until such time as you are supporting only API level 8 or higher.

Leveraging Internet-Aware Android Components

Wherever possible, use built-in Android components that can handle your Internet access for you. Such components will have been fairly rigorously tested and are more likely to handle edge cases well, such as dealing with users on Wi-Fi who move out of range of the access point and fail over to mobile data connections (e.g., 3G).

For example, the WebView widget (introduced in Chapter 15) and the MapView widget (covered in Chapter 40) both handle Internet access for you. While you still need the INTERNET permission, you do not have to perform HTTP requests or the like yourself.

This section outlines some other ways you can take advantage of built-in Internet capability.

Downloading Files

Android 2.3 introduced a DownloadManager, designed to handle a lot of the complexities of downloading larger files, such as:

- Determining whether the user is on Wi-Fi or mobile data and, depending on which, whether the download should occur

- Handling when the user, previously on Wi-Fi, moves out of range of the access point and fails over to mobile data

- Ensuring the device stays awake while the download proceeds

DownloadManager itself is less complicated than the alternative of writing all of it yourself. However, it does present a few challenges. In this section, we will examine the Internet/Download sample project that uses DownloadManager.

The Permissions

To use DownloadManager, you will need to hold the INTERNET permission. Depending on where you elect to download the file, you may also need the WRITE_EXTERNAL_STORAGE permission.

However, at the time of this writing, if you lack sufficient permissions, you may get an error complaining that you are missing ACCESS_ALL_DOWNLOADS. This appears to be a bug in the DownloadManager implementation. It should be complaining about the lack of INTERNET or WRITE_EXTERNAL_STORAGE, or both. You do not need to hold the ACCESS_ALL_DOWNLOADS permission, which is not even documented as of Android 3.0.

For example, here is the manifest for the Internet/Download application:

```
<?xml version="1.0" encoding="utf-8"?>
<manifest xmlns:android="http://schemas.android.com/apk/res/android"
  package="com.commonsware.android.download" android:versionCode="1"
  android:versionName="1.0">
    <!-- <uses-permission android:name="android.permission.ACCESS_ALL_DOWNLOADS" /> -->
    <uses-permission android:name="android.permission.INTERNET"/>
    <uses-permission android:name="android.permission.WRITE_EXTERNAL_STORAGE"/>
    <application android:label="@string/app_name" android:icon="@drawable/cw">
        <activity android:name="DownloadDemo" android:label="@string/app_name">
            <intent-filter>
                <action android:name="android.intent.action.MAIN"/>
```

```
                      <category android:name="android.intent.category.LAUNCHER"/>
                  </intent-filter>
              </activity>
          </application>
       <supports-screens android:largeScreens="true" android:normalScreens="true"
   android:smallScreens="true" android:anyDensity="true"/>
   </manifest>
```

> **NOTE:** You need to make sure your emulator is configured with an SD card for this example. Open the Android SDK and AVD Manager and select your emulator, and then click Edit. You can then set the size of the SD card your emulator uses for storage. If you resize an existing SD card image, note that AVD will delete your existing SD card image, so you should first back up anything of value you wish to keep.

The Layout

Our sample application has a simple layout, consisting of three buttons:

- One to kick off a download

- One to query the status of a download

- One to display a system-supplied activity containing the roster of downloaded files

```xml
<?xml version="1.0" encoding="utf-8"?>
<LinearLayout
  xmlns:android="http://schemas.android.com/apk/res/android"
  android:orientation="vertical"
  android:layout_width="fill_parent"
  android:layout_height="fill_parent"
  >
  <Button
    android:id="@+id/start"
    android:text="Start Download"
    android:layout_width="fill_parent"
    android:layout_height="0dip"
    android:layout_weight="1"
    android:onClick="startDownload"
  />
  <Button
    android:id="@+id/query"
    android:text="Query Status"
    android:layout_width="fill_parent"
    android:layout_height="0dip"
    android:layout_weight="1"
    android:onClick="queryStatus"
    android:enabled="false"
  />
  <Button
    android:text="View Log"
    android:layout_width="fill_parent"
    android:layout_height="0dip"
```

```
      android:layout_weight="1"
      android:onClick="viewLog"
   />
</LinearLayout>
```

Requesting the Download

To kick off a download, we first need to get access to the DownloadManager. This is a system service. We can call getSystemService() on any activity (or other Context), provide it the identifier of the system service we want, and receive the system service object back. However, since getSystemService() supports a wide range of these objects, we need to cast it to the proper type for the service we requested.

So, for example, here is a line from onCreate() of the DownloadDemo activity where we get the DownloadManager:

```
mgr=(DownloadManager)getSystemService(DOWNLOAD_SERVICE);
```

Most of these managers have no close(), release(), or goAwayPlease() sort of methods—we can just use them and let garbage collection take care of cleaning them up.

Given the DownloadManager, we can now call an enqueue() method to request a download. The name is relevant—do not assume that your download will begin immediately, though oftentimes it will. The enqueue() method takes a DownloadManager.Request object as a parameter. The Request object uses the builder pattern, in that most methods return the Request itself, so we can chain a series of calls together with less typing.

For example, the topmost button in our layout is tied to a startDownload() method in DownloadDemo, shown here:

```
public void startDownload(View v) {
  Uri uri=Uri.parse("http://commonsware.com/misc/test.mp4");

  Environment
    .getExternalStoragePublicDirectory(Environment.DIRECTORY_DOWNLOADS)
    .mkdirs();

  lastDownload=
    mgr.enqueue(new DownloadManager.Request(uri)
                .setAllowedNetworkTypes(DownloadManager.Request.NETWORK_WIFI |
                                        DownloadManager.Request.NETWORK_MOBILE)
                .setAllowedOverRoaming(false)
                .setTitle("Demo")
                .setDescription("Something useful. No, really.")
                .setDestinationInExternalPublicDir(Environment.DIRECTORY_DOWNLOADS,
                                                   "test.mp4"));

  v.setEnabled(false);
  findViewById(R.id.query).setEnabled(true);
}
```

We are downloading a sample MP4 file, and we want to download it to the external storage area. To do the latter, we are using getExternalStoragePublicDirectory() on Environment, which gives us a directory suitable for storing a certain class of content. In this case, we are going to store the download in Environment.DIRECTORY_DOWNLOADS, though we could just as easily have chosen Environment.DIRECTORY_MOVIES, since we are downloading a video clip. Note that the File object returned by getExternalStoragePublicDirectory() may point to a not-yet-created directory, which is why we call mkdirs() on it, to ensure the directory exists.

We then create the DownloadManager.Request object, with the following attributes:

- We are downloading the specific URL we want, courtesy of the Uri supplied to the Request constructor.

- We are willing to use either mobile data or Wi-Fi for the download (setAllowedNetworkTypes()), but we do not want the download to incur roaming charges (setAllowedOverRoaming()).

- We want the file downloaded as test.mp4 in the downloads area on the external storage (setDestinationInExternalPublicDir()).

We also provide a name (setTitle()) and description (setDescription()), which are used as part of the notification drawer entry for this download. The user will see these when they slide down the drawer while the download is progressing.

The enqueue() method returns an ID of this download, which we hold onto for use in querying the download status.

Keeping Track of Download Status

If the user taps the Query Status button, we want to find out the details of how the download is progressing. To do that, we can call query() on the DownloadManager. The query() method takes a DownloadManager.Query object, describing what download(s) we are interested in. In our case, we use the value we got from the enqueue() method when the user requested the download:

```java
public void queryStatus(View v) {
  Cursor c=mgr.query(new DownloadManager.Query().setFilterById(lastDownload));

  if (c==null) {
    Toast.makeText(this, "Download not found!", Toast.LENGTH_LONG).show();
  }
  else {
    c.moveToFirst();

    Log.d(getClass().getName(), "COLUMN_ID: "+
        c.getLong(c.getColumnIndex(DownloadManager.COLUMN_ID)));
    Log.d(getClass().getName(), "COLUMN_BYTES_DOWNLOADED_SO_FAR: "+
        c.getLong(c.getColumnIndex(DownloadManager.COLUMN_BYTES_DOWNLOADED_SO_FAR)));
    Log.d(getClass().getName(), "COLUMN_LAST_MODIFIED_TIMESTAMP: "+
        c.getLong(c.getColumnIndex(DownloadManager.COLUMN_LAST_MODIFIED_TIMESTAMP)));
    Log.d(getClass().getName(), "COLUMN_LOCAL_URI: "+
```

```
                c.getString(c.getColumnIndex(DownloadManager.COLUMN_LOCAL_URI)));
      Log.d(getClass().getName(), "COLUMN_STATUS: "+
                c.getInt(c.getColumnIndex(DownloadManager.COLUMN_STATUS)));
      Log.d(getClass().getName(), "COLUMN_REASON: "+
                c.getInt(c.getColumnIndex(DownloadManager.COLUMN_REASON)));

      Toast.makeText(this, statusMessage(c), Toast.LENGTH_LONG).show();
   }
}
```

The query() method returns a Cursor, containing a series of columns representing the details about our download. There are a series of constants on the DownloadManager class outlining what is possible. In our case, we retrieve (and dump to LogCat) the following:

- The ID of the download (COLUMN_ID)

- The amount of data that has been downloaded to date (COLUMN_BYTES_DOWNLOADED_SO_FAR)

- What the last-modified timestamp is on the download (COLUMN_LAST_MODIFIED_TIMESTAMP)

- Where the file is being saved to locally (COLUMN_LOCAL_URI)

- What the actual status is (COLUMN_STATUS)

- What the reason is for that status (COLUMN_REASON)

There are a number of possible status codes (e.g., STATUS_FAILED, STATUS_SUCCESSFUL, and STATUS_RUNNING). Some, like STATUS_FAILED, may have an accompanying reason providing more details.

What the User Sees

The user, upon launching the application, sees our three buttons, as shown in Figure 34–2.

Figure 34–2. *The DownloadDemo sample application, as initially launched*

Clicking the first button disables the button while the download is going on, and a download icon appears in the status bar (though it is a bit difficult to see, given the poor contrast between Android's icon and Android's status bar), as shown in Figure 34–3.

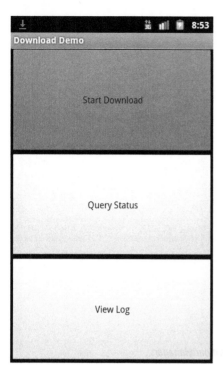

Figure 34–3. *The DownloadDemo sample application, performing a download*

Sliding down the notification drawer shows the user the progress of the download in the form of a ProgressBar widget, as shown in Figure 34–4.

Figure 34–4. *The notification drawer, during a download using DownloadManager*

Tapping the entry in the notification drawer returns control to our original activity, where the user sees a Toast, as shown in Figure 34–5.

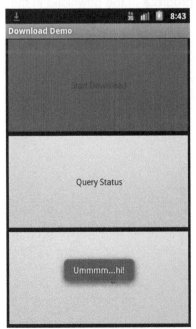

Figure 34–5. *The DownloadDemo sample application, after coming to the foreground from the notification*

If the user taps the middle button during the download, a Toast will appear indicating that the download is in progress, as shown in Figure 34–6.

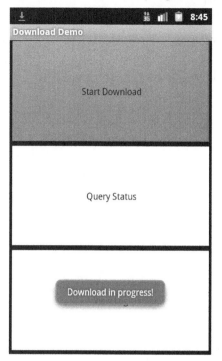

Figure 34–6. *The DownloadDemo sample application, showing the status mid-download*

Additional details are also dumped to LogCat, visible via DDMS or adb logcat:

```
12-10 08:45:01.289: DEBUG/com.commonsware.android.download.DownloadDemo(372):↩
 COLUMN_ID: 12
12-10 08:45:01.289: DEBUG/com.commonsware.android.download.DownloadDemo(372):↩
 COLUMN_BYTES_DOWNLOADED_SO_FAR: 615400
12-10 08:45:01.289: DEBUG/com.commonsware.android.download.DownloadDemo(372):↩
 COLUMN_LAST_MODIFIED_TIMESTAMP: 1291988696232
12-10 08:45:01.289: DEBUG/com.commonsware.android.download.DownloadDemo(372):↩
 COLUMN_LOCAL_URI: file:///mnt/sdcard/Download/test.mp4
12-10 08:45:01.299: DEBUG/com.commonsware.android.download.DownloadDemo(372):↩
 COLUMN_STATUS: 2
12-10 08:45:01.299: DEBUG/com.commonsware.android.download.DownloadDemo(372):↩
 COLUMN_REASON: 0
```

Once the download is complete, tapping the middle button will indicate that the download is, indeed, complete, and final information about the download is emitted to LogCat:

```
12-10 08:49:27.360: DEBUG/com.commonsware.android.download.DownloadDemo(372):↩
 COLUMN_ID: 12
12-10 08:49:27.360: DEBUG/com.commonsware.android.download.DownloadDemo(372):↩
 COLUMN_BYTES_DOWNLOADED_SO_FAR: 6219229
12-10 08:49:27.370: DEBUG/com.commonsware.android.download.DownloadDemo(372):↩
```

```
COLUMN_LAST_MODIFIED_TIMESTAMP: 1291988713409
12-10 08:49:27.370: DEBUG/com.commonsware.android.download.DownloadDemo(372):↵
 COLUMN_LOCAL_URI: file:///mnt/sdcard/Download/test.mp4
12-10 08:49:27.370: DEBUG/com.commonsware.android.download.DownloadDemo(372):↵
 COLUMN_STATUS: 8
12-10 08:49:27.370: DEBUG/com.commonsware.android.download.DownloadDemo(372):↵
 COLUMN_REASON: 0
```

Tapping the bottom button brings up the activity displaying all downloads, including both successes and failures, as shown in Figure 34–7.

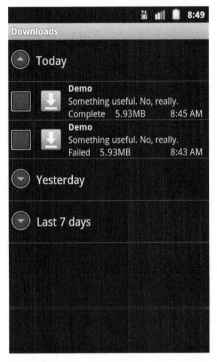

Figure 34–7. *The Downloads screen, showing everything downloaded by the DownloadManager*

And, of course, the file is downloaded. In Android 2.3, in the emulator, our chosen location maps to /mnt/sdcard/Downloads/test.mp4.

Limitations

DownloadManager works with HTTP URLs, but not HTTPS (SSL) URLs. This is unfortunate, as more and more sites are switching to SSL encryption across the board, to deal with various security challenges. Hopefully, in the future, DownloadManager will have more options here.

If you display the list of all downloads, and your download is among them, it is a really good idea to make sure that some activity (perhaps one of yours) is able to respond to an ACTION_VIEW Intent on that download's MIME type. Otherwise, when the user taps the entry in the list, they will get a Toast indicating that there is nothing available to view the download. This may confuse users. Alternatively, use `setVisibleInDownloadsUi()` on your request, passing in `false`, to suppress it from this list.

Continuing Our Escape from Janky Code

The rule is simple: do not access the Internet from the main application thread. Always use a background thread with `HttpClient`, `HttpUrlConnection`, or any other Internet access API you wish to use.

`StrictMode`, introduced in an earlier chapter, will warn you if you attempt to access the Internet on the main application thread. `AndroidHttpClient` will simply crash if you attempt to make web requests on the main application thread. However, these capabilities are available only in newer versions of Android. That being said, there are ways to have `StrictMode` in your application but use it only in newer versions of Android using conditional class loading—this technique was covered earlier in this book.

Services

Part

V

Services

Chapter 35

Services: The Theory

As noted previously, Android services are for long-running processes that may need to keep running even when decoupled from any activity. Examples include playing music even if the player activity gets garbage-collected, polling the Internet for RSS/Atom feed updates, and maintaining an online chat connection even if the chat client loses focus due to an incoming phone call.

Services are created when manually started (via an API call) or when some activity tries connecting to the service via interprocess communication (IPC). Services will live until specifically shut down or until Android is desperate for RAM and destroys them prematurely. Running for a long time has its costs, though, so services need to be careful not to use too much CPU or keep radios active too much of the time, lest the service cause the device's battery to get used up too quickly.

This chapter outlines the basic theory behind creating and consuming services. The next chapter presents a few specific patterns for services, ones that may closely match your particular needs. Hence, this chapter has limited code examples, whereas the next chapter serves up several code examples.

Why Services?

Services are a "Swiss Army knife" for a wide range of functions that do not require direct access to an activity's user interface, such as the following:

- Performing operations that need to continue even if the user leaves the application's activities, such as a long download (e.g., downloading an app from the Android Market) or playing music (e.g., an Android music app)

- Performing operations that need to exist regardless of activities coming and going, such as maintaining a chat connection in support of a chat application

- Providing a local API to remote APIs, such as might be provided by a web service

■ Performing periodic work without user intervention, akin to cron jobs or Windows scheduled tasks

Even things like home screen app widgets often involve a service to assist with long-running work.

Many applications do not need any services. Very few applications need more than one. However, services are a powerful tool in an Android developer's toolbox and their functionality is a subject with which any qualified Android developer should be familiar.

Setting Up a Service

Creating a service implementation shares many characteristics with building an activity. You inherit from an Android-supplied base class, override some lifecycle methods, and hook the service into the system via the manifest.

Service Class

Just as an activity in your application extends either Activity or an Android-supplied Activity subclass, a service in your application extends either Service or an Android-supplied Service subclass. The most common Service subclass is IntentService, used primarily for the command pattern. That being said, many services simply extend Service.

Lifecycle Methods

Just as activities have onCreate(), onResume(), onPause(), and similar methods, Service implementations have their own lifecycle methods, such as the following:

■ onCreate(): As with activities, called when the service process is created, by any means

■ onStartCommand(): Called each time the service is sent a command via startService()

■ onBind(): Called whenever a client binds to the service via bindService()

■ onDestroy(): Called as the service is being shut down

As with activities, services initialize whatever they need in onCreate() and clean up those items in onDestroy(). And, as with activities, the onDestroy() method of a service might not be called if Android terminates the entire application process, such as for emergency RAM reclamation.

The warnings we've provided previously about activities being terminated abruptly in the face of low memory issues apply in a similar fashion with services. However, Android 4.0 Ice Cream Sandwich introduces a new method, onTrimMemory(), that allows the system to better handle low memory situations specifically with services, giving them a chance to release unused or unneeded resources before having to resort to `onDestroy()` (as covered in detail in the next chapter).

The `onStartCommand()` and `onBind()` lifecycle methods will be implemented based on your choice of communicating to the client, as will be explained later in this chapter.

Manifest Entry

Finally, you need to add the service to your `AndroidManifest.xml` file, for it to be recognized as an available service for use. That is simply a matter of adding a `<service>` element as a child of the `application` element, providing `android:name` to reference your service class. So in the following manifest, you'll see `android:name="Downloader"`.

If you want to require some permission of those who wish to start or bind to the service, add an `android:permission` attribute naming the permission you are mandating—see Chapter 38 for more details.

For example, here is a manifest showing the `<service>` element:

```
<?xml version="1.0" encoding="utf-8"?>
<manifest xmlns:android="http://schemas.android.com/apk/res/android"
 package="com.commonsware.android.downloader" android:versionCode="1"
 android:versionName="1.0">
  <uses-permission android:name="android.permission.INTERNET"/>
  <uses-permission android:name="android.permission.WRITE_EXTERNAL_STORAGE"/>
    <application android:label="@string/app_name" android:icon="@drawable/cw">
        <activity android:name="DownloaderDemo" android:label="@string/app_name">
            <intent-filter>
                <action android:name="android.intent.action.MAIN"/>
                <category android:name="android.intent.category.LAUNCHER"/>
            </intent-filter>
        </activity>
        <service android:name="Downloader"/>
    </application>
  <supports-screens android:largeScreens="true" android:normalScreens="true"
 android:smallScreens="true" android:anyDensity="true"/>
</manifest>
```

Communicating to Services

Clients of services—frequently activities, though not necessarily—have two main ways to send requests or information to a service. One approach is to send a command, which creates no lasting connection to the service. The other approach is to bind to the service, establishing a bidirectional communications channel that lasts as long as the client needs it.

Sending Commands with startService()

The simplest way to work with a service is to call startService(). The startService() method takes an Intent parameter, much like startActivity() does. In fact, the Intent supplied to startService() has the same two-part role as it does with startActivity():

- Identify the service to communicate with

- Supply parameters, in the form of Intent extras, to tell the service what it is supposed to do

For a local service (the focus of this book), the simplest form of Intent is one that identifies the class that implements the Intent (e.g., new Intent(this, MyService.class);).

The call to startService() is asynchronous, so the client will not block. The service will be created if it is not already running, and it will receive the Intent via a call to the onStartCommand() lifecycle method. The service can do whatever it needs to in onStartCommand(), but since onStartCommand() is called on the main application thread, it should do its work very quickly. Anything that might take a while should be delegated to a background thread.

The onStartCommand() method can return one of several values, mostly to indicate to Android what should happen if the service's process is killed while it is running. The most likely return values are the following:

- START_STICKY: The service should be moved back into the started state (as if onStartCommand() had been called), but the Intent should not be redelivered to onStartCommand()

- START_REDELIVER_INTENT: The service should be restarted via a call to onStartCommand(), supplying the same Intent as was delivered this time

- START_NOT_STICKY: The service should remain stopped until explicitly started by application code

By default, calling startService() not only sends the command, but tells Android to keep the service running until something tells it to stop. One way to stop a service is to call stopService(), supplying the same Intent used with startService(), or at least one that is equivalent (e.g., identifies the same class). At that point, the service will stop and will be destroyed. Note that stopService() does not employ any sort of reference counting, so three calls to startService() will result in a single service running, which will be stopped by a call to stopService().

Another possibility for stopping a service is to have the service call stopSelf() on itself. You might do this if you use startService() to have a service begin running and doing some work on a background thread, then have the service stop itself when that background work is completed.

Binding with bindService()

Binding allows a service to expose an API to activities (or other services) that bind to it. When an activity (or other client) binds to a service, it primarily is requesting to be able to access the public API exposed by that service via the service's "binder," as returned by the service's onBind() method. When doing this, the activity can also indicate, via the BIND_AUTO_CREATE flag, to have Android automatically start up the service if it is not already running.

The service's binder is usually a subclass of Binder, on which you can put whatever methods you want to expose to clients. For local services, you can have as many methods as you want, with whatever method signatures (parameters, return type, etc.) that you want. The service returns an instance of the Binder subclass in onBind().

Clients call bindService(), supplying the Intent that identifies the service, a ServiceConnection object representing the client side of the binding, and an optional BIND_AUTO_CREATE flag. As with startService(), bindService() is asynchronous. The client will not know anything about the status of the binding until the ServiceConnection object is called with onServiceConnected(). This not only indicates the binding has been established, but, for local services, it provides the Binder object that the service returned via onBind(). At this point, the client can use the Binder to ask the service to do work on its behalf. Note that if the service is not already running and you provide BIND_AUTO_CREATE, the service will be created first before being bound to the client. If you skip BIND_AUTO_CREATE, bindService() will return false, indicating there was no existing service to bind to.

Eventually, the client will need to call unbindService(), to indicate it no longer needs to communicate with the service. For example, an activity might call bindService() in its onCreate() method, then call unbindService() in its onDestroy() method. The call to unbindService() eventually triggers onServiceDisconnected() to be called on the ServiceConnection object—at this point, the client can no longer safely use the Binder object.

If there are no other bound clients to the service, Android will shut down the service as well, releasing its memory. Hence, we do not need to call stopService() ourselves— Android handles that, if needed, as a side effect of unbinding. Android 4.0 also introduces an additional possible parameter to bindService(), called BIND_ALLOW_OOM_MANAGEMENT. Those familiar with OOM know it as the abbreviation for out of memory, and many operating systems employ an "OOM killer" to select processes for destruction in order to avert total memory exhaustion. Binding to a service with BIND_ALLOW_OOM_MANAGEMENT indicates that you consider your application and its bound service to be noncritical, allowing more aggressive consideration for it to be killed and the related service to be stopped in the event of low memory issues.

If the client is an activity, there are two important steps to take to ensure that the binding survives a configuration change, like a screen rotation:

1. Instead of calling bindService() on the activity itself, call bindService() on the Application Context (obtained via getApplicationContext()).

2. Make sure the ServiceConnection gets from the old instance of the activity to the new one, probably via onRetainNonConfigurationInstance().

This allows the binding to persist between activity instances.

Communicating from Services

Of course, the approaches listed in the previous section work only for a client calling out to a service. The reverse is also frequently needed, so the service can let an activity or something know about asynchronous events.

Callback/Listener Objects

An activity or other service client could provide some sort of callback or listener object to the service, which the service could then call when needed. To make this work, you would need to do the following:

1. Define a Java interface for that listener object.

2. Give the service a public API to register and retract listeners.

3. Have the service use those listeners at appropriate times, to notify those who registered the listener of some event.

4. Have the activity register and retract a listener as needed.

5. Have the activity respond to the listener-based events in some suitable fashion.

The biggest catch is to make sure that the activity retracts the listeners when it is done. Listener objects generally know their activity, explicitly (via a data member) or implicitly (by being implemented as an inner class). If the service is holding onto defunct listener objects, the corresponding activities will linger in memory, even if the activities are no longer being used by Android. This represents a big memory leak. You may wish to use WeakReferences, SoftReferences, or similar constructs to ensure that if an activity is destroyed, any listeners it registers with your service will not keep that activity in memory.

Broadcast Intents

An alternative approach, first mentioned in Chapter 21, is to have the service send a broadcast Intent that can be picked up by the activity...assuming the activity is still around and is not paused. The service can call sendBroadcast(), supplying an Intent that identifies the broadcast, designed to be picked up by a BroadcastReceiver. This could be a component-specific broadcast (e.g., new Intent(this, MyReceiver.class)), if the BroadcastReceiver is registered in the manifest. Or, it could be based on some action string, perhaps even one documented and designed for third-party applications to listen for.

The activity, in turn, can register a BroadcastReceiver via registerReceiver(), though this approach will work only for Intent objects specifying some action, not ones identifying a particular component. But, when the activity's BroadcastReceiver receives the broadcast, it can do what it wants to inform the user or otherwise update itself.

Pending Results

Your activity can call createPendingResult(). This returns a PendingIntent, an object that represents an Intent and the corresponding action to be performed upon that Intent (e.g., use it to start an activity). In this case, the PendingIntent will cause a result to be delivered to your activity's implementation of onActivityResult(), just as if another activity had been called with startActivityForResult() and, in turn, called setResult() to send back a result.

Since a PendingIntent is Parcelable, and can therefore be put into an Intent extra, your activity can pass this PendingIntent to the service. The service, in turn, can call one of several flavors of the send() method on the PendingIntent, to notify the activity (via onActivityResult()) of an event, possibly even supplying data (in the form of an Intent) representing that event.

Messenger

Yet another possibility is to use a Messenger object. A Messenger sends messages to an activity's Handler. Within a single activity, a Handler can be used to send messages to itself, as was demonstrated in Chapter 20. However, between components—such as between an activity and a service—you will need a Messenger to serve as the bridge.

As with a PendingIntent, a Messenger is Parcelable, and so can be put into an Intent extra. The activity calling startService() or bindService() would attach a Messenger as an extra on the Intent. The service would obtain that Messenger from the Intent. When it is time to alert the activity of some event, the service would do the following:

1. Call Message.obtain() to get an empty Message object.

2. Populate that Message object as needed, with whatever data the service wishes to pass to the activity.

3. Call send() on the Messenger, supplying the Message as a parameter.

The Handler would then receive the message via handleMessage(), on the main application thread, and thus would be able to update the UI or do whatever is necessary.

Notifications

Another approach is for the service to let the user know directly about the work that was completed. To do that, a service can raise a `Notification`—putting an icon in the status bar and optionally shaking, beeping, or giving some other signal. This technique is covered in Chapter 37.

Basic Service Patterns

Now that you have seen the pieces that make up services and their clients, let's examine a few scenarios that employ services and how those scenarios might be implemented.

The Downloader

If you elect to download something from the Android Market, after the download begins, you are free to exit the Market application entirely. This does not cancel the download—the download and installation run to completion, despite no Android Market activity being shown onscreen.

You may have a similar scenario in your application. Perhaps you want to enable users to download a purchased e-book, download a map for a game, download a file from a "drop box" file-sharing service, or download some other type of material, and you want to allow them to exit the application while the download is taking place in the background.

Android 2.3 introduced the DownloadManager (covered in Chapter 34), which could handle that functionality for you. However, you might need that sort of capability on older versions of Android, at least through 2011. Therefore, this section introduces a downloader that you can incorporate into your application to support earlier versions of Android. The sample project reviewed in this section is Services/Downloader.

The Design

This sort of situation is a perfect use for the command pattern and an IntentService. The IntentService has a background thread, so downloads can take as long as needed. An IntentService will automatically shut down when the work is done, so the service will not linger and you do not need to worry about shutting it down yourself. Your activity can simply send a command via startService() to the IntentService to tell it to go do the work.

Admittedly, things get a bit trickier when you want to have the activity find out when the download is complete. This example will show how to use Messenger for this purpose.

The Service Implementation

Here is the implementation of this IntentService, named Downloader:

```
package com.commonsware.android.downloader;

import android.app.Activity;
import android.app.IntentService;
import android.content.Intent;
import android.os.Bundle;
import android.os.Environment;
import android.os.Message;
import android.os.Messenger;
import android.util.Log;
import java.io.File;
import java.io.FileOutputStream;
import java.io.IOException;
import org.apache.http.client.ResponseHandler;
import org.apache.http.client.HttpClient;
import org.apache.http.client.methods.HttpGet;
import org.apache.http.impl.client.BasicResponseHandler;
import org.apache.http.impl.client.DefaultHttpClient;

public class Downloader extends IntentService {
  public static final String
EXTRA_MESSENGER="com.commonsware.android.downloader.EXTRA_MESSENGER";
  private HttpClient client=null;

  public Downloader() {
    super("Downloader");
  }

  @Override
  public void onCreate() {
    super.onCreate();

    client=new DefaultHttpClient();
  }

  @Override
  public void onDestroy() {
    super.onDestroy();

    client.getConnectionManager().shutdown();
  }

  @Override
  public void onHandleIntent(Intent i) {
    HttpGet getMethod=new HttpGet(i.getData().toString());
    int result=Activity.RESULT_CANCELED;

    try {
      ResponseHandler<byte[]> responseHandler=new ByteArrayResponseHandler();
      byte[] responseBody=client.execute(getMethod, responseHandler);
      File output=new File(Environment.getExternalStorageDirectory(),
```

```
                          i.getData().getLastPathSegment());

      if (output.exists()) {
        output.delete();
      }

      FileOutputStream fos=new FileOutputStream(output.getPath());

      fos.write(responseBody);
      fos.close();
      result=Activity.RESULT_OK;
    }
    catch (IOException e2) {
      Log.e(getClass().getName(), "Exception in download", e2);
    }

    Bundle extras=i.getExtras();

    if (extras!=null) {
      Messenger messenger=(Messenger)extras.get(EXTRA_MESSENGER);
      Message msg=Message.obtain();

      msg.arg1=result;

      try {
        messenger.send(msg);
      }
      catch (android.os.RemoteException e1) {
        Log.w(getClass().getName(), "Exception sending message", e1);
      }
    }
  }
}
}
```

In onCreate(), we obtain a DefaultHttpClient object, as was described in Chapter 34. In onDestroy(), we shut down the client. This way, if several download requests are invoked in sequence, we can use a single DefaultHttpClient object. The IntentService will shut down only after all enqueued work has been completed.

The bulk of the work is accomplished in onHandleIntent(), which is called on the IntentService, on a background thread, every time startService() is called. For the Intent, we obtain the URL of the file to download via a call to getData() on the supplied Intent. Actually downloading the file uses the DefaultHttpClient object, along with an HttpGet object. However, since the file might be binary (e.g., MP3) instead of text, we cannot use a BasicResponseHandler. Instead, we use a ByteArrayResponseHandler, which is a custom ResponseHandler cloned from the source for BasicResponseHandler, but one that returns a byte[] instead of a String:

```
package com.commonsware.android.downloader;

import java.io.IOException;
import org.apache.http.HttpEntity;
import org.apache.http.HttpResponse;
import org.apache.http.StatusLine;
import org.apache.http.client.ResponseHandler;
```

```
import org.apache.http.client.HttpResponseException;
import org.apache.http.util.EntityUtils;

public class ByteArrayResponseHandler implements ResponseHandler<byte[]> {
  public byte[] handleResponse(final HttpResponse response)
                   throws IOException, HttpResponseException {
    StatusLine statusLine=response.getStatusLine();

    if (statusLine.getStatusCode()>=300) {
      throw new HttpResponseException(statusLine.getStatusCode(),
                                      statusLine.getReasonPhrase());
    }

    HttpEntity entity=response.getEntity();

    if (entity==null) {
      return(null);
    }

    return(EntityUtils.toByteArray(entity));
  }
}
```

Once the file is downloaded to external storage, we need to alert the activity that the work is completed. If the activity is interested in this sort of message, it will have attached a `Messenger` object as `EXTRA_MESSENGER` to the Intent. Downloader gets the `Messenger`, creates an empty `Message` object, and puts a result code in the `arg1` field of the `Message`. It then sends the `Message` to the activity. If the activity was destroyed before this point, the request to send the message will fail with a `RemoteObjectException`.

Since this is an `IntentService`, it will automatically shut down when `onHandleIntent()` completes, if there is no more work queued to be completed.

Using the Service

The activity demonstrating the use of `Downloader` has a trivial UI, consisting of one large button:

```
<?xml version="1.0" encoding="utf-8"?>
<Button xmlns:android="http://schemas.android.com/apk/res/android"
  android:id="@+id/button"
  android:layout_width="fill_parent"
  android:layout_height="fill_parent"
  android:text="Do the Download"
  android:onClick="doTheDownload"
/>
```

That UI is initialized in onCreate(), as usual:

```
@Override
public void onCreate(Bundle savedInstanceState) {
  super.onCreate(savedInstanceState);
  setContentView(R.layout.main);

  b=(Button)findViewById(R.id.button);
}
```

When the user clicks the button, doTheDownload() is called to disable the button (to prevent accidental duplicate downloads) and call startService():

```
public void doTheDownload(View v) {
  b.setEnabled(false);

  Intent i=new Intent(this, Downloader.class);

  i.setData(Uri.parse("http://commonsware.com/Android/excerpt.pdf"));
  i.putExtra(Downloader.EXTRA_MESSENGER, new Messenger(handler));

  startService(i);
}
```

Here, the Intent we pass over has the URL of the file to download (in this case, a URL pointing to a PDF), plus a Messenger in the EXTRA_MESSENGER extra. That Messenger is created with an attachment to the activity's Handler:

```
private Handler handler=new Handler() {
  @Override
  public void handleMessage(Message msg) {
    b.setEnabled(true);

    Toast
      .makeText(DownloaderDemo.this, "Download complete!",
                Toast.LENGTH_LONG)
      .show();
  }
};
```

If the activity is still around when the download is complete, the Handler enables the button and displays a Toast to let the user know that the download is complete. Note that the activity ignores the result code supplied by the service, though in principle it could do something different in both the success and failure cases.

The Music Player

Most audio player applications in Android—for music, audiobooks, or whatever—do not require the user to remain in the player application itself to keep it running. Rather, the user can go on and do other things with their device, with the audio playing in the background. This is similar in many respects to the download scenario from the previous section. However, in this case, the *user* is the one who controls when the work (playing audio) ends.

The sample project reviewed in this section is Services/FakePlayer.

The Design

Once again, we will use startService(), since we want the service to run even after the activity that started it has been destroyed. However, this time we will use a regular

Service rather than an IntentService. An IntentService is designed to do work and stop itself, whereas in this case we want the user to be able to stop the music playback.

Since music playback is outside the scope of this book, the service will simply stub out those particular operations.

The Service Implementation

Here is the implementation of this Service, named PlayerService:

```
package com.commonsware.android.fakeplayer;

import android.app.Service;
import android.content.Intent;
import android.os.Bundle;
import android.os.IBinder;
import android.util.Log;

public class PlayerService extends Service {
  public static final String EXTRA_PLAYLIST="EXTRA_PLAYLIST";
  public static final String EXTRA_SHUFFLE="EXTRA_SHUFFLE";
  private boolean isPlaying=false;

  @Override
  public int onStartCommand(Intent intent, int flags, int startId) {
    String playlist=intent.getStringExtra(EXTRA_PLAYLIST);
    boolean useShuffle=intent.getBooleanExtra(EXTRA_SHUFFLE, false);

    play(playlist, useShuffle);

    return(START_NOT_STICKY);
  }

  @Override
  public void onDestroy() {
    stop();
  }

  @Override
  public IBinder onBind(Intent intent) {
    return(null);
  }

  private void play(String playlist, boolean useShuffle) {
    if (!isPlaying) {
      Log.w(getClass().getName(), "Got to play()!");
      isPlaying=true;
    }
  }

  private void stop() {
    if (isPlaying) {
      Log.w(getClass().getName(), "Got to stop()!");
      isPlaying=false;
    }
```

```
    }
}
```

In this case, we really do not need anything for onCreate(), so we skip that lifecycle method. On the other hand, we have to implement onBind(), because that is a required method of Service subclasses. IntentService implements onBind() for us, which is why that was not needed for the Downloader sample.

When the client calls startService(), onStartCommand() is called in PlayerService. Here, we get the Intent and pick out some extras to tell us what to play back (EXTRA_PLAYLIST) and other configuration details (e.g., EXTRA_SHUFFLE). onStartCommand() calls play(), which simply flags that our player is playing and logs a message to LogCat—a real music player would use MediaPlayer to start playing the first song in the playlist. onStartCommand() returns START_NOT_STICKY, indicating that if Android has to kill off this service (e.g., due to low memory), it should not restart it after conditions improve.

onDestroy() stops the music from playing (theoretically, anyway) by calling a stop() method. Once again, this just logs a message to LogCat and updates our internal are-we-playing flag.

In Chapter 37, which discusses notifications, we will revisit this sample and discuss the use of startForeground(), which makes it easier for the user to get back to the music player and lets Android know that the service is delivering part of the foreground experience and therefore should not be shut down.

Using the Service

The UI of the FakePlayer activity demonstrating the use of PlayerService is more complex than the UI in the previous sample, consisting of two large buttons:

```xml
<?xml version="1.0" encoding="utf-8"?>
<LinearLayout xmlns:android="http://schemas.android.com/apk/res/android"
    android:orientation="vertical"
    android:layout_width="fill_parent"
    android:layout_height="fill_parent"
    >
  <Button
      android:layout_width="fill_parent"
      android:layout_height="fill_parent"
      android:layout_weight="1"
      android:text="Start the Player"
      android:onClick="startPlayer"
      />
  <Button
      android:layout_width="fill_parent"
      android:layout_height="fill_parent"
      android:layout_weight="1"
      android:text="Stop the Player"
      android:onClick="stopPlayer"
      />
</LinearLayout>
```

The activity itself is not much more complex:

```
package com.commonsware.android.fakeplayer;

import android.app.Activity;
import android.content.Intent;
import android.os.Bundle;
import android.view.View;

public class FakePlayer extends Activity {
  @Override
  public void onCreate(Bundle savedInstanceState) {
    super.onCreate(savedInstanceState);
    setContentView(R.layout.main);
  }

  public void startPlayer(View v) {
    Intent i=new Intent(this, PlayerService.class);

    i.putExtra(PlayerService.EXTRA_PLAYLIST, "main");
    i.putExtra(PlayerService.EXTRA_SHUFFLE, true);

    startService(i);
  }

  public void stopPlayer(View v) {
    stopService(new Intent(this, PlayerService.class));
  }
}
```

The onCreate() method merely loads the UI. The startPlayer() method constructs an Intent with fake values for EXTRA_PLAYLIST and EXTRA_SHUFFLE, and then calls startService(). After you click the top button, you will see the corresponding message in LogCat. Similarly, stopPlayer() calls stopService(), triggering the second LogCat message. Notably, you do not need to keep the activity running in between those button clicks—you can exit the activity by pressing BACK and come back later to stop the service.

The Web Service Interface

If you are going to consume a REST-style web service, you may wish to create a Java client-side API for that service. This allows you to isolate details about the web service (URLs, authorization credentials, etc.) in one place, enabling the rest of your application to use only the published API. If the client-side API might involve state, such as a session ID or cached results, you may wish to use a service to implement the client-side API. In this case, the most natural form of service would be one that publishes a Binder, so clients can call a "real" API, that the service translates into HTTP requests.

In this case, we want to create a client-side Java API for the National Weather Service's forecast web service, so we can get a weather forecast (timestamps, projected temperatures, and projected precipitation) for a given latitude and longitude (for geographic locations in the United States). As you may recall, we examined this web service in Chapter 34.

The sample project reviewed in this section is `Services/WeatherAPI`.

The Design

To use the binding pattern, we will need to expose an API from a "binder" object. Since the weather forecast arrives in a singularly awful XML structure, we will make the binder be responsible for parsing the XML. Hence, the binder will have a `getForecast()` method to get us an `ArrayList` of `Forecast` objects, each `Forecast` representing one timestamp/temperature/precipitation triple.

Once again, to supply the latitude and longitude of the forecast roster to retrieve, we will use a `Location` object, which will be obtained from GPS. This part of the sample will be described in greater detail in Chapter 39.

Since the web service call may take a while, it is unsafe to do this on the main application thread. In this sample, we will have the service use an `AsyncTask` to call our weather API, so the activity largely can be ignorant of threading issues.

The Rotation Challenge

Chapter 20 noted the issues involved with orientation changes (or other configuration changes) and background threads in activities. The solution given was to use `onRetainNonConfigurationInstance()` with a static inner class `AsyncTask` implementation and manually associate it with the new, post-configuration-change activity.

That same problem crops up with the binding pattern as well, which is one of the reasons binding is difficult to use. If we bind to a service from an activity, that binding will not magically pass to the new activity instance after an orientation change. Instead, we need to do two things:

- Bind to the service not by using the activity as the `Context`, but rather by using `getApplicationContext()`, as that `Context` is one that will live for the lifetime of our process

- Pass the `ServiceConnection` representing this binding from the old activity instance to the new one as part of the configuration change

To accomplish the second feat, we will need to use the same `onRetainNonConfigurationInstance()` trick that we used with threads in Chapter 20.

The Service Implementation

Our service-side logic is broken into three classes, `Forecast`, `WeatherBinder`, and `WeatherService`, plus one interface, `WeatherListener`.

The Forecast

The Forecast class merely encapsulates the three pieces of the forecast data triple—the timestamp, the temperature, and the icon indicating the expected precipitation (if any):

```
package com.commonsware.android.weather;

class Forecast {
  String time="";
  Integer temp=null;
  String iconUrl="";

  String getTime() {
    return(time);
  }

  void setTime(String time) {
    this.time=time.substring(0,16).replace('T', ' ');
  }

  Integer getTemp() {
    return(temp);
  }

  void setTemp(Integer temp) {
    this.temp=temp;
  }

  String getIcon() {
    return(iconUrl);
  }

  void setIcon(String iconUrl) {
    this.iconUrl=iconUrl;
  }
}
```

The Interface

Because we are going to fetch the actual weather forecast on a background thread in the service, we have a slight API challenge—calls on our binder are synchronous. Hence, we cannot have a getForecast() method that returns our forecast. Rather, we need to provide some way for the service to get the forecast back to our activity. In this case, we will pass in a listener object (WeatherListener) that the service will use when a forecast is ready:

```
package com.commonsware.android.weather;

import java.util.ArrayList;

public interface WeatherListener {
  void updateForecast(ArrayList<Forecast> forecast);
  void handleError(Exception e);
}
```

The Binder

The WeatherBinder extends Binder, a requirement for the local binding pattern. Other than that, the API is up to us.

Hence, we expose three methods:

- onCreate(): To be called when the WeatherBinder is set up, so we can get a DefaultHttpClient object to use with the web service

- onDestroy(): To be called when the WeatherBinder is no longer needed, so we can shut down that DefaultHttpClient object

- getForecast(): The main public API for use by our activity, to kick off the background work to create our ArrayList of Forecast objects when given a Location

```
package com.commonsware.android.weather;

import android.app.Service;
import android.content.Context;
import android.content.Intent;
import android.location.Location;
import android.os.AsyncTask;
import android.os.Binder;
import android.os.Bundle;
import java.io.IOException;
import java.io.StringReader;
import java.util.ArrayList;
import javax.xml.parsers.DocumentBuilder;
import javax.xml.parsers.DocumentBuilderFactory;
import org.apache.http.client.ResponseHandler;
import org.apache.http.client.HttpClient;
import org.apache.http.client.methods.HttpGet;
import org.apache.http.impl.client.BasicResponseHandler;
import org.apache.http.impl.client.DefaultHttpClient;
import org.w3c.dom.Document;
import org.w3c.dom.Element;
import org.w3c.dom.NodeList;
import org.xml.sax.InputSource;

public class WeatherBinder extends Binder {
  private String forecast=null;
  private HttpClient client=null;
  private String format=null;

  void onCreate(Context ctxt) {
    client=new DefaultHttpClient();
    format=ctxt.getString(R.string.url);
  }

  void onDestroy() {
    client.getConnectionManager().shutdown();
  }
```

```java
void getForecast(Location loc, WeatherListener listener) {
  new FetchForecastTask(listener).execute(loc);
}

private ArrayList<Forecast> buildForecasts(String raw) throws Exception {
  ArrayList<Forecast> forecasts=new ArrayList<Forecast>();
  DocumentBuilder builder=DocumentBuilderFactory
                          .newInstance()
                          .newDocumentBuilder();
  Document doc=builder.parse(new InputSource(new StringReader(raw)));
  NodeList times=doc.getElementsByTagName("start-valid-time");

  for (int i=0;i<times.getLength();i++) {
    Element time=(Element)times.item(i);
    Forecast forecast=new Forecast();

    forecasts.add(forecast);
    forecast.setTime(time.getFirstChild().getNodeValue());
  }

  NodeList temps=doc.getElementsByTagName("value");

  for (int i=0;i<temps.getLength();i++) {
    Element temp=(Element)temps.item(i);
    Forecast forecast=forecasts.get(i);

    forecast.setTemp(new Integer(temp.getFirstChild().getNodeValue()));
  }

  NodeList icons=doc.getElementsByTagName("icon-link");

  for (int i=0;i<icons.getLength();i++) {
    Element icon=(Element)icons.item(i);
    Forecast forecast=forecasts.get(i);

    forecast.setIcon(icon.getFirstChild().getNodeValue());
  }

  return(forecasts);
}

class FetchForecastTask extends AsyncTask<Location, Void, ArrayList<Forecast>> {
  Exception e=null;
  WeatherListener listener=null;

  FetchForecastTask(WeatherListener listener) {
    this.listener=listener;
  }

  @Override
  protected ArrayList<Forecast> doInBackground(Location... locs) {
    ArrayList<Forecast> result=null;

    try {
      Location loc=locs[0];
      String url=String.format(format, loc.getLatitude(),
```

```
                          loc.getLongitude());
      HttpGet getMethod=new HttpGet(url);
      ResponseHandler<String> responseHandler=new BasicResponseHandler();
      String responseBody=client.execute(getMethod, responseHandler);

      result=buildForecasts(responseBody);
    }
    catch (Exception e) {
      this.e=e;
    }

    return(result);
  }

  @Override
  protected void onPostExecute(ArrayList<Forecast> forecast) {
    if (listener!=null) {
      if (forecast!=null) {
        listener.updateForecast(forecast);
      }

      if (e!=null) {
        listener.handleError(e);
      }
    }
  }
}
}
```

Most of this code is merely doing the web service request using DefaultHttpClient and an HttpGet object, plus using the DOM parser to convert the XML into the Forecast objects. However, this is wrapped in a FetchForecastTask, an AsyncTask that will do the HTTP operation and parsing on a background thread. In onPostExecute(), the task invokes our WeatherListener, either to supply the forecast (updateForecast()) or to hand over an Exception that was raised (handleError()).

The Service

The WeatherService is fairly short, with the business logic delegated to WeatherBinder:

```
package com.commonsware.android.weather;

import android.app.Service;
import android.content.Intent;
import android.os.IBinder;
import java.util.ArrayList;

public class WeatherService extends Service {
  private final WeatherBinder binder=new WeatherBinder();

  @Override
  public void onCreate() {
    super.onCreate();

    binder.onCreate(this);
```

```
  }

  @Override
  public IBinder onBind(Intent intent) {
    return(binder);
  }

  @Override
  public void onDestroy() {
    super.onDestroy();

    binder.onDestroy();
  }
}
```

Our onCreate() and onDestroy() methods delegate to the WeatherBinder, and onBind() returns the WeatherBinder itself.

Using the Service

On the surface, the WeatherDemo activity should be simple:

- Bind to the service in onCreate()

- Arrange to get GPS fixes, in the form of Location objects

- When a fix comes in, use the WeatherBinder to get a forecast, convert it to HTML, and display it in a WebView

- Unbind from the service in onDestroy()

However, our decision to use the binding pattern and to have the activity deal with the background thread means there is more work involved than those bullet points.

First, here is the full WeatherDemo implementation:

```
package com.commonsware.android.weather;

import android.app.Activity;
import android.app.AlertDialog;
import android.content.ComponentName;
import android.content.Context;
import android.content.Intent;
import android.content.IntentFilter;
import android.content.ServiceConnection;
import android.location.Location;
import android.location.LocationListener;
import android.location.LocationManager;
import android.os.AsyncTask;
import android.os.Bundle;
import android.os.DeadObjectException;
import android.os.RemoteException;
import android.os.IBinder;
import android.util.Log;
import android.webkit.WebView;
import java.util.ArrayList;
```

```
public class WeatherDemo extends Activity {
  private WebView browser;
  private LocationManager mgr=null;
  private State state=null;
  private boolean isConfigurationChanging=false;

  @Override
  public void onCreate(Bundle savedInstanceState) {
    super.onCreate(savedInstanceState);
    setContentView(R.layout.main);

    browser=(WebView)findViewById(R.id.webkit);
    state=(State)getLastNonConfigurationInstance();

    if (state==null) {
      state=new State();
      getApplicationContext()
        .bindService(new Intent(this, WeatherService.class),
                   state.svcConn, BIND_AUTO_CREATE);
    }
    else if (state.lastForecast!=null) {
      showForecast();
    }

    state.attach(this);

    mgr=(LocationManager)getSystemService(LOCATION_SERVICE);
    mgr.requestLocationUpdates(LocationManager.GPS_PROVIDER,
                              3600000, 1000, onLocationChange);
  }

  @Override
  public void onDestroy() {
    super.onDestroy();

    if (mgr!=null) {
      mgr.removeUpdates(onLocationChange);
    }

    if (!isConfigurationChanging) {
      getApplicationContext().unbindService(state.svcConn);
    }
  }

  @Override
  public Object onRetainNonConfigurationInstance() {
    isConfigurationChanging=true;

    return(state);
  }

  private void goBlooey(Throwable t) {
    AlertDialog.Builder builder=new AlertDialog.Builder(this);

    builder
```

```
            .setTitle("Exception!")
            .setMessage(t.toString())
            .setPositiveButton("OK", null)
            .show();
    }

    static String generatePage(ArrayList<Forecast> forecasts) {
        StringBuilder bufResult=new StringBuilder("<html><body><table>");

        bufResult.append("<tr><th width=\"50%\">Time</th>"+
                        "<th>Temperature</th><th>Forecast</th></tr>");

        for (Forecast forecast : forecasts) {
            bufResult.append("<tr><td align=\"center\">");
            bufResult.append(forecast.getTime());
            bufResult.append("</td><td align=\"center\">");
            bufResult.append(forecast.getTemp());
            bufResult.append("</td><td><img src=\"");
            bufResult.append(forecast.getIcon());
            bufResult.append("\"></td></tr>");
        }

        bufResult.append("</table></body></html>");

        return(bufResult.toString());
    }

    void showForecast() {
        browser.loadDataWithBaseURL(null, state.lastForecast,
                                "text/html", "UTF-8", null);
    }

    LocationListener onLocationChange=new LocationListener() {
        public void onLocationChanged(Location location) {
            if (state.weather!=null) {
                state.weather.getForecast(location, state);
            }
            else {
                Log.w(getClass().getName(), "Unable to fetch forecast - no WeatherBinder");
            }
        }

        public void onProviderDisabled(String provider) {
            // required for interface, not used
        }

        public void onProviderEnabled(String provider) {
            // required for interface, not used
        }

        public void onStatusChanged(String provider, int status,
                                Bundle extras) {
            // required for interface, not used
        }
    };
```

```
static class State implements WeatherListener {
  WeatherBinder weather=null;
  WeatherDemo activity=null;
  String lastForecast=null;

  void attach(WeatherDemo activity) {
    this.activity=activity;
  }

  public void updateForecast(ArrayList<Forecast> forecast) {
    lastForecast=generatePage(forecast);
    activity.showForecast();
  }

  public void handleError(Exception e) {
    activity.goBlooey(e);
  }

  ServiceConnection svcConn=new ServiceConnection() {
    public void onServiceConnected(ComponentName className,
                                   IBinder rawBinder) {
      weather=(WeatherBinder)rawBinder;
    }

    public void onServiceDisconnected(ComponentName className) {
      weather=null;
    }
  };
}
}
```

Now, let's look at the highlights of the service connection and the background thread.

Managing the State

We need to ensure that our ServiceConnection can be passed between activity
instances on a configuration change. Hence, we have a State static inner class to hold
that, plus two other bits of information: the Activity the state is associated with, and a
String showing the last forecast we retrieved:

```
static class State implements WeatherListener {
  WeatherBinder weather=null;
  WeatherDemo activity=null;
  String lastForecast=null;

  void attach(WeatherDemo activity) {
    this.activity=activity;
  }

  public void updateForecast(ArrayList<Forecast> forecast) {
    lastForecast=generatePage(forecast);
    activity.showForecast();
  }

  public void handleError(Exception e) {
```

```
    activity.goBlooey(e);
  }

  ServiceConnection svcConn=new ServiceConnection() {
    public void onServiceConnected(ComponentName className,
                                   IBinder rawBinder) {
      weather=(WeatherBinder)rawBinder;
    }

    public void onServiceDisconnected(ComponentName className) {
      weather=null;
    }
  };
}
```

The lastForecast String allows us to redisplay the generated HTML after a configuration change. Otherwise, when the user rotates the screen, we would lose our forecast (held only in the old instance's WebView) and would have to either retrieve a fresh one or wait for a GPS fix.

We return this State object from onRetainNonConfigurationInstance():

```
@Override
public Object onRetainNonConfigurationInstance() {
  isConfigurationChanging=true;

  return(state);
}
```

In onCreate(), if there is no nonconfiguration instance, we create a fresh State and bind to the service, since we do not have a service connection at present. On the other hand, if onCreate() gets a State from getLastNonConfigurationInstance(), it simply holds onto that state and reloads our forecast in the WebView. In either case, onCreate() indicates to the State that the new activity instance is the current one:

```
@Override
public void onCreate(Bundle savedInstanceState) {
  super.onCreate(savedInstanceState);
  setContentView(R.layout.main);

  browser=(WebView)findViewById(R.id.webkit);
  state=(State)getLastNonConfigurationInstance();

  if (state==null) {
    state=new State();
    getApplicationContext()
      .bindService(new Intent(this, WeatherService.class),
                   state.svcConn, BIND_AUTO_CREATE);
  }
  else if (state.lastForecast!=null) {
    showForecast();
  }

  state.attach(this);

  mgr=(LocationManager)getSystemService(LOCATION_SERVICE);
```

```
mgr.requestLocationUpdates(LocationManager.GPS_PROVIDER,
                           3600000, 1000, onLocationChange);
}
```

Depending on the subjective importance of your weather forecasting, you might decide that your application and its service aren't necessarily the most important thing running on the device. Recall that the previous chapter highlighted the BIND_ALLOW_OOM_MANAGEMENT parameter, new to Android 4.0, for bindService(). Weather forecasting is probably not as important as maintaining a phone call, so we can opt to modify our bindService() call in the preceding onCreate() method to volunteer for OOM memory reclaim (and process destruction) in the event of low memory:

```
bindService(new Intent(this, WeatherService.class),
                state.svcConn, BIND_AUTO_CREATE |
                BIND_ALLOW_OOM_MANAGEMENT );
```

This does not affect the rest of our logic.

Time to Unbind

We bind to the service when onCreate() is called, if it did not receive a State via getLastNonConfigurationInstance() (in which case, we are already bound). This begs the question: when do we unbind from the service?

We want to unbind when the activity is being destroyed, but not if the activity is being destroyed because of a configuration change.

Unfortunately, there is no built-in way to make that determination from onDestroy(). There is an isFinishing() method we can call on an Activity, which will return true if the activity is going away for good or false otherwise. This does return false for a configuration change, but it will also return false if the activity is being destroyed to free up RAM and the user might be able to return to it via the Back button.

This is why onRetainNonConfigurationInstance() flips an isConfigurationChanging flag in WeatherDemo to true. That flag is initially false. We then check that flag to see whether or not we should unbind from the service:

```
@Override
public void onDestroy() {
  super.onDestroy();

  if (mgr!=null) {
    mgr.removeUpdates(onLocationChange);
  }

  if (!isConfigurationChanging) {
    getApplicationContext().unbindService(state.svcConn);
  }
}
```

Chapter 37

Alerting Users via Notifications

Pop-up messages, tray icons and their associated "bubble" messages, bouncing dock icons...you are no doubt used to programs trying to get your attention, sometimes for good reason. Your phone also probably chirps at you for more than just incoming calls: low battery, alarm clocks, appointment notifications, incoming text and e-mail messages, and so on.

Not surprisingly, Android has a whole framework for dealing with these sorts of things, collectively called *notifications*, as described in this chapter.

Notification Configuration

A service, running in the background, needs a way to let users know something of interest has occurred, such as when e-mail has been received. Moreover, the service may need some way to steer users to an activity where they can act upon the event, such as reading a received message. For this, Android supplies status bar icons, flashing lights, and other indicators collectively known as notifications.

Your current phone may already have such icons, to indicate battery life, signal strength, whether Bluetooth is enabled, and the like. With Android, applications can add their own status bar icons, with an eye toward having them appear only when needed (e.g., a message has arrived).

In Android, you can raise notifications via theNotificationManager, which is a system service. To use it, you need to get the service object via getSystemService(NOTIFICATION_SERVICE) from your activity. The NotificationManager gives you three methods: one to raise a Notification (notify()) and two to get rid of an existing Notification (cancel() and cancelAll()).

The notify() method takes a Notification, which is a data structure that spells out what form your pestering should take. The capabilities of this object are described in the following sections.

Hardware Notifications

You can flash LEDs on the device by setting lights to true, also specifying the color (as an #ARGB value in ledARGB) and what pattern the light should blink in (by providing off/on durations in milliseconds for the light via ledOnMS and ledOffMS). Note, however, that Android devices will apply best efforts to meet your color request, meaning that different devices may give you different colors, or perhaps no control over color at all. For example, the Motorola CLIQ has only a white LED, so you can ask for any color you want, and you will get white. Note that you will need to OR (|) the Notification.FLAG_SHOW_LIGHTS value into the public flags field on the Notification object for flashing of the LED to work.

You can play a sound, using a Uri to a piece of content held, perhaps, by a ContentManager (sound). Think of this as a ringtone for your application.

You can vibrate the device, controlled via a long[], indicating the on/off patterns (in milliseconds) for the vibration (vibrate). You might do this by default, or you might make it an option the user can choose when circumstances require a more subtle notification than a ringtone. To use this, though, you will need to request the VIBRATE permission (permissions are discussed in Chapter 38).

All of these options, by default, happen once (e.g., one LED flash or one playback of the sound). If you want to have them persist until the Notification is canceled, you will need to set the flags public field in your Notification to include FLAG_INSISTENT.

Instead of manually specifying the hardware options, you can also use the defaults field in the Notification, setting it to DEFAULT_LIGHTS, DEFAULT_SOUND, DEFAULT_VIBRATE, or DEFAULT_ALL, which will use platform defaults for all hardware options.

Icons

While the flashing lights, sounds, and vibrations are aimed at getting somebody to look at the device, icons are designed to take them the next step and tell them what's so important.

To set up an icon for a Notification, you need to set two public fields: icon, where you provide the identifier of a Drawable resource representing the icon, and contentIntent, where you supply a PendingIntent to be raised when the icon is clicked. A PendingIntent is a wrapper around a regular Intent that allows the Intent to be invoked later, by another process, to start an activity or whatever. Typically, a Notification will trigger an activity, in which case you would create the PendingIntent via the static getActivity() method and give it an Intent that identifies one of your activities. That being said, you could have the Notification send a broadcast Intent instead, by using a getBroadcast() version of a PendingIntent. Android 4.0 has expanded the variety of send() methods available with PendingIntent, providing for most imaginable circumstance.

You can also supply a text blurb to appear when the icon is put on the status bar (tickerText).

If you want all three, the simpler approach is to call setLatestEventInfo(), which wraps all three of those in a single call.

You can also set a value in the number public field of your Notification. This will cause the number you supply to be drawn over the top of the icon in one corner. This is used, for example, to show the number of unread e-mail messages, so that you don't need to have a bunch of different icons, one for each possible number of unread messages. By default, the number field will be ignored and not used.

Note that thesize of the icons used with a Notification changed with Android 2.3. Before that version, 25-pixel square was the desired size. Now, per-density icons in a more rectangular shape are preferred:

- 24-pixel square (inside a 24-pixel wide by 38-pixel high bounding box) for high-density and extra-high density screens

- 16-pixel square (inside a 16×25-pixel bounding box) for medium-density screens

- 12-pixel square (inside a 12×19-pixel bounding box) for low-density screens

Applications following these rules will want to use specific resource sets for the new icons:

- res/drawable-xhdpi-v9/: For extra-high-density Android 2.3 and later editions

- res/drawable-hdpi-v9/: For high-density Android 2.3 and later editions

- res/drawable-mdpi-v9/: For medium-density Android 2.3 and later editions

- res/drawable-ldpi-v9/: For low-density Android 2.3 and later editions

- res/drawable/: For the icon to use on Android 2.2 and earlier

More details on guidelines for all icons, including status bar icons, can be found in the Android developer documentation.

Notifications in Action

Let's now take a peek at the Notifications/Notify1 sample project, in particular the NotifyDemo class:

```
package com.commonsware.android.notify;

import android.app.Activity;
import android.app.Notification;
import android.app.NotificationManager;
import android.app.PendingIntent;
import android.content.Intent;
import android.os.Bundle;
import android.view.View;

public class NotifyDemo extends Activity {
  private static final int NOTIFY_ME_ID=1337;
  private int count=0;
  private NotificationManager mgr=null;

  @Override
  public void onCreate(Bundle savedInstanceState) {
    super.onCreate(savedInstanceState);
    setContentView(R.layout.main);

    mgr=(NotificationManager)getSystemService(NOTIFICATION_SERVICE);
  }

  public void notifyMe(View v) {
    Notification note=new Notification(R.drawable.stat_notify_chat,
                                "Status message!",
                                System.currentTimeMillis());
    PendingIntent i=PendingIntent.getActivity(this, 0,
                        new Intent(this, NotifyMessage.class),
                                        0);

    note.setLatestEventInfo(this, "Notification Title",
                        "This is the notification message", i);
    note.number=++count;
    note.vibrate=new long[] {500L, 200L, 200L, 500L};
    note.flags|=Notification.FLAG_AUTO_CANCEL;

    mgr.notify(NOTIFY_ME_ID, note);
  }

  public void clearNotification(View v) {
    mgr.cancel(NOTIFY_ME_ID);
  }
}
```

As shown in Figure 37–1, this activity sports two large buttons, one to kick off a notification after a 5-second delay and one to cancel that notification (if it is active).

Figure 37-1. *The NotifyDemo activity main view*

Creating the notification, in notifyMe(), is accomplished in seven steps:

1. Create a Notification object with our icon, a message to flash on the status bar as the notification is raised, and the time associated with this event.

2. Create a PendingIntent that will trigger the display of another activity (NotifyMessage).

3. Use setLatestEventInfo() to specify that, when the notification is clicked, we are to display a certain title and message, and if that is clicked, we launch the PendingIntent.

4. Update the number associated with the notification.

5. Specify a vibration pattern: 500ms on, 200ms off, 200ms on, 500ms off.

6. Include FLAG_AUTO_CANCEL in the Notification object's flags field.

7. Tell the NotificationManager (obtained in onCreate()) to display the notification.

Hence, if we click the top button, our icon will appear in the status bar, along with a brief display of our status message, as shown in Figure 37-2.

Figure 37–2. *Our notification as it appears on the status bar, with our status message*

After the status message goes away, the icon will have our number (initially 1) superimposed on its lower-right corner, as shown in Figure 37–3. You might use this to signify the number of unread messages, for example.

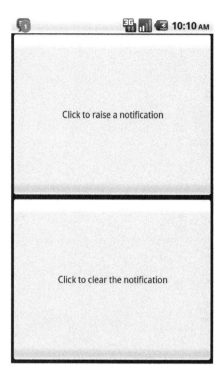

Figure 37–3. *Our notification with the superimposed number*

If you drag down the icon, a drawer will appear beneath the status bar. Drag that drawer all the way to the bottom of the screen to show the outstanding notifications, including our own, as shown in Figure 37–4.

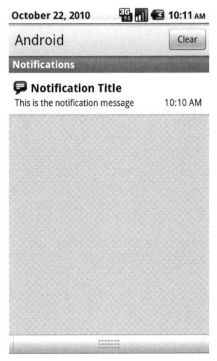

Figure 37–4. *The notifications drawer, fully expanded, with our notification*

If you click the notification entry in the drawer, you'll be taken to a trivial activity displaying a message. In a real application, this activity would do something useful based upon the event that occurred (e.g., take users to the newly arrived mail messages).

Clicking the cancel button, clicking the Clear button in the drawer, or clicking the notification entry in the drawer will remove the icon from the status bar. The latter occurs because we included FLAG_AUTO_CANCEL in the Notification, indicating that a tap on the drawer entry should cancel the Notification itself. Users of Android 4.0 will also have the option of "swipe to clear," where they can simply swipe individual notifications to either side of the screen to dismiss or action them. This aids in situations where a user has multiple notifications active, and wants to return to the remaining notifications after dealing with a particular one.

Staying in the Foreground

Notifications have another use: keeping select services around.

Services do not live forever. Android may terminate your application's process to free up memory in an emergency situation, or just because it seems to have been hanging around memory too long. Ideally, you design your services to deal with the fact that they may not run indefinitely.

However, some services will be missed by the user if they mysteriously vanish. For example, the default music player application that ships with Android uses a service for the actual music playback. That way, users can listen to music while continuing to use their phone for other purposes. The service stops only when the user presses the stop button in the music player activity. If that service were to shut down unexpectedly, the user would wonder what is wrong.

Services like this can declare themselves as being part of the *foreground*. This will cause their priority to rise and make them less likely to be bumped out of memory. The trade-off is that the service has to maintain a Notification, so the user knows that this service is claiming part of the foreground. And, ideally, that Notification should provide an easy path back to some activity where the user can stop the service.

To do this, in onCreate() of your service (or wherever else in the service's life it would make sense), call startForeground(). This takes a Notification and a locally unique integer, just like the notify() method on NotificationManager. It causes the Notification to appear and moves the service into foreground priority. Later on, you can call stopForeground() to return to normal priority.

Note that this method was added with Android 2.0 (API level 5). There was an earlier method, setForeground(), that performed a similar function in earlier versions of Android.

FakePlayer, Redux

The previous chapter, covering service patterns, presented a fake music player, implemented with an Activity (FakePlayer) and a Service (PlayerService). The PlayerService is actually what plays the music, so the music can play even while the FakePlayer activity is not open.

However, Android may not consider PlayerService to be part of the user experience, since services normally interact very little directly with users. This means Android may run PlayerService in a way that caps CPU usage (not necessarily bad) and might elect to shut down the service if it thinks it has been running too long (probably bad).

The answer is to use startForeground() and stopForeground(). We can call startForeground() when we start the music playing in our play() method:

```
private void play(String playlist, boolean useShuffle) {
  if (!isPlaying) {
    Log.w(getClass().getName(), "Got to play()!");
    isPlaying=true;

    Notification note=new Notification(R.drawable.stat_notify_chat,
                                       "Can you hear the music?",
                                       System.currentTimeMillis());
    Intent i=new Intent(this, FakePlayer.class);

    i.setFlags(Intent.FLAG_ACTIVITY_CLEAR_TOP|
            Intent.FLAG_ACTIVITY_SINGLE_TOP);

    PendingIntent pi=PendingIntent.getActivity(this, 0,
```

```
                                          i, 0);

    note.setLatestEventInfo(this, "Fake Player",
                            "Now Playing: \"Ummmm, Nothing\"",
                            pi);
    note.flags|=Notification.FLAG_NO_CLEAR;

    startForeground(1337, note);
  }
}
```

The plus side is that our service will have more CPU availability if needed and will be far less likely to be killed by Android. Users will see an icon in the status bar. If they slide down the notification drawer and tap our Notification's entry, they will be taken back to FakePlayer—the existing instance, if there is one, or a fresh instance otherwise, courtesy of our Intent flags (Intent.FLAG_ACTIVITY_CLEAR_TOP| Intent.FLAG_ACTIVITY_SINGLE_TOP). For a music player, this UI pattern makes it easy for users to quickly go back to stop the music when needed.

Stopping the music, via our stop() method, will call stopForeground():

```
private void stop() {
  if (isPlaying) {
    Log.w(getClass().getName(), "Got to stop()!");
    isPlaying=false;
    stopForeground(true);
  }
}
```

The true value passed to stopForeground() tells Android to remove the Notification, which would be the typical approach for this pattern.

Notifications in Ice Cream Sandwich and Honeycomb

The Honeycomb UI introduced in Android 3.0, and its successor in Android 4.0, Ice Cream Sandwich, support notifications, just like all previous versions of Android. However, the user experience is a bit different, owing to the tablet metaphor and its additional screen space.

Figure 37–5 shows the unmodified Notifications/Notify1 project, as seen in a tablet-sized emulator.

Figure 37–5. *Notify1 as seen on an Android 3.0 tablet-sized emulator*

Other than the newer style of the status bar, and the extra-huge buttons, this is no different from what you would see on a pre-Honeycomb phone.

If we click the top button, our Notification appears, this time in the lower-right corner, with the icon and ticker text, as shown in Figure 37–6.

Figure 37–6. *Notify1 with a notification added*

Note that if the user taps the ticker, it triggers our PendingIntent, just as if they had tapped the notification drawer entry on a phone.

When the ticker is removed, our icon remains...without the number, as shown in Figure 37–7.

Figure 37–7. *Notify1 with a numberless notification icon*

If the user taps that icon, a notification drawer–style pop-up appears nearby, as shown in Figure 37–8.

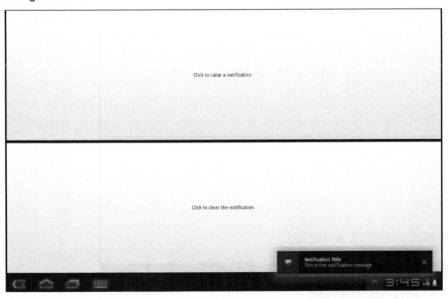

Figure 37–8. *Notify1 with the notification content appearing*

Tapping the icon or the text triggers the `PendingIntent`, while tapping the × on the right cancels this `Notification`.

Part VI

Other Android Capabilities

Part IV

Other Android Capabilities

Chapter 38

Requesting and Requiring Permissions

In the late 1990s, a wave of viruses spread through the Internet, delivered via e-mail, using contact information culled from Microsoft Outlook. A virus would simply e-mail copies of itself to each of the Outlook contacts that had an e-mail address. This was possible because, at the time, Outlook did not take any steps to protect data from programs using the Outlook API, since that API was designed for ordinary developers, not virus authors.

Nowadays, many applications that hold onto contact data secure that data by requiring that a user explicitly grant rights for other programs to access the contact information. Those rights could be granted on a case-by-case basis or all at once at install time.

Android is no different, in that it requires permissions for applications to read or write contact data. Android's permission system is useful well beyond contact data, and for content providers and services beyond those supplied by the Android framework.

You, as an Android developer, will frequently need to ensure that your applications have the appropriate permissions to do what you want to do with other applications' data. You may also elect to require permissions for other applications to use your data or services, if you make those available to other Android components. This chapter covers how to accomplish both these ends.

Mother, May I?

Requesting the use of other applications' data or services requires the uses-permission element to be added to your AndroidManifest.xml file. Your manifest may have zero or more uses-permission elements, all as direct children of the root manifest element.

The uses-permission element takes a single attribute, android:name, which is the name of the permission your application requires:

```
<uses-permission
  android:name="android.permission.ACCESS_LOCATION" />
```

All of the stock system permissions begin with android.permission and are listed in the Android SDK documentation for Manifest.permission. Third-party applications may have their own permissions, which, hopefully, they have documented for you. Here are some of the more useful permissions:

- INTERNET, if your application wishes to access the Internet through any means, from raw Java sockets through the WebView widget

- WRITE_EXTERNAL_STORAGE, for writing data to the SD card (or whatever the device has designated as external storage)

- NFC, for performing I/O with the near-field communication (NFC) radio on newer devices

- ACCESS_COARSE_LOCATION and ACCESS_FINE_LOCATION, for determining where the device is located

- CALL_PHONE, to allow the application to place phone calls directly, without user intervention

Permissions are confirmed at the time the application is installed. The user will be prompted to confirm that it is acceptable for your application to do what the permission calls for. Hence, it is important that you ask for as few permissions as possible and justify those you seek, so users do not elect to skip installing your application because you ask for too many unnecessary permissions. This prompt will not appear when loading an application via USB, such as during development.

If you do not have the desired permission and try to do something that needs it, you should get a SecurityException informing you of the missing permission. Note that you will fail on a permission check only if you forgot to ask for the permission—it is impossible for your application to be running and *not* have been granted your requested permissions.

Halt! Who Goes There?

The other side of the coin is to secure your own application. If your application is mostly activities, security may be just an "outbound" thing, where you request the right to use resources of other applications. If, on the other hand, you put content providers or services in your application, you will want to implement "inbound" security to control which applications can do what with the data.

Note that the issue here is less about whether other applications might mess up your data, but rather about privacy of the user's information or use of services that might incur expense. That is where the stock permissions for built-in Android applications are focused: whether you can read or modify contacts, send SMS messages, and so forth. If your application does not store information that might be considered private, security is less of an issue. If, on the other hand, your application stores private data, such as medical information, security is much more important.

The first step to securing your own application using permissions is to declare said permissions, once again in the `AndroidManifest.xml` file. In this case, instead of `uses-permission`, you add `permission` elements. Once again, you can have zero or more `permission` elements, all as direct children of the root `manifest` element.

Declaring a permission is slightly more complicated than using a permission. You need to supply three pieces of information:

- *The symbolic name of the permission*: To keep your permissions from colliding with those from other applications, you should use your application's Java namespace as a prefix.

- *A label for the permission*: Choose something short that would be understandable by users.

- *A description for the permission*: Choose something a wee bit longer that is understandable by your users.

Following is an example:

```
<permission
  android:name="vnd.tlagency.sekrits.SEE_SEKRITS"
  android:label="@string/see_sekrits_label"
  android:description="@string/see_sekrits_description" />
```

This does not enforce the permission. Rather, it indicates that it is a possible permission; your application must still flag security violations as they occur.

There are two ways for your application to enforce permissions, dictating where and under what circumstances they are required. The easier option is to indicate in the manifest where permissions are required. The more difficult option is to enforce permissions in your code. Both options are discussed next.

Enforcing Permissions via the Manifest

Activities, services, and receivers can all declare an attribute named `android:permission`, whose value is the name of the permission that is required to access those items:

```
<activity
  android:name=".SekritApp"
  android:label="Top Sekrit"
  android:permission="vnd.tlagency.sekrits.SEE_SEKRITS">
  <intent-filter>
    <action android:name="android.intent.action.MAIN" />
    <category
      android:name="android.intent.category.LAUNCHER" />
  </intent-filter>
</activity>
```

Only applications that have requested your indicated permission will be able to access the secured component. In this case, "access" means the following:

- Activities cannot be started without the permission.

- Services cannot be started, stopped, or bound to an activity without the permission.

- Intent receivers ignore messages sent via sendBroadcast() unless the sender has the permission.

Enforcing Permissions Elsewhere

In your code, you have two additional ways to enforce permissions.

First, your services can check permissions on a per-call basis via checkCallingPermission(). This returns PERMISSION_GRANTED or PERMISSION_DENIED depending on whether the caller has the permission you specified. For example, if your service implements separate read and write methods, you could require separate read and write permissions in code by checking those methods for the permissions you need from Java.

Second, you can include a permission when you call sendBroadcast(). This means that eligible broadcast receivers must hold that permission; those without the permission are ineligible to receive it. We will examine sendBroadcast() in greater detail elsewhere in this book.

May I See Your Documents?

There is no automatic discovery of permissions at compile time; all permission failures occur at runtime. Hence, it is important that youdocument the permissions required for your public APIs, including content providers, services, and activities intended for launching from other activities. Otherwise, programmers who are attempting to interface with your application will have to find out the permission rules by trial and error.

Furthermore, you should expect that users of your application will be prompted to confirm any permissions your application says it needs. Hence, you need to document for your users what they should expect, lest they get confused by the question posed by the device and elect to not install or use your application. You may wish to use string resources for this, so you can internationalize your permission details the way you internationalize all the other messages and prompts in your application. You should also be mindful that your users will be reading your permission details on a phone or tablet screen, so keep your justifications short and to the point.

New Permissions in Old Applications

Sometimes, Android introduces new permissions that govern behavior that formerly did not require permissions. WRITE_EXTERNAL_STORAGE is one example. Originally, applications could write to external storage without any permission at all. Android 1.6 introduced WRITE_EXTERNAL_STORAGE, which is required before you can write to external storage. However, applications that were written before Android 1.6 could not possibly request that permission, since it did not exist at the time. Breaking those applications would seem to be a harsh price for progress.

What Android does is grandfather in certain permissions for applications supporting earlier SDK versions. In particular, if you have <uses-sdk android:minSdkVersion="3"> in your manifest, saying that you support Android 1.5, your application will automatically request WRITE_EXTERNAL_STORAGE and READ_PHONE_STATE, even if you do not explicitly request those permissions. People installing your application on an Android 1.5 device will see these requests.

The number of new permissions introduced grows as the handsets take on new capabilities and users' attitudes toward underlying features mature, requiring more fine-grained approaches to managing access. New permissions in Android 4.0 include the following:

- ADD_VOICEMAIL: Allows an application to inject voicemail into the system
- BIND_TEXT_SERVICE: Required for any service you write that derives from TextService
- BIND_VPN_SERVICE: Required for any service you write that derives from VpnService
- READ_PROFILE: Provides access to read a user's personal profile data
- WRITE_PROFILE: Allows an application to update or change a user's personal profile data

Eventually, when you drop support for the older version of permissions (e.g., switch to <uses-sdk android:minSdkVersion="4">), Android will no longer automatically request those permissions. Hence, if your code really *does* need those permissions, you will need to ask for them yourself.

Permissions: Up Front or Not at All

The permission system in Android is not especially flexible. Notably, you have to ask for all permissions you might ever need up front, and the user has to agree to all of them or abandon the installation of your app.

This means you cannot do the following:

- Create optional permissions, ones the user could say "no, thanks" to, that your application could react to dynamically

- Request new permissions after installation, which means that even if a permission is needed only for some lightly used feature, you have to ask for it anyway

Hence, as you determine the feature list for your app, it is important that you keep permissions in mind. Every additional permission that you request is a filter that will cost you some portion of your prospective audience. Certain combinations—such as INTERNET and READ_CONTACTS—will have a stronger effect, as users may fear what the combination can do. You will need to decide for yourself whether attracting additional users by offering the feature is worth the cost of requiring the permissions the feature needs to operate.

Chapter 39

Accessing Location-Based Services

A popular feature on current mobile devices is GPS capability, so the device can tell you where you are at any point in time. While the most popular uses of GPS service are for mapping and getting directions, there are other things you can do with it if you know your location. For example, you might set up a dynamic chat application based on physical location, so users can chat with those people who are nearest to them. Or, you could automatically geo-tag posts to Twitter or similar services.

GPS is not the only way a mobile device can identify your location. Alternatives include the following:

- The European equivalent to GPS, called Galileo, which is still under development at the time of this writing

- Cell tower triangulation, where your position is determined based on signal strength to nearby cell towers

- Proximity to public Wi-Fi hotspots that have known geographic locations

Android devices may have one or more of these services available to them. You, as a developer, can ask the device for your location, plus details on which providers are available. There are even ways for you to simulate your location in the emulator, for use in testing your location-enabled applications.

Location Providers: They Know Where You're Hiding

Android devices can have access to several different means of determining your location. Some will have better accuracy than others. Some may be free, while others may have a cost associated with them. Some may be able to tell you more than just your current position, such as your elevation over sea level or your current speed.

Android has abstracted all this out into a set of `LocationProvider` objects. Your Android environment will have zero or more `LocationProvider` instances, one for each distinct locating service that is available on the device. Providers know not only your location, but their own characteristics, in terms of accuracy, cost, and so on.

You, as a developer, will use a `LocationManager`, which holds the `LocationProvider` set, to figure out which `LocationProvider` is right for your particular circumstance. You will also need a permission in your application, or the various location APIs will fail due to a security violation. Depending on which location providers you wish to use, you may need `ACCESS_COARSE_LOCATION`, `ACCESS_FINE_LOCATION`, or both (see Chapter 38).

Finding Yourself

The obvious thing to do with a location service is to figure out where you are right now. To do that, you first need to get a `LocationManager`, so call `getSystemService(LOCATION_SERVICE)` from your activity or service and cast it to be a `LocationManager`. The next step is to get the name of the `LocationProvider` you want to use. Here, you have two main options:

- Ask the user to pick a provider
- Find the best-match provider based on a set of criteria

If you want the user to pick a provider, calling `getProviders()` on the `LocationManager` will give you a `List` of providers, which you can then present to the user for selection.

If you want to find the best-match provider based on a set of criteria, create and populate a `Criteria` object, stating the particulars of what you want out of a `LocationProvider`. Following are some of the methods that you can use to specify criteria:

- `setAltitudeRequired()`: Indicates whether or not you need the current altitude
- `setAccuracy()`: Sets a minimum level of accuracy, in meters, for the position
- `setCostAllowed()`: Controls whether the provider must be free or can incur a cost on behalf of the device user

Given a filled-in `Criteria` object, call `getBestProvider()` on your `LocationManager`, and Android will sift through the criteria and give you the best answer. Note that not all of your criteria may be met; all but the monetary cost criterion might be relaxed if nothing matches.

You are also welcome to hard-wire in a `LocationProvider` name (e.g., `GPS_PROVIDER`), perhaps just for testing purposes.

Once you know the name of the `LocationProvider`, you can call `getLastKnownPosition()` to find out where you were recently. However, unless something else is causing the desired provider to collect fixes (e.g., unless the GPS radio is on), getLastKnownPosition() will return null, indicating that there is no known position. On the other hand, getLastKnownPosition() incurs no monetary or power cost, since the provider does not need to be activated to get the value.

These methods return a Location object, which can give you the latitude and longitude of the device in degrees as a Java double. If the particular location provider offers other data, you can get that as well:

- For altitude, hasAltitude() will tell you if there is an altitude value, and getAltitude() will return the altitude in meters.

- For bearing (i.e., compass-style direction), hasBearing() will tell you if there is a bearing available, and getBearing() will return it as degrees east of true north.

- For speed, hasSpeed() will tell you if the speed is known, and getSpeed() will return the speed in meters per second.

A more likely approach to getting the Location from a LocationProvider, though, is to register for updates, as described in the next section.

On the Move

Not all location providers are necessarily immediately responsive. GPS, for example, requires activating a radio and getting a fix from the satellites before you get a location. That is why Android does not offer a getMeMyCurrentLocationNow() method. Combine that with the fact that your users may not want their movements to be reflected in your application, and you are probably best off registering for location updates and using that as your means of getting the current location.

The Internet/Weather and Service/WeatherAPI sample applications show how to register for updates—call requestLocationUpdates() on your LocationManager instance. This method takes four parameters:

- The name of the location provider you wish to use

- How long, in milliseconds, *should* have elapsed before we might get a location update

- How far, in meters, the device must have moved before we might get a location update

- A LocationListener that will be notified of key location-related events, as shown in the following example:

```
LocationListener onLocationChange=new LocationListener() {
  public void onLocationChanged(Location location) {
    if (state.weather!=null) {
      state.weather.getForecast(location, state);
    }
    else {
      Log.w(getClass().getName(), "Unable to fetch forecast - no WeatherBinder");
```

```
    }
  }

  public void onProviderDisabled(String provider) {
    // required for interface, not used
  }

  public void onProviderEnabled(String provider) {
    // required for interface, not used
  }

  public void onStatusChanged(String provider, int status,
                              Bundle extras) {
    // required for interface, not used
  }
}
```

Here, all we do is trigger a FetchForecastTask with the Location supplied to the onLocationChanged() callback method.

Bear in mind that the time parameter is only a guide to help steer Android from a power consumption standpoint. You may get many more location updates than this. To get the maximum number of location updates, supply 0 for both the time and distance constraints.

When you no longer need the updates, call removeUpdates() with the LocationListener you registered. If you fail to do this, your application will continue receiving location updates even after all activities and such are closed up, which will also prevent Android from reclaiming your application's memory.

There is another version of requestLocationUpdates() that takes a PendingIntent rather than a LocationListener. This is useful if you want to be notified of changes in your position even when your code is not running. For example, if you are logging movements, you could use a PendingIntent that triggers a BroadcastReceiver (getBroadcast()) and have the BroadcastReceiver add the entry to the log. This way, your code is in memory only when the position changes, so you do not tie up system resources while the device is not moving.

Are We There Yet? Are We There Yet?

Sometimes, you are not interested in where you are now, or even when you move, but want to know when you get to where you are going. This could be an end destination, or it could be getting to the next step on a set of directions, so you can give the user the next instruction.

To accomplish this, LocationManager offers addProximityAlert(). This registers a PendingIntent, which will be fired off when the device gets within a certain distance of a certain location. The addProximityAlert() method takes the following as parameters:

- The latitude and longitude of the position of interest.

- A radius, specifying how close you should be to that position for the Intent to be raised.

- A duration for the registration, in milliseconds. After this period, the registration automatically lapses. A value of -1 means the registration lasts until you manually remove it via removeProximityAlert().

- The PendingIntent to be raised when the device is within the target zone expressed by the position and radius.

Note that it is not guaranteed that you will actually receive an Intent. There may be an interruption in location services, or the device may not be in the target zone during the period of time the proximity alert is active. For example, if the position is off by a bit, and the radius is a little too tight, the device might only skirt the edge of the target zone, or it might go by the target zone so quickly that the device's location isn't sampled during that time.

It is up to you to arrange for an activity or receiver to respond to the Intent you register with the proximity alert. What you do when the Intent arrives is up to you. For example, you might set up a notification (e.g., vibrate the device), log the information to a content provider, or post a message to a web site. Note that you will receive the Intent whenever the position is sampled and you are within the target zone, not just upon entering the zone. Hence, you may get the Intent several times, perhaps quite a few times, depending on the size of the target zone and the speed of the device's movement.

Testing... Testing...

The Android emulator does not have the ability to get a fix from GPS, triangulate your position from cell towers, or identify your location by some nearby Wi-Fi signal. So, if you want to simulate a moving device, you will need to have some means of providing mock location data to the emulator.

For whatever reason, this particular area has undergone significant changes as Android itself has evolved. It used to be that you could provide mock location data within your application, which was very handy for demonstration purposes. Alas, those options were all removed as of Android 1.0.

One option for supplying mock location data is the Dalvik Debug Monitor Service (DDMS). This is an external program, separate from the emulator, which can feed the emulator single location points or full routes to traverse, in a few different formats. There is a specific permission to include in your manifest file called ACCESS_MOCK_LOCATION, to enable access to the data. You will also need to ensure that the "Allow mock locations" option is enabled under Developer Settings for your emulator. The "Step 6: Set Up the Device" section in Chapter 2 explains how to access those settings. DDMS itself is described in greater detail in Chapter 43.

Chapter 40

Mapping with MapView and MapActivity

One of Google's most popular services—after Search, of course—is Google Maps, which enables you to map everything from the location of the nearest pizza parlor to directions from New York City to San Francisco (only 2571 miles, or 4135 kilometers for the metric-inclined), and includes street views and satellite imagery.

Most Android devices, not surprisingly, integrate Google Maps. For those that do, there is a mapping activity available to users straight from the main Android launcher. More relevant to you, as a developer, are MapView and MapActivity, which allow you to integrate maps into your own applications. Not only can you display maps, control the zoom level, and allow people to pan around, but you can tie in Android's location-based services to show where the device is and where it is going.

Fortunately, integrating basic mapping features into your Android project is fairly easy. And with a bit more effort, you can integrate more sophisticated mapping features.

Terms, Not of Endearment

Integrating Google Maps into third-party applications requires agreeing to a fairly lengthy set of legal terms. These terms include clauses that you may find unpalatable.

If you are considering Google Maps, please review these terms closely to determine if your intended use will run afoul of any clauses. You are strongly recommended to seek professional legal counsel if there are any potential areas of conflict.

Also, keep your eyes peeled for other mapping options, based on other sources of map data, such as OpenStreetMap (www.openstreetmap.org/).

Piling On

As of Android 1.5, Google Maps is not strictly part of the Android SDK. Instead, it is part of the Google APIs Add-On, an extension of the stock SDK. The Android add-on system provides hooks for other subsystems that may be part of some devices but not others.

> **NOTE:** Because Google Maps is not part of the Android open source project, some devices lack Google Maps due to licensing issues. For example, at the time of this writing, the Archos 5 Android tablet does not have Google Maps.

By and large, the fact that Google Maps is in an add-on does not affect your day-to-day development. However, bear in mind the following:

- You will need to create your project with an appropriate target to ensure the Google Maps APIs will be available.

- To test your Google Maps integration, you will also need an AVD that uses an appropriate target.

The Key to It All

If you download the source code for this book, compile the Maps/NooYawk project, install it in your emulator, and run it, you will probably see a screen with a grid and a couple of pushpins, but no actual maps. That's because the API key in the source code is invalid for your development machine. Instead, you will need to generate your own API key(s) for use with your application. This also holds true for any map-enabled projects you create on your own from scratch.

Full instructions for generating API keys, for development and production use, can be found on the Android web site. In the interest of brevity, let's focus on the narrow case of getting NooYawk running in your emulator. Doing this requires the following steps:

1. Visit the API key signup page and review the terms of service.

2. Reread those terms of service and make really sure you want to agree to them.

3. Find the MD5 digest of the certificate used for signing your debug-mode applications (described in detail following this list).

4. On the API key signup page, paste in that MD5 signature and submit the form.

5. On the resulting page, copy the API key and paste it as the value of apiKey in your MapView-using layout.

The trickiest part is finding the MD5 signature of the certificate used for signing your debug-mode applications. Much of the complexity is merely in making sense of the concept.

All Android applications are signed using a digital signature generated from a certificate. You are automatically given a debug certificate when you set up the SDK, and there is a separate process for creating a self-signed certificate for use in your production applications. This signature process involves the use of the Java `keytool` and `jarsigner` utilities. For the purposes of getting your API key, you only need to worry about `keytool`.

To get your MD5 digest of your debug certificate, if you are on Mac OS X or Linux, use the following command:

```
keytool -list -alias androiddebugkey -keystore ~/.android/debug.keystore↵
 -storepass android -keypass android
```

On other development platforms, such as Windows, you will need to replace the value of the `-keystore` switch with the location for your platform and user account (where `<user>` is your account name):

- On Windows XP, use `C:\Documents and Settings\<user>\.android\debug.keystore`.

- On Windows Vista or Windows 7, use `C:\Users\<user>\.android\debug.keystore`.

The second line of the output contains your MD5 digest, as a series of pairs of hex digits separated by colons.

The Bare Bones

To put a map into your application, you need to create your own subclass of `MapActivity`. Like `ListActivity`, which wraps up some of the smarts behind having an activity dominated by a `ListView`, `MapActivity` handles some of the nuances of setting up an activity dominated by a `MapView`. A `MapView` can be used only by a `MapActivity`, not by any other type of `Activity`.

In your layout for the `MapActivity` subclass, you need to add an element named `com.google.android.maps.MapView`. This is the "longhand" way to spell out the names of widget classes, by including the full package name along with the class name. This is necessary because `MapView` is not in the `android.widget` namespace. You can give the `MapView` widget whatever `android:id` attribute value you want, plus handle all the layout details to have it render properly alongside your other widgets.

However, you do need to have the following items:

- `android:apiKey`, your Google Maps API key

- `android:clickable = "true"`, if you want users to be able to click and pan through your map

For example, from the `Maps/NooYawk` sample application, here is the main layout:

```xml
<?xml version="1.0" encoding="utf-8"?>
<RelativeLayout xmlns:android="http://schemas.android.com/apk/res/android"
  android:layout_width="fill_parent"
  android:layout_height="fill_parent">
```

```
    <com.google.android.maps.MapView android:id="@+id/map"
      android:layout_width="fill_parent"
      android:layout_height="fill_parent"
      android:apiKey="00yHj0k7_7vxbuQ9zwyXI4bNMJrAjYrJ9KKHgbQ"
      android:clickable="true" />
</RelativeLayout>
```

In addition, you will need a couple of extra things in your AndroidManifest.xml file:

- The INTERNET and ACCESS_FINE_LOCATION permissions (the latter for use with the MyLocationOverlay class, described later in this chapter)

- Inside your <application>, a <uses-library> element with android:name = "com.google.android.maps", to indicate you are using one of the optional Android APIs

Here is the AndroidManifest.xml file for NooYawk:

```
<?xml version="1.0" encoding="utf-8"?>
<manifest xmlns:android="http://schemas.android.com/apk/res/android"↩
 package="com.commonsware.android.maps">
  <uses-permission android:name="android.permission.INTERNET"/>
  <uses-permission android:name="android.permission.ACCESS_FINE_LOCATION"/>

  <application android:label="@string/app_name" android:icon="@drawable/cw">
    <uses-library android:name="com.google.android.maps"/>
    <activity android:name=".NooYawk" android:label="@string/app_name">
      <intent-filter>
        <action android:name="android.intent.action.MAIN"/>
        <category android:name="android.intent.category.LAUNCHER"/>
      </intent-filter>
    </activity>
  </application>
  <supports-screens android:largeScreens="true" android:normalScreens="true"↩
 android:smallScreens="true" android:anyDensity="true"/>
</manifest>
```

That is pretty much all you need for starters, in addition to subclassing your activity from MapActivity. If you were to do nothing else, and built that project and tossed it in the emulator, you'd get a nice map of the world. Note, however, that MapActivity is abstract—you need to implement isRouteDisplayed() to indicate whether you are supplying some sort of driving directions. Since displaying driving directions is not supported by the current edition of the terms of service, you should have isRouteDisplayed() return false.

Optional Maps

While most mainstream Android devices have Google Maps, a small percentage do not, because their manufacturers did not elect to license it from Google. Therefore, you need to decide whether Google Maps is essential to your application's operation.

If Google Maps is essential, then include the <uses-library> element in your application, as shown previously, as that will require any device running your app to have Google Maps.

If Google Maps isn't essential, you can make it optional, via the android:required attribute available on <uses-library>. Set that to false, and Google Maps will be loaded into your application if it is available, but your application will run fine regardless. You will then need to use something like Class.forName("com.google.android.maps.MapView") to see if Google Maps is available to your application. If it is not, you can disable the menu items for it, or whatever would lead the user to your MapActivity.

> **NOTE:** In older documentation, the android:required attribute was "undocumented" and its use and support was questionable. Google has now officially documented it, and it is available in Android 4.0 Ice Cream Sandwich and future releases.

Exercising Your Control

You can find your MapView widget by findViewById(), just as with any other widget. The widget itself then offers a getController() method. Between the MapView and MapController, you have a fair bit of capability to determine what the map shows and how it behaves. Zoom and center are two features you will likely want to use, so they are covered next.

Zoom

The map of the world you start with is rather broad. Usually, people looking at a map on a phone will be expecting something a bit narrower in scope, such as a few city blocks.

You can control the zoom level directly via the setZoom() method on the MapController. This takes an integer representing the level of zoom, where 1 is the world view and 21 is the tightest zoom you can get. Each level is a doubling of the effective resolution: 1 has the equator measuring 256 pixels wide, while 21 has the equator measuring 268,435,456 pixels wide. Since the phone's display probably does not have 268,435,456 pixels in either dimension, the user sees a small map focused on one tiny corner of the globe. A level of 17 will show several city blocks in each dimension, which is probably a reasonable starting point for you to experiment with.

If you wish to allow users to change the zoom level, call setBuiltInZoomControls(true);, and the user will be able to zoom in and out of the map via zoom controls found at the bottom center of the map.

Center

Typically, you will need to control what the map is showing, beyond the zoom level, such as the user's current location or a location saved with some data in your activity. To change the map's position, call setCenter() on the MapController.

The setCenter() method takes a GeoPoint as a parameter. A GeoPoint represents a location, via latitude and longitude. The catch is that the GeoPoint stores latitude and longitude as integers representing the actual latitude and longitude in *microdegrees* (degrees multiplied by 1E6). This saves a bit of memory versus storing a float or double, and it greatly speeds up some internal calculations Android needs to do to convert the GeoPoint into a map position. However, it does mean you have to remember to multiply the real-world latitude and longitude by 1E6.

Layers Upon Layers

If you have ever used the full-size edition of Google Maps, you are probably used to seeing things overlaid atop the map itself, such as pushpins indicating businesses near the location being searched. In map parlance (and, for that matter, in many serious graphic editors), the pushpins are on a separate layer from the map itself, and what you are seeing is the composition of the pushpin layer atop the map layer.

Android's mapping allows you to create layers as well, so you can mark up the maps as you need to based on user input and your application's purpose. For example, NooYawk uses a layer to show where select buildings are located on the island of Manhattan.

Overlay Classes

Any overlay you want to add to your map needs to be implemented as a subclass of Overlay. There is an ItemizedOverlay subclass available if you are looking to add pushpins or the like; ItemizedOverlay simplifies this process.

To attach an overlay class to your map, just call getOverlays() on your MapView and add() your Overlay instance to it, as we do here with a custom SitesOverlay:

```
marker.setBounds(0, 0, marker.getIntrinsicWidth(),
                       marker.getIntrinsicHeight());

map.getOverlays().add(new SitesOverlay(marker));
```

We will look at that marker in the next section.

Drawing the ItemizedOverlay

As the name suggests, ItemizedOverlay allows you to supply a list of points of interest to be displayed on the map—specifically, instances of OverlayItem. The overlay, then, handles much of the drawing logic for you. Here are the minimum steps to make this work:

1. Override ItemizedOverlay<OverlayItem> as your own subclass (in this example, SitesOverlay).

2. In the constructor, build your roster of OverlayItem instances, and call populate() when they are ready for use by the overlay.

3. Implement size() to return the number of items to be handled by the overlay.

4. Override createItem() to return OverlayItem instances given an index.

5. When you instantiate your ItemizedOverlay subclass, provide it with a Drawable that represents the default icon (e.g., a pushpin) to display for each item, on which you call boundCenterBottom() to enable the drop-shadow effect.

The marker from the NooYawk constructor is the Drawable used for step 5, which shows a pushpin.

For example, here is SitesOverlay:

```
private class SitesOverlay extends ItemizedOverlay<OverlayItem> {
  private List<OverlayItem> items=new ArrayList<OverlayItem>();
  private Drawable marker=null;

  public SitesOverlay(Drawable marker) {
    super(marker);
    this.marker=marker;

    boundCenterBottom(marker);

    items.add(new OverlayItem(getPoint(40.748963847316034,
                                       -73.96807193756104),
                              "UN", "United Nations"));
    items.add(new OverlayItem(getPoint(40.76866299974387,
                                       -73.98268461227417),
                              "Lincoln Center",
                              "Home of Jazz at Lincoln Center"));
    items.add(new OverlayItem(getPoint(40.765136435316755,
                                       -73.97989511489868),
                              "Carnegie Hall",
                "Where you go with practice, practice, practice"));
    items.add(new OverlayItem(getPoint(40.70686417491799,
                                       -74.01572942733765),
                              "The Downtown Club",
                    "Original home of the Heisman Trophy"));

    populate();
  }

  @Override
  protected OverlayItem createItem(int i) {
    return(items.get(i));
  }

  @Override
  protected boolean onTap(int i) {
    Toast.makeText(NooYawk.this,
                   items.get(i).getSnippet(),
                   Toast.LENGTH_SHORT).show();
```

```
      return(true);
    }

    @Override
    public int size() {
      return(items.size());
    }
  }
}
```

Handling Screen Taps

An Overlay subclass can also implement onTap(), to be notified when the user taps the map, so the overlay can adjust what it draws. For example, in full-size Google Maps, clicking a pushpin pops up a bubble with information about the business at that pin's location. With onTap(), you can do much the same in Android.

The onTap() method for ItemizedOverlay receives the index of the OverlayItem that was tapped. It is up to you to do something worthwhile with this event.

In the case of SitesOverlay, as shown in the preceding section, onTap() looks like this:

```
@Override
protected boolean onTap(int i) {
  Toast.makeText(NooYawk.this,
                   items.get(i).getSnippet(),
                   Toast.LENGTH_SHORT).show();

  return(true);
}
```

Here, we just toss up a short Toast with the snippet from the OverlayItem, returning true to indicate we handled the tap.

My, Myself, and MyLocationOverlay

Android has a built-in overlay to handle two common scenarios:

- Showing where you are on the map, based on GPS or other location-providing logic

- Showing where you are pointed, based on the built-in compass sensor, where available

All you need to do is create a MyLocationOverlay instance, add it to your MapView's list of overlays, and enable and disable the desired features at appropriate times.

The "at appropriate times" notion is for maximizing battery life. There is no sense in updating locations or directions when the activity is paused, so it is recommended that you enable these features in onResume() and disable them in onPause().

For example, NooYawk will display a compass rose using `MyLocationOverlay`. To do this, we first need to create the overlay and add it to the list of overlays (where `me` is the `MyLocationOverlay` instance as a private data member):

```
me=new MyLocationOverlay(this, map);
map.getOverlays().add(me);
```

Then, we enable and disable the compass rose as appropriate:

```
@Override
public void onResume() {
  super.onResume();

  me.enableCompass();
}

@Override
public void onPause() {
  super.onPause();

  me.disableCompass();
}
```

This gives us a compass rose while the activity is onscreen, as shown in Figure 40–1.

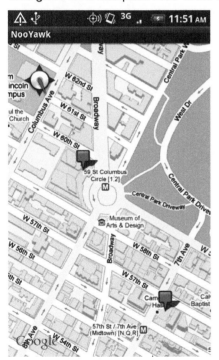

Figure 40–1. *The NooYawk map, showing a compass rose and two OverlayItems*

Rugged Terrain

Just as the Google Maps you use on your full-size computer can display satellite imagery, so too can Android maps.

MapView offers toggleSatellite(), which, as the name suggests, toggles on and off the satellite perspective on the area being viewed. You can allow the user to trigger this via an options menu or, in the case of NooYawk, via key taps:

```
@Override
  public boolean onKeyDown(int keyCode, KeyEvent event) {
    if (keyCode == KeyEvent.KEYCODE_S) {
      map.setSatellite(!map.isSatellite());
      return(true);
    }
    else if (keyCode == KeyEvent.KEYCODE_Z) {
      map.displayZoomControls(true);
      return(true);
    }

    return(super.onKeyDown(keyCode, event));
  }
```

Figure 40–2 shows a satellite view in NooYawk, courtesy of tapping the S key.

Figure 40–2. *The NooYawk map, showing a compass rose and two OverlayItems, overlaid on the satellite view*

Maps and Fragments

You might think that maps would be an ideal place to use fragments. After all, on a large tablet screen, you could allocate most of the space to the map but still have other stuff alongside it. Alas, over the last two major releases of Android, maps and fragments remain two great tastes that do not taste so great together.

First, MapView requires you to inherit from MapActivity. This has a few ramifications:

- You cannot use the Android Compatibility Library (ACL), because that requires you to inherit from FragmentActivity, and Java does not support multiple inheritance. Hence, you can use maps in fragments only on Android 3.0 and higher, requiring that you fall back to some alternative implementation on older versions of Android.

- Any activity that might host a map in a fragment has to inherit from MapActivity, even if in some cases it might not host a map in a fragment.

Also, MapView makes some assumptions about the timing of various events, in a fashion that makes setting up a map-based fragment a bit more complex than it might otherwise have to be.

It is entirely possible that someday these problems will be resolved, through a combination of an updated Google APIs Add-On for Android with fragment support, and possibly an updated ACL. In the meantime, here is the recipe for getting maps to work, as well as they can, in fragments.

Limit Yourself to the Latest Android Versions

In the manifest, make sure that you set both your android:minSdkVersion and your android:targetSdkVersion to at least 11, so your application runs only on Android 3.0 and newer. For example, here is the manifest from the Maps/NooYawkFragments sample project:

```xml
<?xml version="1.0" encoding="utf-8"?>
<manifest xmlns:android="http://schemas.android.com/apk/res/android"
          package="com.commonsware.android.maps">
  <uses-permission android:name="android.permission.INTERNET"/>
  <uses-permission android:name="android.permission.ACCESS_FINE_LOCATION"/>

  <application android:label="@string/app_name"
               android:icon="@drawable/cw"
               android:hardwareAccelerated="true">
    <uses-library android:name="com.google.android.maps"/>
    <activity android:name=".NooYawk" android:label="@string/app_name">
      <intent-filter>
        <action android:name="android.intent.action.MAIN"/>
        <category android:name="android.intent.category.LAUNCHER"/>
      </intent-filter>
    </activity>
  </application>
  <uses-sdk android:minSdkVersion="11" android:targetSdkVersion="11" />
```

```
    <supports-screens android:largeScreens="true" android:normalScreens="true"
android:smallScreens="true" android:anyDensity="true"/>
</manifest>
```

Use onCreateView() and onActivityCreated()

A map-based fragment is simply a Fragment that shows a MapView. By and large, this code can look and work much like a MapActivity would, configuring the MapView, setting up an ItemizedOverlay, and so on.

However, there is a timing problem: you cannot reliably return a MapView widget, or an inflated layout containing such a widget, from onCreateView(). For whatever reason, it works fine the first time, but on a configuration change (e.g., screen rotation) it fails.

The solution is to return a container from onCreateView(), such as a FrameLayout, as shown here in the MapFragment class from NooYawkFragments:

```
@Override
public View onCreateView(LayoutInflater inflater, ViewGroup container,
                         Bundle savedInstanceState) {
  return(new FrameLayout(getActivity()));
}
```

Then, in onActivityCreated()—once onCreate() has been completed in the hosting MapActivity—you can add a MapView to that container and continue with the rest of your normal setup:

```
@Override
public void onActivityCreated(Bundle savedInstanceState) {
  super.onActivityCreated(savedInstanceState);

  map=new MapView(getActivity(), "00yHj0k7_7vxbuQ9zwyXI4bNMJrAjYrJ9KKHgbQ");
  map.setClickable(true);

  map.getController().setCenter(getPoint(40.76793169992044,
                                         -73.98180484771729));
  map.getController().setZoom(17);
  map.setBuiltInZoomControls(true);

  Drawable marker=getResources().getDrawable(R.drawable.marker);

  marker.setBounds(0, 0, marker.getIntrinsicWidth(),
                   marker.getIntrinsicHeight());

  map.getOverlays().add(new SitesOverlay(marker));

  me=new MyLocationOverlay(getActivity(), map);
  map.getOverlays().add(me);

  ((ViewGroup)getView()).addView(map);
}
```

Note that we are creating a MapView in Java code, which means our Maps API key resides in the Java code (or something reachable from the Java code, such as a string resource). You could inflate a layout containing a `MapView` here if you wished—the change for `MapFragment` was simply to illustrate creating a `MapView` from Java code.

Host the Fragment in a MapActivity

You must make sure that whatever activity hosts the map-enabled fragment is a `MapActivity`. So, even though the NooYawk activity no longer has much to do with mapping, it must still be a `MapActivity`:

```
package com.commonsware.android.maps;

import android.os.Bundle;
import com.google.android.maps.MapActivity;

public class NooYawk extends MapActivity {
  @Override
  public void onCreate(Bundle savedInstanceState) {
    super.onCreate(savedInstanceState);
    setContentView(R.layout.main);
  }

  @Override
  protected boolean isRouteDisplayed() {
    return(false);
  }
}
```

The layout now points to a `<fragment>` instead of a `MapView`:

```
<?xml version="1.0" encoding="utf-8"?>
<fragment xmlns:android="http://schemas.android.com/apk/res/android"
  class="com.commonsware.android.maps.MapFragment"
  android:id="@+id/map_fragment"
  android:layout_width="fill_parent"
  android:layout_height="fill_parent"
/>
```

The resulting application, shown in Figure 40–3, looks like the original NooYawk activity would on a large screen, because we are not doing anything much else with the fragment system (e.g., having other fragments alongside in a landscape layout).

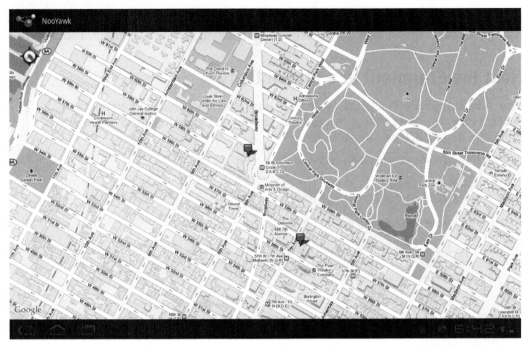

Figure 40–3. *The NooYawkFragments map, rendered on a Motorola XOOM*

A Custom Alternative for Maps and Fragments

The Android developer community was understandably frustrated at the limitations of maps within fragments, and grappled with the limitation of a MapView needing to be within a MapActivity. You can see the history of experimentation and discussion on the StackOverflow Android Developers forum, which led one of the contributors, Pete Doyle, to release the android-support-v4-googlemaps custom compatibility library.

Doyle's custom compatibility library is a working solution to make FragmentActivity extend MapActivity. This in turn allows you to use a MapView object in a fragment.

You can download the support-v4-googlemaps custom compatibility library from GitHub at https://github.com/petedoyle/android-support-v4-googlemaps.

Chapter 41

Handling Telephone Calls

Many, if not most, Android devices will be phones. As such, not only will users be expecting to place and receive calls using Android, but you will have the opportunity to help them place calls, if you wish.

Why might you want to?

- Maybe you are writing an Android interface to a sales management application (*a la* Salesforce.com) and you want to offer users the ability to call prospects with a single button tap, and without them having to keep those contacts both in your application and in the phone's contacts application.

- Maybe you are writing a social networking application, and the roster of phone numbers that you can access shifts constantly, so rather than try to sync the social network contacts with the phone's contact database, you want to let people place calls directly from your application.

- Maybe you are creating an alternative interface to the existing contacts system, perhaps for users with reduced motor control (e.g., the elderly), sporting big buttons and the like to make it easier for them to place calls.

Whatever the reason, Android has the means to let you manipulate the phone just like any other piece of the Android system.

Report to the Manager

To get at much of the phone API, you use the TelephonyManager class. That class lets you do things like the following:

- Determine if the phone is in use via getCallState(), with return values of CALL_STATE_IDLE (phone not in use), CALL_STATE_RINGING (call requested but still being connected), and CALL_STATE_OFFHOOK (call in progress)

- Find out the SIM ID (IMSI) via getSubscriberId()
- Find out the phone type (e.g., GSM) via getPhoneType() or find out the data connection type (e.g., GPRS or EDGE) via getNetworkType()

You Make the Call!

You can also initiate a call from your application, such as from a phone number you obtained through your own web service. To do this, simply craft an ACTION_DIAL Intent with a Uri of the form tel:NNNNN (where NNNNN is the phone number to dial) and use that Intent with startActivity(). This will not actually dial the phone; rather, it activates the dialer activity, from which the user can then tap a button to place the call.

For example, let's look at the Phone/Dialer sample application. Here's the crude but effective layout:

```
<?xml version="1.0" encoding="utf-8"?>
<LinearLayout xmlns:android="http://schemas.android.com/apk/res/android"
    android:orientation="vertical"
    android:layout_width="fill_parent"
    android:layout_height="fill_parent"
    >
  <LinearLayout
    android:orientation="horizontal"
    android:layout_width="fill_parent"
    android:layout_height="wrap_content"
    >
    <TextView
      android:layout_width="wrap_content"
      android:layout_height="wrap_content"
      android:text="Number to dial:"
      />
    <EditText android:id="@+id/number"
      android:layout_width="fill_parent"
      android:layout_height="wrap_content"
      android:cursorVisible="true"
      android:editable="true"
      android:singleLine="true"
    />
  </LinearLayout>
  <Button android:id="@+id/dial"
    android:layout_width="fill_parent"
    android:layout_height="wrap_content"
    android:layout_weight="1"
    android:text="Dial It!"
    android:onClick="dial"
  />
</LinearLayout>
```

We have a labeled field for typing in a phone number, plus a button for dialing that number.

The Java code simply launches the dialer using the phone number from the field:

```
package com.commonsware.android.dialer;
```

```
import android.app.Activity;
import android.content.Intent;
import android.net.Uri;
import android.os.Bundle;
import android.view.View;
import android.widget.EditText;

public class DialerDemo extends Activity {
  @Override
  public void onCreate(Bundle icicle) {
    super.onCreate(icicle);
    setContentView(R.layout.main);
  }

  public void dial(View v) {
    EditText number=(EditText)findViewById(R.id.number);
    String toDial="tel:"+number.getText().toString();

    startActivity(new Intent(Intent.ACTION_DIAL, Uri.parse(toDial)));
  }
}
```

The activity's own UI is not that impressive, as shown in Figure 41–1.

Figure 41–1. *The DialerDemo sample application, as initially launched*

However, the dialer you get from clicking the dial button is better, showing you the number you are about to dial, as shown in Figure 41–2.

Figure 41-2. *The Android Dialer activity, as launched from DialerDemo*

No, Really, You Make the Call!

The good news is that ACTION_DIAL works without any special permissions. The bad news is that it takes the user only to the dialer. The user still has to take action (press the green call button) to actually place the phone call.

An alternative approach is to use ACTION_CALL instead of ACTION_DIAL. Calling startActivity() on an ACTION_CALL Intent will immediately place the phone call, without any other UI steps required. However, you need the CALL_PHONE permission to use ACTION_CALL (see Chapter 38).

Chapter 42

Fonts

The question you'll inevitably get when developing any type of application is, "Hey, can we change this font?" The answer depends on which fonts come with the platform, whether you can add other fonts, and how fonts are applied to the widget or whatever needs the font change. Android is no different. It comes with some fonts, plus a means for adding new fonts. However, as with any new environment, there are a few idiosyncrasies to deal with, as described in this chapter.

Love the One You're With

Android natively knows three fonts, by the shorthand names sans, serif, and monospace. These fonts are actually the Droid series of fonts, created for the Open Handset Alliance by Ascender Corp. (www.ascendercorp.com/), a division of Monotype Imaging. To use these three fonts, you can just reference them in your layout XML, such as the following layout from the Fonts/FontSampler sample project:

```xml
<?xml version="1.0" encoding="utf-8"?>
<TableLayout
  xmlns:android="http://schemas.android.com/apk/res/android"
  android:layout_width="fill_parent"
  android:layout_height="fill_parent"
  android:stretchColumns="1">
  <TableRow>
    <TextView
      android:text="sans:"
      android:layout_marginRight="4dip"
      android:textSize="20sp"
    />
    <TextView
      android:id="@+id/sans"
      android:text="Hello, world!"
      android:typeface="sans"
      android:textSize="20sp"
    />
  </TableRow>
  <TableRow>
    <TextView
```

```
    android:text="serif:"
    android:layout_marginRight="4dip"
    android:textSize="20sp"
  />
  <TextView
    android:id="@+id/serif"
    android:text="Hello, world!"
    android:typeface="serif"
    android:textSize="20sp"
  />
</TableRow>
<TableRow>
  <TextView
    android:text="monospace:"
    android:layout_marginRight="4dip"
    android:textSize="20sp"
  />
  <TextView
    android:id="@+id/monospace"
    android:text="Hello, world!"
    android:typeface="monospace"
    android:textSize="20sp"
  />
</TableRow>
<TableRow>
  <TextView
    android:text="Custom:"
    android:layout_marginRight="4dip"
    android:textSize="20sp"
  />
  <TextView
    android:id="@+id/custom"
    android:text="Hello, world!"
    android:textSize="20sp"
  />
</TableRow>
<TableRow android:id="@+id/filerow">
  <TextView
    android:text="Custom from File:"
    android:layout_marginRight="4dip"
    android:textSize="20sp"
  />
  <TextView
    android:id="@+id/file"
    android:text="Hello, world!"
    android:textSize="20sp"
  />
</TableRow>
</TableLayout>
```

This layout builds a table showing short samples of five fonts. Notice that the first three have the android:typeface attribute, whose value is one of the three built-in font faces (e.g., "sans").

Additional Fonts

The three built-in fonts are very nice. However, a designer, a manager, or a customer may want a different font. Or perhaps you want to use a font for specialized purposes, such as a dingbats font instead of a series of PNG graphics. The easiest way to accomplish this is to package the desired font(s) with your application. To do this, simply create an assets/ folder in the project root, and put your TrueType (TTF) fonts in that folder. You might, for example, create assets/fonts/ and put your TTF files in there.

Then, you need to tell your widgets to use that font. Unfortunately, you can no longer use layout XML for this, since the XML does not know about any fonts you may have tucked away as an application asset. Instead, you need to make the change in Java code:

```java
import android.widget.TextView;
import java.io.File;

public class FontSampler extends Activity {
  @Override
  public void onCreate(Bundle icicle) {
    super.onCreate(icicle);
    setContentView(R.layout.main);

    TextView tv=(TextView)findViewById(R.id.custom);
    Typeface face=Typeface.createFromAsset(getAssets(),
                                   "fonts/HandmadeTypewriter.ttf");

    tv.setTypeface(face);

    File font=new File(Environment.getExternalStorageDirectory(),
                  "MgOpenCosmeticaBold.ttf");

    if (font.exists()) {
      tv=(TextView)findViewById(R.id.file);
      face=Typeface.createFromFile(font);

      tv.setTypeface(face);
    }
    else {
      findViewById(R.id.filerow).setVisibility(View.GONE);
    }
  }
}
```

Here, we grab the TextView for our custom sample, and then create a Typeface object via the static createFromAsset() builder method. This takes the application's AssetManager (from getAssets()) and a path within your assets/ directory to the font you want.

Then, it is just a matter of telling the TextView to setTypeface(), providing the Typeface we just created. In this case, we are using the Handmade Typewriter font. You can also load a font out of a local file and use it. The benefit is that you can customize your fonts after your application has been distributed. On the other hand, you have to somehow arrange to get the font onto the device. But, just as you can get a Typeface via createFromAsset(), you can get a Typeface via createFromFile(). In our FontSampler, we look in the root of "external storage" (typically the SD card) for the MgOpenCosmeticaBold TrueType font file, and if it is found, we use it for the fifth row of the table. Otherwise, we hide that row.

Figure 42–1 shows the results.

Figure 42–1. *The FontSampler application*

We will go into more details regarding assets and local files in an upcoming chapter.

Note that Android does not seem to like all TrueType fonts. When Android dislikes a custom font, rather than raise an Exception, it seems to substitute Droid Sans ("sans") quietly. So, if you try to use a different font and it does not appear to be working, it might be incompatible with Android, for whatever reason.

Here a Glyph, There a Glyph

TrueType fonts can be rather pudgy, particularly if they support an extensive subset of the available Unicode characters. The Handmade Typewriter font used in the previous section runs over 70KB; the DejaVu free fonts can run upwards of 500KB apiece. Even compressed, these add bulk to your application, so be careful not to go overboard with custom fonts, lest your application take up too much room on your users' phones.

Conversely, bear in mind that fonts may not have all of the glyphs that you need. As an example, let's talk about the ellipsis.

Android's TextView class has the built-in ability to "ellipsize" text, truncating it and adding an ellipsis if the text is longer than the available space. You can use this via the android:ellipsize attribute, for example. This works fairly well, at least for single-line text.

The ellipsis that Android uses is not three periods. Rather, it uses an actual ellipsis character, where the three dots are contained in a single glyph. Hence, any font that you use for which you also use the "ellipsizing" feature will need the ellipsis glyph.

Beyond that, though, Android pads out the string that gets rendered on the screen, such that the length (in characters) is the same before and after ellipsizing. To make this work, Android replaces one character with the ellipsis, and replaces all other removed characters with the Unicode character ZERO WIDTH NO-BREAK SPACE (U+FEFF). As a result, the extra characters after the ellipsis do not take up any visible space onscreen, yet they can be part of the string. However, this means any custom fonts you use for TextView widgets that you use with android:ellipsize must also support this special Unicode character. Not all fonts do, and you will get artifacts in the onscreen representation of your shortened strings if your font lacks this character (e.g., rogue *X*s appear at the end of the line). Another side-effect of this approach is that it can be dicey to predict whether any string length arithmetic, such as a simple length() Java call, will return the value you expect. It's almost counter-intuitive, but Android is trying to present you with a consistent answer, whereas your previous experience with Java and fonts might have conditioned you to expect variable results.

And, of course, Android's international deployment means your font must handle any language your users might be looking to enter, perhaps through a language-specific input method editor.

Hence, while using custom fonts in Android is very possible, there are many potential problems, and so you must weigh carefully the benefits of the custom fonts versus their potential costs.

Chapter 43

More Development Tools

The Android SDK is more than a library of Java classes and API calls. It also includes a number of tools to assist in application development. Eclipse, of course, tends to dominate the discussion. However, that is not the only tool at your disposal, so let's take a quick tour of what else is available to you.

Hierarchy Viewer: How Deep Is Your Code?

Android comes with a Hierarchy Viewer tool, designed to help you visualize your layouts as they are seen in a running activity in a running emulator. So, for example, you can determine how much space a certain widget is taking up, or try to find where a widget that does not appear on the screen is hiding.

To use Hierarchy Viewer, you first need to fire up your emulator, install your application, launch your activity, and navigate to the spot you wish to examine. Note that you cannot use Hierarchy Viewer with a production Android device.

You can launch Hierarchy Viewer via the `hierarchyviewer` program, found in the `tools/` directory in your Android SDK installation, or from inside of Eclipse. The main window is shown in Figure 43–1.

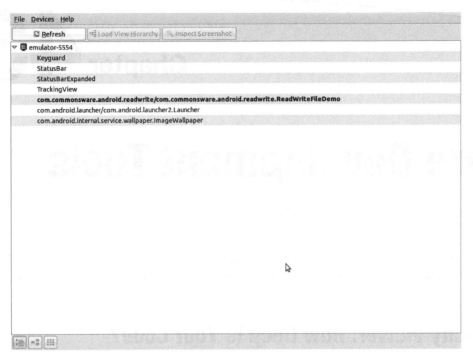

Figure 43–1. *Hierarchy Viewer main window*

The roots of the table show the emulator instances presently running on your development machine. The leaves represent applications running on that particular emulator. Your activity will be identified by application package and class (e.g., `com.commonsware.android.files/...`).

Things get interesting when you choose a window and click Load View Hierarchy. After a few seconds, the details spring into view, as shown in Figure 43–2.

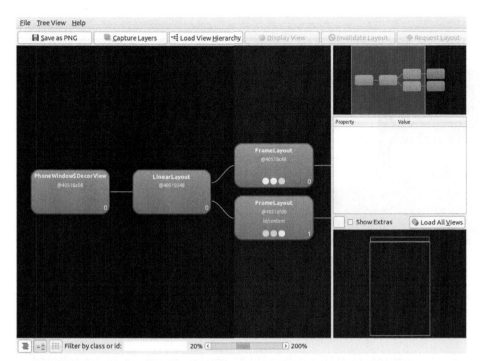

Figure 43–2. *Hierarchy Viewer Layout View*

The main area of the Layout View shows a tree of the various widgets and stuff that make up your activity, starting from the overall system window and driving down into the individual UI widgets that users will interact with. This includes both the widgets and containers defined by your application and others that are supplied by the system, including the title bar.

Clicking one of the views adds more information to this perspective, as shown in Figure 43–3.

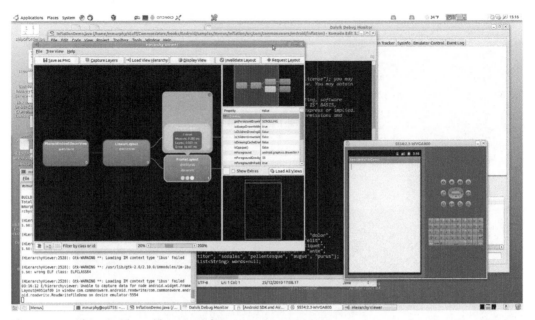

Figure 43–3. *Hierarchy Viewer View properties*

Now, in the middle-right region of Hierarchy Viewer, you see properties of the selected widget or container, plus timing details for how long it took to render that container and its children.

Also, the widget is highlighted in red in the wireframe of the activity, shown beneath the properties (by default, views are shown as white outlines on a black background). This can help you to ensure that you have selected the right widget, if, say, you have several buttons and cannot readily tell from the tree which button is which.

You can also do the following in the main Hierarchy Viewer window:

- Save the tree diagram as a PNG file

- Save the UI as a Photoshop PSD file, with different layers for the different widgets and containers

- Force the UI to repaint in the emulator or reload the hierarchy, in case you have made changes to a database or to the app's contents and need a fresh diagram

Instead of clicking Load View Hierarchy in the main window, you can click Inspect Screenshot. This puts Hierarchy Viewer in a whole new perspective, called the Pixel Perfect View, as shown in Figure 43–4.

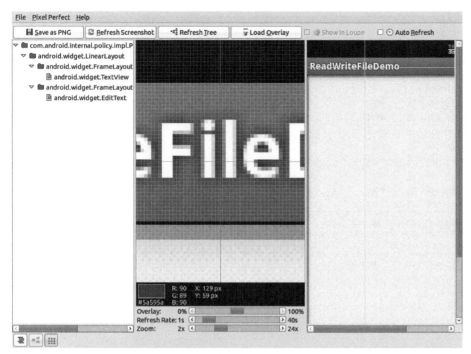

Figure 43–4. *Hierarchy Viewer Pixel Perfect View*

On the left, you see a tree representing the widgets and other Views in your activity. In the middle, you see a zoomed view of your activity, which is shown at normal size on the right.

The crosshairs overlaying the activity show the position being zoomed. Just click a new area to change what you are seeing. There is a slider to control the level of zoom. Clicking a pixel also indicates the position and color of that pixel.

If you check the Auto Refresh check box in the toolbar, Hierarchy Viewer will poll and reload the UI from your activity periodically, with the frequency controlled by another slider.

DDMS: Under Android's Hood

Another tool in the Android developer's arsenal is the Dalvik Debug Monitor Service (DDMS). This is like a Swiss army knife, allowing you to do everything from browse log files, update the GPS location provided by the emulator, simulate incoming calls and messages, and browse the on-emulator storage to push and pull files.

To launch DDMS, run the ddms program inside the tools/ directory in your Android SDK distribution or open the DDMS perspective in Eclipse. It will initially display just a tree of emulators and running programs on the left, as shown in Figure 43–5.

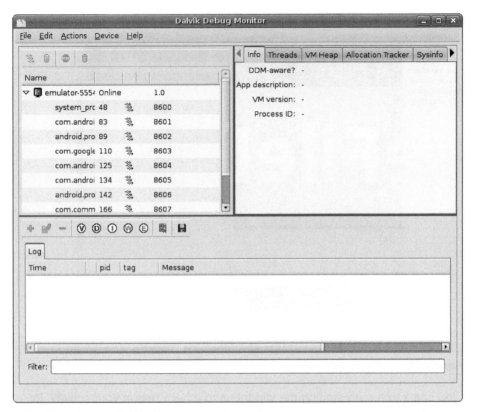

Figure 43–5. *DDMS initial view*

Clicking an emulator allows you to browse the event log on the bottom and manipulate the emulator via the tabs on the right, as shown in Figure 43–6.

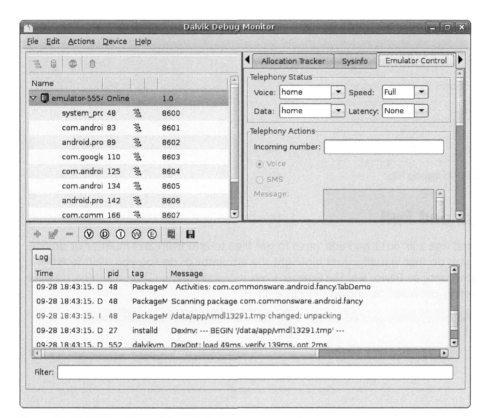

Figure 43–6. *DDMS, with emulator selected*

Logging

Rather than use `adb logcat`, DDMS lets you view your logging information in a scrollable table. Just highlight the emulator or device you want to monitor, and the bottom half of the screen shows the logs.

In addition, you can do the following:

- Filter the Log tab by any of the five logging levels, shown as the V through E toolbar buttons.

- Create a custom filter, so you can view only those entries tagged with your application's tag, by clicking the + toolbar button and completing the form (shown in Figure 43–7). The name you enter in the form will be used as the name of another logging output tab in the bottom portion of the DDMS main window.

- Save the log information to a text file for later perusal, or for searching.

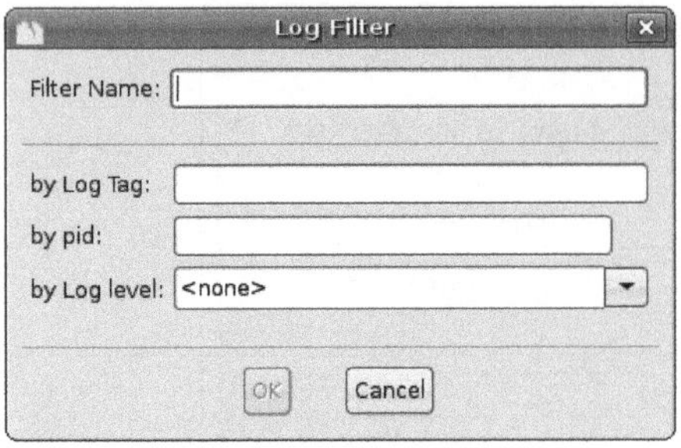

Figure 43–7. *DDMS logging filter*

File Push and Pull

While you can use adb pull and adb push to get files to and from an emulator or device, DDMS lets you do that visually. Just highlight the emulator or device you wish to work with, and then choose **Device** ➤➤ **File Explorer** from the main menu. That will bring up your typical directory browser, as shown in Figure 43–8.

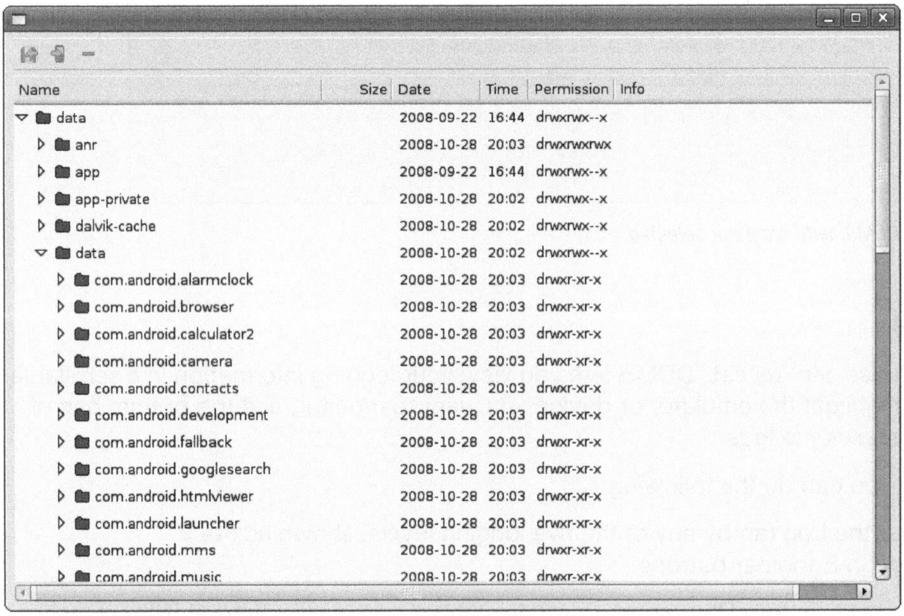

Figure 43–8. *DDMS File Explorer*

Just browse to the file you want and click either the pull (leftmost) or push (middle) toolbar button to transfer the file to or from your development machine. To delete a file, click the delete (rightmost) toolbar button.

Using File Explorer has a few caveats:

- You cannot create directories through this tool. You will need to either use adb shell or create them from within your application.

- While you can putter through most of the files on an emulator, you can access very little outside of /sdcard on an actual device, due to Android security restrictions.

Screenshots

To take a screenshot of the Android emulator or device, switch to the DDMS perspective in Eclipse, and press the screen capture toolbar button (displayed as a camera). This will bring up a dialog box containing an image of the current screen, as shown in Figure 43–9.

Figure 43–9. *DDMS screen capture*

From here, you can click Save to save the image as a PNG file somewhere on your development machine, click Refresh to update the image based on the current state of the emulator or device, or click Done to close the dialog box.

Location Updates

To use DDMS to supply location updates to your application, the first thing you must do is have your application use the gps LocationProvider, as that is the one that DDMS is set to update. Then, click the Emulator Control tab and scroll down to the Location Controls section. Here, you will find a smaller tabbed pane with three options for specifying locations: Manual, GPX, and KML, as shown in Figure 43–10.

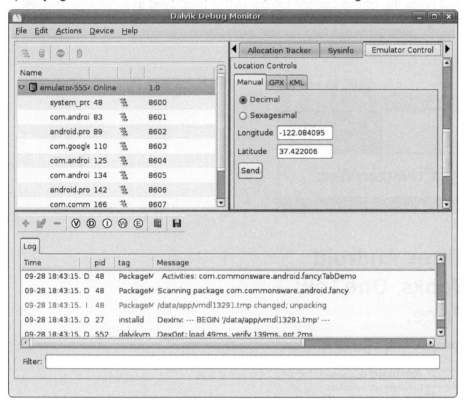

Figure 43–10. *DDMS location controls*

To use the Manual tab, provide a latitude and longitude and click the Send button to submit that location to the emulator. The emulator, in turn, will notify any location listeners of the new position.

Placing Calls and Messages

If you want to simulate incoming calls or SMS messages to the Android emulator, DDMS can handle that as well. On the Emulator Control tab, above the Location Controls group, is the Telephony Actions group, as shown in Figure 43–11.

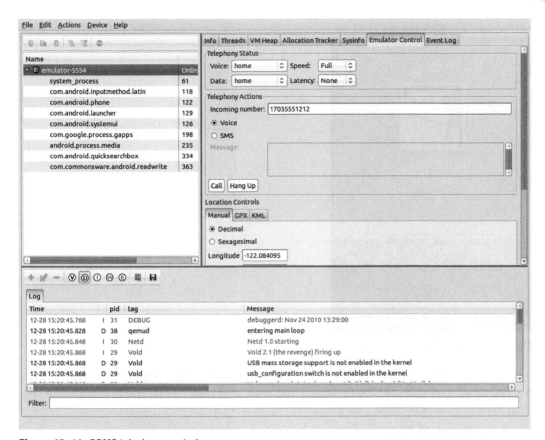

Figure 43–11. *DDMS telephony controls*

To simulate an incoming call, fill in a phone number, choose the Voice radio button, and click Call. At that point, the emulator will show the incoming call, allowing you to accept it or reject it, as shown in Figure 43–12.

Figure 43–12. *Simulated incoming call*

To simulate in an incoming text message, fill in a phone number, choose the SMS radio button, enter a message in the provided text area, and click Send. The text message will then appear as a notification, as shown in Figure 43–13.

Figure 43–13. *Simulated text message*

And, of course, you can click on the notification to view the message in the full-fledged Messaging application, as shown in Figure 43–14.

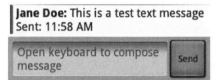

Figure 43–14. *Simulated text message, in Messaging application*

Memory Management

DDMS also helps you diagnose issues related to how your application uses memory, particularly heap space.

On the Sysinfo tab, you can see a pie chart of the overall memory allocation for the emulator, as shown in Figure 43–15.

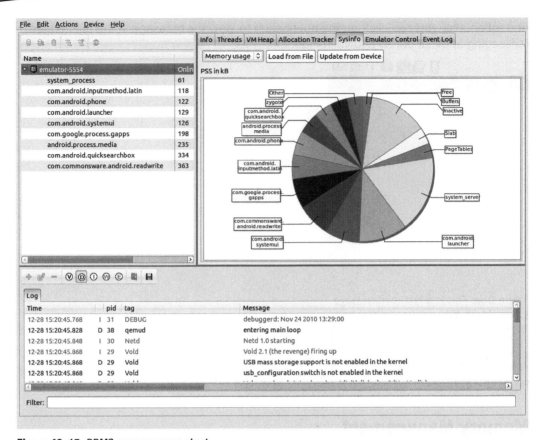

Figure 43–15. *DDMS memory usage chart*

On the Allocation Tracker tab, you can record every time your code (or code you call inside of Android) allocates memory. Simply highlight your application's process in the tree table, and then click the Start Tracking button. When you want to see what you have allocated since you clicked Start Tracking, click the Get Allocations button, which will fill in a table showing each allocation, how much memory was allocated, and where in the code the memory was allocated, as shown in Figure 43–16.

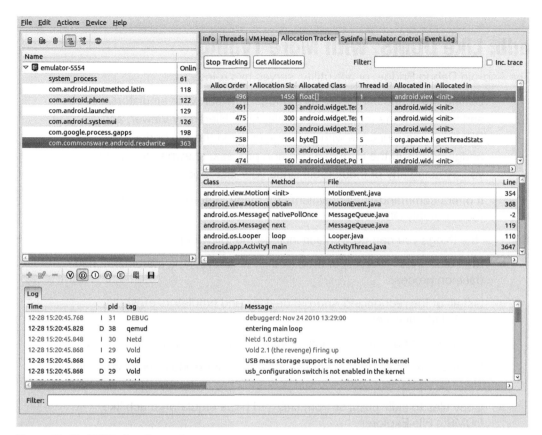

Figure 43–16. *DDMS allocation tracker*

And, you can even dump the entire heap for your application via the Dump HPROF option, which is the toolbar button that looks like a half-empty can with a red downward-pointing arrow to its right. The resulting HPROF file can be used with MAT, an add-in for Eclipse, to see which objects are still on the heap and who is causing them to stick around.

Before dumping the HPROF file, you may wish to force a garbage collection run on your process. You do so by clicking the toolbar button that looks like a classic metal garbage can.

adb: Like DDMS, with More Typing

The Android Debug Bridge, or adb utility, serves two roles:

- Behind the scenes, it serves as a bridge between your emulators/devices and the rest of the tools. For example, ADT, Hierarchy Viewer, and DDMS all communicate with your emulator via the adb bridge. This bridge comes in the form of a daemon process, spawned the first time you try using any of those tools since your last reboot.

- It offers command-line equivalents for many features of the other tools, notably DDMS.

Some of the things you can do with adb include the following:

- Start (adb start-server) or stop (adb kill-server) the aforementioned daemon process

- List all of the recognized Android devices and emulators presently visible (adb devices)

- Get access to a Linux shell inside your device or emulator (adb shell)

- Install or uninstall Android applications on your device or emulator (adb install)

- Copy files to (adb push) or from (adb pull) the emulator, much like DDMS's File Explorer

- Examine LogCat (adb logcat)

Getting Graphical

The latest release of Android Developer Tools, released with Android 4.0 (ADT editions 14 and 15), introduces the new Android Asset Studio. This companion tool is designed to allow you to quickly and easily create graphic assets such as launcher icons, action bar and tab icons, and more, and takes care of many of the tedious aspects of creating a coherent set of images that looks good at each possible device size, resolution, and so forth.

There are at least two ways to access and use Android Asset Studio. For the hardcore developer, the code is open source and available on Google Code at http://code.google.com/p/android-ui-utils/. You can download the code, and build your solution, giving you your own instance of Android Asset Studio running in your environment. The downside to this approach is that Android Asset Studio is still flagged as a beta version, and you may well find yourself encountering issues that are still being corrected in development.

> **NOTE:** As an example of one of the issues yet to be corrected, the author can consistently send his graphics card haywire by attempting to add text to a launcher icon under Firefox.

The alternative approach is to use the hosted version of Android Asset Studio from your favorite browser. The developers of Android Asset Studio recommend that you use Chrome as the browser, but you'll have some success using other browsers.

The hosted version of Android Asset Studio is currently at `http://android-ui-utils.googlecode.com/hg/asset-studio/dist/index.html`. Opening that page in your browser presents you with the currently available options for Android Asset Studio, shown in Figure 43–17.

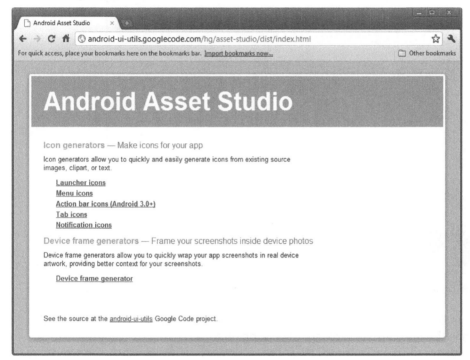

Figure 43–17. *Android Asset Studio home page*

For example, choosing to create a launcher icon takes you to a very simple palette, where you can see icons in Android-scaled sizes like `ldpi`, `mdpi`, `hdpi`, and `xhdpi` come to life as you add graphics and text to your new icon. Figure 43–18 demonstrates some quick results (and the fact that your author is not exactly the next Picasso).

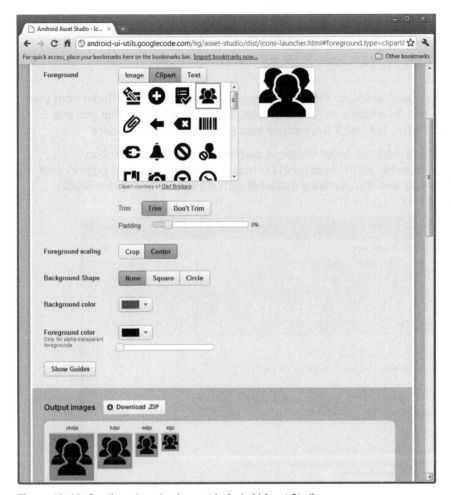

Figure 43–18. *Creating a launcher icon set in Android Asset Studio*

When you've finished creating your masterpieces, you can download the assets and place them in the relevant res/ folders of your project.

Alternative Application Environments

Part

VII

Alternative Application
Environments

Chapter **44**

The Role of Alternative Environments

You might think that Android is all about Java. The official Android Software Development Kit (SDK) is for Java development, the build tools are for Java development, the Android discussion groups and blog posts are all about Java, and, yes, most Android books are for Java development. Heck, most of this book is about Java.

However (and with apologies to William Goldman), it just so happens that Android is only mostly Java. There's a big difference between mostly Java and all Java. Mostly Java is slightly not Java.

So, while Android's "sweet spot" will remain Java-based applications for the near term, you can still create applications using other technologies. This chapter and the three that follow introduce some of those alternative technologies.

This chapter starts with an examination of the pros and cons of Android's Java-centric strategy. It then enumerates some reasons why you might want to use something else for your Android applications. The downsides of alternative Android application environments—lack of support and technical challenges—are also discussed.

In the Beginning, There Was Java...

The core Android team made a fairly reasonable choice of language when they chose Java. It is a very popular language, and in the mobile community it had a clear predecessor in Java 2 Platform, Micro Edition (J2ME). Lacking direct access to memory addresses (so-called pointers), a Java-based application will be less prone to developer errors that might lead to buffer overruns and expose the application to possible hacks. And there is a fairly robust ecosystem around Java, in terms of educational materials, existing code bases, integrated development environments (IDEs), and so on.

However, while you can program Android in the Java language, an Android device does not run a Java application. Instead, your Java code is converted into something that runs on the Dalvik virtual machine. This is akin to the technology used for regular Java applications, but Dalvik is specifically tuned for Android's environment. Moreover, it limits the dependency of Android on Java itself to a handful of programming tools, which is important as Java's stewardship moves from Sun to Oracle to wherever.

The Dalvik virtual machine is also capable of running code from other programming languages, a feature that makes possible much of what this book covers.

...And It Was OK

No mobile development environment is perfect, and the combination of Java and Android is no exception.

In the beginning, Java, as implemented for the Dalvik virtual machine, was interpreted, without any of the just-in-time (JIT) compiler tricks regular Java uses to boost performance. This is a bigger problem in mobile, since the devices Android runs on tend to be less powerful than your average desktop, notebook, or web server. Android 2.3 added a JIT compiler, which helps a lot, but it is still slow compared to native compiled code. Hence, there will be some things you just can't do on Android with Java because it is too slow.

Java uses garbage collection to save people from having to keep track of all their memory allocations. That works for the most part, and is generally a boon to developer productivity. However, it is not a cure-all for every memory and resource allocation problem. You can still have what amounts to "memory leaks" in Java, even if the precise mechanics of those leaks differ from the classic leaks you get in C, C++, and other languages.

Most importantly, though, not everybody likes Java. It could be because they lack experience with it, or perhaps they have had experience with it and did not enjoy that experience. Certainly, Java is often seen as a language for big enterprise systems and, therefore, not necessarily "cool." Advocates of other languages will have their own pet peeves with Java as well (e.g., to a Ruby developer, Java is really verbose).

So, while Java was not a bad choice for Android, it was not perfect, either.

Bucking the Trend

Just because Java is the dominant way to build apps for Android, that does not mean it is the only way, and for you, it may not even be the best way.

Perhaps Java is not in your existing skill set. You might be a web developer, more comfortable with HTML, CSS, and JavaScript. There are frameworks to help you with that. Or, maybe you cut your teeth on server-side scripting languages like Perl or Python—there are ways to sling that code on Android as well. Or perhaps you already have a bunch of code in C/C++, such as game physics algorithms, that would be painful to rewrite in Java. You should be able to reuse that code, too.

Even if you would be willing to learn Java, it may be that your inexperience with Java and the Android APIs will just slow you down. You might be able to get something built much more quickly with another framework, even if you wind up replacing it with a Java-based implementation in the future. Rapid development and prototyping is frequently important, to get early feedback with minimal investment in time.

And, of course, you might just find Java programming to be irritating. You would not be the first, nor the last, to have that sentiment. If you are getting into Android as a hobby, rather than as part of your "day job," having fun will be particularly important to you, and you might not find Java to be much fun.

Fortunately, Android is friendly toward alternative ways of building applications, unlike some mobile platforms.

Support, Structure

However, "friendly" and "fully supported" are two different things. Some alternatives to Java-based development are officially supported by the core Android team, such as C/C++ development via the Native Development Kit (NDK) and web-style development via HTML5. Some alternatives to Java-based development are supported by companies. Adobe supports the Adobe Integrated Runtime (AIR), and recently also acquired Nitobi, famous for their support of PhoneGap (described in detail in Chapter 46), Rhomobile supports Rhodes, and so on. Other alternatives are supported by standards bodies. For example, the World Wide Web Consortium (W3C) supports HTML5. Still others are just tiny projects with the backing of only a couple of developers.

You will need to make the decision for yourself which of these levels of support will meet your requirements. For many development activities, support is not much of an issue, but in some cases, support might be paramount (e.g., enterprise application development).

Caveat Developer

Of course, going outside the traditional Java environment for Android development has its issues, beyond just how much support might be available.

Some environments may be less efficient, in terms of processor time, memory, or battery life, than Java. C/C++, on the whole, is probably better than Java, but HTML5 may be worse, for example. Depending on what you are writing and how heavily it will be used will determine how critical that inefficiency will be.

Some environments may not be available on all devices. Right now, Flash is the best example of this; some devices offer some amount of Flash support, while other devices have no Flash support at all. Similarly, HTML5 support was added to Android only as of

Android 2.0, so devices running older versions of Android do not have HTML5 as a built-in option.

Every layer between you and officially supported environments makes it that much more difficult for you to ensure compatibility with new versions of Android, when they arise. For example, if you create an application using PhoneGap, and a new Android version becomes available, there may be incompatibilities that only the PhoneGap team can address. While they will probably address those quickly—and they may provide to you some measure of insulation from those incompatibilities—the response time is outside of your control. In some cases, that is not a problem, but in other cases, that might be bad for your project.

Hence, just because you are developing outside of Java does not mean everything is perfect. You simply have to trade off between these problems and the ones Java-based development might cause you. Where the balance lies is up to each individual developer or firm.

Chapter 45

HTML5

Prior to the current wave of interest in mobile applications, the technology *du jour* was web applications. A lot of attention was paid to AJAX, Ruby on Rails, and other techniques and technologies that made the experience of using web applications close to, and sometimes even superior to, the experience of using a desktop application.

The explosion of web applications eventually drove the next round of enhancements to web standards, collectively called HTML5. Android 2.0 was the first version to add support for these HTML5 enhancements. Notably, Android supports offline applications and Web Storage, meaning that HTML5 becomes a relevant technique for creating Android applications, without dealing with Java.

Offline Applications

The linchpin for using HTML5 for offline applications—on Android or elsewhere—is that those applications can be used when there is no Internet connectivity, either on the client side (e.g., on an airplane sans Wi-Fi) or on the server side (e.g., due to web server maintenance).

What Does It Mean?

Historically, web applications have had this annoying tendency to require web servers. This led to all sorts of workarounds for offline use, up to and including shipping a web server and deploying it to the desktop.

HTML5 solves this problem by allowing web pages to specify their own caching rules. A web app can publish a *cache manifest*, describing which resources

- Can be safely cached, such that if the web server is unavailable, the browser can use the cached copy.

- Cannot be safely cached, such that if the web server is unavailable, the browser should fail as it normally would.

■ Have a "fallback" resource, such that if the web server is unavailable, the cached fallback resource should be used instead.

For mobile devices, this means that a fully HTML5-capable browser should be able to load all its assets up front and keep them cached. If the user loses connectivity, the application will still run. In this respect, the web app behaves almost identically to a regular app.

How Do You Use It?

For this chapter, we will use the Checklist "mini app" created by Alex Gibson. While the most up-to-date version of this app can be found at the MiniApps web site (http://miniapps.co.uk/), this chapter will review the HTML5/Checklist copy found in the Source Code/Download area of the Apress web site (www.apress.com). This copy is also hosted online on the CommonsWare site, and you can easily locate it directly via the shortened URL http://bit.ly/cw-html5.

About the Sample App

Checklist is, as the name suggests, a simple checklist application. When you first launch it, the list will be empty, as shown in Figure 45–1.

Figure 45–1. *The Checklist app, as initially launched*

You can enter some text in the top field and click the Add button to add it to the list, as shown in Figure 45–2.

Figure 45–2. *The Checklist, with one item added*

You can "check off" individual items, which are then displayed in strikethrough, as shown in Figure 45–3.

Figure 45–3. *The Checklist, with one item marked as completed*

You can also delete the checked entries (via the Delete Checked button) or all entries (via the Delete All button), which will pop up a confirmation dialog box before proceeding, as shown in Figure 45–4.

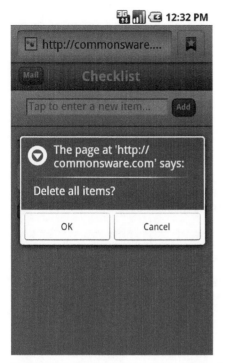

Figure 45–4. *The Checklist's delete confirmation dialog box*

"Installing" Checklist on Your Android Device

To access Checklist on your Android device, visit the hosted edition at http://bit.ly/cw-html5. You can then add a bookmark for it (choose More ➤ Add bookmark in the browser's options menu) to come back to it later.

You can even set up a shortcut for the bookmark on your home screen, if you so choose—just long-tap the background, choose Bookmark, and then choose the Checklist bookmark you set up before.

Examining the HTML

All the functionality in the Checklist app is accomplished using just a handful of lines of HTML:

```
<!DOCTYPE html>
<html lang="en" manifest="checklist.manifest">
<head>
<meta http-equiv="Content-Type" content="text/html; charset=utf-8" />
<title>Checklist</title>
<meta name="viewport"
  content="width=device-width; initial-scale=1.0; maximum-scale=1.0;↩
 user-scalable=0;" />
<meta name="apple-mobile-web-app-capable" content="yes" />
```

```
<meta name="apple-mobile-web-app-status-bar-style" />
<link rel="apple-touch-startup-image" href="splashscreen.png" />
<link rel="stylesheet" href="styles.css" />
<link rel="apple-touch-icon-precomposed"
      href="apple-touch-icon-precomposed.png" />
</head>
<body>
<section>
 <header>
 <button type="button" id="sendmail">Mail</button>
 <h1>Checklist</h1>
 </header>
 <article>
    <form id="inputarea" onsubmit="addNewItem()">
    <input type="text" name="name" id="name" maxlength="75"
                autocorrect placeholder="Tap to enter a new item&hellip;" />
    <button type="button" id="add">Add</button>
  </form>
  <ul id="maillist">
    <li class="empty"><a href="" id="maillink">Mail remaining items</a></li>
  </ul>
  <p id="totals"><span id="tally1">Total: <span id="total">0</span></span>
        <span id="tally2">Remaining: <span id="remaining">0</span></span></p>
  <ul id="checklist">
    <li class="empty">Loading&hellip;</li>
  </ul>
 </article>
 <fieldset>
  <button type="button" id="deletechecked">Delete Checked</button>
  <button type="button" id="deleteall">Delete All</button>
 </fieldset>
</section>
<script src="main.js"></script>
</body>
</html>
```

For the purposes of offline applications, though, the key is the manifest attribute of our html element:

```
<html lang="en" manifest="checklist.manifest">
```

Here, we specify the relative path to a manifest file, indicating what the rules are for caching various portions of this application offline.

Examining the Manifest

Because the manifest is where all the fun is, let's look at Checklist's manifest:

```
CACHE MANIFEST
#version 54
styles.css
main.js
splashscreen.png
```

The HTML5 manifest format is extremely simple. It starts with a CACHE MANIFEST line, followed by a list of files (technically, relative URLs) that should be cached. It also supports comments, which are lines beginning with #.

The manifest can also have a NETWORK: line, followed by relative URLs that should never be cached. Similarly, the manifest can have a FALLBACK: line, followed by pairs of relative URLs: the URL to try to fetch off the network, followed by the URL of a cached resource to use if the network is not available.

In principle, the manifest should request caching for everything that the application needs to run, though the page that requested the caching (index.html in this case) is also cached.

Web Storage

Caching the HTML5 application's assets for offline use is all well and good, but that will be rather limiting on its own. In an offline situation, the application would not be able to use AJAX techniques to interact with a web service. So, if the application is going to be able to store information, it will need to do so on the browser itself.

Everything from cookies through to Google Gears has been used to grapple with this problem, with the latter tool blazing the trail for what is now variously called Web Storage or DOM Storage for HTML5 applications. An HTML5 app can store data persistently on the client, within client-imposed limits. That, in conjunction with offline asset caching, means an HTML5 application can deliver far more value when it lacks an Internet connection, or for data that just does not make sense to store "in the cloud."

> **NOTE:** Technically, Web Storage is not part of HTML5, but rather is a related specification. However, it tends to get lumped in with HTML5 in common conversation.

What Does It Mean?

On a Web Storage–enabled browser, your JavaScript code will have access to a localStorage object, representing your application's data. More accurately, each *origin* (i.e., domain) will have a distinct localStorage object on the browser.

The localStorage object is an *associative array*, meaning you can work with it via either numerical indexes or string-based keys. Values typically are strings. You can do the following with localStorage:

- Find out how many entries are in the array via length()
- Get and set items by key via getItem() and setItem()
- Get the key for a numerical index via key()
- Remove individual entries via removeItem() or remove all items via clear()

This means you do not have the full richness of a SQL database, like you might have with SQLite in a native Android application. But, for many applications, this should suffice.

How Do You Use It?

Checklist stores the list items as keys in the associative array, with a value of 0 for a regular item and 1 for a deleted item. Here, we see the code for putting a new item into the checklist:

```
try {
  localStorage.setItem(strippedString, data);
}
catch (e) {
  if (e == QUOTA_EXCEEDED_ERR) {
    alert('Quota exceeded!');
  }
}
```

Following is the code where those items are pulled back out of storage and put into an array for sorting and, later, display as DOM elements on the web page itself:

```
/*get all items from localStorage and push them one by one into an array.*/
for (i = 0; i <= listlength; i++) {

  var item = localStorage.key(i);
  myArray.push(item);
}

/*sort the array into alphabetical order.*/
myArray.sort();
```

When the user checks the check box next to an item, the storage is updated to toggle the checked setting persistently:

```
/*toggle the check flag.*/
if (target.previousSibling.checked) {
  data = 0;
}
else {
  data = 1;
}
/*save item in localStorage.*/
try {
  localStorage.setItem(name, data);
} catch (e) {

  if (e == QUOTA_EXCEEDED_ERR) {
    alert('Quota exceeded!');
  }
}
```

Checklist also has code to delete items from storage, either all items marked as checked or all items. Following is the code to delete all checked items:

```
/*remove every item from localStorage that has the data flag checked.*/
while (i <= localStorage.length-1) {

  var key = localStorage.key(i);
  if (localStorage.getItem(key) === '1') {
    localStorage.removeItem(key);
  }
  else { i++; }
}
```

And here is the code to delete all items:

```
/*deletes all items in the list.*/
deleteAll: function() {

  /*ask for user confirmation.*/
  var answer = confirm("Delete all items?");

  /*if yes.*/
  if (answer) {

    /*remove all items from localStorage.*/
    localStorage.clear();
    /*update view.*/
    checklistApp.getAllItems();
  }
  /*clear up.*/
  delete checklistApp.deleteAll;
},
```

Web SQL Database

Android's built-in browser also supports a Web SQL Database option, which enables you to use SQLite-style databases from JavaScript. This adds a lot more power than basic Web Storage provides, albeit at a complexity cost. It is also not part of an active standard—the Web Hypertext Application Technology Working Group (WHATWG) team working on this standard has set it aside for the time being.

You might consider evaluating Lawnchair, which is a JavaScript API that allows you to store arbitrary JavaScript Object Notation (JSON)-encoded objects. It will use whatever storage options are available, and therefore will help you deal with cross-platform variety.

Going to Production

Creating a little test application requires nothing magical. Presumably, though, you are interested in having other people use your application—perhaps many others. Classic Java-based Android applications have to deal with testing, having the application digitally signed for production, distributing it through various channels (such as the Android Market), and providing updates to the application by one means or another. Those issues do not all magically vanish because HTML5 is used as the application environment. However, HTML5 does change things significantly from what Java developers have to do.

Testing

Since HTML5 works in other browsers, testing your business logic could easily take advantage of any number of HTML and JavaScript testing tools, from Selenium to QUnit to Jasmine.

For testing on Android proper—to ensure there are no issues related to Android's browser implementation—you can use Selenium's Android Driver or Remote Control modes.

Signing and Distribution

Unlike native Android applications, you do not need to worry about signing your HTML5 applications. The downside of this is that there is no support for distribution of HTML5 applications through the Android Market, which today supports only native Android apps. Users will have to find your application by one means or another, visit it in the browser, bookmark the page, and possibly create a home screen shortcut to that bookmark.

Updates

Unlike native Android applications, which by default must be updated manually, HTML5 applications will be transparently updated the next time the user runs the app while connected to the Internet. The offline caching protocol will check the web server for new editions of files before falling back to the cached copies. Hence, there is nothing more for you to do other than publish the latest web app assets.

Issues You May Encounter

Unfortunately, nothing is perfect. While HTML5 may make many things easier, it is not a panacea for all Android development problems.

This section covers some potential areas of concern you will want to consider as you move forward with HTML5 applications for Android.

Android Device Versions

Not all Android devices support HTML5—only those running Android 2.x or higher. Ideally, therefore, you should do a bit of user-agent sniffing on your web server and redirect older Android users to some other page explaining the limitations in their device.

Here is the user-agent string for a Google/HTC Nexus One device running Android 2.1:

```
Mozilla/5.0 (Linux; U; Android 2.1-update1; en-us; Nexus One Build/ERE27)⏎
 AppleWebKit/530.17 (KHTML, like Gecko) Version/4.0 Mobile Safari/530.17
```

As you can see, it is formatted like a typical modern user-agent string, meaning it is quite a mess. It does indicate it is running `Android 2.1-update1`.

Eventually, somebody will create a database of user-agent strings for different device models, and from there we can derive appropriate regular expressions or similar algorithms to determine whether a given device can support HTML5 applications.

Screen Sizes and Densities

HTML5 applications can be run on a wide range of screen sizes, from QVGA Android devices to 1080p LCDs and beyond. Similarly, screen densities may vary quite a bit, so while a 48×48-pixel image on a smartphone may be an appropriate size, it may be too big for a 1080p television, let alone a 24-inch LCD desktop monitor.

Other than increasing the possible options on the low end of screen sizes, none of this is unique to Android. You will need to determine how best to design your HTML and CSS to work on a range of sizes and densities, even if Android were not part of the picture.

Limited Platform Integration

HTML5, while offering more platform integration than ever before, does not come close to covering everything an Android application might want to be able to do. For example, an ordinary HTML5 application cannot do the following:

- Launch another application

- Work with the contacts database

- Raise a notification with the stock browser (note that Firefox for Android has a solution for this)

- Do work truly in the background (though web workers may alleviate this somewhat someday)

- Interact with Bluetooth devices

- Record audio or video

- Use the standard Android preference system

- Use speech recognition or text-to-speech

Many applications will not need these capabilities, of course. And other application environments, like PhoneGap (covered in Chapter 46), will likely evolve into "HTML5 Plus" for Android. That way, you could create a stock application that works across all devices and a separate enhanced Android application that leverages greater platform integration, at the cost of some additional amount of programming.

Performance and Battery

There has been a nagging concern for some time that HTML-based user interfaces are inefficient compared to native Android UIs, in terms of processor time, memory, and battery. For example, one of the stated reasons for avoiding BONDI-style web widgets for the Android home screen is the performance impact.

Certainly, it is possible to design HTML5 applications that will suck down the battery. For example, if you have a hunk of JavaScript code running every second indefinitely, that is going to consume a fair amount of processor time. However, outside of that, it seems unlikely that an ordinary application would be used so heavily as to materially impact battery life. Certainly, more testing will need to be done in this area.

Also, an HTML5 application may start up a bit slower than other applications, particularly if the browser has not been used in a while or if the network connection is there but has minimal bandwidth to your server.

Look and Feel

HTML5 applications can certainly look very slick and professional—after all, they are built with web technologies, and web apps can look very slick and professional.

However, HTML5 applications will not necessarily look like standard Android applications, at least not initially. Some enterprising developers will, no doubt, create some reusable CSS, JavaScript, and images that will, for example, mirror an Android native `Spinner` widget (a type of drop-down control). Similarly, HTML5 applications will tend to lack options menus, notifications, or other UI features that a native Android application may well use.

This is not necessarily bad. Considering the difficulty in creating a very slick-looking Android application, HTML5 applications may tend to look better than their Android counterparts. After all, there are many more people skilled in creating slick web apps than there are people skilled in creating slick Android apps.

However, some users may complain about the look-and-feel disparity, just because it is different.

Distribution

HTML5 applications can be trivially added to a user's device—browse, bookmark, and add a shortcut to the home screen. However, HTML5 applications will not show up in the Android Market, so users trained to look at the Market for available applications will not find HTML5 applications, even ones that may be better than their native counterparts.

It is conceivable that, someday, the Android Market will support HTML5 applications. It is also conceivable that, someday, Android users will tend to find their apps by means other than searching the Android Market, and will be able to get their HTML5 apps that way. However, until one of those becomes true, HTML5 applications may be less "discoverable" than their native equivalents.

Browser Changes Post Ice Cream Sandwich

Google has announced that their future direction for the stock Android browser will be Chrome (or a version of Chrome derived for Android). No indication was given with the Android 4.0 release as to whether the change will come through an incremental process slowly converging on a Chrome-like browser, or via a big-bang change in a future release. When the change does occur, some of the nuances of using HTML5, and indeed some of the supported features, are likely to change. This will impact all of your users for any HTML5 apps, barring those using alternative browsers.

HTML5 and Alternative Android Browsers

While the built-in Android browser will be the choice of many Android users, there are other browsers available. Here is how some of the better-known alternatives stand in terms of HTML5 support:

- *Firefox Mobile*: Still in beta form after quite some time, supports offline caching and local storage. However, it is unable to run the Checklist sample correctly at this time.

- *Opera Mobile*: A steadily improving offering, recently adding features like haptic feedback support. Does not support local storage, rendering Checklist moot. It also does not support offline caching at this time.

- *Dolphin Browser HD 4.0*: Supports offline caching and local storage. While there are slight rendering problems—perhaps CSS-related—in Checklist, the application otherwise runs fine, even without an Internet connection.

HTML5: The Baseline

HTML5 is likely to become rather popular for conventional application development. It gives web developers a route to the desktop. It may be the only option for Google's Chrome OS. And, with ever-improving support on popular mobile devices—Android among them—developers will certainly be enticed by another round of "write once, run anywhere" promises.

It is fairly likely that, over time, HTML5 will be the number two option for Android application development, after the conventional Java application written to the Android SDK. That will make HTML5 the baseline for comparing alternative Android development options—not only will those options be compared to using the SDK, they will be compared to using HTML5.

Chapter **46**

PhoneGap

PhoneGap is perhaps the original alternative application framework for Android, arriving on the scene in early 2009. PhoneGap (www.phonegap.com/) is open source, backed by Nitobi, which traditionally offered a mix of open source and commercial products, along with consulting and training services. As of October 2011, Nitobi had agreed to be acquired by Adobe. To ensure the longevity of the PhoneGap code, Nitobi submitted the PhoneGap code base to the Apache Software Foundation, where the project is now named Apache Callback. Most people still know the project by its original name, and much of the documentation still refers to PhoneGap, so we'll stick to the traditional name.

What Is PhoneGap?

PhoneGap is a platform built around HTML5 that enables you to develop apps from one code base and deploy them to multiple platforms. Using PhoneGap is as easy as following these steps:

1. Build your application using web standard languages such as HTML5 and JavaScript.

2. Wrap your application with PhoneGap to gain access to native APIs.

3. Deploy your application to multiple platforms.

Read more about PhoneGap and how it works at www.phonegap.com/about.

What Do You Write In?

A PhoneGap application is made up of HTML, CSS, and JavaScript, no different from a mobile web site or HTML5 application, except that in PhoneGap the web assets are packaged with the application rather than downloaded on-the-fly.

A preinstalled PhoneGap application, therefore, can contain comparatively large assets, such as complex JavaScript libraries, that might be too slow to download over slower

EDGE connections. However, PhoneGap is still limited by the speed of mobile devices and how quickly the WebKit browser can load and process those assets.

Also, development for WebKit for mobile differs from development for WebKit for desktops, particularly with respect to touch versus mouse events. You may want to develop using mobile layers of JavaScript frameworks (e.g., jQTouch versus plain jQuery) where practical.

What Features Do You Get?

As with an HTML5 application, PhoneGap gives you the basic capabilities of a web browser, including AJAX support. Beyond that, PhoneGap adds a number of JavaScript APIs to allow you to get at the underlying features of the Android platform. At the time of this writing, that includes the following:

- Accelerometer access, for detecting movement of the device
- Audio recording
- Camera access, for taking still pictures
- Compass access, for orientation-based activities
- Contacts access, for working with the built-in contacts provider
- Database access, both to databases that you create (SQLite) and to others built into Android (e.g., contacts)
- File system access, such as to the SD card or other external storage
- Geolocation, for determining where the device is
- Notification services, including alerts and sound effects
- Storage, both on-device and SD card
- Vibration, for shaking the phone (e.g., force-feedback)

Since some of these are part of the HTML5 specification (e.g., geolocation), you have your choice of APIs. Also, this list will change over time, but you'll see that the preceding list is a pretty comprehensive list of the native features on most contemporary Android devices.

What Do Apps Look Like?

PhoneGap apps look like web pages, more so than native Android apps, as shown in Figure 46–1, a screenshot of the example application that ships with PhoneGap. You can use CSS and images to mimic the Android look and feel to some extent, but only for those sorts of widgets that can be created in both Android and HTML. For example, the Android Spinner widget, which resembles a drop-down list, may be difficult to mimic in HTML.

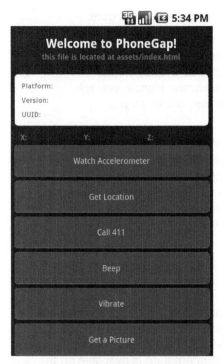

🄳🄳 📶 🄴 5:34 PM

Welcome to PhoneGap!
this file is located at assets/index.html

Platform:

Version:

UUID:

X: Y: Z:

Watch Accelerometer

Get Location

Call 411

Beep

Vibrate

Get a Picture

Figure 46–1. *The example application that comes with PhoneGap*

How Does Distribution Work?

Distributing a PhoneGap application is pretty much identical to distributing any other standard Android application, with some additional options available. Using stand-alone PhoneGap, after testing, you create a standard APK file with the Android build tools, from an Android project generated for you by PhoneGap. This project will contain the Java, XML, and other necessary bits to wrap around your HTML, CSS, and JavaScript to make up your application. Then, you digitally sign the application and upload it to the Android Market or any other distribution mechanism you wish to use. Nitobi also makes available a hosted build service, called PhoneGap Build, which we'll discuss a bit later in the chapter.

What About Other Platforms?

PhoneGap is not just for Android. You can create PhoneGap applications for iPhone, Blackberry, some flavors of Symbian, Microsoft Windows Phone, Samsung Bada, and Palm's WebOS. In theory, at least, you can create one application using HTML, CSS, JavaScript, and the PhoneGap JavaScript APIs, and have it run across many devices.

There are a couple of limitations that will hamper your progress to that goal:

- The web browsing component used by PhoneGap across all those platforms is not identical. Even multiple platforms using WebKit will have different WebKit releases, based on what was available when WebKit was integrated into a given device's firmware. Hence, you will want to test to ensure that your CSS, in particular, works as you expect on as many devices as possible.

- Not all PhoneGap JavaScript APIs are available on all devices yet, due to a variety of factors (e.g., not exposed in the platform's native APIs, lack of engineering time to hoist the capability into the PhoneGap APIs, etc.). The PhoneGap wiki can keep you apprised of what works and what does not across the devices. You will want to restrict your feature use to match your desired platforms, or restrict your platforms to match your desired features.

Using PhoneGap

Now, let's look at more of the mechanics for using PhoneGap. PhoneGap's installation and usage, as of the time of this writing, normally requires an expert in Java-based Android development. You need to install a whole bunch of tools, edit configuration files by hand, and so forth. If you want to do all of that, documentation is available on the PhoneGap web site and we'll cover it briefly below. If you are reading this chapter, there's a decent chance that you would rather skip all of that. Once again, you can use the PhoneGap Build service (http://build.phonegap.com/), which we'll cover shortly.

Installation

You can download the latest PhoneGap tools as a ZIP archive from the PhoneGap web site, which acts as a redirect to the Apache Callback incubator repository at the Apache Software Foundation. Unpack those tools wherever it makes sense for your development machine and platform. For Android development, that is all the PhoneGap-specific installation you will need. However, you will need the Android SDK and related tools (e.g., Eclipse, if you wish to use Eclipse) for setting up the project.

Creating and Installing Your Project

A PhoneGap Android project is, at its core, a regular Android project, which you can create following the instructions outlined earlier in this book. To convert the standard generated "Hello, World" application into a PhoneGap project, you need to do the following:

1. From the `Android/` directory of wherever you unzipped the PhoneGap ZIP file, copy the PhoneGap JAR file to the `libs/` directory of your project. If you are using Eclipse, you also need to add it to your build path.

2. Create an `assets/www/` directory in your project. Then, copy over the PhoneGap JS file from the `Android/` directory of wherever you unzipped the PhoneGap ZIP file.

3. Adjust the standard "Hello, World" activity to inherit from `DroidGap` instead of `Activity`. This requires you to import `com.phonegap.DroidGap`.

4. In your activity's `onCreate()` method, replace `setContentView()` with `super.loadUrl("file:///android_asset/www/index.html");`.

5. In your manifest, add all the permissions that PhoneGap requests, listed later in this chapter.

6. Also in your manifest, add a suitable `<supports-screens>` element based on what screen sizes you want to test and support.

7. Also in your manifest, add `android:configChanges=` `"orientation|keyboardHidden"` to your `<activity>` element, as `DroidGap` handles orientation-related configuration changes.

At this point, you can create an `assets/www/index.html` file in your project and start creating your PhoneGap application using HTML, CSS, and JavaScript. You need to include a reference to the PhoneGap JavaScript file (e.g., `<script type="text/javascript" charset="utf-8" src="phonegap.1.2.0.js" />`). When you want to test the application, you can build and install it like any other Android application (e.g., `ant clean install` if you are using the command-line build process).

For somebody experienced in Android SDK development, setting this up is not a big challenge.

PhoneGap Build

PhoneGap Build is a tools-as-a-service (TaaS) hosted approach to creating PhoneGap projects. All of the Android build process is handled for you by PhoneGap-supplied servers. You just focus on creating your HTML, CSS, and JavaScript as you see fit.

When you log into PhoneGap Build, you are first prompted to create your initial project, by supplying a name and the web assets to go into the app, as shown in Figure 46–2.

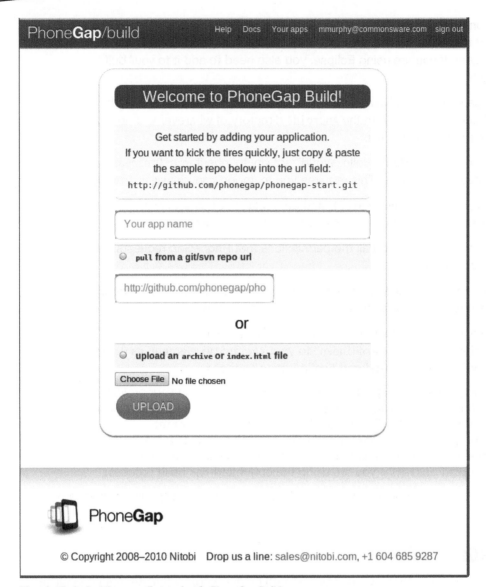

Figure 46–2. *Creating your first project in PhoneGap Build*

You will be able to add new projects later via a New App button, which gives you the same set of options.

Your choices for supplying the assets are to upload a ZIP file containing all of them or to specify the URL to a public GitHub repository that PhoneGap Build can pull from. The latter method tends to be more convenient, if you are used to using Git for version control and your project is open source (and therefore has a public repository).

Once you click the Upload button, the PhoneGap Build server immediately starts building your application for Android, plus Blackberry, Symbian, and the other supported platforms, or platforms you have chosen, as shown in Figure 46–3.

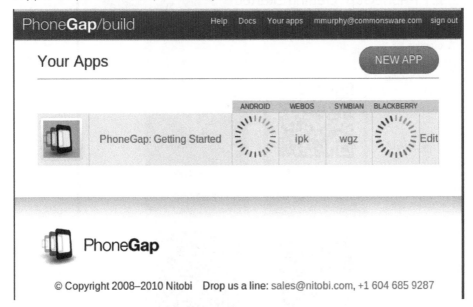

Figure 46–3. *Building your first project in PhoneGap Build*

Each of the targets has its own file extension (e.g., apk for Android). Clicking that link will let you download that file. Or, click the name of the project, and you get Quick Response (QR) codes to enable downloads straight to your test device, as shown in Figure 46–4.

Figure 46–4. *Your project's QR codes in PhoneGap Build*

This page also gives you a link to update the app from its GitHub repository (if you chose that option). Or, you can click Edit to specify more options, such as the version of your application or its launcher icon, as shown in Figure 46–5.

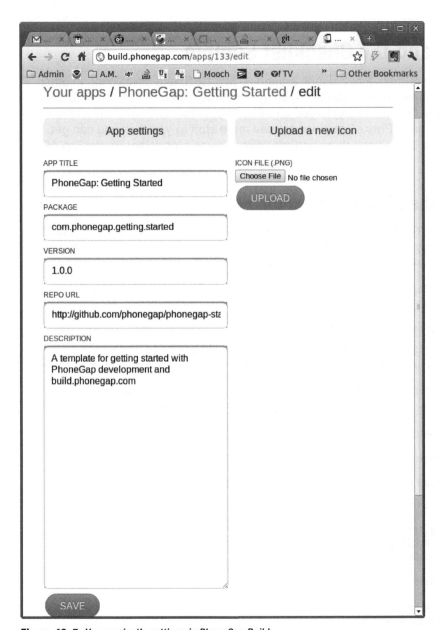

Figure 46–5. *Your project's settings in PhoneGap Build*

All in all, if you do not otherwise need the Android SDK and related tools on your development machine, PhoneGap Build certainly simplifies the PhoneGap building process.

Nitobi launched PhoneGap Build as a commercial service for non–open source applications, with rates available from the PhoneGap Build web site.

PhoneGap and the Checklist Sample

The beauty of PhoneGap is that it wraps around HTML, CSS, and JavaScript. In other words, you do not have to do much of anything PhoneGap-specific to be able to take advantage of PhoneGap delivering to you an APK suitable for installation on an Android device. That being said, PhoneGap does expose more stuff to you than you can get from the standards, if you need them and are willing to use proprietary PhoneGap APIs for them.

Sticking to the Standards

Given an existing HTML5 application, all you need to do to make it an installable APK is wrap it in PhoneGap. For example, to convert the HTML5 version of `Checklist` (from Chapter 45) into an APK file, you need to do the following:

1. Follow the steps to create an empty PhoneGap project, as outlined earlier in this chapter.

2. Copy the HTML, CSS, JavaScript, and images from the HTML5 project into the `assets/www/` directory of the PhoneGap project (note that you do not need anything unique to HTML5, such as the cache manifest).

3. Make sure that your HTML entry point file name matches the path you used with the `loadUrl()` call in your activity (e.g., `index.html`).

4. Add a reference to the PhoneGap JavaScript file from your HTML.

5. Build and install the project.

Here is the `DroidGap` activity for our app, from the `PhoneGap/Checklist` project:

```
package com.commonsware.pg.checklist;

import android.app.Activity;
import android.os.Bundle;
import com.phonegap.DroidGap;

public class Checklist extends DroidGap {
  @Override
  public void onCreate(Bundle savedInstanceState) {
    super.onCreate(savedInstanceState);
    super.loadUrl("file:///android_asset/www/index.html");
  }
}
```

Here is the manifest, with all of the PhoneGap-requested settings added:

```
<?xml version="1.0" encoding="utf-8"?>
<manifest xmlns:android="http://schemas.android.com/apk/res/android"
      package="com.commonsware.pg.checklist"
      android:versionCode="1"
      android:versionName="1.0">
```

```
<application android:label="@string/app_name" android:icon="@drawable/cw">
    <activity android:name="Checklist"
            android:configChanges="orientation|keyboardHidden"
            android:label="@string/app_name">
        <intent-filter>
            <action android:name="android.intent.action.MAIN" />
            <category android:name="android.intent.category.LAUNCHER" />
        </intent-filter>
    </activity>
</application>
<supports-screens
    android:largeScreens="true"
    android:normalScreens="true"
    android:smallScreens="true"
    android:resizeable="true"
    android:anyDensity="true"
/>
<uses-permission android:name="android.permission.CAMERA" />
<uses-permission android:name="android.permission.VIBRATE" />
<uses-permission android:name="android.permission.ACCESS_COARSE_LOCATION" />
<uses-permission android:name="android.permission.ACCESS_FINE_LOCATION" />
<uses-permission android:name="android.permission.ACCESS_LOCATION_EXTRA_COMMANDS" />
<uses-permission android:name="android.permission.READ_PHONE_STATE" />
<uses-permission android:name="android.permission.INTERNET" />
<uses-permission android:name="android.permission.RECEIVE_SMS" />
<uses-permission android:name="android.permission.RECORD_AUDIO" />
<uses-permission android:name="android.permission.MODIFY_AUDIO_SETTINGS" />
<uses-permission android:name="android.permission.READ_CONTACTS" />
<uses-permission android:name="android.permission.WRITE_CONTACTS" />
<uses-permission android:name="android.permission.WRITE_EXTERNAL_STORAGE" />
<uses-permission android:name="android.permission.ACCESS_NETWORK_STATE" />
</manifest>
```

And here is the HTML, which is almost identical to the HTML5 original, but with some HTML5 offline stuff removed (e.g., iPhone icons) and the reference to PhoneGap's JavaScript file added:

```
<!DOCTYPE html>
<html lang="en" manifest="checklist.manifest">
<head>
    <meta http-equiv="Content-Type" content="text/html; charset=utf-8" />
    <title>Checklist</title>
    <meta name="viewport"
      content="width=device-width; initial-scale=1.0; maximum-scale=1.0;↵
  user-scalable=0;" />
    <link rel="stylesheet" href="styles.css" />
    <script type="text/javascript" charset="utf-8" src="phonegap.1.2.0.js"></script>
</head>
<body>
    <section>
        <header>
          <button type="button" id="sendmail">Mail</button>
          <h1>Checklist</h1>
        </header>
        <article>
          <form id="inputarea" onsubmit="addNewItem()">
              <input type="text" name="name" id="name" maxlength="75"
```

```
                        autocorrect placeholder="Tap to enter a new item&hellip;" />
          <button type="button" id="add">Add</button>
        </form>
        <ul id="maillist">
        <li class="empty"><a href="" id="maillink">Mail remaining items</a></li>
      </ul>
        <p id="totals"><span id="tally1">Total: <span id="total">0</span></span>
        <span id="tally2">Remaining: <span id="remaining">0</span></span></p>
      <ul id="checklist">
        <li class="empty">Loading&hellip;</li>
      </ul>
    </article>
    <fieldset>
      <button type="button" id="deletechecked">Delete Checked</button>
      <button type="button" id="deleteall">Delete All</button>
    </fieldset>
    </section>
    <script src="main.js"></script>
</body>
</html>
```

For many applications, this is all you will need. You are simply looking at PhoneGap to give you something you can distribute on the Android Market, on the iOS App Store, and so on.

Adding PhoneGap APIs

If you want to take advantage of more device capabilities, you can augment your HTML5 application to use PhoneGap-specific APIs. These run the gamut from telling you the device's model to letting you get compass readings. Hence, their complexity will vary. For the purposes of this chapter, we will look at some of the simpler ones.

Set Up Device-Ready Event Handler

For various reasons, PhoneGap will not be ready to respond to all of its APIs right away when your page is loaded. Instead, you need to look for a deviceready event to confirm that it is safe to use PhoneGap-specific JavaScript globals. The following is the typical recipe:

1. Add an onload attribute to your <body> tag, referencing a global JavaScript function (e.g., onLoad()).

2. In onLoad(), use addEventListener() to register another global JavaScript function (e.g., onDeviceReady()) for the deviceready event.

3. In onDeviceReady(), start using the PhoneGap APIs.

Use What PhoneGap Gives You

PhoneGap makes a number of methods available to you through a series of virtual JavaScript objects. Here, "virtual" means that you cannot check to see if the objects exist, but you can call methods and read properties on them. So, for example, there is a device object that has a handful of useful properties, such as phonegap to return the PhoneGap version and version to return the OS version. These virtual objects are ready for use in or after the deviceready event.

For example, here is a JavaScript file (props.js from the PhoneGap/ChecklistEx project) that implements an onLoad() function (to register for deviceready) and an onDeviceReady() function (to use the device object's properties):

```javascript
// PhoneGap's APIs are not immediately ready, so set up an
// event handler to find out when they are ready

function onLoad() {
  document.addEventListener("deviceready", onDeviceReady, false);
}

// Now PhoneGap's APIs are ready

function onDeviceReady() {
  var element=document.getElementById('props');

  element.innerHTML='<li>Model: '+device.name+'</li>' +
                    '<li>OS and Version: '+device.platform +' '+device.version+'</li>' +
                    '<li>PhoneGap Version: '+device.phonegap+'</li>';
}
```

The onDeviceReady() function needs a list element with an id of props. That, plus loading this JavaScript in the first place, will require some minor modifications to our HTML:

```html
<!DOCTYPE html>
<html lang="en" manifest="checklist.manifest">
<head>
    <meta http-equiv="Content-Type" content="text/html; charset=utf-8" />
    <title>Checklist</title>
    <meta name="viewport"
      content="width=device-width; initial-scale=1.0; maximum-scale=1.0;↵
 user-scalable=0;" />
    <link rel="stylesheet" href="styles.css" />
    <script type="text/javascript" charset="utf-8" src="phonegap.1.2.0.js"></script>
    <script type="text/javascript" charset="utf-8" src="props.js"></script>
</head>
 <body onload="onLoad()">
    <section>
 <header>
 <button type="button" id="sendmail">Mail</button>
 <h1>Checklist</h1>
 </header>
 <article>
    <form id="inputarea" onsubmit="addNewItem()">
    <input type="text" name="name" id="name" maxlength="75"
                autocorrect placeholder="Tap to enter a new item&hellip;" />
    <button type="button" id="add">Add</button>
  </form>
  <ul id="maillist">
    <li class="empty"><a href="" id="maillink">Mail remaining items</a></li>
```

```
  </ul>
  <p id="totals"><span id="tally1">Total: <span id="total">0</span></span>
       <span id="tally2">Remaining: <span id="remaining">0</span></span></p>
  <ul id="checklist">
    <li class="empty">Loading&hellip;</li>
  </ul>
</article>
<fieldset>
  <button type="button" id="deletechecked">Delete Checked</button>
  <button type="button" id="deleteall">Delete All</button>
</fieldset>
    <footer>
        <h2>Device Properties</h2>
        <ul id="props"></ul>
    </footer>
    </section>
    <script src="main.js"></script>
  </body>
</html>
```

Figure 46–6 shows what the resulting app looks like.

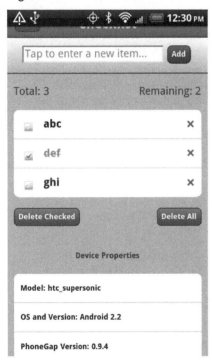

Figure 46–6. *The PhoneGap Checklist application with device properties*

Obviously, reading a handful of properties is far simpler than, say, taking a picture with the device's camera. However, the difference in complexity is mostly in what PhoneGap's virtual JavaScript objects give you and how you can use them, more so than anything peculiar to Android.

Issues You May Encounter

PhoneGap is a fine choice for creating cross-platform applications. However, it is not without its issues. Some of these issues may be resolved in time; some may be endemic to the nature of PhoneGap.

Security

Android applications use a permission system to request access to certain system features, such as making Internet requests or reading the user's contacts. Applications must request these permissions at install time, so the user can elect to abandon the installation if the requested permissions seem suspect.

A general rule of thumb is that you should request as few permissions as possible, and make sure that you can justify why you are requesting them.

PhoneGap, for a new project, requests quite a few permissions:

- CAMERA

- VIBRATE

- ACCESS_COARSE_LOCATION

- ACCESS_FINE_LOCATION

- ACCESS_LOCATION_EXTRA_COMMANDS

- READ_PHONE_STATE

- INTERNET

- RECEIVE_SMS

- RECORD_AUDIO

- MODIFY_AUDIO_SETTINGS

- READ_CONTACTS

- WRITE_CONTACTS

- WRITE_EXTERNAL_STORAGE

- ACCESS_NETWORK_STATE

Leaving this roster intact will give you an application that can use every API that PhoneGap makes available to your JavaScript...and an application that will scare away many users. After all, it is unlikely that your application will be able to use, let alone justify, all of these permissions.

It is certainly possible for you to trim down this list, by modifying the AndroidManifest.xml file in the root of your PhoneGap project. However, you will then need to thoroughly test your application to make sure you did not get rid of a permission that you actually need. Also, it may be unclear to you which permissions you can safely remove.

Eventually, the PhoneGap project may have tools to help guide you in the choice of permissions, perhaps by statically analyzing your JavaScript code to see which PhoneGap APIs you are using. In the meantime, though, getting the proper set of permissions will involve a lot of trial and error.

Screen Sizes and Densities

Normal web applications primarily focus on screen resolution and window sizes as their primary variables. Mobile web applications do not have to worry about window sizes, as browsers and apps typically run full-screen. Mobile web applications need to deal with physical size and density, though—issues that are off the radar for traditional web development.

Netbooks can have screens that are 10 inches or smaller, whereas desktops can have screens that are 24 inches or larger. So physical screen size would seem to be something web developers need to address. However, screen resolution (in pixels) generally tracks well with physical size in the netbook/notebook/desktop realm. That is because screen density is fairly consistent across their LCDs, and that density is fairly low.

Smartphones, on the other hand, have several different densities, causing the connection between resolution and size to be broken. Some low-end phones, particularly with small (e.g., 3 inch) LCDs, have densities on par with nice monitors. Midrange phones have twice the density (240 dpi versus 120 dpi). Apple's iPhone 4 has even higher density, and there likely will soon be some Android devices with so-called retina displays as well. Hence, an 800×480 resolution could be on a screen ranging anywhere from 4 inches to 7 inches, for example. Tablets add even more possible sizes to the mix.

This is compounded by the problems caused by touchscreens. A mouse can get pixel-level precision in its clicks. Fingers are much less precise. Hence, you may need to make your buttons and such bigger on a touchscreen, so that it is finger-friendly. This causes some problems with scaling of assets, particularly images. What might be finger-friendly on a low-density 3-inch device might be entirely too small for a high-density 4-inch device.

Native Android applications have built-in logic for dealing with this issue, in the form of multiple sets of resources (e.g., images) that can be swapped in based on device characteristics. Eventually, PhoneGap and similar tools will need to provide relevant advice to their users for how to create applications that can similarly adapt to circumstances.

Look and Feel

A web app never quite looks like a native one. This is not necessarily a bad thing. However, some users may find it disconcerting, particularly since they will not understand why their newly installed app (made with PhoneGap, for example) looks so different from any other similar app they may already have.

As HTML5 applications become more prominent on Android, this issue should decline in importance. However, it is something to keep in mind. If you are creating your own graphic elements (icons, etc.) you will almost certainly benefit from using Android Asset Studio, covered in Chapter 43, to take on some of the chores: crafting icons in the necessary sizes, creating web images sympathetic to your icon and other styles, and so forth.

For More Information

At the time of this writing, there are no books available dedicated to PhoneGap development. At the moment, the best information on PhoneGap can be found on the PhoneGap web site, including its API documentation, and in a number of other publicly available tutorials on other web sites.

Chapter **47**

Other Alternative Environments

The alternative application environments described in the preceding chapters represent but a few of the growing flood of such technologies. Here, we will take a brief look at a few other alternative application environments.

> **NOTE:** This area is changing rapidly, so by the time you read this chapter, the material may be somewhat out of date relative to the progress each of these technologies has made. Check the web site of each of the application environments for the latest updates.

Rhodes

Rhodes (http://rhomobile.com/) is similar to PhoneGap insofar as you develop an Android application whose user interface is defined via HTML, CSS, and JavaScript. The difference is that Rhodes bakes in a full Ruby environment, with a Rails-esque framework. Your Ruby code generates HTML and such to be "served" to an activity via a WebView widget, much like a server-side Ruby web app would generate HTML to be served to a stand-alone web browser.

Similar to PhoneGap, you can either build the project on your development machine or use their hosted build process, RhoHub. The latter method is recommended, partly because the requirements for local builds are higher than those for PhoneGap—notably, Rhodes requires the Native Development Kit (NDK) for building and linking the Ruby interpreter to your application.

Rhodes winds up creating larger applications than does PhoneGap, due to the overhead of the Ruby interpreter (~1.5MB). However, if you are used to server-side web development, picking up Rhodes may be easier for you than picking up PhoneGap.

One area in which Rhodes differentiates itself is by providing a set of connectors and a server-side service known as RhoConnect, all of which act to offer integration between Rhodes-developed Android applications and various enterprise and business systems.

Flash, Flex, and AIR

Adobe worked long and hard to extend its Flash, Flex, and AIR technologies to the mobile space. Histroically, you could use Flex (the "Hero" edition) and Flash Builder (the "Burrito" edition) to create Android APK files that can be distributed on the Android Market and deployed to Android devices. Those devices would need to have the Adobe Integrated Runtime (AIR) installed, which is free, but is a large download and works only on Android 2.2 or later devices with later-model ARM processors (specifically, ARM v7 or later processors, so some early model devices that run Android 2.2 or 2.3 are out of luck, such as the LG Optimus V).

Then in November 2011, Adobe announced that Flash for mobile devices (Android and other platforms) would be no more. If you read the preceding chapter on PhoneGap, you can probably draw your own conclusions about where Adobe is going in the mobile space. Adobe certainly has been gathering a lot of technology and know-how in the realm of tools to build Flash code and then convert it to HTML5 and related non-Flash technologies. Only time will tell if this move is a success for them in the mobile space.

AIR is not as tightly integrated with the platform as PhoneGap is (e.g., AIR provides no access to the device's contacts), though this is an area to which Adobe likely will devote more resources now, likely leveraging the know-how it acquired with the purchase of Nitobi.

JRuby and Ruboto

JRuby (www.jruby.org/) is one of the most popular languages designed to run on the JVM—besides Java itself. JRuby was quickly ported to run on Android, but with some optimizations disabled, since JRuby is actually running on the Dalvik virtual machine that underlies the Android environment, not on a classic JVM.

However, JRuby alone cannot create Android applications. As a scripting language, there is no way for it to define an activity or other component—those need to be registered in the application's manifest as regular Java class files.

This is where Ruboto (http://ruboto.org/) comes in. Ruboto is a framework for a generic JRuby/Android application. It provides skeletal activities via a code generator and allows JRuby scripts to define handlers for all of the lifecycle methods (e.g., onCreate()), define user interfaces using JRuby code, and so forth. The result can be packaged as an APK file using supplied Rake script. The results can be uploaded to the Android Market or distributed however else you desire.

Mono for Android

Mono is an open source reimplementation of C# and .NET for non-Windows environments. Mono has had its fair share of controversies, mostly stemming from Microsoft, such as whether Microsoft will someday squash Mono over patent considerations.

Mono for Android has been in the works for some time. This would allow Mono developers to target Android for their apps. In principle, one could develop C# applications for Android this way.

While Mono itself is an open source project, Mono for Android "is a commercial product...licensed on a per-developer basis," hosted by Xamarin (http://android.xamarin.com/). This may come as a bit of a shock to developers who are expecting Mono on Android to remain open source. As of late 2011, the Xamarin web site lists prices starting from $399 per developer.

App Inventor

App Inventor (http://appinventor.googlelabs.com/) is an Android application development tool made available by Google, but outside of the normal Android developer site. App Inventor was originally developed for use in education, but Google has been inviting others into their closed beta.

App Inventor is theoretically a web-based development tool. Here, "theoretically" means that, in practice, users have to do a fair amount of work outside of the browser to get everything set up:

- Have Java 1.6 or later installed and functioning in the browser, capable of running Java Web Start (.jnlp) applications
- Download and install a large (~55MB) client-side set of tools

Once you set it up, App Inventor gives you a drag-and-drop GUI editor, as shown in Figure 47–1.

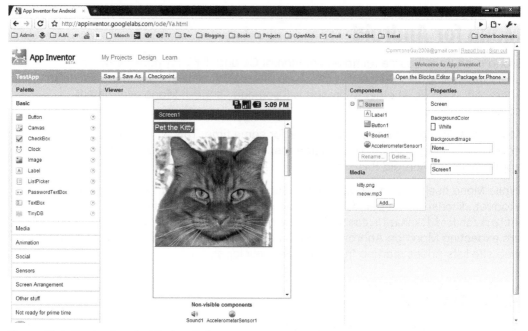

Figure 47–1. *The App Inventor "Designer" view*

App Inventor also gives you a Blocks Editor (see Figure 47–2), where you attach behaviors to events (e.g., button clicks) by snapping together various "blocks" representing events, methods, and properties.

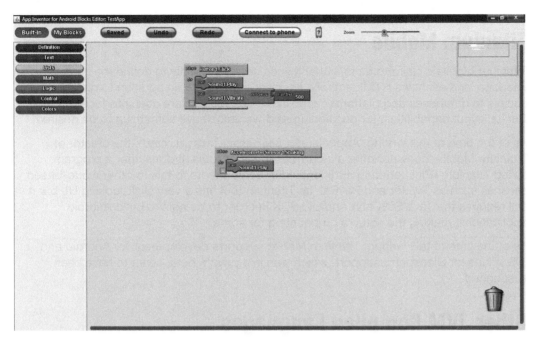

Figure 47–2. *The App Inventor Blocks Editor*

While working in the GUI editor, if you've chosen to build your applications directly to an attached device, you see what you are building live on the attached device and can test it in real time. Later, when you are ready, you can package the application into a standard APK file.

However, App Inventor is not really set up for production application use today:

■ You cannot distribute App Inventor apps on the Android Market. Google claims this is due to technical limitations that were being actively worked on, but this status has not changed for much of 2011.

■ It has more components aimed at "sizzle" (e.g., Twitter integration) and fewer components delivering capabilities that a typical modern app might need (e.g., relational databases and lists).

■ Shared development is primitive, where additional developers upload and download ZIP files of the project code.

■ Perhaps the biggest limitation is its single-screen focus, meaning having additional activities with different screens is beyond App Inventor's scope.

In the future, it is possible that App Inventor will become a solid option, or that App Inventor will trigger other firms to create similar sorts of programming-free development options for Android.

Titanium Mobile

Titanium Mobile's claim to fame is that it uses JavaScript only to define the user interface, and eschews HTML entirely. Its JavaScript library, in addition to providing access to databases and platform capabilities, lets you declare user interface widgets. But its layout capabilities, for positioning said widgets, leave something to be desired.

As of the time of this writing, Appcelerator (www.appcelerator.com/), the creator of Titanium Mobile, does not offer a cloud-based set of tools. It does offer a program called Titanium+Plus, offering additional SDK components to talk to other cloud-based services such as Twitter and PayPal. Its Titanium tool has a very slick-looking UI, but it still requires the Java SDK and Android SDK in order to be able to build Android applications, making the setup a bit daunting for some.

As of the time of this writing, Titanium Mobile supports development for Android and iOS. Plans for Blackberry support, which was in a private beta, seem to have been suspended.

Other JVM Compiled Languages

If you are happy with regular Android development, but you just do not like Java, any language that can generate compatible JVM bytecode should work with Android. You would have to modify the build chain for that other language to do the rest of the Android build process (e.g., generate R.java from the resources and create the APK file in the end).

Scala (www.scala-lang.org/) and Clojure (http://clojure.org/) are two such languages, whose communities have put together instructions for using their languages for Android development.

Part VIII

The Ever-Evolving Android

Chapter 48

Dealing with Devices

Android is open source and made available freely for device manufacturers. Hence, device manufacturers have *carte blanche* to do what they want with Android as they put it on their devices. This means a breadth of choices for device users, who can choose among Android devices in a variety of shapes, sizes, and colors. This also means developers have some device differences and idiosyncrasies to take into account.

This chapter will give you some tips and advice for dealing with these device-specific issues, to go along with the screen size material in earlier chapters.

This App Contains Explicit Instructions

Originally, the only Android device was the T-Mobile G1. Hence, if you were writing an Android application, you could assume the existence of a hardware QWERTY keyboard, a trackball for navigation, and so on. Now, though, hundreds of other devices exist, many with different hardware capabilities (e.g., no keyboard, multiple screens, game controller buttons, and more!).

Ideally, your application can work regardless of the existence of various types of hardware. Some applications, though, will be unusable without certain hardware characteristics. For example, a full-screen game may rely on a hardware keyboard or trackball to indicate player actions—soft keyboards and touchscreens may be insufficient.

Fortunately, starting with Android 1.5, you can add explicit instructions that tell Android what you need, so that your application is not installed on devices lacking such hardware. We'll look at that now, and then move on to implied feature requests.

Explicit Feature Requests

In addition to using the target ID system to indicate the level of device your project is targeting, you can use an `AndroidManifest.xml` element to specify hardware that is required for your application to run properly. You can add one or more `<uses-configuration>` elements inside the `<manifest>` element. Each `<uses-configuration>` element specifies one valid configuration of hardware that your application will work with. At the present time, there are five possible hardware requirements you can specify this way:

- android:reqFiveWayNav: Indicates you need a five-way navigation pointing device of some form (e.g., android:reqFiveWayNav = "true")

- android:reqNavigation: Restricts the five-way navigation pointing device to a specific type (e.g., android:reqNavigation = "trackball")

- android:reqHardKeyboard: Specifies whether a hardware (physical) keyboard is required (e.g., android:reqHardKeyboard = "true")

- android:reqKeyboardType: Used in conjunction with android:reqHardKeyboard, indicates a specific type of hardware keyboard is required (e.g., android:reqKeyboardType = "qwerty")

- android:reqTouchScreen: Indicates what type of touchscreen is required, if any (e.g., android:reqTouchScreen = "finger")

Starting in Android 1.6, there is a similar manifest element, <uses-feature>, that is designed to document requirements an application has for other optional features on Android devices. For example, the following attributes can be placed in a <uses-feature> element:

- android:glEsVersion: Indicates that your application requires OpenGL, where the value of the attribute indicates the level of OpenGL support (e.g., 0x00010002 for OpenGL 1.2 or higher)

- android:name = "android.hardware.camera": Indicates that your application needs a camera

- android:name = "android.hardware.camera.autofocus": Indicates that your application specifically needs an autofocus camera

Each Android release adds more features that you can require. A great example is the recently added android:hardware:nfc feature, for using near-field communication (NFC). These requests will cause the Android Market—and other, third-party markets, one hopes—to filter your application out from being loaded on devices for which it is unsuitable.

The <uses-feature> element has an android:required attribute that you can specify. By default, it is set to true, meaning your application absolutely needs this feature. If you set it to false, you are advertising that your application can take advantage of the feature if it exists, but does not absolutely need it. To find out at runtime whether the feature exists on the device, you can use the hasSystemFeature() method on PackageManager to interrogate the device.

Implied Feature Requests

If you have requested permissions like `CALL_PHONE` or `SEND_SMS`, unless you take the proper steps, your application will not be available for the Motorola XOOM, nor presumably for other Wi-Fi-only Android tablets.

Some permissions imply that you need certain hardware features. Scroll down to the "Permissions that Imply Feature Requirements" section on the `<uses-feature>` page to find the list.[1]

The Android Market treats a request for a permission like `CALL_PHONE` as though it is also a request for the following:

```
<uses-feature android:name="android.hardware.telephony" />
```

The XOOM was the first Android device to lack telephony; several other devices have followed in its footsteps. While the XOOM can have a data plan, it has no voice or SMS capability, so it is treated as not having `android.hardware.telephony`. But, if you request permissions like `CALL_PHONE`, the Android Market by default will assume you *need* `android.hardware.telephony`. As a result, you will be filtered out of the Android Market for the XOOM.

The solution is simple: for any hardware features that might be implied by permissions but that your application does not absolutely need, manually add the appropriate `<uses-feature>` element to your manifest with `android:required="false"`:

```
<uses-feature
  android:name="android.hardware.telephony"
  android:required="false"
/>
```

Then, before you try placing a phone call or sending an SMS or something, use `PackageManager` and `getSystemAvailableFeatures()` to find out if `android.hardware.telephony` is available on the device. For example, you might check for telephony early on and disable various menu choices, such as buttons that might lead the user to place a call or send an SMS.

If your application absolutely needs telephony, then the implied `<uses-feature>` will work, though you may wish to consider putting one in explicitly. However, just bear in mind that this means your app will not work on the XOOM or other tablets that lack telephony.

A Guaranteed Market

As mentioned in the introduction to the chapter, Android is open source. Specifically, it is mostly available under the Apache Software License 2.0. This license places few restrictions on device manufacturers. Therefore, it is very possible for a device

---

[1] `http://developer.android.com/guide/topics/manifest/uses-feature-element.html`

manufacturer to create a device that, frankly, does not run Android very well. It might work fine for standard applications shipped on the device but do a poor job of handling third-party applications, like the ones you might write.

To help address this, Google has some applications, such as the Android Market, that it has not released as open source. While these applications are available to device manufacturers, the devices that run the Android Market are tested first, to help ensure that a user's experience with the device will be reasonable.

Hence, the existence of the Android Market on a device, beyond providing a distribution means for your applications, also serves as a bit of a seal of approval that the device should support well-written third-party applications. Specifically, any device that has the Android Market

- Meets the criteria outlined in the Compatibility Definition Document (CDD)
- Has passed the Compatibility Test Suite (CTS)

Other Stuff That Varies

Other things that vary from device to device include the following:

- Which location technologies are available (e.g., GPS, cell tower proximity, Galileo)
- Which camera features are available (e.g., flash, autofocus, sepia tone)
- Which sensors are available (e.g., accelerometer, gyroscope, barometer)

The strategy for dealing with these variables is to interrogate the system first to find out what the possibilities are, and then decide which to use, where the decision could be made solely by you or with user input. For example, you can use `Criteria` to determine which is the best location provider to use with `LocationManager`.

Bugs, Bugs, Bugs

Unfortunately, devices inevitably have bugs. Some bugs are truly accidental. Some are side effects from changes the device manufacturer made to achieve some business aims. Some are actually intentional, though the engineers who implemented them may not have fully understood their ramifications.

There is not much you can do tactically about these bugs, beyond try to work around them. The `Build` class, in the `android.os` package, can tell you the make and model of the device that is running your app. That, plus your own hard-won experience with certain problems, will help you identify where you need to route around firmware damage.

Strategically, if you find something that is clearly a device bug, you should file an issue to have this bug detected via the CTS. The CTS is supposed to filter out devices that cannot faithfully run Android applications. However, the CTS has many holes, and device bugs slip through. By collectively improving the CTS, we can help prevent problems from cropping up in the future. You can file an issue at the Public Issue Tracker for Android Bugs, `http://code.google.com/p/androidbugs/issues/list`.

Device Testing

Ideally, you should try to test your apps on a variety of hardware. However, this can get expensive. Here are some options for doing it more cheaply:

- Sign up for Keynote DeviceAnywhere's independent developer plan, which is a lower-cost way of being able to access their device farm for remote testing.

- Some device manufacturers hold device labs at various events, such as Motorola held at AnDevCon 2011.

- Some carriers have perpetual device labs, such as Orange's developer centres.

- You may be able to arrange short-term (e.g., 15-minute) device swaps as part of a Meetup or Google Technology User Group with fellow Android developers.

Chapter 49

Where Do We Go from Here?

Obviously, this book does not cover everything. And while your primary resource (besides the book) is the Android SDK documentation, you are likely to need information from additional sources.

Searching online for "android" and a class name is a good way to locate tutorials that reference a given Android class. However, bear in mind that Android's pace of change means tutorials written even only a few years ago are probably written for much earlier SDK versions and, as such, will require considerable adjustment to work properly in current SDKs.

Instead of randomly hunting around for tutorials, you can use some of the resources outlined in this chapter to narrow your search.

Questions, Sometimes with Answers

The official places to get assistance with Android are the Android Google Groups. With respect to the SDK, there are two to consider:

- Android Developers (http://groups.google.com/group/android-developers), for SDK questions and answers

- Android Discuss (http://groups.google.com/group/android-discuss), designed for free-form discussion of anything Android-related, not necessarily for programming questions and answers

You might also consider the following resources, particularly StackOverflow, which is increasingly considered the best place to receive help:

- StackOverflow's android tag (http://stackoverflow.com/questions/tagged/android)

- The Android tutorials and programming forums at www.anddev.org

- The Open Mob for Android wiki (http://andmob.wikidot.com/)

- The #android-dev IRC channel on freenode (http://freenode.net/)

- The Android Forum at JavaRanch (www.coderanch.com/forums/f-93/Android)

It is important, particularly for StackOverflow and the Google Groups, to write informative questions. Following are some tips for writing effective questions:

- Include relevant portions of the source code (e.g., the method in which you are getting an exception).

- Include the stack trace from LogCat, if the problem is an unhandled exception.

- On StackOverflow, make sure your source code and stack trace are formatted as source code; on Google Groups, consider posting long listings on http://gist.github.com or a similar code-paste site.

- Explain thoroughly what you are trying to do, how you are trying to do it, and why you are doing it this way (especially if you think your goal or approach may be a little offbeat). Be prepared for people to try to steer you toward a completely different approach rather than actually trying to help you solve your current problem. Consider other approaches, but be wary of compromising the integrity of your vision.

- On StackOverflow, respond to answers and comments with your own comments, addressing the person using the @ syntax (e.g., @CommonsWare), to maximize the odds you will get a reply.

- On the Google Groups, do not "ping" or reply to your own message to try to elicit a response until a reasonable amount of time has gone by (e.g., 24 hours).

Heading to the Source

The source code to Android is now available, albeit several versions behind the current Android 4.0 release. Mostly, this is for people who are looking to enhance, improve, or otherwise fuss with the insides of the Android operating system. But it is possible that you will find the answers you seek in that code, particularly if you want to see how some built-in Android component does its thing.

> **NOTE:** Google has promised it will release the source code for Android 4.0, Ice Cream Sandwich, in the near future. Such a release is becoming increasingly important, as the existing version available on http://source.android.com is 2.3, which is growing long in the tooth. As previously stated by Google, the source for the 3.x versions is unlikely ever to be released, as 4.0 is the preferred merged code base for all future editions.

The source code and related resources can be found at `http://source.android.com`, where you can do the following:

- Download or browse the source code

- File bug reports against the operating system itself

- Submit patches and learn about the process for how such patches are evaluated and approved

- Join a separate set of Google Groups for Android platform development

Rather than download the multigigabyte Android source code snapshot, you may wish to use Google Code Search (`www.google.com/codesearch`) instead. Just add the `package:android` constraint to your search query, and it will search only in Android and related projects.

Getting Your News Fix

Ed Burnette, a nice guy who happened to write his own Android book, is also the manager of Planet Android (`www.planetandroid.com`), a feed aggregator for a number of Android-related blogs. Subscribing to Planet Android's feed enables you to monitor quite a few Android-related blog posts, though not exclusively related to programming.

To try to focus more on programming-related, Android-referencing blog posts, you can search DZone (`www.dzone.com`) for "android" and subscribe to a feed based on that search.

Index

S

CPSIA information can be obtained at www.ICGtesting.com
Printed in the USA
LVOW010217190912

299382LV00006B/11/P

9 781430 239840